THE KERRY ANTHOLOGY

The Arts Council
An Chomhairle Ealaíon

First published in 2000 by Marino Books, an imprint of Mercier Press
16 Hume Street Dublin 2
e.mail: books@marino.ie
Tel: (01) 661 5299; Fax: 661 8583

Trade enquiries to CMD Distribution, 55A Spruce Avenue, Stillorgan Industrial Park,
Blackrock, Co Dublin.
Tel: 294 2556; Fax: 294 2556
e.mail: cmd@columba.ie

Introduction © Gabriel Fitzmaurice 2000
The acknowledgements page is an extension of this copyright notice

ISBN 1 86023 121 7

10 9 8 7 6 5 4 3 2 1

A CIP record for this title is available from the British Library

Cover design by SPACE
Printed in Ireland by ColourBooks, Baldoyle Industrial Estate, Dublin 13

THE KERRY ANTHOLOGY

EDITED BY GABRIEL FITZMAURICE

Contents

INTRODUCTION

Here is yet another Kerry book! Another act of faith in the Kerry people, a ship of hope launched on a sea of love. But, for all that, not an uncritical book – not an uncritical look at life through the eyes of writers who have been inspired by the Kerry experience.

I was born in Kerry – in Moyvane, a small, sleepy straggle of a village seven miles north-east of Listowel on the Limerick border. I have lived here all my life. I am inspired by community and community life. And yet it's fair to say that I'm a loner, an outsider. Both in the community and outside it. The eye I cast on my community is not a cold one. It is not dispassionate. Rather it is compassionate. There are too many exiles in literature. Too many people writing from outside.

The role of a writer in his or her community is to tell the truth. Some people confuse truth-telling with destruction. As if the function of telling the truth is to destroy. It might be a misreading of Christ's impulse to destroy the temple. But Christ destroyed the temple (i.e. himself) with the stated purpose of raising it up in three days. So we tell the truth to remake ourselves and our communities. This is how I see literature. If literature is to have any function (and I'm not at all sure that it should have anything as functional as a function!), this is it. In raising the matter of the function of literature, I beg the question – is writing, then, purely an aesthetic matter? The answer to this is that a writer is answerable to himself or herself and to the community out of which he or she writes.

So, another Kerry book! Why? Aren't there enough already? Maybe the purpose of a book such as this, in gathering a diverse body of writing *as Gaeilge* and in English, is to bring to our attention the often unnoticed energy of the county. This energy may be its real genius. The Cork poet Seán Ó Ríordáin (1917–77) wrote of Dún Chaoin that the native Irish speakers didn't hear the music of their language *('Ceol ceantair/Ná chloiseann lucht a labhartha')* – that only the stranger hears this particular lilt. Maybe so. But the music is there. This book, then, is a symphony drawing the different themes and tones into a coherent representation of the county of Kerry – a place that exists in the mind as surely as it does on any map.

People keep telling me that they sense the energy in Kerry. Arts officers, writers, singers, musicians, travelling salesmen and women, lorry and van drivers have told me this. I always supposed that they were unconsciously picking up on the many community activities, cultural, sporting and otherwise, they saw, or half-saw, advertised on posters and other notices. Others, believing in psychic energy, have told me that they can pick up 'vibes' of extraordinary energy on crossing the county bounds! Be that as it may, there is energy in the place. Football, books (at least one per week, every week throughout the year reported in the local newspapers), greyhounds, horse races, arts festivals, music festivals, drama festivals, regattas, fairs – the place is bursting with energy. And when this energy is channelled into literature, it makes good reading.

And literature is important in Kerry. It is one of the things you'd get a bloody nose for. The only time I was ever assaulted since I grew into a man was over a short story – a genre, I hasten to add, I do not practise. In condemning the fatwa on Salman Rusdie, Fintan O'Toole (I think it was he) pointed out that literature was a matter of life and death to Muslims. It has slipped considerably in the West. Well, I got assaulted over a short story in Kerry. Not quite a matter of life or death, but pretty important nonetheless! And, indeed, there's the story of the Moyvane farmer who, a number of years ago, when hay-making was the only way to secure winter fodder, was asked by the wife of a big farmer busy with hay, 'Paddy, have you the hay saved?' Paddy, a man of uncommon intelligence, smiled at her. 'Missus,' he replied, 'I have a good book!' The hay could wait.

In this book I have tried to be inclusive. It wasn't possible to include everybody I would have liked to. In reparation for my sins of omission, I exclude myself too. I know what it's like to be excluded, but the true writer will write on nevertheless.

Perhaps a note on the Irish-language content of the book would not be amiss here. Kerry has two vibrant, living languages – *Gaeilge* and English. Everybody in the county has fluent English, more or less. Alas, the reverse is not the case. Irish is not the first language of most Kerry people outside of the

Gaeltacht, and even there Irish is declining. There is, however, significant interest in the Irish language throughout the English-speaking areas. Irish is available to every pupil in primary and secondary school, and a growing number of students now attend Irish-speaking schools. Kerry has produced first-rate literature in the Irish language throughout the centuries, particularly in Sliabh Luachra and Corca Dhuibhne. In compiling a representative selection from this corpus, I wondered about the feasibility of providing accompanying translations. I consulted *Gaeilgeoirí* writers and editors and English-language writers and editors, and the general feeling was that the Irish should not be translated. For the following reasons: (i) the integrity of the original (ii) many people who would be able to read the originals might be tempted to read the translations only, and (iii) space – I could devote more space to work *as Gaeilge* if I didn't have to devote space to translations. The solution (not to provide translations) isn't entirely satisfactory, but it is a workable one nonetheless.

I am not satisfied with the number of women vis-à-vis men in this anthology. But I plead a mixture of my own ignorance and their unavailability. I can say, however, that times are changing, that patriarchy is no longer in the ascendant and that more and more women are being published – many of them by Irish publishers. I welcome this, and hope that when next someone like me is foolhardy enough to attempt another Kerry anthology, the gender imbalance will be redressed. As to this present book, this is the best I could do.

This is my reading of my native place. Inevitably there will be others. '*Ní lia daoine ná tuairimí*', as the proverb goes. All I can say is that it is an honest and celebratory reading. I couldn't live here otherwise. I hope you enjoy the book.

Gabriel Fitzmaurice
Moyvane, October 2000

SIGERSON CLIFFORD
I AM KERRY

I am Kerry like my mother before me,
And my mother's mother and her man.
Now I sit on an office stool remembering,
And the memory of them like a fan
Soothes the embers into flame.
I am Kerry and proud of my name.

My heart is looped around the rutted hills
That shoulder the stars out of the sky,
And about the wasp-yellow fields
And the strands where the kelp-streamers lie;
Where, soft as lovers' Gaelic, the rain falls,
Sweeping into silver the lacy mountain walls.

My grandfather tended the turf fire
And, leaning backward into legend, spoke
Of doings old before quills inked history.
I saw dark heroes fighting in the smoke,
Diarmuid dead inside his Iveragh cave
And Deirdre caoining upon Naoise's grave.

I see the wise face now with its hundred wrinkles,
And every wrinkle held a thousand tales
Of Finn and Oscar and Conawn Maol,
And sea-proud Niall whose conquering sails,
Raiding France for slaves and wine,
Brought Patrick to mind Milchu's swine.

I should have put a noose about the throat of time
And choked the passing of the hobnailed years,
And stayed young always, shouting in the hills
Where life held only fairy fears.
When I was young my feet were bare
But I drove cattle to the fair.

'Twas this I lived, skin to skin with the earth,
Elbowed by the hills, drenched by the billows,
Watching the wild geese making black wedges
By Skelligs far west and Annascaul of the willows.
Their voices came on every little wind
Whispering across the half-door of the mind,
For always I am Kerry.

WILLIAM PEMBROKE MULCHINOCK
THE ROSE OF TRALEE

The pale moon was rising above the green mountain,
The sun was declining beneath the blue sea,
When I stray'd with my love to the pure crystal fountain
That stands in the beautiful vale of Tralee.

She was lovely and fair as the rose of the summer,
Yet 'twas not her beauty alone that won me,
Oh, no, 'twas the truth in her eyes ever beaming
That made me love Mary, the Rose of Tralee.

The cool shades of evening their mantle were spreading,
And Mary, all smiling, was list'ning to me.
The moon through the valley her pale rays was shedding
When I won the heart of the Rose of Tralee.

Tho' lovely and fair as the rose of that summer,
Yet 'twas not her beauty alone that won me,
Oh, no, 'twas the truth in her eyes ever beaming
That made me love Mary, the Rose of Tralee.

MICK O'CONNELL
MOST MEMORABLE MOMENTS

Apart from a few medals and trophies and being recognised in the football world it would seem to most people that I have gained nothing else. This I cannot dispute if one is thinking in terms of material gain. However, I have accumulated a store of something that can only be valued by myself personally, memories. My reservoir is filled with them, those ecstatic moments when it was great to be alive and on which it is now pleasant to reminisce. But there are also those preferred-to-be-forgotten ones which come floating to the surface far too often. this time I will concern myself with the more cheerful memories.

Fitzgerald Stadium, Killarney is a ground that I have fond memories of and has probably given me more great moments than anywhere else. I will always remember a bout of play towards the end of a National League play-off against Cork in March, 1960. As Kerry attacked, the Cork left full-back intercepted and kicked clear and from the moment it left his boot I had a feeling that this ball was mine. I know that a man should always have a positive approach and think that every ball he goes to field is his but the ball was tailor-made for me. It did not drop in the form of a lob in which situation there are usually several men tussling for possession, making it difficult to effect a clean catch. This ball had just the right amount of height for a good man-to-man contest. I read its flight perfectly and having edged out in front of my man, with eyes focused firmly I made contact. Without changing pace or hesitating, I pulled that ball down and in one continuous movement swung at it left-footed. From a position outside the fifty-yards line that ball sailed unerringly between the posts for what was to turn out the score of my lifetime, off play. I have often since reconstructed in my mind a picture of that score at the western end of that well laid-out Killarney stadium. The instant that the ball splits the space between the goal-posts, with Carrantohill and the McGillicuddy Reeks in the background, is the moment I will never forget. As one sportswriter put it, 'poetry in motion'. It felt good to me at any rate. In football, like everything else, it is true to say that nothing succeeds like success. That day I had a particularly good game and played a major part in having a Kerry victory almost assured at the time I scored that point. This gave me the confidence to take a sporting chance from long distance. That great deterrent, fear, fear of a wide as it would be in my case, was nowhere in sight.

Place-kicking or free kicks off the ground, no matter how good it looked, never gave me any satisfaction. There was a lack of competitiveness that I did not like. Nevertheless, to point a placed ball that you are not expected to or that a few others have done leaves you with a certain sense of achievement. In the All-Ireland semi-final of 1962 against Dublin, I experienced this. A sideline ball was awarded to Kerry thirty-five yards out from the Dublin goal, on the left under the Hogan Stand. This I stepped up to and curled the ball in between the posts for a good point and no more, I thought. A light breeze blowing into the goal facilitated me in turning it in. Better was to follow. In the second half, again under the Hogan Stand about forty-five yards out another sideline kick was given to us. Because of the half-time change of ends, this time the ball was to the right of the posts and I was kicking into the wind. A point from that position would need deadly accuracy combined with a powerful kick, two things that seldom go hand in hand. Accuracy is sacrificed with too much concentration on getting the distance and the reverse is also true. So when Paudie Sheehy beckoned me to take the kick my intention was to centre the ball. Aiming for the centre of the crossbar with force, I was allowing for the wind to swing the ball across the face of the goal, into the danger zone for the forwards' benefit. Nobody was more surprised than I was when that ball sailed cleanly through the posts for a great point. In the relaxed atmosphere of the practise ground, I and I am sure that sure that most footballers, have performed feats that seem beyond them on an important occasion. This is another reason I have for thinking that this second-half point of the 1962 deserved to be called great and one of the few ground ball kicks that I think worth recalling.

Some of my greatest fielding thrills have been in Croke Park and none better than one later that very same year. It was in the Grounds Tournament final with Dublin again providing the opposition. In the second half, a Dublin defender halted the Kerry attack and hurriedly kicked clear. The ball was dropping into an open space out towards the middle of the field when it became obvious that it would be a man-for-man situation between myself and an opponent. However, we were approaching the ball from different directions. He was more or less coming with the ball from the direction of his own goal and had to look askance to track it. I was running straight into it and naturally in the more favourable position. In these circumstances I knew from experience that my opponent had a poor chance of competing successfully, so ignoring any possible challenge and with total concentration on the the ball, I took to the air. I fielded the ball firmly but simultaneously my boots caught and tripped over the shoulders of my opponent. Down I came, head and shoulders first. It was not a smooth landing but that did not matter as I still had the ball securely gripped. The Dublin midfielders that day were John Timmons, an amazingly tidy player despite the heavy physique, and Paddy Holden who was a great trier. But it was one of the half-backs who happened to contest that ball with me. Why do I single out this particular catch from so many? I cannot say exactly why it has lingered so long in the memory when others have long been forgotten. Chiefly, I think it is because for once in my lifetime I knew how high my feet were off the ground. My gauge was that Dublin man's shoulders.

Whenever I am asked what was the greatest game I have played, I am never stuck for the answer. Without reservation, that charmed hour was the National League Final of 1961 against Derry. Everything, and I really mean everything, that I contested in the air, I won and every kick must have seemed guided by some supernatural control. And so effortlessly was the whole operation that I must have, that day, reached the very pinnacle of my physical form. By half-time Kerry had taken the lead, my contribution being a good supply of the ball to the forwards and three points, two long range off play and one from a fifty yards placed ball. In the second half we increased our lead so that the 'all over' stage was reached long before the final whistle. It was only natural that we eased off the pressure, not that I ever ostensibly did this because the feelings of opposing players have to be considered. Nothing can be as hurtful to another player as to give the impression that he is unworthy of further contest. With this in mind, when a fifty yards kick was awarded to Kerry near the end of the game, I went through the normal motions of taking it. I intentionally intended to lob the ball somewhere in front of the Derry goal and did not want to score and widen the margin on the scoreboard. Imagine my amazement when that fifty not alone cleared the crossbar but went far beyond it, another instance of how easily it all came that day. Phil Stuart was one of the many Derrymen sent to oppose me during the game. The previous year he had played well against me when he was a member of the Queen's University team that toured South Kerry and played a club game against us in Cahirciveen. Maybe it was the determination to turn the tables of him that spurred me on. Whatever it was, that performance of mine in May, 1961, was the highest standard over one game I ever attained and time has confirmed my opinion on that.

While scoring is not the be-all and end-all of the game, it plays a big part. Many a man has his game brightened by scoring at a vital time, and I am no exception. When playing for Munster against Ulster in Breffni Park, Cavan, in the Railway Cup semi-final of 1958, my winning point came very timely. Like the boxer down on points and endeavouring to win the fight with a knock-out, I was in a somewhat similar position. I had to do something special to obliterate the stains of not too good performance. With the sides level and only minutes left to play, I dashed into a broken ball at midfield and hared towards goal on a solo run. When within range about thirty-five yards out, I shot on the run and scored the winning point; the final whistle went with the kickout. The Press headline the following day said: 'O'Connell steers Munster through'. Whatever about the steering, that score was the result of wanting very badly to justify my presence. Another last-minute point in the 1972 Railway Cup final against Leinster in Croke Park was also my redeemer. Having done little else during the game, I shot the equalising point from a forty-five yards free away out on the left under the Cusack Stand.

While on the subject of equalisers, I cannot forget that one in the Munster final of 1961 and which was another last-minute effort. Kerry, as League winners, were outright favourites but Cork always gave us a run for our money. That day they looked like creating a major upset when they took a one-point lead near the end. Gene McCarthy, then their outstanding player, should have consolidated this lead had he not shot an inexplicable wide immediately afterwards. If he had not, the score that followed from myself would not have mattered. It was desperation time when I got the ball at midfield and headed for the Blackrock goal in the Cork Athletic Grounds. As two Corkmen converged to cover my attempted right-footed kick, I changed my mind. Instead, I pivoted on that foot and, wrong-footing my opponents, swung with the left to score a very precious point from the right-hand side of the posts. In sporting terms, the value of that point was the guarantee of a replay which we won well but in economic terms, to the town of Killarney it was equivalent to a tourist season with the influx of over thirty thousand people for the day. The late Pat O'Mara, treasurer of the Kerry County Board and a publican himself, told me that my point of the drawn game was worth several thousand pints of the other kind. If only I could have charged accordingly, it would have paid me well.

While I have, for personal reasons, very fond memories of that game against Derry in 1961, in broader terms I think that a game (or half a game) I played in New York in 1969 surpasses it. Having beaten Offaly in May of that year in the home League Final, Kerry travelled to New York the following month to take on the exiles in the proper final. Nothing more than a formality and a bit of sightseeing thrown in or so we thought but what a surprise we were in for. This final was played in the two-leg system. A game was played on two consecutive Sundays with the overall aggregate score taken into account to decide the winners. The first day, I was not long on the field when I was consigned to the sidelines with an injury, intentionally inflicted, I thought. Whether it was or not, the toss I took on the concrete hard ground damaged my back and I spent the following week in bed. This first game was drawn and Kerry were deemed lucky not to have lost heavily. So immobilised was I with my back that I feared some permanent injury. Needless to say, the second leg of the final was far from my mind.

In New York, I always found a home from home with a fellow-Valentiaman and ex-Young Islander footballer, John Cooper. On the Saturday before the second game, I was amazed and delighted to find that I was able to walk unhindered and John persuaded me to go down to Van Cortland Park for a try out. I managed to trot a little but anything more strenuous brought me back to reality once more, my back was not fit. So I packed up, unhappy with myself. Why should I expect a miracle to happen, but still I expected one. Believe it or not, some miracle did happen. The following morning as I walked to Mass with some of the Kerry lads I felt so good that I jumped for a few signposts and there was no remainder from the back. Still, playing a physical contact game was far more demanding than jumping up to any signpost, I knew well. It was not any optimism on my part that made me tog-out with the rest of the team that afternoon but only to comply with the wishes of the trainer Jackie Lyne who put me on stand-by duty. Putting on my playing gear that day was a fateful decision. As halftime approached and Kerry doing badly, Jackie whispered to me 'you will be wanted'. For the second half, I was assigned the full-forward position. I played a very unorthodox game, in fact I played everywhere except in front of the square so that Peter Nolan, the New York full-back, did not know where to look for me next. Astonishingly I played very well, scoring six points and none more important than the last one. The special clock at the back of the goal posts in Gaelic Park had the hour visibly registered and the buzzer to signal the end was about to go off at any second. With New York in front by a point, Eamon O'Donoghue won possession out near the left sideline and placed me in a position thirty-five yards out in front of goal. Without a step, for fear of hearing the final whistle any moment, I transferred the ball between the posts for the equalising point. In the extra time, we pulled out well in front to finish decisive winners. It was hard luck on New York, to have victory snatched from them.

The second-half display, in one hundred degrees temperature of New York on the last day of June has overshadowed many of my better midfield games. Apart from playing well there was the surprise aspect of it. The unexpected gift is most appreciated and my form that day certainly surprised me. It might sound vain to suggest it but the consequential benefit of that victory to the Kerry team of recent years was immense. If we had returned defeated from New York I doubt if Kerry would have succeeded the winning of the following two All-Ireland championships and several league titles. Since the 1962 victory, the county had gone through a rather barren spell. This victory provided the breakthrough.

Football is a team game and therefore some of the greatest moments are shared with other players. In this respect I can recall a great goal scored by Brendan Lynch a few years ago in a National League semi-final against Westmeath. Early in the first half as I fielded a ball about forty yards out from the Railway End goal of Croke Park, at a glance I spotted Brendan sprinting diagonally between myself and goal. Without hesitation, I fisted the ball out in front of him which he took at full speed to score in typical left-footed fashion. To contribute a little towards another's great moment was very satisfying to me.

With contribution to another's game in mind, I was lucky in having Mick O'Dwyer as a regular companion during my playing days. Being the only two team members from South Kerry, most of the time at any rate, meant more miles travelling for us for games and training. At all hours of the night as we drove homeward we debated and re-debated the game, expounding our theories openly. Discussion has not been associated with football, Gaelic anyway, but in my opinion it is of great value. I doubt if any two sportsmen in Ireland know each other's game and thoughts on the game as well as we did.

As a left half-back, I saw Mick make many a spectacular catch from behind his opponent. He was quite unique in this regard because most outfield players prefer to take the frontal position when fielding. In later times as a forward, it was the accuracy and power of his right-footed kick that stood out and I remember particularly the nine points which he scored in the first leg of the National League Final against New York in 1969. Yes, some of my best days were in association with 'Dwyer' as he is popularly known in Kerry football circles.

Apart from what happens on the field there are other incidental factors in football that have been most rewarding. As a corner-forward, I remember playing a minor (under-age) game in Currow, a village near Castleisland, County Kerry, in 1954. In the intervening years my thoughts often harked back to that little game played in the fields in the picturesque woodland setting. I never saw or set foot on that field again until this year, 1974, when I returned there to play a club game. Maybe I was a little nostalgic but not too sad that twenty good years had passed because those years have given me some great memories. And I was happy to know that I was still fit enough to play.

from A KERRY FOOTBALLER (1974)

SIGERSON CLIFFORD
THE BOYS OF BARR NA SRAIDE

O the town it climbs the mountain and looks upon the sea,
And sleeping time or waking 'tis there I long to be,
To walk again that kindly street, the place I grew a man
And the Boys of Barr na Sraide went hunting for the wran.

With cudgels stout we roamed about to hunt the droileen
We looked for birds in every furze from Letter to Dooneen:
We sang for joy beneath the sky, life held no print or plan
And we Boys in Barr na Sraide, hunting for the wran.

And when the hills were bleeding and the rifles were aflame,
To the rebel homes of Kerry the Saxon stranger came,
But the men who dared the Auxies and beat the Black and
        Tan
Were the Boys of Barr na Sraide hunting for the wran.

And here's a toast to them tonight, the lads who laughed with
        me,
By the groves of Carhan river or the slopes of Beenatee,
John Dawley and Batt Andy, and the Sheehans Con and
        Dan,
And the Boys of Barr na Sraide who hunted for the wran.

And now they toil on foreign soil, where they have gone their
        way
Deep in the heart of London town or over in Broadway.
And I am left to sing their deeds, and praise them while I
        can
Those Boys of Barr na Sraide who hunted for the wran.

And when the wheel of life runs down and peace comes over
        me,
O lay me down in that old town between the hills and sea,
I'll take my sleep in those green fields the place my life began,
Where the Boys of Barr na Sraide went hunting for the wran.

TOMÁS Ó CRIOMHTHAIN
as AN TOILEÁNACH (1929)

Lá Breá Domhnaigh ghluais naomhóg isteach ón dtír agus daoine strainséartha inti. Ní fheadair aoinne cérbh iad féin nó gur shroicheadar na daoine ar bharr an chalaidh.

Sriosúnach d'fhear mór ard lom a b'ea é, agus cuma dhrochshláinteach air, agus cuma chríonna ina theanntasan air. Bhí sé pósta agus a bhean in éineacht leis, agus beirt leanbh acu. Bhí trí cosa faoin mbean, cos chliste, cos ghearr, agus cos mhaide. Lig duine thoir agus duine thiar giota gáire as, agus dúirt duine eile: 'Dá aimlitheacht atá siad, nach maith atá na páistí acu!' 'Is é sin toil Dé, a dhuine,' arsa fear eile á fhreagairt, a raibh breis d'aitheanta a chreidimh aige.

Níorbh fhada ón áit iad; ó pharóiste an Fheiritéaraigh an fear, agus de threibh Dhún Chaoin a b'ea an bhean. Bhaineadar tigh na scoile amach, mar bhí deighilt sa scoil chun múinteoirí a lonnú ann. Ghlacadar seilbh ann. Thug na daoine a ndóthain tine chucu, agus shrocraíodar iad féin síos ann chun a ngnó a chur ar bun.

Seanshaighdiúir a fuair cúpla gráinne san arm a b'ea é, agus bhí réal sa ló aige. Ní raibh sé ina chumas a bhróga a dhúnadh ná cromadh chuige de dheasca an ghráinne a chuaigh ina chliathán. B'aimlithe an bheirt iad, ní á chasadh leo é, ach b'fhearr bean na dtrí gcos pic ná eisean, mar bheadh sí sa bhaile mór go rábach roimh aon bhean dhá chois.

Bhí bliain nach mór dúnta ag an scoil san am seo, agus deineadh í a oscailt ar maidin Dé Luain. Ní raibh aoinne in easnamh ar an scoil an lá seo; múinteoir nua, dar ndóigh, is beag nár chuaigh na daoine aosta ag féachaint conas mar a bheadh an máistir ag déanamh.

Bhí oidí scoile tearc an uair úd, agus chuaigh den sagart aon duine a fháil; agus nuair a b'fhada leis a bhí an scoil gan aoinne chuir sé é seo ann go ceann tamaill. Ní raibh sé in aon choláiste riamh ná é rómhaith ar an mbunscoil ach a oiread. Pé scéal é, b'eo leis an léann ar siúl ar maidin Dé Luain.

Is cruinn díreach a bhí an Rí ar a shuíochán féin romham, agus sméid sé orm teacht in aice leis. Thug cogar dom: 'Nach pollta atá an craiceann ar an scolardach!' ar seisean. 'Tá sé mionphollta go maith,' arsa mise. Bhí a fhios agamsa ó m'athair go raibh rian na bolgaí ann, ach ní fheadair an Rí cad é an bholgach chuige an t-am seo dá shaol.

Níor mhór an léann a ghlac ceann na gramaisce an lá seo, mar nach ag féachaint ar leabhar ná pháipéar a bhíodar ach ag tabhairt bhean na dtrí gcos faoi ndeara a thugadh í féin le taispeáint anois agus arís. Duine fíormhacánta a b'ea an múinteoir, agus ní bhíodh a oiread de chritheagla roimhe agus a bheadh roimh fhear eile a bheadh mallaithe. Tar éis an tsaoil, bhíodh na scoláirí go maith aige.

Uair sa ráithe théadh sé go dtí an baile mór, agus thugadh sé bosca milseán leis agus úlla do na hóga ar scoil, agus pé lá a d'fhanfadh aon leanbh istigh thagadh sé ag triall air agus úll nó milseán aige chuige. Toisc é a bheith tláth, is beag a d'fhanadh istigh aon lá uaidh.

Is é seo an múinteoir deánach a rabhas aige, agus an Rí, leis, agus a lán eile againn, mar thug sé tamall maith ann. Is í an drochshláinte a chuir as sa deireadh é; bhí sé chun Corcaigh a bhaint amach ach cailleadh faoi shlí é timpeall Thrá Lí.

Sular fhág sé, ní raibh faic eile ina phlaicide ná raibh pioctha suas agamsa agus ag an Rí agus ag a lán eile chomh maith. Níorbh fhada gur bheartaigh sé ormsa chun a bheith ag múineadh na coda eile agus é féin a fhágaint ag stádar dó féin, mar nárbh fhéidir leis faic eile a mhúineadh dom féin. Fuaireas leor leis tamall, ach nuair a chuaigh an scéal rófhada b'ait liom é.

Lá dár thug sé eolas mo ghnótha dom le déanamh, bhuail sé féin amach faoin spéir, ach nuair a b'fhonn leis teacht bhí an gnó gan déanamh. B'ait leis sin agus tháinig sórt paisiúin air. B'é sin an chéad lá ar bhraitheamar sin ag baint leis. Luigh sé féin isteach leis an ngnó gan puinn cainte, mar smachtaigh sé é féin ar eagla gurbh é féin a bheadh thíos leis ar é a dhul chun cinn.

Cé gur lom buí an cuntanós a bhí air, ba dhóigh leat nárbh é an fear céanna nuair a bhuail an cigire an doras isteach chuige lá. Tháinig spionnadh beag suas ina aghaidh faoi mar a bheadh duine a bheadh beagán éadrom ina chiall agus ní deirim ná go raibh sin ag baint leis an uair seo, pé rud eile a bhí ina theannta air.

Is mise nár thóg sin air a bheith athraithe roimh an mbearránach a tháinig, mar tháinig critheagla ar a raibh de ghramaisc ar scoil roimhe. Bhí ceithre súile ann a thabharfadh a dhóthain solais don dtigh, gan lá ná lampa a bheith ann. Ní raibh aoinne is mó a chuir suim iontu ná an Rí, cé gur tháinig an galar céanna air féin ina dhiaidh sin go raibh ceithre súile ann, agus ceann breá maisiúil á n-iompar air!

An seithe ramhar buí a bhí ar an gcigire, ba dhóigh leat gur i bpáirt den tSín a cuireadh don chliabhán é. Maidir le scéanshúilí, ba dhóigh leat gur san arm a bhí sé riamh, agus níorbh aon ionadh an scoláire a bhí faoina smacht critheagla a bheith air, agus bhí, leis.

Bhí gach duine beag agus mór againn ar bheagán cainte an uair seo, ach pé gnó a bhí idir lámha againn á dhéanamh go ciúin. Níorbh fhada dom gur ghabh an máistir chugam agus figiúirí ar shlinn aige, agus dúirt sé liom iad a chaitheamh suas chomh luath agus b'fhéidir liom é. Ba bhearna réidh liomsa sin a dhéanamh agus dheineas gan mhoill. Is é an cigire a chuir chuige féin iad, ach ní raibh sé ina chumas iad a chur le chéile.

Toisc ná raibh an t-oide róshláintiúil, thug sé taom breoiteachta as an gcritheagla a chuir an cigire air, cé go raibh an scoil ar oscailt gach lá. Dúirt an máistir liom go mbeadh sé buíoch go deo díom ach seasamh i measc na gramaisce, agus go mbeadh an Rí do mo chúnamh. M'aintín a b'ea bean na dtrí gcos, leis, agus tháinig sí go dtí mo mháthair agus dúirt léi comhairle a thabhairt domsa chun mé a ghríosadh chun na scoile faid a bheadh an máistir breoite. 'Agus má tá cuilt nó aon rud le déanamh agat, déanfad duit é,' ar sise. Bhí fáth leis an gcomhairle sin ar eagla go gcuirfinnse stailc suas.

Bhíos féin agus an Rí inár dhá mhúinteoir ar feadh mí, agus ní á bhreith as seo é, ba bheirt sin ná raibh le moladh, mar pé rud a bhí inár gcumas a dhéanamh ní ligfeadh an mífhortún ná na crosa dúinn é a dhéanamh. Bhí balcairí déanta láidir ar scoil an Bhlascaeid an uair úd, agus ba mhó go mór a bhíodh de chlis na cúirtéireachta ar siúl againn ná dintiúirí an léinn, ach pé scéal é, breacadh an mhí amach ar an gcuma seo, gan bhuairt gan bhrón.

Is gairid ó cailleadh bean na dtrí gcos. Thug an scoil tamall eile dúnta agus bhíos fein agus an Rí arís le chéile chun sealgaireachta i gcnoc agus ar chósta na farraige. Má bhí mianach an pheata ag baint liomsa féin, bhí an mianach céanna sa Rí toisc gurbh é an chéad duine den ál é. D'fhág sin cead oilc agus maitheasa againn, nach mór.

Maidin áirithe, ghluais sé chugam go moch. 'Preab i do shuí,' ar seisean, 'go ragham ag fiach.'

'Ach níl gléas maith fiaigh againn,' arsa mise.

'Tá a bhuachaill,' ar seisean. 'Tabharfadsa an firéad liom. Goidfead ó m'athair críonna í.'

Chuir mo mháthair mo chuid bídh chugam agus ní rabhas i bhfad á shlogadh, agus an méid de ná raibh oiriúnach le slogadh bhí an muileann go faobhrúil chuige, cliathán de chíste déanta de mhin bhuí agus liathuisce bainne. B'eo le beirt againn. Buaileann seisean an firéad síos ina bhrollach. Bhí dhá mhadra mhaithe againn, agus ramhann agamsa ar mo ghualainn. Chun cnoic linn go fuadrach. Nuair a bhíomar i dtreo leis na coiníní, bhuail coinicéar linn.

Tharraing an Rí an firéad amach as a bhrollach, chuir sreang léi agus scaoil isteach í, agus leath líon ar gach poll a bhí ar an gcoinicéar. Níorbh fhada gur rop coinín amach, ach ghabh an líon é go tapaidh; dhein fuairnín de, mar bhí béalshreang faoi. Bhain sé amach as an líon é, agus chuir an líon ar tinneall arís mar a bhí sé cheana. Ní raibh ach an méid sin déanta aige nuair a rop ceann eile amach i malairt poill. Níor ghabh an firéad anial nó gur chuir sí an ceann deiridh chugainn. Casann sí aniar nuair ná buaileann aon ní eile léi. Bhí seacht gcinn de sheibineacha coiníní curtha ag an bhfiréad chugainn as an bpoll, agus iad gafa ag na líonta.

B'eo linn go dtí lantán eile. Scaoil sé isteach í, agus bhí sí tamall istigh sular ghabh aon ní amach. Faoi dheireadh, sháigh coinín mór láidir amach faoin bpoll. Ghabh an líon é, ach tharraing sé an staic a bhí á choimeád agus b'eo leis le fánaidh ach tháinig an dhá mhadra suas leis.

Nuair a bhí sé um ard an tráthnóna agus an ghrian ag druidim siar, dúirt an Rí: 'Tá an scéal go maith anois againn, ach ní fhéadfam na coiníní a thabhairt abhaile leis an ocras.'

'Ní fhaca aon fhear riamh d'fhear garbh mar tú is túisce a thiteann leis an ocras i gcónaí ná tú,' arsa mise leis, 'agus tabharfad féin iad ar fad abhaile liom mura mbeidh a thuilleadh againn.'

'Ó, ní bheidh. Ní ligfeam in aon pholl eile í mar tá sí cortha, agus nuair a bhíonn firéad cortha bíonn sí contúrthach ar fhanacht istigh,' ar seisean.

Bhí dosaen go leith marbh an uair seo againn, beart maith

agus sinn beartaithe ar a bheith ag tabhairt ár n-aghaidh ar an
dtigh. Bhí lomchasóg agam féin, agus bhí póca maith mór uirthi
ón dtaobh istigh agus canta maith aráin ann. Ní mise a chuir
ann é ach mo mháthair. Dúirt sí go raibh an lá fada agus go
mbíonn na daoine óga géarghoileach, rud a b'fhíor di.

Tharraingíos amach é agus dheineas dhá leath de, agus
thugas leath don Rí. Ní raibh rite chomh deacair a shásamh an
uair úd agus atáid inniu. Ach ní raibh an choróin air seo fós.
Phramsáil sé siar é go milis. Nuair a bhí sé meilte aige bhraith
sé láidir é féin, agus chuir an firéad i bpoll nó go raibh dosaen
ag an duine againn ag teacht abhaile agus réiltín in airde.

FIONA BRENNAN
FEEDING THE MUSE

for Audrey Favier

And still
the ordinary things must be done.

I prune the small thyme bush
trying to save its younger shoots

plan how to stop the dog from walking
on the lemon-scented floor

watch the week-old washing
drag along the muddy path

switch off Gaybo's radio wisdom
to sit down with pen and paper.

The young cairn trots in
from the garden,

falls into a hero's sleep
at my feet, beneath the table.

He ignores my futile efforts
at recording mundane moments.
I bend down and leave him
a tasty first draft to eat.

DOROTHY MACARDLE
BALLYSEEDY CROSS

But for one accident, so incomprehensible as to seem miraculous, what happened at Ballyseedy Cross could never be rightly known. That early on Wednesday morning a shattering explosion was heard, that a great rent in the roadside and hideous evidence of bloodshed were discovered later in the day, that nine coffins containing the mutilated remains of prisoners were sent out from the barrack and that for days afterwards 'the birds were eating the flesh off the trees at Ballyseedy Cross' – these facts and these only would be known.

The explanation put out by the Free State authorities was known in the locality to be untrue. They said that the prisoners were blown up by mines attached to barricades set up by the Republicans in Killorglin Road.

No barricade was placed by Republicans in that neighbourhood on that night.

They had, however, at Knocknagoshel, attached a trigger mine to a dump. The following statement was issued on 10 March from IRA Headquarters, Kerry No. 1 Brigade: 'A trigger mine was laid in Knocknagoshel for a member of the Free State Army, Lieutenant O'Connor, who had made a hobby of torturing Republican prisoners in Castleisland. On Tuesday, a party of Free State troops, including Lieutenant O'Connor, proceeded to the place, and two captains, Lieutenant O'Connor, and two privates were killed.'

Reprisals on prisoners, instituted by the Free State Government in Mountjoy on 8 December, 1922, had become a systematic practice in their jails. It was concluded that the slaughter of eight prisoners at Ballyseedy and of four at Killarney and of five at Cahirciveen were reprisals for the Knocknagoshel mine.

Every precaution against disclosure was taken by the

murderers; every preparation was made to make Ireland believe a lie; yet every detail of those three massacres 'by most miraculous organ' has been revealed.

Nine prisoners were taken from Tralee to be killed at Ballyseedy, and nine coffins were sent out from the jail, but only eight men had been killed. Their names were John Daly, George Shea, Timothy Twomey, Patrick Hartnett, James Connell, John O'Connor, Patrick Buckley and James Walsh.

Patrick Buckley, who had five children, was thought by some of his friends to be safe in jail – he had done so much for Michael Brennan in Limerick in the trouble with the Black-and-Tans.

There were others who knew that his action then would be little protection to him now.

John Daly was captured on 4 February. He had been in the Republican Army for seven years or more, and was known to the enemy. They beat him until his spine was injured beyond recovery, in Tralee Jail.

Michael Connell was only twenty-two years old, but since the Conscription menace he had been a Volunteer. He was taken in the middle of February at a dance; he was unarmed, and his mother had no fear for him. She saw him looking out of the prison window on Tuesday evening. 'I'll write tomorrow,' he called. She would not believe that he was one of the victims until a girl who had seen the bodies told her there was a 'black curly boy', she went up and looked then, and knew her son.

James Walsh was well known to be in danger, being a leader and a man with great influence among the people.

George Shea, Tim Twomey, John Shanahan and Stephen Fuller were captured on 21 February in a dugout. They were taken, to be interrogated, to Ballymullen Barracks in Tralee.

'Interrogation', by Neligan in Ballymullen Barracks was an ordeal under which reason might give way. The prisoner, in the usual practice, was first blindfolded, then his arms were tied to his sides, and 'interrogation' began.

This time a hammer was used.

The prisoners were taken in separately. When Shanahan came out his head was covered with blood and his spine was injured, but he was still able to walk.

The hammer failed. The prisoners were taken out to be shot, and shots were fired around their heads. They were then sentenced, for their obdurate silence, to be executed at midnight and were then locked in their cells.

At midnight Stephen Fuller heard his comrades being taken out, one by one, and heard shots fired in the yard.

The guards came for him and took him down to a dark cell.

He saw nine coffins there with the lids closed.

'Three of those have their men,' they told him, 'and this is yours,' and they stopped to unscrew the lid.

For half-an-hour more they were questioning him, he wishing only for a sharp end. Then they locked him into his cell again.

The prisoners were given some kind of trial in the Workhouse on March 3, but no sentence was told. They were kept there for three days more. Shanahan's back had grown weak since the beating in Ballymullen, and before March 6 he collapsed. His illness saved him when his comrades were taken out.

Very early on Wednesday, while it was still dark, Stephen Fuller was called out of his cell. He was taken to the guardroom. George Shea and Timothy Twomey were with him and they found six more prisoners there. An officer was shouting at Patrick Buckley, accusing him of having deserted from the RIC, raging against him for giving over a barrack to Michael Brennan before the Truce. It was true: he had done it: he was to get his punishment now.

The prisoners looked ill; one had a broken arm; all were scarred and bruised and suffering; James Welsh had a bandage on his broken wrist.

The soldiers searched them in the guardroom and took their cigarettes.

They were put into a lorry with a heavy escort and driven along the Castleisland Road. They were being taken, they were told, to remove barricades. They did not believe that – sick men with useless hands and arms.

One of the soldiers handed each of them a cigarette.

'The last smoke you'll have,' he said.

The lorry pulled up near the corner of the Killorglin Road, beside Ballyseedy Wood. They saw a log lying across the road. They were made to get out of the lorry and stand in a close circle around the log.

The soldiers had strong ropes and electric cord. Each prisoner's hands were tied behind him, then his arms were tied above the elbow to those of the men on either side of him. Their feet were bound together above the ankles and their legs were bound together above the knees. Then a strong rope was passed round the nine and the soldiers moved away.

The prisoners had their backs to the log and the mine, which was beside it; they could see the movement of the soldiers and knew what would happen next. They gripped one another's hands, those who could, and prayed for God's mercy upon their souls.

The shock came, blinding, deafening, overwhelming. For Stephen Fuller it was followed by a silence in which he knew that he was alive. Then sounds came to him – cries and low moans, then the sounds of rifle fire and exploding bombs. Then silence again: the work was done.

He turned over; he was not hurt; he was lying under a ditch in the wood. His clothes were scorched and torn to shreds; cords with burnt and broken ends were knotted on both his wrists. The explosion that killed the two men to whom he was bound had severed the cords and thrown him, uninjured, into the ditch.

The soldiers had no means of counting their victims. They went back to their breakfast, and Stephen Fuller crawled away to safety over the fields.

The Military thought him dead; his name was on one of the nine coffins which they sent out.

There was madness among the people of Tralee. What prisoners were in those coffins? No one could tell. The people opened them in the streets.

The frenzy that followed was terrible; the women seemed demented; Free State soldiers were stoned; the funerals of those Republicans kindled a fire through Kerry that it would be difficult to subdue.

The Free State Government issued a new regulation to their Kerry command:-

'Prisoners who die while in military custody in the Kerry command shall be interred by the troops in the area in which the death has taken place.'

It was published in the Dublin press on 21 March.

from TRAGEDIES OF KERRY (1924)

ÉAMON KELLY
FIGHTING AMONG OURSELVES

I was over seven years of age when I went to school in the autumn of 1921. I was always a delicate child and my mother thought she'd never rear me. She swore by beef tea and chicken broth as body builders, but the sustenance failed to fill out my spare shanks.

Molly and Nell Murphy called for me that first morning. They were a few years older than me. My mother held back the tears as I went out the front door in a navy suit, Eton collar and no shoes. All the scholars went barefoot until the winter months.

'How old are you, Edmund?' Mrs O'Leary, the school-mistress, asked me. Jerry Mac, Jer Daniels and Con Dineen nearly burst out laughing when they heard her calling me Edmund. To them and everyone at home I was Ned, young Ned. 'How old are you, Edmund?' she said again.

'I am seven years since last March,' I replied.

'And why did it take so long for you to come to school, Edmund?'

'Well the way it was, Ma'am,' I said, settling myself and talking like one of the men in my father's rambling house. 'The way it was, we were every day waiting for the Tan war to be over!'

'Now that you are here, Edmund,' she told me, 'you'll have to learn very fast to make up for lost time.' And she gave me a new penny. My mother had taught me how to count up to twenty, and I knew most of the letters of the alphabet. Indeed I recognised words like 'cat' and three-lettered words in a sentence like, 'Ned put his leg in the tub.' I had a little head start and I made good progress.

As the autumn died and the winter came, a fire was lit in the school. The pupils supplied the fuel. Well-to-do farmers brought a creel of turf, heeled it out at the gate and boys in the big classes brought it in the armfuls and put it in the turf box in the hall. Those of us who couldn't afford to bring fuel by the creel brought a sod of turf to school each morning. My mother went through the turf shed to find a small sod for me.

With my mother looking after me at home, the two Murphy

girls taking me to school and Mrs O'Leary's daughter teaching me, I began to feel that I was too much under petticoat rule. Having so many women around me was bad for my image. I made friends fast with boys of my own age and even though of a shy nature I managed to get into a few fights. In the playground one day I got a puck of a fist into the throat, sinking the big stud of the Eton collar into my Adam's apple. I cried from pain but soon dried my tears. That belt of a fist hardened me. I left the house on my own every morning and sought the company of the boys going and coming from school. I never again sat down with the girls as they played the game of gobs on the grassy patch by Mac's Well.

Older brothers of the boys going to school were out in the IRA. Not yet carrying arms, they acted as scouts, and one morning we saw Jimmy Williams with a spyglass scanning the countryside. He wasn't on the lookout for English troops. It was 1922 and the Civil War was on. That war divided neighbours. In one case it divided a household as two brothers fought on opposite sides. And it divided us schoolchildren. In the playground and on the way home from school we fought the Republican and the Free State cause. I was on the Republican side. I didn't know what it meant. All I knew was that my Uncle Larry, who worked in Dublin, was a prisoner of the Free State Government and was on hunger strike.

We fought with our fists. We squared out in front of an opponent and called, 'Come on! Put up the dukes!' and the boy who couldn't keep his guard ended up with a bloodied nose. Boys whose fathers accepted the Treaty called us Republicans murderers and looters. And looting did go on. The men talked about it around my father's fire. They told of a prominent citizen who took a cartload of furniture out of the Great Southern Hotel before it was taken over by the regular army. He unloaded his booty in a laneway off College Street and went back to the hotel for a second load. When he returned to College Street the first load was gone. Lifting his eyes to heaven he shouted to the clouds, 'This town is nothing but the seed and breed of robbers! A man couldn't leave anything out of his hand!'

Running battles took place along the road when we were freed from school. Opposing armies lined up and threw stones and clods of earth at each other. The Dineens and I soon found that our Republican allies deserted us, not through cowardice, but because of the fact that they had reached their homes. Now that we were greatly outnumbered by Free State forces, we had to leg it out of the firing line, and take the short-cut home through Mick Sullivan's fields.

But our schoolboy war came to an end when we were brought face to face with the real thing. One day when we were out to play, two Republican soldiers, young Mick Sullivan and Dinny Connor, passed by the school. I can still see their gaitered legs, the rifles slung from their shoulders and the bandoliers about their breasts. One wore a hat and the other a cap. They didn't slope along. They walked as if they were marching to music. The big boys out of fifth and sixth classes walked along with them, chatting all the while. 'We heard shots,' the big boys said. 'The military are somewhere near.' 'That firing,' one of the men replied, 'is as far away as Millstreet.' We watched them as they passed by Jer Leary's house until they were out of sight around the bend towards Fordes' cottage.

Playtime over, the bell rang for us to go back to the classroom. Some time afterwards we heard gunfire, then the sound of lorries. Standing on a desk and looking out, one of the boys said there were soldiers everywhere. It seems when the two Republicans had got around the bend out of our view they looked down into the village of Knockanes and saw that the place was full of military. They decided to engage them and fired into the village. If the soldiers advanced they could easily retreat. They were local men and knew the countryside. Advance the soldiers did, and some say that, hiding behind fences, they put their caps on the tops of their rifles to draw the Irregulars' fire, while others fanned out to encircle the two men. Realising that they could soon be trapped, Connor and Sullivan split up and made a dash for it. In the getaway Mick Sullivan was wounded in the arm. Dinny Connor made his escape and Sullivan barely made it to Jer Leary's house. The Free State advance party was there as soon. Because of his wounded arm Mick Sullivan couldn't use his gun. The soldiers burst into the kitchen. Sullivan surrendered but despite the protests of Jer Leary and his wife they dragged Mick Sullivan outside the front door and shot him dead.

When news came to the school that he was shot, the school

missus and her daughter, later Mrs Spillane, were overcome with grief. We, seeing the anguish in their faces, tried to hold back the tears, and the big girls in the upper classes cried openly. It was then I saw my first Free State soldier. He came into the classroom and stood under the clock. He was a doctor. He wore a white coat which was open at the front and we could see his uniform and his Sam Browne belt. He spoke to Mrs O'Leary very quietly. As far as we could make out he said there was no need to be afraid, that the fighting was over. When he went out we heard the lorries going away. We knelt down and prayed for the soul of the young man lying dead two doors away. In a while's time, as no one could settle down to work again, the school was closed and we went home.

There was no stone-throwing on the road that afternoon. We went quietly and told our parents of the dreadful happening. 'You are too young,' my mother said, 'to be a witness to such terrible things.' I was put to bed early that night and when I came down in the morning there on the window-sill I saw a clay pipe and I knew that my father had spent the night at young Mick Sullivan's wake. The men sitting at our fireside talked the next night and for many a night about the shooting and the refusal of the parish priest to come and give the last rites to the man who died.

Other nights brought other stories. Young Republicans in Kenmare climbed a lean-to roof in the night time, entered a bedroom and shot dead two Free State soldiers as they slept. They were brothers, killed in their father's house when they were home on furlough. Stories of horror vied with each other for our attention: the blowing up of Republican prisoners at Ballyseedy, and forever etched in our minds remains the image of Dave Nelligan, a military officer, taking off his cap and combing his hair as he walked down Fair Hill in Killarney at the head of his troops after they had blown to pieces young Republicans on a mined barricade at the Countess Bridge.

The Civil War was a black time. It blackened the people's minds. Neighbours disagreed as they followed their different loyalties. Old feuds, long dead, were reopened, and hatred was the prevailing emotion. Men in Tralee who were being given back the dead body of a Republican by the regular army refused to accept the remains in a Free State coffin. They went down the town and brought a new one, and with hatchets smashed to pieces the coffin in which he had lain.

Our parish priest, who had refused the last rites to Mick Sullivan, preached continually against the Irregular soldiers. One Sunday he lit the church with language. So fiery was his condemnation of what he called looters and murderers that men of the same way of thinking as Mick Sullivan and Dinny Connor rose from their seats in the body of the church and walked out. A loose heeltip went clanging at every second step on the tiles of the aisle, as if in protest against the reviling of the Republican cause.

from THE APPRENTICE (1995)

SEÁN Ó TUAMA
THE WORLD OF AOGÁN Ó RATHAILLE

Very few details of the life and career of Aogán Ó Rathaille have been established with any certainty. On the meagre evidence available, I think it probable – as was suggested by a nineteenth-century scholar – that his father was a County Cavan man who travelled to the Killarney area to study for the priesthood. Killarney seems to have been noteworthy at this period (c.1650–1690) for its schools and seminaries where *inter alia* Greek and Latin were taught. That seminaries flourished there at the time is due mostly, one thinks, to the fact that the principal English colonists (the Brownes), who had supplanted the native aristocrats (mainly McCarthys and O'Donoghues), were themselves staunch Catholics committed to supporting the activities of their Church.

It is likely that Ó Rathaille's father met and married in the vicinity of Killarney the daughter of one of the hereditary *ollaves* ('poets and learned men') attached to the principal McCarthy family in the district, the McCarthymores of Palice. Her family name was probably Egan, in Irish Mac Aogáin. Some special arrangements would have to be made, of course, so that the landless spoiled priest from northern Ireland and his wife would have a comfortable holding. That holding was secured. I would guess, by the McCarthymores from the Brownes in a barren and remote part of Sliabh Luachra, called *Screathan a' Mhíl* (Scrahana-veel), about ten miles east of Killarney where one of the minor McCarthy nobles was a close neighbour.

Ó Rathaille's mother and father married probably about the years 1670–75, and had a son called Aogán (Egan) – a name absolutely untraditional in the Ó Rathaille family annals in Kerry.

The two influential families, the Brownes and the McCarthy-mores, with whom the poet's parents probably had strong links, played a dominant role in the highly complex social scene in Kerry at the time. The McCarthymore family, like Irish aristocratic families in general, had gradually lost most of its power and territory, during the seventeenth (and late sixteenth) century. By various legal and other subterfuges, however, they had retained a substantial estate (10,000 acres perhaps) at Palice, five miles east of Killarney. They also held, by traditional right, small parcels of land in other districts, one of them in the Sliabh Luachra district close to that granted *c.*1670 to the Ó Rathaille family.

The McCarthymores, in older times the chief family amongst the widespread McCarthy clan, were beginning at this period to accumulate vast debts, and in addition, were being rapidly Anglicised. The particular McCarthymore Aogán Ó Rathaille would have known in his youth was married to the daughter of an English lord, Lord Brittas, who fought on the side of the Catholic King James in 1690, but quite soon afterwards declared for the Protestant winner, King William. (His grandson, known as the last McCarthymore, was to become an officer in the British Army). Even though the McCarthymore in Aogán Ó Rathaille's time still maintained poets and learned men such as the Egans, their estate documents were now being written in English to comply with English legal requirements.

The Browne family on the other hand had prospered during the seventeenth century. They had come to Ireland as colonists in early Elizabethan times (*c.*1854) and during the following century had gradually acquired the confiscated estates of the McCarthys and other Irish families in Kerry, Cork and Limerick, so that in Ó Rathaille's time their vast holdings were in the region of 140,000 acres. The Brownes, like some early Elizabethan planters, were Catholic and in time intermarried with Irish aristocratic families. In fact the mother of the poet's landlord, Sir Nicholas Browne, was a McCarthy, sister of the chief McCarthy figure in County Cork.

It is in no way surprising that the Brownes were highly sympathetic to the Irish Catholic cause, and quite generous in their dealings with families such as the McCarthys – whose acquiescence in the new order of things was, of course, doubly assured by their acceptance of Browne generosity. Several minor McCarthy nobles, for instance, held large tracts of land from the Brownes at a nominal rent. Aogán Ó Rathaille's neighbour and friend, Captain Eoghan McCarthy, was one of these. He held an estate of *c.*3,600 acres on Sliabh Luachra for a mere two shillings a year. This arrangement ensured that Captain McCarthy, gentleman-tenant, having collected quite substantial rents from his undertenants, and having paid his own meagre rent to the Browns, was able to live lavishly and maintain an open house in traditional Irish fashion for poets, scholars, musicians and wandering people.

We have no record of what rent Ó Rathaille's father paid but it is quite likely that it was also a nominal sum, enabling him to live comfortably as gentleman-tenant on the rents collected from whatever undertenants resided on his 300-450 (?) acre farm. So while the family holding may have been bleak, rough and remote, Aogán Ó Rathaille grew up, to some extent, in the privileged position enjoyed by poets from earliest times in Irish society.

We know nothing of his boyhood upbringing. We can only surmise that he herded cows like other children of his age, played games, listened to music and storytelling. He certainly received, somehow or other, a comprehensive education. It would appear from his poetry that he read some Latin; Ovid and Virgil, in particular. He read Old and Medieval Irish prose and verse from manuscripts, and wrote manuscripts himself. He probably knew English and perhaps a little Greek; there is some evidence (for instance his mention of Sancho Panza in a prose satire written in 1713) that he was not unaware of post-Renaissance literature in other countries.

Both his parents could have played an active part in his education. His father, the ex-seminarian, may have given him at home the rudiments of Latin and Greek; his mother may have helped him with his general reading and have sent him from time to time to study with his learned Egan grandfather on the McCarthymore estate, some twenty miles away. The likelihood, however, is that the greater part of his education occurred locally in Gaelic Big Houses and castles, several of which still existed within a radius of a few miles of the Ó Rathaille home. It is certain, for instance, that he visited the O'Donoghue castle in Glenflesk (eight or nine miles away), the home of a renowned aristocratic and poetic family. But it is altogether more likely that the home of his patron and friend, Captain Eoghan McCarthy, at Headford (four or five miles away) was his particular open university. In a poem (c.1700) lamenting Captain Eoghan's dispossession, he tells us how one frequently encountered at Headford gatherings of poets, bards, priests and learned men. There cannot be much doubt that Ó Rathaille was accepted from an early age amongst this privileged band.

Ó Rathaille was possibly fifteen years of age, or thereabouts, when King James and the Jacobite cause was dealt a severe blow at the Battle of the Boyne (1690). In the next few decades the fairly stable world he had grown up in collapsed slowly but inexorably around him. In 1693 the 140,000 acre Browne estate – of which Scrahanaveel was a minute parcel – was confiscated because of Sir Nicholas Browne's allegiance to the defeated Catholic King. The confiscation, however, was to last only for the lifetime of Sir Nicholas (who fled for a time to England, and later to Belgium). Different sons-in-law – one of them an English MP – managed by stealth to keep legal or nominal possession of the estate for a lengthy period, but this did not prevent wholesale destruction and desecration of the property by the new Williamite colonists and by some local entrepreneurs. Trees from the great woods were hacked down and sold at sixpence each; various mining and smelting operations were set up in the Killarney area. Deploying a kind of image familiar to people in a nuclear age. Ó Rathaille declares that the sun had been blotted out by the smoke of these new 'smithies': *'sa ghréin níl taitneamh os fearannaibh, féachaidh,/is ceo na ceártan tá ar a sléibhtibh.'* He likens the young men who had fled abroad after the Boyne to 'young sapling trees, hacked down, dispersed': *'a slata fáis go scáinte réabtha/i gcríochaibh eachtrann scaipthe ó chéile.'* It is clear that he was being shocked into poetry by the stark details of the horror which was now engulfing his boyhood world.

Ironically enough, while the Anglo-Irish Brownes were dispossessed, the old Irish McCarthy family of Palice managed to retain possession of their heavily-burdened estate; this was probably due to their late switch of allegiance to King William. Other McCarthys, however, were not so fortunate. The poet's friend, Captain Eoghan McCarthy who had sided with King James, was singled out for dispossession. So also in time it seems were the O'Rahillys and a number of other important families in the Sliabh Luachra district. It would appear indeed that Sliabh Luachra, compared with other Browne territories, was given very rough treatment indeed. The reason for this calls for some comment.

It seems – and this is a further complicating factor in the social picture of the time – that a great part of Sliabh Luachra c.1700 was a particularly lawless no man's land, a centre of continuing resistance not alone to the new Williamite colonists but also to the old Anglo-Irish colonists such as the Brownes. Chief amongst the resistance leaders were the O'Donoghues of Glenflesk, admired by Aogón Ó Rathaille and feared by gentlemen-tenants of the Brownes such as the Herberts, who were settled on former O'Donoghue lands. The O'Donoghues, who roamed the mountainy Sliabh Luachra district at will, struck terror into the hearts of all colonists. As late as 1729, the probable year of Ó Rathaille's death (at a time he had given up all hope for the restoration of the old order), a report on O'Donoghue activity against a new planter, who had got possession of a farm on Sliabh Luachra, shows clearly that the O'Donoghues, at any rate, had not given up. 'They burnt his crops,' the report states, 'and lifted his cattle . . . his steward was attacked . . . they cut off his ears and tongue, gouged his eyes, and finished their hellish work by stabbing his wife who was enceinte, and cutting out her tongue.' That the forces of the new Williamite order would wish to root out such kinds of traditional resistance on Sliabh Luachra is quite understandable. Aogán Ó Rathaille was one of those who suffered grievously as a consequence.

from REPOSSESSIONS (1985)

Aogán Ó Rathaille
Is Fada Liom Oíche Fhírfliuch

Is fada liom oíche fhírfliuch gan suan, gan srann,
gan ceathra, gan maoin caoire ná buaibh na mbeann;
anfa ar toinn taoibh liom do bhuair mo cheann,
's nár cleachtas im naíon fíogaigh ná ruacain abhann.

Dá maireadh an rí díonmhar ó bhruach na Leamhan
's an ghasra do bhí ag roinn leis lér thrua mo chall
i gceannas na gcríoch gcaoin gcluthar gcuanach gcam,
go dealbh i dtír Dhuibhneach níor bhuan mo chlann.

An Carathach groí fíochmhar lér fuadh an mheang
is Carathach Laoi i ndaoirse gan fuascladh fann;
Carathach, rí Chinn Toirc, in uaigh 's a chlann,
's is atuirse trím chroí gan a dtuairisc ann.

Do shearg mo chroí im chlíteach, do bhuair mo leann,
na seabhaic nár fríth cinnte, agár dhual an eang
ó Chaiseal go Toinn Chlíona 's go Tuamhain thall,
a mbailte 's a dtír díthchreachta ag sluaghaibh Gall.

A thonnsa thíos is airde géim go hard,
meabhair mo chinnse cloíte ód bhéiceach tá;
cabhair dá dtíodh arís ar Éirinn bhán,
do ghlam nach binn do dhingfinn féin id bhráid.

PATRICK GIVEN
ON VISITING THE GRAVES
OF THE GAELIC POETS AT MUCKROSS

That Nature here erupts beyond her measure
In riches vast and varied to awe the eye,
And with a spendthrift's hand spills out her treasure,
Is sure no wonder, for here great poets lie.
They know what sorrow is, what broken heart,
They saw, alas, the tongue they served diminish,
Patrons, from prince to beggar, change their part,
They saw the Gaelic world all but finish.
They lie in exile here among their own,
For no one greets them in the ancient tongue,
– Shattered their dream, the world they had known –
And we, who make in foreign words a song,
    Only intrude upon their sacred haunt,
    We bear no tribute here, instead a taunt.

SEAN McCARTHY
DARLING KATE

You are fair of face, dear Kate, now you're nearing twenty-one,
I hesitate to spoil your dreams, when your life has just begun.
Your father he is old, *a grah,* and I am far from strong,
A dowry from John Hogan's son would help us all along.

Just think of it, my darling Kate, you would own a motor car,
You'd wear fine linen next your skin and travel near and far.
Hogan's lands stretch far and wide, from Rathea to Drummahead;
He owns sheep and cows and fine fat sows; pyjamas for the bed!

I know he's tall and skinny, Kate, and his looks are not the best,
But beggars can't be choosers, love, when you're feathering
          your nest!
He's been to college in the town, his shirts are always new,

What does it matter if he's old, he's just the man for you!
I know you love young Paddy Joe, him with the rakish eye,
I've seen the way you glance at him whenever he goes by.
I will admit he's handsome, Kate, but he doesn't own a car,
Sure he likes to fight and drink all night above in Sheehan's bar.

Did I ever tell, you, Kate *a grah*, that I was pretty too?
The summer days seemed longer then, and the sky was
        always blue!
I was only gone nineteen, and your father fifty-three,
But he owned the land on which we stand, and he seemed
        the man for me.

There was a young man lived next door, I loved with all my
        might,
It was his face that haunted me when your father held me tight;
I longed, dear Kate, down through the years, for the soft
        touch of his hand,
But young love is no substitute for ten acres of fine land.

You will wear a long white dress and a red rose in your hair,
I will throw confetti, Kate, the whole town will be there;
You will make your promise true, to honour and obey,
I will stand on your right hand, and I'll send my love away.

Tears are not for daytime, Kate, but only for the night,
You'll have a daughter of your own and teach her wrong from
        right;
Rear her strong and healthy, Kate, pray guidance from above.
Then one fine day when she's nineteen – she might marry
        just for love.

PAT SPILLANE
A BORN FOOTBALLER

There was little in the way of organised under-age football when I was growing up in Templenoe in the sixties. Back then the only football field in the area was at the other end of the parish in Dromore, five or six miles away from our house. To me, football meant playing around in the yard or kicking the ball against the garage door.

My first real taste of competitive football came when I enrolled in 'The Sem', or to give it its official name, St Brendan's College, Killarney. I was twelve at the time. Prior to that I played no more than one or two games a year. Indeed, I saw very few competitive matches and never played outside the Kenmare District Board area. So I had no idea if I was any good.

The only reason I remember my first day at secondary school was because we played a game of Gaelic football. During it I realised I was one of the best players on the field. Fr Pierce, a teacher in the college, gave me and the rest of the my classmates our first ever formal coaching session in the skills of Gaelic football.

Attending St Brendan's as a boarder helped my football education as well as my academic education. If I hadn't gone there, I would never have made it to third level college and qualified as a teacher. Studying was compulsory – three and half hours every evening. It seemed like a terrible chore at the time, but I know had I attended a day school it would have been both impossible and impractical to study for that period of time while living over a bar.

The college was big into sport, particularly Gaelic football. I was very lucky because my first year there coincided with St Brendan's first ever victory in the All-Ireland colleges' final in 1969. John O'Keeffe captained the team and other players included Ger O'Keeffe and his brother Tony, who is now the Kerry County Board GAA secretary. Those guys were our heroes. It made our day when John O'Keeffe nodded to us in the corridor.

The ambition of virtually every youngster in Brendan's was to make the college's senior football team. Observing how the students on the All-Ireland winning team were treated, we quickly realised there were a lot of perks to be had if you were lucky enough to make the senior squad. There were training sessions during study periods, the senior players got better food, they travelled to matches in the best carriages on the train and they were a big hit with the girls from the nearby convent schools.

As first years we were envious of them and this fuelled a desire to be part of this scene. I made the senior team in my last two years there. In 1972 we reached the All-Ireland final. In the semi-final we beat Franciscan College, Gormanstown. Their star midfielder was Ogie Moran – who won an All-Ireland Colleges' medal the following year – while his opposite number on our team was Páidí Ó Sé.

On April 16, 1972 I made my Croke Park debut in the All-Ireland Colleges' final against St Patrick's, Cavan. We felt like professional footballers in the weeks leading up to the final. We travelled to Dublin by train the day before the match and stayed in the Spa Hotel in Lucan. Our coach, Fr Hegarty, took us to the Phoenix Park for a kick-around before the match.

We worked on a preplanned move which we put into use straight from the throw-in. It worked and we scored one of the quickest points ever seen in an All-Ireland final at Croke Park. However, it was downhill all the way afterwards. There was no age-limit in colleges football at the time and I think our opponents had a lot of guys who were repeating their Leaving Certificate. They completely dominated us physically, with players like Kieran O'Keeffe and Ollie Brady causing us all kinds of problems. They won by nine points.

It was a particularly forgettable day for me as I was substituted in the second half. Nobody could have envisaged then that Croke Park would eventually become a happy hunting ground for me. Within five months I was back on the Croke Park pitch. But I wasn't supposed to be there. Kerry qualified to play title holders Offaly in the 1972 All-Ireland final. Páidí Ó Sé and myself got permission from the college authorities to attend the game.

After the match, which ended in a draw, Páidí met a few acquaintances from West Kerry and, of course, being a social animal I willingly joined the party. We had a few drinks and missed the train back to Killarney. We didn't panic. We booked into a bed and breakfast on Clonliffe Road. Later that night we attended a dance in the Ierne ballroom on Parnell Square.

Walking back to the B&B after the dance we noticed the gates of Croke Park were still open. So Páidí and I ended up kicking an imaginary ball around the pitch at two o'clock in the morning watched by a bemused female – an old flame of Páidí's if memory serves me right. Little did we realise then that within three years we would be back in the stadium playing with a real football in an All-Ireland final.

Not surprisingly, there was consternation around St Brendan's when we failed to return on Sunday night and the college authorities notified our respective mothers.

Páidí and I hadn't a care in the world. In fact, we didn't even bother making the early train the following day. We eventually got back to Killarney on Monday night. We received what could only be described as a severe verbal warning from the college authorities, but escaped any serious punishment. I'm sure the fact that we were star footballers on the college team helped our case.

In 1973 I was captain of Brendan's and my brother, Mike, was also a member of the team. We retained the Munster title, beating Tralee CBS – who had Mike Sheehy on their side – in the final. I produced my best ever performance for the Sem in that match and I won the Man of the Match award.

Incidentally on the night of the Munster final a new alcohol-free disco bar was opened in St Mary's Parish Hall in Killarney. The Munster trophy was filled with lemonade and one of the first men to drink from it was the then Bishop of Kerry Eamonn Casey, who officially opened the new bar. The dormitory I stayed in for three of my five years in St Brendan's was situated in what was known as the new wing. Just a concrete block away from my bed was the Bishop's Palace where Dr Casey lived and, indeed, it was during my college days that Annie Murphy was entertained there!

We were beaten in the 1973 All-Ireland semi-final by St Jarlath's, Tuam, who lost to Gormanstown College in the final. Even though my football career with the Sem ended on a disappointing note, I reckon that the roving tactics I later became famous for evolved during my days in secondary school. Back then, colleges' football was a 13-a-side game. There were two players in the full-back line opposed by two inside forwards. But there were no real set positions. I was one of those inside forwards and during matches I started to drift across the entire full forward line.

I developed a kind of free spirit and I loved to roam, not just along the full forward line, but all over the field. Thankfully nobody ever stopped me. Perhaps, if there was a dictatorial type manager in charge of the Brendan's team, I would have been whipped back into line and told to stay in one position. However, nobody told me to stop and roving became one of my trademarks.

I played on the Kerry minor teams in 1972 and 1973 but we were beaten in successive Munster finals by Cork, who went on to complete a hat-trick of provincial titles. The 1972 Cork team, which included Jimmy Barry Murphy and Tom Creedon, went on to win the All-Ireland. Kerry had quite a good team and many of the players on it had great success later at senior level.

I was unfortunate at under-age level because I was born on 1 December, 1956. My brother Mike, who was born in January 1957 was just 13 months younger than me. But from a football perspective there are two years between us: the GAA use January 1st as the cut off date for under-age competition. This meant I missed out on what should have been my best year as a minor.

Quite honestly, I was nothing more than an average county minor. While I did stand out in my late year at colleges level I don't think the standard was particularly high. There was no indication back then that one day I would become a famous footballer.

I failed to get an honour in Irish in the Leaving Certificate and, while it wasn't my favourite subject, I always blamed football for this. On the day of the oral Irish exam in 1973 we had a trial game as we were busy preparing for the All-Ireland series. Somebody, presumably the team coach, got the time of my exam changed so that I could play in the match. I can only assume the examiner, a female, wasn't impressed at the idea of her schedule being changed because of a football match and she gave me an awful grilling.

I'm often asked how did I manage to reach the top in Gaelic football in such a short space of time. Within two years of failing to impress as a minor I won an All-Ireland at senior level.

I wasn't the kind of footballer who would feature in a coaching manual. I used my left foot for standing on most of the time although, curiously enough, I managed to score a few soft goals with it. I wasn't a tremendous fielder although I played at midfield when I first made my name at club level with Kenmare. In 1973 I was Man of the Match in the county semi-final between Kenmare and Austin Stacks, even though we lost. It was this performance which first brought me to the attention of the Kerry selectors.

Studying physical education at Thomond College in 1973 gave me a head start. But the main reason I became a great footballer was because I worked hard at it. I don't think any player trained as hard as I did. I made unbelievable sacrifices: I constantly practised the various skills, be it picking up the ball, soloing or kicking.

One of the main reasons why the skills levels have dropped in Gaelic football in the last decade is because the majority of players are not prepared to go off on their own and practice the skills.

I regarded myself as a skilful player – although I wasn't perceived as such. I have a theory that the majority of players who are regarded as skilful have a questionable work rate. Southampton soccer player Matt Le Tissier would be a prime example. People seemed to think that because I spent all day running up and down the field it hid weaknesses in my game. It annoyed me that I was regarded as a workaholic type player rather than a skilful one.

I devoured all the manuals written about Gaelic football and, from closely watching other sports, I came to appreciate how important it is for forwards to run off the ball and create space. Even in my current arthritic state, I am still very good at losing my marker and making space for myself. It was one of the strongest characteristics of my game. My chief tutor in this area was Kenny Dalglish. I learned a great deal from watching him play. His work rate off the ball was tremendous and he could lose his marker by a 'shimmy' or running in one direction and then veering off in another.

I simply cannot understand why footballers don't practice kicking the ball more. In golf, if a pro has a bad day on the greens he goes out early the next morning with a hundred balls and practises his putting until he feels he has got his rhythm back. Unfortunately, in Gaelic football, very few players who kick badly go out the next day and practice what is essentially a very simple technique. The reason I was good at kicking was because I tried to practise every day for at least one hour – sometimes two. There are a few simple principles involved. If you are kicking with your right foot then your left foot must be firmly on the ground, you lean towards the target and follow through.

Nowadays many talented under-age players lose interest in Gaelic football once they sample wine, women and song. So why didn't I follow that path? It's not that I wasn't tempted. I'm now 28 years playing for Templenoe. I had my first senior match when I was fourteen. As a result I mixed with adults from a very early age. I had my first drink when I was sixteen. Templenoe won a carnival tournament in Kenmare to capture our first trophy for many years. In true Templenoe fashion, it was an occasion which demanded a major celebration. I drank several pints of cider in recognition of our achievement.

I chose cider because I couldn't be seen drinking Guinness or Smithwicks. Cider looked like Cidona so it was all right – or so I thought. Later that night I got as sick as a dog in bed and my mother wasn't too pleased. It was one of the rare times she gave out to me even though it wasn't really a telling off. She just said: 'You let me down.' I never drank cider again. The other beverage I never touch is wine. My dislike of it was the result of another binge much later in life.

Given the fact that my mother is a devout Catholic the Pope's visit to Ireland in 1979 was a big event in our family. My brother, Mike, presented an oak sapling to the Pope in Galway on behalf of the youth of Ireland, my mother went to see the Holy Father in Limerick and I was sent to Dublin to the open-air mass in the Phoenix Park. I travelled up by train and was collected at the station by ex-Republic of Ireland soccer international Ray Treacy and World Superstars champion Brian Budd. They knew each other from playing soccer in Canada and I got friendly with Budd while competing in the World Superstars the previous year.

As far as I can recall all the pubs closed early that night in Dublin and the only drink to be had was wine in the night clubs in Leeson Street. I didn't like the taste of it but somebody suggested I mix orange juice with it. So I ended up drinking pints of wine laced with orange juice.

I woke up the following morning in Ray Treacy's house feeling awful. I muttered to Ray that I better head off to the Phoenix Park. He said: 'Come in here to the sitting room. There's about ten minutes of it left on television.' That was it – I never again drank wine.

But even though I didn't practise a life of temperance it must be remembered that in the early seventies there wasn't nearly as much excessive teenage drinking as there is nowadays. We didn't have as much money in our pockets as youngsters have now and, in general, there weren't as many distractions as there are now. We might go for a few drinks one night a week. Of course, living at home helped me to keep on the straight and narrow.

Much later, when I should have had sense, the wheels came off the wagon – albeit occasionally. Three weeks before the 1985 All-Ireland final, I wrote off my car returning home from the Rose of Tralee festival in the early hours of the morning. In fact it's not quite accurate to say that I wrote off the car – it was a friend who was driving at the time. After a night at the festival I was so inebriated I couldn't drive so I left the job to a friend. Four of us headed for home in the car and we all fell asleep.

We went off the road at Looscannagh on the Killarney-Kenmare road. The car landed on its four wheels parallel to a lake. When I got out the passenger door I stepped into water. Had it plunged a few yards further from the road we would probably all have drowned. A local wag reckoned that when the black box was recovered the only thing heard on it was snoring!

In general I stayed away from the drink in the run-up to matches. Normally I didn't touch the stuff for three weeks before a big game. Naturally, I had to spend a few days quenching my thirst afterwards.

from SHOOTING FROM THE HIP
THE PAT SPILLANE STORY (1998)

MUIRIS Ó SÚILLEABHÁIN
LÁ SEILGE

Lá arna mháireach dob é an Domhnach é, bhi sé an-bhreá ar fad. Bhí an fharraige ina báinté, gan fuaim le cloisint ach glór na dtonn ag briseadh isteach ar an dTráigh Bháin agus coiscéimeanna na bhfear ag siúl an Tóchar anuas fé dhéin an chaladh le dul go dtí an Aifreann.

Bhí sé nó seacht do naomhóga Lár Bá amach anois agus na fearaibh stripálta go dtí sna léinte geala iontu. Is gearr go bhfeicim Tomás anuas chugham – Dia dhuit, a Thomáis, arsa mise. – An Dia céanna dhuit, ar seisean, nach breá an lá ar an gcnoc é? an mbeadh aon mhisneach ort? ar seisean. – Th'anam 'on riabhach, téanam, arsa mise.

Seo linn gan an tarna focal do rá nó go rabhamair bóthar an chnoic amach agus ceol binn ag imeacht trím chluasa ag na cearca fraoigh a bhí ag seimint gan staonadh ar a mhullach. Bhí madra agam féin agus madra eile ag Tomás. – B'fhéidir, arsa Tomás, go mbeadh dosaen cánóga thiar i mBun na Raithni againn agus dosaen eile coiníní. Tá an-mhadra agamsa chúchu, ar seisean.

Ní fada go rabhamair thiar ag Loc na gCapall, teas na gréine ag scoilt na gcloch an uair sin agus ceann allais orainn féin. Luíomair síos ar thortóig. An riabhach do Thomás ná go raibh pip agus tobac aige. Tharraig amach í agus do dhearg í ar a shástacht. I gceann tamaill, sineann sé chugham féin í. – Á, ní chaithim í, arsa mise. – Tástáil í, ar seisean. Bheireas uirthi. Nuair a bhí mo dhóthain ólta agam di, shíneas chuige arís í. – An maith leat í? ar seisean. – Is maith, arsa mise.

Do shíneas siar ansan fé theas na gréine, ach ambriathar nach fada a bhíos nuair a bhraitheas Loc na gCapall ag imeacht timpeall orm. Tháinig scanradh agus liathbhuí orm. Bhí Tomás an uair sin ag amhrán dó féin. – A Thomáis, arsa mise, tá rud éigin ag teacht orm. D'fhéach sé orm agus dhein gáire: – Ó, ní faic é sin, ar seisean, an iomad don bpíp a chaithis; má chuireann tú amach, beidh tú go maith. B'fhearr liom bheith marbh ná an chuma go rabhas. Bhíos ag seitreach agus ag piastáil riamh agus choíche nó gur chuireas amach, agus ansan dar fia bhíos comh maith agus bhíos riamh.

Amach linn agus ní raibh na madraí le fáil againn. Seo liom ag feadaíl, ach ní raibh an madra ag teacht. Do ghlaos go hard ansan: – Beauty, Beauty, Beauty! mar b'shin é an ainm a bhí ar mo mhadra agam. Bhí Tomás taobh thiar díom agus gach glaoch aige ar a mhadra féin: – Topsy, Topsy, Topsy! I gceann tamaill, tháinig Beauty agus coinín trasna ar a bhéal aige. – Mo chroí go deo thú, a Bheauty, arsa mise. Is gearr ina dhiaidh sin gur tháinig Topsy agus gan faic aige. – Féach anois, a Thomáis, arsa mise, ciacu is fearr do sna madraí? Níor fhan focal aige.

Seo linn siar ansan go dtí Bun an Raithní, agus ambriathar gur gearr gur bhraith mo mhadrasa cánóg. Seo linn ag taighdeadh an phoill, thugamir uair go leith ag taighdeadh linn, ach bhí sé ródhaingean agus chaitheamair tabhairt suas. B'shiúd linn arís comh fada siar leis na Clocháin Gheala. – Tá an-sheans anois linn ar dhosaen coinín, arsa Tomás, mar tá na rapaí an-éadrom anso. – Féach, arsa mise, tá rud éigin braite ag Beauty. – Tá go díreach, arsa Tomás.

Seo linn síos ins na cosa in airde, shás féin siar mo lámh, agus dar fia gur tharraigíos aniar coinín breá saille. – Th'anam 'on diucs, arsa Tomás ag cur glam as, tá ceann eile braite ag Topsy. Seo leis síos, sháigh siar a lámh, agus tharraig amach stumpa do choinín mhór. Bhí ag rith linn go maith anois, agus is gearr go raibh dosaen go leith coiníní againn.

– Tá sé comh maith againn ár scíth do thógaint anois, arsa Tomás ag suí ar thortóig agus ag tarrac a phípe amach arís. Síneann chugham féin í. – Á mhuise, beannaím uaim í, fuaireas ciall cheannaigh cheana uaithi, arsa mise.

Bhí sé meán lae anois, an ghrian i bpríomh a maitheasa, agus brothall thar barr ann. Sa chaint dúinn éiríonn Tomás aniar ar a uillinn. – An bhfuil a fhios agat cá raghaimíd an chuid eile don lá? ar seisean. – Cén áit? arsa mise. – Ag bailiú uibhe faoileann ó thuaidh sa Scornaigh, ar seisean. – An-mhaith, arsa mise.

Seo linn le gach deabhadh nó gur thánamair go dtí béal na Scornaí. D'fhéachas uaim síos ar an bhfaill, agus dar fia tháinig meadhrán im cheann. – Cad é an mac máthar a dh'fhéadfadh dul ansan síos, a Thomáis? arsa mise. – Dhera a dhuine, ar seisean ag déanamh gáire, ceal taithí atá ort. Sin é mar a bhíos féin an chéad lá a chuas in aonacht le Seán Ó Sé, bhí sé liom riamh agus choíche nó gur thoilíos le dul síos in aonacht leis. – B'fhéidir an ceart a bheith agat, arsa mise. Tá comh maith

againn na coiníní a chur in bhfolach anso ar barra agus gan a
bheith á n-iompar síos agus aníos, arsa mise.
   – An-sheift, arsa Tomás. Siúd linn ag cuardach poill mhaith
oiriúnach chun iad a chur ann. – Tá poll maith anso, a Thomáis,
arsa mise. – Á an riabhach, ar seisean, gheobhaidh na caobacha
amach ansan iad. Fuaireamair poll maith sa deireadh, agus mise
á rá leat nár fhágamair oiread agus poll bioráin gan clúdach
timpeall orthu le rabháin agus scraithíní. Nuair a bhí san déanta
againn, thugamair ár n-aghaidh síos fén bhfaill.
   Bhí Tomás romham síos agus mise ina dhiaidh. Tomás comh
pocléimeach le haon ghabhar trí sna screathain, ach níorbh
ionadh dhó bheith, mar is iontu a chaitheadh sé a shaol. – Tóg
go breá réidh é, ar seisean liomsa, le heagla go mbainfeá aon
chloch led chois agus ansan mé féin do bhualadh san cheann le
linn di imeacht le fánaidh – sin é an uair a bheadh an liútar-
éitear agat, a Mhuiris, nuair a bheifeá ag féachaint ormsa ag
imeacht le haill ar nós na cloiche. – Ná bí ag caint mar sin, a
Thomáis, arsa mise, mar chuirfeá diamhaireacht orm.
   Bhí saghas fuarallais ag teacht tríom amach le diamhaireacht na
háite. Stadas ar bharra stocáin agus d'fhéachas tharm in airde. Ba
mhó ná san an criothán a tháinig orm nuair a thugas fé ndeara an
com dubh méiscreach agus é ina sheasamh suas díreach. D'fhéachas
síos agus gan fém bun ach an poll gorm. A Dhia na bhfeart, arsa
mise, nach dainséarach an áit go bhfuilim! Chonac Tomás ins an
am chéanna fém bun síos ag strapadóireacht ar nós an ghabhair gan
cíos cás ná cathú air. Ba mhór go léir an macalla a bhí sa bhfaill
agus í bán gléigeal ag tuar na n-éanlaithe mara – na héin dearga,
na faoileáin bheaga, na faoileáin gheala, na cánóga, na fochain, na
crosáin, na fiaigh mhara, na caobacha agus na guardail, agus a scread
féin ag gach ceann dóibh agus a nead féin déanta isteach sa chloich
aige. Is gearr anois go raibh an diamhaireacht ag imeacht dom, agus
mé ag machnamh gur chruaidh an saol a bhí acu ar an gcuma go
rabhadar ag soláthar ar nós aon pheacach.
   Sa mhachnamh dom, do chonac éan dearg ag déanamh orm
isteach tríd an aer lom díreach, bhí sé ag druideam liom go mear,
bhí sé an-ghairid dom anois, agus cad a bhí ach beart salán trasna
ar a ghob aige. Bhí sé ag druideam liom agus ag druideam liom
riamh agus choíche nó go raibh sé i ngiorracht cúig slata dhom.
B'ait liom é, dúrt liom féin gur dhócha go raibh sé chun stad
ar an stocán, luíos féin síos ins an chraobh mhór fhada a bhí ag

fás im thimpeall, dhein sé orm isteach go neamheaglach, thugas fogha fé lem láimh go mbéarfainn air, ach cá mbeadh sé dulta ach isteach i bpoll a bhí taobh liom. D'éiríos, d'fhéachas ar an bpoll, poll rapaí a bhí ann, é lán do thuar amuigh ina bhéal. Seo liom ag taighdeadh, ach geallaim duit gurbh fhuirist é thaighdeadh, mar nár dheineas faic ach mo lámh do shá siar agus an scailp a thógaint in airde. Cad a bhuailfeadh liom ach fuipín breá ramhar. Shás siar mo lámh arís chun an t-éan dearg do tharrac aniar, ach más ea b'fhearr liom ná déanfainn, mar do bheir sé orm go dóite lena ghob géar. Tharraigíos aniar go tapaidh í agus thugas fogha eile fé. Bheireas suas ar scornaigh air, ach do chuir san na gathaí go dóite i bhfeidhm orm. D'fhéachas ar dhrom mo láimhe, agus bhí sé go léir scrabhaite gearrtha aige, ach ba chuma liom, ón uair go raibh dhá éan agam, bhíos an-shásta liom féin.

D'éiríos im sheasamh. D'fhéachas uaim síos. Ní raibh Tomás agam le feiscint. Chuireas glam asam: – A Thomáis! arsa mise go hard. A Thomáis, arsa an macalla am fhreagairt féin. – Sea! arsa Tomás i bhfad síos. Sea! arsa an macalla á fhreagairt, sa tslí go dtabharfá an leabhar go raibh ceathrar sa bhfaill. Tuigeadh dom an uair sin go raibh Tomás na mílte ó bhaile uaim. A Dhia na bhfeart, arsa mise liom féin, is le haill a raghaidh sé, má mhairim beo – ní raghad féin a thuilleadh, pé ar domhan é.

Seo liom ansan ag máineáil liom ar mo shuaimhneas anonn is anall tríd an screathan, nó gur thána trasna ar pholl rapaí eile agus tuar thar barr amuigh ina bhéal. Tháinig misneach dom. Dar fia go bhfuil fuipín eile agam. Seo liom ag taighdeadh ar an bpoll, agus ambriathar nach fada a bhíos nuair a tharraigíos aniar pataire do fhuipín mhór. B'é críoch agus deireadh na mbeart é go raibh trí dosaen fuipín agam tar éis mo mháineála dhom. Bhíos anois ar an bhfiagaí ba shásta ar shléibhte Chiarraí. Shuíos ar stocán agus tharraigíos chugham an foiscealach aráin a bhí agam in gcomhair an lae, agus deirim leat gur itheas go sásta agus go hocrasach é. D'éiríos ansan agus d'fhéachas ar na fuipíní a bhí caite in ngabhal a chéile sa chlais agam. Stadas ag breithniú orthu. Do mhachnaíos láithreach ar conas a bhéarfainn abhaile iad. Sa deireadh chuimhníos go raibh rópa timpeall mo choim. Scaoileas é, bheireas ar dhosaen fuipín, chuireas a gcinn le chéile, agus chuireas aon tsnaidhm amháin ar an ndosaen san. Dheineas an cleas céanna le dosaen agus dosaen eile nó go raibh na trí dosaen istigh ar an rópa agam.

Bhí an ghrian anois ar nós pláta do dhroim na Tiarachta siar faid mo radhairce do bhóthar a bhí comh buí leis an ór, agus é ag glioscarnaigh ag gathaí na gréine sínte uaim siar sa bhfarraige. D'fhéachas síos fém bun, ach ní raibh Tomás ag teacht fós, mar fear ab ea é ná raibh deabhadh ná deithneas riamh air an fhaid a bheadh ailp aige á fháil. Lena linn sin, do ligeas fead air, agus do fhreagair an macalla mé ar an nós céanna. Ní fada ina dhiaidh sin gur chuala Tomás ag rá, Táim ag teacht anois! Shuíos síos arís ag brath leis. Bhí na céadta éan ag eiteallaigh im thimpeall, coiníní ag pocleimrigh ó rabhán go rabhán, boladh cumhra ón mbláth gheal a bhí ag fás ar an gcraobh agus ón raithnigh, árthaí móra agam le feiscint fé íor na spéire, agus dar fia ba dhóigh leat gur ar lasadh a bhíodar ag an ngréin, ceo brothaill anso is ansúd ins na cumaracha, agus clocha scáil timpeall orm ag lagú mo radhairce lena nglioscarnaigh.

Is gearr go bhfeaca Tomás faid mo radhairce síos fém bun agus é ag déanamh chugham aníos go mall, aghaidh shalach smeartha air do dheascaibh na cré, agus gan aon gheansaí air. Chaitheas gáire breá a dhéanamh nuair a chonac an cló a bhí air – bhí a gheansaí bainte aige dhó, corda fáiscithe ar a bhéal aige, agus pé seilg a bhí aige, is ann thíos a bhí sé, agus é caite siar ar a dhrom. Tháinig sé aníos mar a rabhas féin agus lig uaidh an geansaí go haiclí.

– Th'anam 'on diabhal, a Thomáis, arsa mise, cad atá sa gheansaí agat? – Tá, a bhuachaill, ar seisean ag cuimilt a chaipín dona éadan d'iarraidh an t-allas a thiormú dhó féin, uibhe forchain agus uibhe crosáin agus uibhe faoileáin. – Dar fia, tá an-lámh déanta agat, arsa mise. – Th'anam 'on riabhach, canathaobh nár chuais síos? Bheadh a dhá oiread eile againn, a dhuine, dá raghfá. – Tháinig an iomad scanradh ormsa, arsa mise, ag ligint orm ná raibh aon seilg déanta agam féin – ní fheacaidh sé na fuipíní fós. Is dócha go bhfuil sé comh maith againn bheith ag imeacht, arsa mise ag éirí im sheasamh agus ag dul go dtí an mbeart agus á bhualadh ar mo dhrom. D'fhéach Tomás orm: – Cad tá agat? ar seisean. – Tá fuipíní go leor, arsa mise. – Cá bhfuairis iad? ar seisean go hiontaiseach. – Fuaireas anso sa screathan iad gan corraí as, arsa mise. – Dar fia, is tú an fiagaí is fearr a bhuail trasna ormsa riamh, ar seisan.

Bhíomair go bogadh linn anois in gcoinne na faille in airde. Seo linn ó strapa go strapa agus ó thortóig go tortóig nó gur bhaineamair amach barra.

Thógamair ár scíth ansan. – Fan go bhfeicfidh tú na huibhe atá agamsa, arsa Tomás ag oscailt an gheansaí. Ba ghleoite leat féachaint orthu, iad lán do spotaí dubha agus do spotaí dearga. – Tá ard-sheilg againn, arsa mise. – An-mhaith, arsa Tomás, ach an mó fuipín atá agatsa? – Tá trí dosaen, arsa mise. – Och, ar mh'anam féin ná tabharfam abhaile go deo iad, mar sin, arsa Tomás, Is é an áit go bhfuil an obair anois, ar seisean, mura bhfuil na huibhe glan tar éis na trioblóide go léir. – Ná feiceann tú féin go bhfuil siad glan? arsa mise ag déanamh gáire. – Ó, ní hé sin an glanachar atá agam á rá, ar seisan, ach téanam ort agus beidh a fhios againn má táid, ag imeacht leis síos agus mise ina dhiaidh ó dheas go dtí loig mhór uisce a bhí i bportach.

– Féach anois, ar seisean ag breith ar ubh, má tá glogar san ubh so, fanfaidh sé ar snámh ar bharra an uisce, agus má tá sé glan raghaidh sé síos ar tóin. Lena linn sin, cuireann sé an t-ubh san uisce, ach más ea fanann sé ar snámh. – Och, th'anam 'on diabhal, ar seisean, tá an gearrcach ansan, ag breith air amach as an uisce agus á smiotadh i gcoinne carraige, agus cad a bheadh ann ach an gearrcach. – Dar fia, ar seisean, gur maith an tosnú é. Chuir sé isteach ceann eile, agus más ea b'é an dálta céanna é. – Ó, an riabhach ceann glan agat, arsa mise. – Is dóigh liom é, ar seisean. Bhí ó cheann go ceann aige á chur isteach, ach b'é an dálta céanna acu go léir é.

Thit an lug ar an lag aige ansan tar éis ar shiúlaigh sé i rith an lae agus gan faic dá bharr aige. D'aithníos air go raibh sé an thromchroíoch mar gheall air sin. – Sea, ná bac san, arsa mise, ná fuil ár ndóthain againn tar éis an lae? ná beidh dosaen go leith coinín agus dosaen go leith fuipín ag gach éinne againn? – Tá an ceart agat, ar seisean, ní ceart dúinn bheith ag cnáimhseáil in aon chor.

Roinneamair an tseilg ansan, agus deirimse leat gur maith tóstalach a bhíomair nuair a bhíodar déanta suas ina mbeartáin againn i gcomhair an bhóthair abhaile. D'fhéachas ar Tomás arís agus dheineas gáire. – Ní fheadar 'on domhan, arsa Tomás, canathaobh go bhfuileann tú ag gáiri fúm ó mhaidean. – Táim, arsa mise, mar ba dhóigh le duine gur ápa thú, tánn tú comh salach san. – Dar fia, ar seisean, má táim comh salach leatsa, tá an riabhnach buí ar fad orm.

– Cad ba dhóigh leat, arsa mise, dá dtabharfaimís tumadh maith dhúinn féin sa loig – nár mhaith an tseift é? – An-cheart, arsa Tomás. Chaitheamair dínn anuas a raibh orainn agus chuamair isteach inti, agus dar fia, nuair a bhí an tumadh san tabhartha againn agus sinn fáiscithe suas, go rabhamair comh húr agus go siúlfaimís an cnoc fé dhó arís. – An riabhach, a Thomáis, gurbh iontach é an tumadh san. – Dhera a dhuine, éist, ar seisean, ach ní mé an duine céanna in aon chor. Anois in ainm Dé tugaimís ár n-aghaidh ar an dtigh.

Bhí sé ag éirí déanach. Bhí an ghrian ina luí in íor na spéire, an drúcht ag titeam go trom, mar bhí an t-aer ag fuarú, na cupóga ag dúnadh isteach ar a chéile in gcomhair na hoíche, éanlaithe na mara ag screadaigh mar thagaidis fé dhéin na ngearrcach, glór ag na coiníní á bhaint as an raithnigh ag teacht amach as an gcoinigéar dóibh mar ba ghnách, glioscarnach, na gclocha scáil imithe as amharc, agus cuma uaigneach ag teacht ar na cumaracha. – Tá sé ina óiche, a Thomáis, arsa mise. – Tá, ar seisean, an dóigh leat ná gur maith an cliathán atá ag an lá? – Ambriathar féin gur maith, arsa mise, agus dar fia gur dócha go mbeidh imni ar mo mhuintir im thaobhsa, mar níl a fhios acu cá bhfuilim agus dá dheascaibh sin tuigfidh siad gur in bpoll éigin atáim dulta. – Dhé mo léir, arsa Tomás, is minic a bhíos-sa agus gurb é lár na hoíche a thabharfadh abhaile mé. – Ó, ní mar a chéíle mise agus tusa, arsa mise. – Canathaobh nach ea? ar seisean, nach duine mé comh maith leatsa? – Ó, arsa mise, seanmhadra is ea tusa sa chnoc, agus tá taithí ag do mhuintir ort a bheith amuigh moch déanach, ach is é an chéad lá agamsa é. – Ach nílimse riamh ar an saol, arsa Tomás, agus dá bhrí sin do chaitheas an chéad lá amuigh déanach.

Ní fada anois go raibh radharc ar an mbaile againn. Bhí na lampaí ar lasadh ins gach tigh agus fothram ag na madraí ag sceamhaíl, scáth na dtithe agus na gcarraigeacha máguairt go soiléir le feiscint sa bhfarraige a bhí ansúd ina luí gan corraí ach ar nós tobar fíoruisce, an ghealach ag cur di aníos do dhroim Chnoc an Choma, í go mórleathan agus comh buí leis an ór. Chuaigh Tomás i dtreo a thí féin agus mise an gcéanna tar éis slán a dh'fhágaint ag a chéile.

as FICHE BLIAN AG FÁS (1933)

SEAMUS HEANEY
THE GIVEN NOTE

On the most westerly Blasket
In a dry-stone hut
He got this air out of the night,

Strange noises were heard
By others who followed, bits of a tune
Coming in on loud weather

Though nothing like melody.
He blamed their fingers and ear
As unpractised, their fiddling easy

For he had gone alone into the island
And brought back the whole thing.
The house throbbed like his full violin.

So whether he calls it spirit music
Or not, I don't care. He took it
Out of wind off mid-Atlantic.

Still he maintains, from nowhere.
It comes off the bow gravely,
Rephrases itself into the air.

PORT NA BPÚCÁI

Inis Icíleáin is a source of much folklore, and the story of the
folk air 'Caoineadh na bhFairies'. 'Caoineadh na bPúcaí', 'Port
na bPúcaí' or 'The Fairies' Lament' is one of the best known.
This is how Tom Daly na hInishe or Tomás Ó Dála, a former
inhabitant of Inis Icíleáin, told the story.

Tháinig an bhean lasmuigh dhon dtigh, agus í ag amhrán, ag rá an phoirt – an t-aer, abair, an fonn aici – agus bhí duine éigin istigh acu go raibh cluas aige, bhí sé ag fheín ar maidin, bhí an bhean bailithe lei. Bhí focail leis:

The fairy woman came to the outside of the house and she was singing, saying the tune and there was someone inside who had an ear for music: he had the tune by morning. The woman vanished. There were words to it:

Is bean ón slua sí mé, tháinig thar toinn
Agus go goideadh san oíche mé tamall thar lear,
'S go bhfuilim sa ríocht, fé gheasa mná sí,
Agus ní bheadsa ar an saol so, ach go nglaofaidh an coileach
Caithfeadsa féin tabhairt fén lios isteach,
Ní taitneamh liom é ach caithfead tabhairt fé
Agus a bhfuil ar an saol so caithfead imeacht as.

I'm a woman from the fairy host, who came over the wave
I was carried off by night for a while over sea
I'm in their kingdom, under control of fairy women
And I shall not be in this world after the cock crows
Then will I go into the lios (fairy fort)
It is not a pleasure for me but there must I go,
And all in this world must I leave.

Ní Fios Cé a Scríobh

Bryan MacMahon
from The Master (1992)

I had been appointed principal of one of the schools, the previous principal having died before his time, largely because of the appalling conditions under which he worked. Having contracted pneumonia, he survived only a few weeks. The principal of the adjoining school, in which I had served up to then, was unwilling to start or support any kind of protest against conditions; he was approaching pensionable age and did not want to risk an upheaval. I perfectly understood his position and his reluctance to protest. He too collapsed and died before his time.

As I pondered my predicament, a resolute man in the person of Frank Sheehy, afterwards chairman of the Munster Council of the GAA, was appointed to the adjoining principalship. He had been headmaster of an endowed school in Oldcastle in County Meath. Although he had been a pupil of our school and, like my brother, also a monitor, he could not credit his ears, eyes and nose at the conditions prevailing when he took up his duties.

We decided on a course of action. It was a very simple one, and, despite some harrowing experiences, it proved to be successful.

Frank and I drew up a document. We had already decided that the practice of having a small group of boys, all of whom were on or just above the poverty line, clean out the vile toilets every afternoon would not be continued. What if some of these boys contracted a disease while engaged in this filthy work? We could be held responsible, as we had failed to officially inform the very reverend manager of the conditions obtaining. Any court of law might find us personally culpable. So we dispatched a letter on the following lines:

> Very Reverend and Dear Manager:
> As you are aware, the practice in these schools has been and still is for the poorer section of the pupils to brush the classroom floors and clean the lavatories each afternoon. When one considers that the lavatory seats are damp and as a consequence the boys do not use the toilets properly, with the result that a pile of faeces remains on the boards, you will readily appreciate our predicament. Therefore we ask you to give this matter your very urgent attention with a view to having the matter rectified.
> We remain your obedient servants . . .

The result was a silence as of the tomb.

After a discreet delay we wrote another letter outlining our growing concern. Still no reply. Finally I drafted a long memorandum setting out the absolute impossibility of educating pupils in this type of school. There followed a detailed list of the problems.

A copy of this document signed by Frank and myself was sent

to the manager and also to the bishop, requesting each of them to countersign to the effect that it was a true presentation of the facts. A third copy was sent to the County Medical Officer, and a fourth to the head office of the teachers' union, the INTO. Finally, when nothing seemed to be moving, we informed the then secretary of the INTO, Dave Kelleher, that we were stopping the cleaning of the toilets on a certain day.

The Central Executive Council of the INTO agreed to back us in any action we would take, even if it resulted in a strike on our part. Our last letter on the matter was sent to the manager stating that we were ending our cleaning rota for the toilets and that the results would have serious repercussions in the town. We relied on him to make alternative arrangements.

In addition to this we had done something that clearly portrayed the conditions we worked under. We had asked a local photographer to take pictures of boys floundering in the winter muck, together with further unsavoury aspects of the building. These we held in reserve. Then we waited.

To his credit the bishop countersigned, confirming that our complaints were well founded; the County Medical Officer did likewise. Meanwhile the piles of faeces mounted. If the toilet was objectionable after a day, it was unbearable after a week, and incredible after a month.

The parents began to take notice. They visited the school, saw the disgusting state of affairs, and announced that they were withdrawing their children from this vile building. As staff we had no objection whatsoever. So began a strike of parents. For a while the school struggled on, until eventually the attendance was reduced to the teachers' children. The teachers continued to attend in empty classrooms, waiting for events to reach a climax.

At this point I pause to say that I am aware that this may seem a local problem, but it had its importance as a test case and as being a struggle for a school. It stood for many hundreds of sub-standard – to use a mild word – schools in Ireland in which hundreds or even thousands of teachers were forced to teach and which children had to attend. This, thirty or more years after the foundation of our adventurous new state!

A brave curate stepped in at this point. Calling out the fire brigade, he asked them to hose down the piles of excrement that had mounted in the cubicles. It was a memorable day in the town when the fire brigade was called out for this most unusual purpose.

A public meeting ended in fireworks. One speaker compared the reverend manager to a ship sunk at the mouth of a harbour so that no vessel could go in or out.

Eventually our document found its way to the office of the Minister for Education. A meeting in Dublin was arranged with the minister, Dick Mulcahy, to be attended by a deputation of the INTO, with Frank Sheehy and myself present.

The meeting opened formally. Our presentation lay on the table; so did the series of photographs. Our complaints were voiced and received courteously, and the meeting rambled on. Presently I began to chafe at the apparent insouciance with which the matter was being treated by the authorities, which could end with Frank and myself returning to Kerry with little achieved, the whole matter destined to rumble on in the bowels of bureaucracy.

I watched my opportunity carefully. When the sheaf of photographs was being examined, with the minister equably asking, 'What have we here?' I, until then a back-room boy, broke in in Irish saying, 'I will explain, minister.' Walking forward to the table, I said, 'You see these mud-spattered children?' 'Yes,' he said. 'The first boy there is a grand-nephew of Michael Collins. The second boy covered in mud in the schoolyard is the grandson of a man who sat in the first Dáil with you and was a member of your party. Thirdly, this boy clothed in muck from head to foot is a nephew of Thomas Ashe, who, as history records, fought with you in north Dublin in the Easter Rising, a man who subsequently died as a result of forced feeding while on hunger strike. You will bear with me, minister, if I say that these, the inheritors of your revolution, were rewarded with squalor.'

I then walked back to my seat. There was silence for a moment or two. I heard the minister speak under his breath to the secretary of his department – a man for whom I had the highest regard. 'Cé hé sin?' The answer, from Tarlach Ó Raifeartaigh, a fine teacher and scholar well known to us from our St Pat's days, was, 'Bryan MacMahon, one of the principals; he writes a bit.' The rest was inaudible, but I had the feeling that Tarlach was on our side and had probably contributed in bringing matters to a head, if not a successful conclusion.

JOHN MONTAGUE
MOUNT EAGLE

The eagle looked at this changing world;
sighed and disappeared into the mountain.

Before he left he had a last reconnoitre:
the multi-coloured boats in the harbour

Nodded their masts, and a sandy white
crescent of strand smiled back at him.

How he liked the slight, drunk lurch
of the fishing fleet, the tide hoist-

ing them a little, at their ropes' end.
Beyond, wrack, and the jutting rocks

emerging slowly, monsters stained
and slimed with strands of seaweed.

Ashore, beached boats and lobster
pots, settled as hens in the sand.

II

Content was life in its easiest form;
another was the sudden, growling storm

which the brooding eagle preferred
bending his huge wings into the winds'

wild buffeting, or thrusting down along
the wide sky, at an angle, slideways to

survey the boats, scurrying homewards,
tacking against the now contrary winds,

all of whom he knew by their names.
To be angry in the morning, calmed

by midday, but brooding again in
the evening was all in a day's quirk

with lengthy intervals for silence,
gliding along, like a blessing, while

the fleet toiled on earnestly beneath
him, bulging with a fine day's catch.

III

But now he had to enter the mountain.
Why? Because a cliff had asked him?
The whole world was changing, with one
language dying, and another encroaching,
bright with buckets, cries of children.
There seemed to be no end to them,
and the region needed a guardian –
so the mountain had told him. And

A different destiny lay before him:
to be the spirit of that mountain.
Everyone would stand in awe of him.
When he was wrapped in the mist's caul
they would withdraw because of him,
peer from behind blind, or curtain.
When he lifted his wide forehead
bold with light, in the morning,
they would all laugh and smile with him.
It was a greater task than an eagle's
aloofness, but sometimes, under his oilskin
of coiled mist, he sighed for lost freedom.

ONE DAY FOR RECREATION

I

One day for recreation,
Is gan éinne beo i m'chuideachta,
I spied a charming fair maid
Na' haonar is í i siopa istigh.
She was singing like an angel
'S mé ag éisteacht lena binneghuth,
I whispered soft and aisy
Sé dúirt sí stad den radaireacht.

Curfá
'S anonn 's anall a Mháirin
Do mhálaí's do bheilteanna
'S a bhean na stocaí mbána
Ba bhreá liom bheith ag iomaidh leat.
(faoi dhó)

II

Her amber locks most nately
Go dréimreach ag titim lei,
Adown her back and waist
'S gur phreab mo chroí le taitneamh di.
I axed was she the fair one
A' bandia úd 'bhí ag Iúpatar
Or the brightsome vestal deity
Chaith seal in Ifreann.

Curfá

III

She answered me most daintily
Ní héinne mar do thuigis mé,
I fear you are a réice
'S ná taobhaigh a thuille mé.
Indeed I am no réice
Ná straeire bhréagfadh bruinneall seal.
I'm a pupil of Jack Lahey's
Sí'n áit a gcónaim Mucaros.

Curfá

IV

I axed her who her father was
'Sé dúirt sí liom 'an ministéir'
I knew I stood in danger
'S gur baolach dom dá bhfeicfí sinn.
If I had you in a nate grove
Idir Claodach is Mucaros
Your sparkling eyes do tase me
Trí lár mo chroí tá taithneamh duit.

Curfá

V

Her syllables so charming –
'S gur bhreá liom bheith 'na cuideachta,
'S gur bhinne liom ná 'n chláirseach
Gach ardphort dá seinneadh sí.
You'll get my stock and farm
Má théann tú liom go Mucaros,
And then she sang most charming:
'A ghrá geal I'm fond of you.'

ANONYMOUS

JOHN B. KEANE
from SELF-PORTRAIT (1964)

People will find it hard to understand the strange ambition of a writer.

Ambition is hardly the right word. Search for fulfilment or expression covers it better. It isn't easy to become a writer, particularly a play-writer. Anyhow, there is no such thing as the perfect play, or, for that matter, the perfect anything. Anything that is conceived by a human being is no better, or no worse, than the human being.

Nobody ever accepts a writer. He accepts himself. To be a writer, a recognised writer, you have to dream about it from the age of reason onwards. You have to hold this thing into yourself and you have to listen to taunts and jibes far removed from clinical and detached criticism. You have to be conscious of jealousies and the criticism that arises from them but you have the consciousness to realise that you are not without jealousy yourself. It is being eternally conscious of oneself that develops the writer.

You have to suffer punches from behind, in the shape of lies and anonymous letters, all delivered by unknown assailants for tragic reasons known only to themselves. You have to listen to, and read, things about yourself far removed from the truth and you must say nothing whatsoever about it. You'll be called anything from communist to anti-clerical and if you dare to deny it you succeed only in hanging yourself.

You have to perpetually preach the gospel of charity to yourself and, most important of all, whether they be friends or enemies, you have to feel deeply for the hurt in other people. You never stop making allowances, if that is possible. You hope that some day a budding, blossoming writer will come along and say, 'Friends, listen to this! Listen to what this fellow wrote!' and hope that one out of a throng of people will later acknowledge and receipt the quoted comments by writing something better in the same vein himself.

I have always wanted to be a writer. I have needed to be accepted as a writer at any level. It doesn't matter so much now because I am beginning to accept myself. I have lived with other writers – not with their beings but with their books and with their poems, with their plays, essays and journals. To me writing matters, because I believe that it can be the most ennobling profession of all. It is the last of the free professions and a man doesn't need Leaving Cert or Matriculation to enter it. All he needs is heart, guts, courage, and never to be ashamed of himself or of his own people.

A writer isn't a freak, a man to be watched or made suspect. He is a human being with one of the finest of God's gifts at his disposal – the power to convey the great joys, the great sorrows, the great madnesses and the great hurts in himself and others.

I am a kind of writer. Nobody knows what kind of writer I am, least of all myself. My ambition is that people will say, some time, 'He was a kind of writer. He said things a different way from others.'

Nowadays, unfortunately, it is not enough to write. You must be a likeable fellow, too. It is almost necessary to be a hypocrite. What I mean is that people who have met you must leave you, saying, 'My God! Isn't he a most unassuming fellow!' or, 'He's just like ourselves!' Well, he's not like yourselves, because no two people are alike.

It isn't enough to be a successful writer, any more. You must be a nice likeable fellow, too. But writers can no more be plausible than anybody else. His head is crammed with the seedlings of ideas. A writer gets an idea every day of his life, and he is subject, too, like other human beings, to the occasional retarding obsession, to the waylaying and seductive external influences.

> For we are tired of meanings dimmed by placid phrases
> Wearied of all thinking and its philosophic mazes
> Jargons of the tongues have foiled the great expression
> And beauty ever pleasing has but kept us in procession.

As Dickeen Roche says, 'The more you think about it, the less you're able to think about it!'

The easiest and the surest way of expressing real values is to hug the rails of truth and to hell with those who prefer the diplomacy of justifiable lying.

But the truth is the hardest thing of all to write. There are too many past liaisons, when I personally face the moment of truth or have to make decisions about truth, too many sins committed, too many past ordeals resulting in the nowaday blush, too many occasions of weakness which could all contrive to hang a man. All these manage to blackmail the mind, to obscure the courageous truth which every man longs to express but daren't. But, thanks to God! you can't blackmail the heart, no matter how hard one tries, because the heart has great moments of love and honesty and great moments of truth and beauty.

PIARAS FEIRITÉAR
LÉIG DHÍOT TH'AIRM, A MHACAOIMH MNÁ

Léig dhíot th'airm, a mhacaoimh mná,
muna fearr leat cách do lot;
muna léige th'airmse dhíot,
cuirfead bannaidhe ón rígh ort.

Má chuireann tú th'airm ar gcúl,
folaigh feasta do chúl cas;
ná léig leis do bhráighe bhán
nach léig duine de chách as.

Má shaoileann tú féin, a bhean,
nár mharbhais aon theas ná thuaidh,
do mharbh silleadh do shúl mín
cách uile gan scín gan tuaigh.

Dar leat féin gé maol do ghlún,
dar leat fós gé húr do ghlac,
do lot gach aon – tuig a chiall –
ní fearra dhuit scian nó ga.

Folaigh orthu an t-ucht mar aol,
ná faiceadh siad do thaobh bog,
ar ghrádh Chríost ná faiceadh cách
do chíoch roigheal mar bhláth dos.

Folaigh orthu do rosc liath,
má théid ar mharbhais riamh leat;
ar ghrádh th'anma dún do bhéal,
ná faiceadh siad do dhéad geal.

Ní beag dhuit ar chuiris d'éag,
cé shaoile nach cré do chorp;
folaighthear leat th'airm go cóir –
ná déana níos mó de lot.

Más lór leat ar chuiris tim,
sula gcuirthear sinn i gcré,
a bhean atá rem ro-chloí,
na hairmsin díotsa léig.

Do shloinneadh, a mhacaoimh mná,
ní beag liom ar chách mar cheist:
do chuirfeadh soin th'ainm i gcéill
dá mbeith a agus é leis.

COLE MORETON
from HUNGRY FOR HOME
LEAVING THE BLASKETS (2000)

Whenever an islandman died, the body was carried to his home.
The eyes and mouth were closed and the legs and arms pulled
down so that he appeared to be at rest. The mother, if she was
still alive, or the wife, or a sister, washed the corpse all over and
combed his hair, and tied his jaw closed with a white handkerchief
before dressing him in the finest shirt available, and his Sunday
suit. Over this was pulled a seamless brown cloak, like the habit
of a monk. It had no pockets, because the dead could take no
belongings into the next world with them.

Every family's most urgent need was to raise a crew for the canoe
which must travel to the mainland to fetch a coffin and supplies
for the wake. Some men in the island could work with driftwood,
after a fashion, but the skill of the coffin-maker in Dingle was
respected and admired. A dead body demanded care and generous
attention. Tobacco and a box of clay pipes were required for the

wake, along with white bread and jam, tea, a barrel of porter and
a bottle or two of whiskey. These could also be bought in Dingle,
so two of the crew usually hired a cart or car to take them there
from Dunquin. Superstition demanded that they be accompanied
by a woman, either an islander or a relative on the mainland. The
other two set out on foot for Ballyferriter, five miles away in the
opposite direction, to fetch the priest.

If it was a fine day, and the sea was calm, the coffin and supplies
could be back in the island within twelve hours. In the meantime,
the tearful relatives at home continued to prepare the body. It was
laid on a white sheet which covered the kitchen table, and a pillow
was placed under the head. More white sheets were sewn together
and hung over ropes suspended from the rafters to make a canopy
covering the body, onto which a cross was tied. Twelve long white
candles representing the disciples of Christ stood in bottles around
the body, and eleven of them were lit. The twelfth gave out no light,
in memory of Judas the betrayer.

Grief could not be private. A father or a sister might turn for
a moment to the window, or disappear to the strand for a while,
but the house was already filling up with relatives and neighbours,
each expecting to help or to offer words of comfort. There were
tears, of course, and the tremulous sound of women beginning their
keen, an unearthly combination of wailing, groaning and singing
that lamented the dead man and praised him. Planks of wood were
balanced along the walls as benches, and *punann na marbh*, the sheaf
of straw for the dead, laid on the floor beside the corpse so that
those who came to pray could kneel by him.

The rest of the village gathered with the family when they
saw the coffin being lifted from the returned *naomhóg* and
carried up to the house. There was a clay pipe and tobacco in
a box by the door for each mourner, the men removing their caps
and the women pulling shawls tighter around their heads as they
stooped to pass through the doorway, going to the body with
a prayer for the soul of the dead man. Some whispered their
words, overcome with emotion. Others spoke loud and strong,
beseeching the Mother of God to find this soul a bed in heaven.

'The old people here say that if you would touch his hand
or forehead when dead, that you would never again be afraid of
him to see him or anything,' wrote the islandwoman Eibhlís Ní
Shúilleabháin to a friend in 1932. A neighbour had died. Some

[71]

kissed the forehead, others wove their fingers around his. 'I felt his hand, dear me, he was as cold as ice.'

Such an act would banish all danger of being haunted by the dead man. The bravest of children allowed their hands to be pulled out towards the corpse by an elder, but younger ones shied away in fear.

As the wailing abated and the night drew in, the assembled company turned from the body to the hearth and began to tell stories and sing songs about the dead. Faith, he was a fine strong fellow. Never a word of trouble on his lips. By God, it is rare we see the like of him in this life. A thousand years for the parents that lose such a boy. As the hours passed jam was spread on the bread, the tea made by the women, the porter and whiskey uncorked by the men. Around midnight, the company settled on its knees and the Rosary was spoken: '. . . blessed art thou among women, and blessed is the fruit of thy womb, Jesus,' said a single voice, the leader, reciting the Hail Mary. The room responded: 'Holy Mary, Mother of God, pray for us sinners, now and at the hour of our death . . .'

NUALA NÍ DHOMHNAILL
CEIST NA TEANGAN

Cuirim mo dhóchas ar snámh
i mbáidín teangan
faoi mar a leagfá naíonán
i gcliabhán
a bheadh fite fuaite
de dhuilleoga feileastraim
is bitiúman agus pic
bheith cuimilte lena thóin

ansan é a leaghadh síos
i measc na ngiolcach
is coigeal na mban sí
le taobh na habhann
féachaint n'fheadaraís
cá dtabharfaidh an sruth é,
féachaint, dála Mhaoise,
an bhfóirfidh iníon Fharoinn?

John B. Keane
Death Be Not Proud

The land meant everything to Mick Henderson. The cardinal rule of his long life was its preservation. Envious neighbours whose own land had become run-down through neglect and laziness would have outsiders believe that he loved the land more than he loved his wife and certainly more than he loved his family. This was not so. He had been fond of his wife when he married. He had remained fond of her through storm and calm over the years and even now when the physical aspect of his marriage was becoming something of a memory he treasured her companionship in a way that only long attachment can foster.

He would have been hard put to explain his obsession with the land. His wife understood fully and there were others like himself in the valley who felt as he did. These would be silent, tight-lipped men, not without humour and not given to vindicating or modifying what would seem to be an extraordinary preoccupation with the soil.

At seventy Mick Henderson found himself in a quandary. Labour was becoming impossible to come by. Factories were shooting up like thistles in the nearby towns and cities. Whatever work-force was available in the area was almost completely absorbed. Even his regular workman had deserted him for lucrative shift work and a five-day week. The latter was something of a joke amongst the farming community. All the holdings supported herds of milch cows and during the heavy milking periods these needed constant attention.

Once when endeavouring to hire a workman Mick was asked if he would settle for a five-day week.

'You can have a one-day week in the winter,' Mick had told him, 'but until such time as we have a five-day cow there will be no five-day week.'

He had gone so far as to offer free Sundays during the peak periods and occasional days off for special events but there was no competing with the attractions of the factories. He cut down his herd to a manageable size although he was still heavily in debt from having put three sons and two daughters through boarding schools and colleges. There was another son, Mikey, named after himself, a black sheep of sorts, who disappeared one morning when he was barely sixteen after a vicious row regarding his attitude towards further schooling. That was nearly ten years before. Mick Henderson knew his son's address in England, knew he was doing well as a charge-hand in a Coventry factory, knew enough in fact to make Mikey feel downright uncomfortable if he ever suspected such paternal interest.

The others had no feeling for the land, no concern about it. On his seventieth birthday he had betaken himself to the city to consult with his eldest son, Maurice, who was a solicitor there. After listening carefully for over half an hour Maurice submitted his opinion.

'Your safest and your easiest course,' he said dispassionately, 'is to sell out and live here in Dublin or if city life has no appeal for you there is nothing to prevent you from buying a comfortable house in the country. The money you would make from the sale would clear your debts and leave you with more than sufficient to ensure a comfortable life for Mother and yourself until the end of your days.'

His second son, Eddie, was a dentist. Married with two children, he operated from a small surgery attached to his home in the suburbs. Late as it was when Tom called he found Eddie up to his eyes in work. Very late that night they sat round the sitting room fire and talked about the land. It was impossible not to like Eddie and his wife but they had little to offer by way of a solution. They also felt that selling the land would be the best way out.

It was the third son, Martin, a civil servant, who supplied the obvious answer. Mick had a job finding his house in the sprawling, estate-cluttered northside of the metropolis. Snugly seated in the back seat of a taxi he passed row after row of newly-erected, two-storied houses. After numerous enquiries they eventually discovered the estate. Another search and they located the house. It stood amid hundreds of others which looked exactly alike.

'How in the name of God does anyone live here?' he had asked undiplomatically when Martin and his wife met him at the door.

'You get used to it,' Martin said enjoying his father's innate rustic perplexity.

In spite of his first impression he was pleasantly surprised by the interior of the house. It had a heartening spaciousness in contrast to what he had expected.

'You have a fine home Martin,' he announced by way of conciliation.

'It's only a few hundred yards from the school,' Martin's wife said, 'and that's what really matters.'

After the usual preliminaries Mick settled down to the business of outlining his problems. Martin and his wife listened sympathetically while he explained about the new factories and the scarcity of labour.

'The last thing I want to do is sell it,' he finished.

'The logical thing as far as I can see is to bring Mikey back from Coventry,' Martin suggested.

'Will he want to come back?' Mick asked.

'I have no doubt that he will,' Martin assured him.

Mick Henderson considered this for some time. It was a thought that had always been at the back of his head. All he needed was someone, other than himself, to suggest it. He was aware that Martin and Mikey were as close as brothers could be despite the distance that separated them. In age there was hardly a year between them. It was to be expected, therefore, that Martin would put forward a strong case for the youngest brother. Mick Henderson decided that he would find out how forceful Martin's advocacy might be.

'That's all very fine,' he said disinterestedly, 'but has he the feel for the land?'

'Why wouldn't he?' Martin hastened to reply, 'he's your son isn't he?'

'You're my son and you have no feel for it. Neither have Maurice or Eddie.'

'Look,' Martin pleaded, 'Mikey is different. He's only good with his hands. He was a hopeless scholar. If you had kept him at home when he kicked off the traces that first time he'd know it all now and you wouldn't be worrying about labour.'

"Tis easy be wise after the event,' Mick Henderson said. He suspected that Mikey might have the true feeling for the land but there was no way he could be certain. He resolved to probe further.

'What guarantee have I that he won't flog the farm as soon as I pass on?' he asked.

'That's a chance you'll have to take but let me tell you this.

Mikey is hardly likely to flog it when it's going to be his livelihood. You know as well as I that he knew how to handle livestock. That time before he ran away he had no objection to working on the farm. What he objected to was school.'

'Agreed,' Mick Henderson returned, 'but there's many a young lad will volunteer for anything to escape school.'

'I happen to know,' Martin's tone was really serious now, 'that if he doesn't come home this year he won't come home at all.'

'Did he say this?'

'Yes.'

'Then I suppose I had better contact him. What if he says no?'

'That's one thing he won't say,' Martin assured him.

After this conversation Mick Henderson had no doubt in his mind that Martin and Mikey had discussed the latter's position in depth. On his way home by train he had ample time to think. His one fear was that the land might be sold after his death but this would happen anyway if Mikey refused to come home. He remembered when the farm had been signed over to him by his own father. It had been a bright May morning close on forty years before. He had no idea what his father's business in the neighbouring town might be when he instructed him to tackle the black mare to the family trap. By mid-day he was the legal owner of the land. He had in no way pressurised his father although he had dropped hints that he was thinking of getting married. It was somewhat different in his case. The true feeling for the land was there. His father knew this, knew that the green pastures to which he had devoted the best years of his life would be safe for another generation. It was so important that Mikey have this feeling for the acres which would shortly be under his care. Mick Henderson knew everything there was to be known about the land. Over the years he had discovered its idiosyncrasies and failings and learned painstakingly how to turn deficiencies into advantages. The land had its own unique characteristics, its own vague, imperceptible contours, its inexplicable portions of soft and hard, wet and dry, barren and lush.

On the surface the fields were like any other in the district but he knew better. His father had been a source of constant help as he endeavoured to discover the true lie of the land. Now that he knew all there was to be known it was high time the knowledge was passed on. He would announce his decision to his wife Julia as soon as he got home. She would be pleased. He was aware that she secretly pined after her youngest son although, like all mothers, she became somewhat resigned to his absence as time went by.

The proper thing for me to do, Mick thought, is to impress upon him without seeming to do so the value of well-treated land. I will show him that while human life is to be valued more than anything else, that which sustains it should be valued no less. I will pass over and my wife will pass over but the land will remain. We are only passing through, mere tenants at best. The land will be there forever to nurture my seed and the seed of my seed. Somehow he would try to get these feelings through to Mikey. If the genuine consciousness was there this would be no problem. If Mikey did not fully respond all would not be lost. At least he would not sell and the land would be saved. If one generation failed to throw up a man with love for the land the next generation was sure to compensate. Who could tell but he might live to see a grandson blessed with the appropriate and peculiar disposition so difficult to define.

Mikey Henderson arrived home during the second week of spring. The roadside hedgebanks were bright with clusters of early primroses and along the sides of the avenue leading to the old farmhouse were healthy clumps of daffodils and irises in various stages of flower. It was a good time to come home. During the first months he made many mistakes but Mick was not slow to notice that he never made the same mistake a second time. He was uncannily adept with all sorts of machinery. He understood cattle and most important of all he knew how to husband his strength. He fitted perfectly into the pattern of things.

Mick watched his progress with the keenest interest. Who knew but some evening he might see Mikey with his hands on his hips surveying the sheen of a freshly ploughed tillage field or shading his eyes against a summer sun on the headland of a meadow ripe for cutting.

With the coming of summer the new green grass, luscious and fleecy, returned to the fields. The hedgerows no longer bare hosted a thousand songbirds and the first of the long herbage took the naked look from the broad meadows.

The meadows would prove to be the chief of Mikey's problems that first summer. It wasn't a particularly good year for growth. The new crops were light and late and to crown the general misfortune of the farming community there was no labour available when the outlook was favourable for harvesting. The weather too was unkind. To say the least it was inconsistent. Fine days were few and far between and rarely succeeded each other. During this time came the worst calamity that could possibly befall. Julia Henderson took ill and had to be removed to hospital. All thoughts of harvesting had to be abandoned until she recovered.

It was two weeks before she was released. She had undergone a mild coronary. Her doctor warned that unless she cut down considerably in her everyday work there would be a recurrence. After her short stay in the hospital she felt refreshed and the tiredness which had nagged her for so long seemed to have disappeared altogether. She herself declared that she felt twenty years younger and insisted in shouldering her full quota of chores. A young girl was found locally to help her. She agreed to stay until the schools reopened in September. Outwardly, at any rate, Julia Henderson seemed very much rejuvenated. She looked the picture of health and there was none of the breathlessness which she so often endured before her visit to hospital.

There was a general air of excitement all over the district when the weather changed for the better. Despite the fact that there was no immediate prospect of labour Mick and Mikey Henderson decided to make an all-out assault on the uncut meadows. All day they followed each other on two tractors. In their wake the tall grass fell in long parallel swathes. Julia and the girl brought their meals to the meadow. There was no tarrying for small-talk afterwards. As soon as they had eaten they mounted the cumbersome machines. The onslaught lasted until the first faint stars appeared in the late evening sky. The moment they finished they headed straight for the local pub. It wasn't that they especially needed a drink. It was the only place where they were likely to recruit labour. They were partly successful. It was first necessary to invest in several rounds of drink and to exhibit an interest in the welfare of likely prospects that was tantamount to fawning. This, with the offer of almost double the normal wage, was responsible for the extraction of three promises. Both Mick and Mikey were well aware that the trio in question were not exactly the cream of the crop. They would be late and they would put no great strain on themselves but they were labourers and if the weather held the produce of the combined meadows might be saved at the end of three days.

For most of the first day they turned and then tossed the freshly mown swathes. Late in the afternoon they made it up into wind-rows in preparation for the following day's cocking. This completed they broke off. That night the Hendersons listened avidly to the weather forecast. The prospects were still good. Mick and Mikey rose with the dawn. First the cows had to be milked. Then the milk had to be cooled and transported to the creamery. After that it was straight to the meadow. Everything else was secondary. The labourers arrived at ten o'clock and then the business of cocking commenced. First the crisp hay had to be gathered by the tractor-drawn, iron-toothed rake. Mikey attended to this particular function. He worked furiously supplying the needs of the cock-makers who worked in pairs. When the supply exceeded the demand he would jump from the tractor and shoulder huge pikefuls of hay to the base of the developing cock. This was the hardest part of haymaking. One by one, slowly and painfully, the cocks went up until by the end of the second day half the entire crop was safe. The third day followed the same pattern as the second. The mid-day meal was brought to the meadow by Julia Henderson and the girl. On the third day Julia came alone. The girl had not showed up. Enquiry revealed that she had been at a dance the night before and was unable to get out of bed. Julia was not unprepared. She arrived at the meadow shortly after noon, just as the sky was undergoing a murky suffusion in the southwest. If rain was to come this would be the direction from which it would threaten. After the meal one of the labourers announced that he was unable to continue because of a stomach ailment. Mick guessed that the pace was not to his liking. The same man had shown himself to be somewhat of a shirker from the beginning. Mikey had heard him derogatorily remarking to one of his colleagues that if he was to die he wouldn't like it to be for a farmer.

Despite her husband's protestations Julia insisted in falling in by his side. They worked together, silently, at a corner of the meadow far removed from the other pair. Julia Henderson was the ideal farmer's wife. Always she had been by her husband's side when the need was there. Of solid farming stock herself, she was aware of her obligations although these had often ranged from milking the entire herd to deputising at weddings and funerals. This was the unwritten law when labour was not to be had.

Now and then Mick would glance anxiously to the west and south where the ominous turgescence of massing clouds was slowly enveloping the otherwise clear sky. By his own reckoning he estimated that there were three, maybe four good hours left. Given that much time all the hay would undoubtedly be saved. He redoubled his own efforts and then without warning of any kind Julia Henderson heaved a massive, choking sigh. Mick stood helpless and appalled while she attempted to restrain with clutching fingers the terrible upheaval in her chest. Then just as suddenly her hands fell listlessly to her sides and she fell backwards noiselessly in a crumpled heap. Urgently Mick Henderson bent and whispered an act of contrition into her ear. There was no disputing the fact that she was dead. He stretched her legs gently and folded her hands across her bosom.

Then he sat by her side awaiting the arrival of Mikey with the next rake of hay. The young man sensed that something was wrong. He dismounted slowly from the tractor and read the news in his father's face. He knelt by his mother's side and kissed her on the lips and forehead. He smoothed back the hair from her face and lifted her head so that he could rest it on the pillow of hay. Then he rose and looked at the sky.

'Let's get on with it,' he said. At first Mick Henderson looked at him uncomprehendingly. Then the logic of it dawned on him.

'What about the two?' he asked, pointing to where the labourers were building a cock at the other end of the meadow.

'What they don't know won't trouble them,' said Mikey dismissing the question. Slowly his father rose. Already Mikey was adding to the half-made cock. Instinctively his father followed his example.

Before departing for another rake-up Mikey laid a hand on his father's shoulder.

'She would understand,' he said. 'I don't have to tell you that. When the job is done we'll take her indoors. Then I'll go for a priest.'

So saying he mounted the machine and in a matter of seconds

was again raking the ever-decreasing wind rows. Mick Henderson cast a glance at his dead wife and then his eyes followed his youngest son. Beyond doubt here was a man with a sound sense of values, a man with a true feel for the land.

AN FEAIRÍN
SEÁN Ó RÍORDÁIN

Ní Ezra Pound atá in gceist anseo, ach duine de na cainteoirí dúchais Gaeilge is binne agus is oilte sa tír. Ní fear beag é ach an oiread ach taibhsítear don té a chíonn é go bhfuil gach ball dá bhaill beag toisc go bhfuil cuma na huaisleachta ar a phearsa.

'Theastódh tigh is gort ón bhfeairín bocht,'
A dúirt an bhean 'dtaobh Pound,
Is bhailigh Pound isteach sa bhfocal di
Is chónaigh ann.

Ní fhaca Pound iomlán go ndúirt sí é,
Is do scrúdaíos é ó bhonn
Fé ghnéithe an teidil sin a bhaist sí air,
Is dar liom gur dheas a rogha.

Tá beirthe ar Phound sa bhfocal sin aici,
Mar feairín is ea Pound,
Do réitigh gach a bhfuil dá chabhail sa bheatha léi,
Ó bharr a chinn go bonn.

Tá buanaíocht age Pound sa bhfocal sin,
Tá suaimhneas aige ann,
Is pé duine eile 'bheidh míshocair inár n'aigne,
Ní mar sin a bheidh Pound.

MICHÈLE VASSAL
CLEAN SHEETS

The strange topography of your absence
Carves in the frozen ocean of our bed
Stagnant waves and currents of icy dread.
The void under my hand makes little sense
Rounded hollows empty of your presence
Your soft belly on which I laid my head
Fragrant and warm like a fresh loaf of bread.
Maybe I'll find the ghost of your essence
In the starched storm of a white cotton sea
(I wish I hadn't changed the sheets.) I miss you.
You said to love, we have to feel the pain
Burning bright and sharp like our ecstasy.
Searching for scattered reefs to hold on to,
I miss and mourn the lack of coffee stains.

JULIE O'CALLAGHAN
THE GREAT BLASKET ISLAND

Six men born on this island
have come back after twenty-one years.
They climb up the overgrown roads
to their family houses
and come out shaking their heads.
The roofs have fallen in
and birds have nested in the rafters.
All the white-washed rooms
all the nagging and praying
and scolding and giggling
and crying and gossiping
are scattered in the memories of these men.
One says, 'Ten of us, blown to the winds –
some in England, some in America, some in Dublin.
Our whole way of life – extinct.'
He blinks back the tears
and looks across the island

past the ruined houses, the cliffs
and out to the horizon.

Listen, mister, most of us cry sooner or later
over a Great Blasket Island of our own.

AOGÁN Ó RATHAILLE
MAC AN CHEANNAÍ

Aisling ghéar do dhearcas féin
ar leaba 's mé go lagbhríoch,
an ainnir shéimh darbh ainm Éire
ag teacht im ghaor ar marcaíocht,
a súile glas, a cúl tiubh casta,
a com ba gheal 's a mailí,
dá mhaíomh go raibh ag tíocht 'na gar
a díogras, Mac an Cheannaí.

A beol ba bhinn, a glór ba chaoin,
is ró-shearc linn an cailín,
céile Bhriain dár ghéill an Fhiann,
mo léirchreach dhian a haicíd:
fá shúistibh Gall dá brú go teann,
mo chúileann tseang 's mo bhean ghaoil;
beidh sí 'na spreas, an rí-bhean deas,
go bhfillfidh Mac an Cheannaí.

Na céadta tá i bpéin dá grá
le géarshearc shámh dá cneas mhín,
clanna ríthe, maca Míle,
dragain fhíochta is gaiscígh;
gnúis ná gnaoi ní mhúsclann sí
cé dubhach fá scíos an cailín –
níl faoiseamh seal le tíocht 'na gar
go bhfillfidh Mac an Cheannaí.

A ráite féin, is cráite an scéal,
mo lánchreach chlé do lag sinn,
go bhfuil sí gan chel ag caoi na ndeor,
's a buíon gan treoir gan maithghníomh,
gan fiach gan feoil, i bpian go mór,
'na hiarmsa fó gach madaí,
cnaíte lag ag caoi na ndearc
go bhfillfidh Mac an Cheannaí.

Adúirt arís an bhúidhbhean mhíonla
– turnadh ríthe 'cleacht sí,
Conn is Art ba lonnmhar reacht,
ba foghlach glac i ngleacaíocht,
Críomhthainn tréan tar toinn tug géill,
is Luighdheach Mac Céin an fear groí,
go mbeadh sí 'na spreas gan luí le fear
go bhfillfeadh Mac an Cheannaí.

Do-bheir súil ó dheas gach lá fá seach
ar thráigh na mbarc an cailín,
Is súil deas-soir go dlúth tar muir,
mo chumha anois a haicíd,
a súile siar ag súil le Dia,
tar tonntaibh fiara gainmhe;
cloíte lag beidh sí gan phreab
go bhfillfidh Mac an Cheannaí.

A bráithre breaca táid tar lear
na táinte shearc an cailín;
níl fleadh le fáil, níl gean ná grá
ag neach dá cairdibh, admhaím;
a gruanna fliuch, gan suan gan sult,
fá ghruaim is dubh a n-aibíd,
's go mbeidh sí 'na spreas gan luí le fear
go bhfillfidh Mac an Cheannaí.

Adúrtsa léi ar chlos na scéal,
i rún gur éag do chleacht sí,
thuas sa Spáinn go bhfuair an bás –
's nar thrua le cách a ceasnaí;

ar chlos mo ghotha i bhfogas di
chorraigh a cruth 's do scread sí
is d'éalaigh an t-anam d'aonphreib aisti –
mo léansa an bhean go neamhbhríoch.

PATRICK KENNELLY
from SAUSAGES FOR TUESDAY (1969)

The year was coming to an end. On the first of June those boys
not sitting for public examinations went home on summer
holidays. You waved goodbye to them, half wondering why your
feelings were not purely happy. Dizzy Dick gave you a holy
medal and you didn't know how to accept it.

'Do you like it?' he asked.

'I'd rather a button for my fly.'

He was disappointed and it showed on his face. It was this
image of him that you retained in your mind.

Because the number of students was now reduced and because
the danger of the impending examinations hung constantly, like a
cloud, a new atmosphere manifested itself, so radically different
from anything you were accustomed to that it seemed unreal. The
little band of students grew more united every day. Nicknames were
no longer used. Boys treated each other with an almost brotherly
affection, sensitive and understanding.

The priests as well as the students behaved differently and
the change was most evident in Fr Daly. He treated boys with
a maturity of understanding that was completely at variance, it
seemed, with his former terrifying attitudes.

Before the examination the President gave his last talk to the
Seniors. He wished everybody success and said he would help those
who found it difficult to secure positions when they had left St
Andrew's. He had tried as best he could to make boys happy in the
college and though some might believe that he had been harsh at
times he had always acted with the common good in mind. He
asked those who considered themselves mistreated to forgive him.

During these last few days you studied till your eyes grew
sore. At night in bed, using a torch as a light, you revised page
after printed page.

The night before the Leaving Certificate began you stole out of the college and went down town. It was a very risky thing to do, for you could not run with the crutches, only hobble along as quickly as your injured ankle would allow.

When you reached the town you limped into the nearest pub and there, for the second time ever, you got drunk. Not for a long time after that night did you taste drink.

You sat by yourself in the nearest corner, alone and sultry, not enjoying your drink because you were afraid that a priest would walk in each time the pub door opened.

It was a stupid fear, for you should have known, you did know, that priests don't walk into pubs. But you were afraid all the same, even when the drink started going to your brain and you decided to get very drunk.

Afraid you bloody idiot, afraid because time is running out and there is an exam to do and you might not do well. Afraid because you're leaving St Andrew's! Jesus! you are afraid to be at school and afraid to be out of it. Nothing can satisfy you.

You must be a fierce bore you know, with certain people anyway, because you hate being introduced and having to talk to them about nothing and wondering what you should say next. Why the hell don't they dispense with all the Goddamn formalities.

'Could I have a beer please, if you don't mind?' Drinking too fast.

The next time you're introduced to a man you'll say: 'Listen, bud, we're both stuck with each other and I don't want to talk to you and you don't want to talk to me. So let's be honest. Let's – let's just look at each other.'

And if it's a woman, by Christ you won't start off by saying that the weather is good, or bad, or fair.

'I'm talking to you,' you'll say, 'because you're sexy. So let's stop talking and get down to business. Down to sex.' No, you shouldn't say 'Down to sex.' Sex is lovely. Isn't it bloody marvellous how a man can go demented over legs and thighs and skin and things like that.

So you'll say to her instead 'Let's get up to sex. If it's wan thing I like it's sex. Up sssex.'

Afraid, you bloody idiot, afraid of the heat. Loosen your tie to cool the red fire along your throat.

'This scutterin' pub is too hot.'

And the lady will be shocked but you'll keep saying, 'Up sex.'
'Up sex.'

Barman was tapping you on the shoulder.

'That's enough of that kind of language, mate. This is a respectable place.'

You looked at him coldly. Then you drank your beer, never taking your eyes from him. Plant the empty glass heavily on the table.

'Alright, Mister Barman, I'm leaving your pub anyhow because 'tis too scutterin' hot.'

For no reason you were angry and when the barman began to laugh as you took up your crutches this anger mounted.

'And another reason I'm leaving is that you are only a Primary-Cert man. Just like the Gardai. Ignorant Primary-Cert men, the lot of ye.'

That fixed him, you thought while you hobbled out to the street fumbling with your crutches. You walked, or staggered till you came to a dark street. Put your arse to the wall, arching outwards, hands dug deep into your pockets, elbows leaning heavily on your crutches.

For some time you stood there, bloating heavily because of the strain of walking from the pub. The injury to your ankle depressed you more than ever, so that you believed that you would never be able to walk properly again.

You watched the passers-by, vaguely registering their faces in your mind. If you were sober, you'd be trying to figure out what goes on behind the skin of those faces. But, you were drunk, and heavy and wheezing.

And then you saw a beautiful girl. Remember your thought in the pub. Up sex!

'Pssst, Pssst, hi! lady! Psst, Pssst!' But she was gone from your sight before you had finished.

Another girl passed by. She was beautiful too. All women were beautiful.

'Hi, lady! Pssst, Psst.' She threw you a very cold stare, the vicious flashing of her eyes arousing you, and passed on.

Something must be done about this. Take the crutches in hand and hobble after her.

'Hey lady! Lady – I say!'

She stopped abruptly and turned to face you, very annoyed looking. You knew what to say, by God.

'I just . . . just want to talk to you . . . that's all.'

'About what?'

'About . . . the weather. The weather is fair at the moment, don't you think?'

'Anything else?'

'Not particularly.'

In those few seconds your sense had sharpened and you had observed everything about the girl. Young, about twenty, wth her hands neatly arranged around her handbag. She had a sharp, instinctive temper, but she could smile too. a kind smile. You thought that she understood you, or at least forgave you. She was amused when other would be mad with rage. You liked her.

'You're a true liberal,' you stuttered.

'Thanks for the information about the weather.' She seemed suddenly bored and turned to walk away.

'Hold on a minute.'

'Yes.' She hissed her answer and flung her hands to the sky in a gesture of impatience. Yet, it amazed you that she was interested enough to talk.

'I just want to talk to you, lady, because you're beautiful. I love talking to beautiful women.'

She laughed happily so that you wondered if you had succeeded in giving a compliment.

Easy to see, too, that you amused her. She eyed you coquettishly.

'You're drunk,' she said.

'You're beautiful.'

'What's wrong with your legs?'

'I tore ligaments above my right ankle. But I won't have these crutches for long. I'll be able to walk again soon, honest.'

'I see.'

'I hurt it playing football. I was a great footballer before this happened, honest.'

'I'd say that.'

'But honestly I was. Ask anyone. Really.'

She looked at her watch.

'I must go, now.'

Your face dropped with disappointment and you thought she

must have noticed it, but you could say nothing, nothing at all, while she walked away, because she was too bloody nice to be asking her for a court, too nice for you. Look at yourself! Drunk and unfit and wheezy. One leg gone wrong. Worked too hard for the past month. Smelly.

The feeling of tenderness passed and you became extremely disgruntled. From this you passed into a rage and began to shout at the passers-by.

'Smelly. You're all smelly. Dirty smelly things.'

And when this fit had passed you took your crutches in your hand and headed back towards the college.

You left it a bit late for it was half past nine and you had only a half-hour of hobbling before the doors were shut. Easy, Easy!

And then you fell. Such a stupid way to fall.

You missed a step in the pavement and your ankle fell from under you. And then the pain came back. The sharp pain, and the swelling just as on the day of the football match. Only this time you panicked.

You tried to rise and succeeded. Then you took a step forward but fell again. You should not have allowed your right leg to touch the ground, but the pain, and the thought that you would not reach the college on time, clogged your reasoning.

You tried to rise again, clinging to some iron bars that were bounding a garden, but when you had pulled yourself halfway up the bars and had almost got to your feet you felt the pains preading from your ankle along your legs, through your stomach, to your head.

Then you fainted.

When you woke, Hegarty was standing over you. He circled round you, eyeing you closely as if you were an oddity from space with a contagious disease.

'How did you get here?' he asked.

The pain had sobered you and you were conscious of the cruel throbbing on your ankle. And even more conscious that Hegarty was the fellow you had kicked between the legs the day Dizzy Dick was 'baptised'. You noticed that his question was quiet, too quiet, and knew that he remembered the day also, and was ill at ease.

'I stole out and got drunk, and fell on my ankle again. I'm sober now.'

'I stole out, too,' he said, 'but I'm still drunk. Can you walk?'

'No, I can't walk an inch.'

'What are you going to do?'

'Will you get a taxi for me, please? Please!'

'Shit, man. Don't you know well that there's no chance of getting a taxi at this hour of the night.' He seemed angry at your asking so stupid a question.

'What will I do,' you said.

Hegarty looked around cautiously, trying to think.

'Hop on my back,' he said, his face expressionless.

'D'you mean that you'll take me back?'

'Take it or leave it.'

Hegarty was a strong fellow, and he lifted you easily onto the bonnet of a car that was parked on the roadside. Then he bent down and you glided on to his back.

'Thanks,' you said.

'You're too heavy,' he said but he kept you on his back, sometimes running, sometimes walking while you held on tightly, your arms round his neck, the crutches dangling awkwardly from your hands.

You were tempted to thank him with humour and soon might have started doing the clown on his back pretending that you were a jockey, and he a horse, only that he began complaining. You grew afraid.

'Your hands are too bloody tight and you're sitting too bloody far down on my back. Can you be a little more bloody helpful?'

The cold of his voice iced through you, jolting you back to the day of the 'Baptism'.

'I'm sorry for the time I kicked you in the balls.'

'By God, but 'tis expedient to apologise at a time like this.'

'I'm sincerely sorry.'

'Why did you do it?' he asked. 'It was all only in fun.'

'I don't know. I don't know.'

'Why did you do it?' his voice was insistent.

'I thought you were a savage at the time.'

He stopped dead in his tracks, and turned his head angrily, so that his face was very close to yours. He snorted.

'You didn't think I was a savage,' he said, 'but you tried to make me into one. But I was never a savage.'

'I know. But I thought you were at the time.'

He was still at a halt.

'I had that idea about you,' he said.

'What idea?'

'I knew you considered us all to be savages. I suppose you think you're the only fucking civilised person around.'

'No . . . that's not . . . '

'Shut up – if you want to get back to College in time,' he said, starting off again and quickening his pace to a mad run.

You woke at six the following morning and immediately began to study the subject due for examination that day. The pattern was set. From now until the end of the examination you would cram your mind with a million facts and formulae. Enter the Examination Hall each morning, your mind soaked with information on the subject in hand. A quick prayer at the beginning of each session. Then read the papers with a starved curiosity. Then – the only reward for all your work – finding out that you knew the questions and that you could do a good paper.

Allocate a certain amount of time for each question, and write. Write without thinking, for the knowledge required was at the surface of your brain and flowed easily from your pen. Ten minutes after the session was over much of what you had written was forgotten.

Afterwards you met your classmates and discussed the questions with them. You would try to assess your own marks. Again and again. Then you would resume study, cramming your brain once more.

This timetable lasted eight days. Everything went smoothly and the only trouble you had was the pain in your ankle. It had swollen very much when you had fallen on it, the night before the examinations began, and now your concentration was often broken by a sharp jab of pain. Eventually you went to the college doctor who tightened the bandages and told you that the tendons had received another jolt which would delay the healing.

You met Hegarty again, too, for he had hurt you with his words and you needed to apologise to him to pacify your scruples. You went to his cubicle one night. He was washing his teeth when you entered, the white foam spewed around his lips.

'I came to say I'm sorry for calling you a savage.'

He rinsed his mouth without acknowledging your apology. Then suddenly he wheeled on you.

'What colour is a cow's shite?' he asked.

'Brown!'

'How many black keys on a piano?'

'I don't know.'

'I have a real excuse for calling you a savage – you know more about shite than music.'

You laughed. For the last few days, at least, you were good friends.

On the night before going home, when you had all your things packed, you went to Moran's cubicle. Dunne and Hynes were already there, and some members of the football team.

Talk long into the night, discussing long-forgotten moments of humour and glory.

Dunne called for silence and stood up on the bed:

'As a reporter of the "Times" I can now reveal that it was I and some of my colleagues who pissed into the milk in the priests' refectory.'

'The kidneys are still bad, Dunne,' somebody said.

It was the only embarrassing remark of the night.

'I have an idea,' said Moran. 'We'll go out into the grounds and make a bonfire of our books.'

It must have been a queer sight. Some fifty students dressed in pyjamas, like fleeting, noisy ghosts, skitting about in the darkness. Book upon book was thrown into the ring at the centre of the lawn. Somebody produced a match. Very slowly at first, and then quickly the ring of enlightenment took fire. You had remembered to bring your flash camera from the cubicle and, since your ankle prevented you from participating, you took photos of your friends as they danced wildly around the blaze like Indians around a warfire.

'It is all over now,' said Hynes, 'and thanks be to jazus. I never want to see a book again.'

Everybody echoed his sentiments and danced wilder than ever around the ring shouting, 'Thanks be to jazus' until Father Daly came on the scene and asked that you return to the dormitory.

Before returning shake each other's hands.

'Good luck, whatever.'

Dunne took your hand half apologetically and said 'Thanks.' You wondered for what. Probably because you had never called him 'Pee-wee'.

Moran was the last to take your hand.

'Good luck, buddy.'

'Same to you, boyo.'

'You won't forget your promise?' he asked.

'Of course not.'

By licking flames of firelight you could see his hand reaching into the top pocket of his pyjamas.

'This photo of my parents – take it.'

You took it, foolishly.

''Tis from me.'

He left immediately, shuffling his great body into the night.

You did not go to bed. As always at night, stare out the window of your cubicle, searching the field, the thick darkness. The long wait of four years, the recent cramming of your mind tended to draw a weary curtain of heaviness over your thoughts but something within, a mixture of joy and sadness and fear, drove you on.

Fear above all else. What would it be like outside? Would you still have time to question and deliberate or would some great force, unknown and unexperienced, sweep you on its path? Things would be different altogether. You would have to stop looking for the hidden meaning then, or you would leave yourself open to hurt and insult.

You would have to assume a new character. Toughen yourself up and don't be thinking, don't stop to think, of how or why you might hurt others. Be frank, and expose yourself so that in the end nobody would be able to hurt you.

Stare out the window, through the night, to the slow breaking of dawn and the shattered fragments of light appearing out beyond St Andrew's. A waking town! Bracing itself, like you, half in fear, half in the simmering excitement of anticipation for the challenge of the coming day. And maybe the waking city for all its appearances of calm, was just as nervous as you.

At six in the morning it occurred to you that you should undress but you decided against this and took out your Racine, to prepare for the coming French examination. And after the examination, what?

You could not study.

The dark blue clouds shedding the last effects of night reminded you that day would soon be here. You had remained at the window all night, often leaning on your injured ankle, but you had no pain at all, and were not in the least bit tired.

One hour later you were still standing by the window. The morning had come.

The last examination was over.

Lug the old case down along the terrazzo corridor and out the main door. Consider calling to the room of Father Bransfield to tell him that you appreciated his efforts and kindnesses over the years. Decide against this. You would only have made a fool of yourself.

Your father, mother and sister were waiting in the car.

'Well, son, you're finished with College now.' Your father would be lonely. He hated to see you growing up.

'It's great to be going home,' you answered, because this was the way you were expected to answer.

'How did you do in the exam?' asked your mother. She could always distinguish the important from the sentimental.

When she asked this question you remembered your resolve. Be frank.

'I did very well.'

'How do you know?' asked your sister. 'The results will not be known for another two months.'

'I marked my own papers. Conservatively.'

'There's something about you that maddens me,' said your sister.

'What?'

'You're too sure of yourself. Too cocky. I think you have a swelled head.'

You smiled at her for a reply. You liked getting on her nerves.

'Leave him alone,' said your mother. 'I'm sure he will do well for himself yet.'

'Of course he'll do well,' said your sister. 'But he does not have to be so cocky about it. He simply can't imagine himself a failure.'

Think about your sister's words and smile at her again. You would have to try something else besides being frank. That created the wrong impression altogether. How are you going to get on with people from now on?

What could succeed, or Christ! would you be floundering around forever, and not succeed at all?

Nuala Ní Dhomhnaill
Fear

Bain díot do chuid éadaigh
ceann ar cheann,
do threabhsar is do bheist
líontánach liath.
Cuir do chuid spéaclaí
ar an gclabhar
in aice do chíor
is do haincisiúr.

Is siúil chugham trasna
an urláir ar dheis
go bun na leapan
chun go bhfaighead deis
mo shúile a shíneadh
thar an niamh dorcha id chneas
thar na míorúiltí is ailleachtaí
i do chabhail.

Is ná bí grod ná giorraisc
liom anocht,
ná fiafraigh díom 'cén chaoi?',
ná brostaigh ort,
tuig nach lú a fhéadaim
in bhfianaise do dhea-nocht
mo shúile a líonadh
ná iad a dhúnadh ort.

A fhir atá chomh fada
as do ghéag
chomh leathan as do ghualainn
is do thaobh,
fainge fionn fireann
ó bhaitheas go bearradh iongan
is do bhall fearga

cumtha dá réir,
ba chóir go mórfaí tú
os comhair an tslua,
go mbronnfaí ort
craobh is próca óir,
ba chóir go snoífí tú
id dhealbh marmair
ag seasamh romham
id pheilt is uaireadóir.

PÁDRAIG Ó CÍOBHÁIN
as AR GACH MAOILINN TÁ SÍOCHÁIN (1998)

1

Deir Eoin Aspal linn go raibh tosach ag an bhfocal. Ní thugann sé le haon chinnteacht aon tuairim dúinn conas mar a bheidh ag an ndeireadh nó conas a shaorfar sinn ó ghaoth an fhocail. Is falla an timpeallú so a dheinim ar m'eachtra, ach i dtaobh nach cumadóir ceoil mé a chuirfeadh nótaí ar foluain os do chionn in aoibhneas a gcruthaitheachta, i dtaobh nach péintéir mé a chuirfeadh dathanna go hildaite ag rince ar chanbhás duit, tabharfad liom tú trí bhóithrín seo na marbhfhocal a rithfidh ina ribín bán go dtí buacphointe éigin nó bunphointe éigin de m'eisint mar gur chun é sin a thuiscint a mhairim. Pé scéal é, seans nach scéal éinne amháin é mar gur minic don gcomhtharlú a bheith mar mháistreás ar an gcinniúint agus eachtraithe dar linn go leithliseach ná baineann le héinne ach linn á dháileadh go fial ar dhaoine eile aici.

Mar gur baisteadh mé táim faoin a dhaorbhroid. Ceann de na cuingeacha a bhraithim ina gcéadta anuas sa mhullach orm do mo bhrú i nguta m'intinne. Curtha faoi chéachta na Críostaíochta, mé fós i mo bhraimichín gan bhriseadh. Agus fé mar a dúirt an fear fadó agus mar a dúirt an té a dúirt muran cuing amháin é agus sinn snaidhmte di is cuing eile é, mar go n-iarraimid cúis. Is ó chúis go cúis dúinn siar chomh fada siar is atá siar ann ag criathrú agus ag scagadh gan teacht againn sa duibheagán ar faic gur fuaim asainn féin é. Ní hea ach macalla de thuiscintí tuirsiúla traochta dhaoine eile.

Féachaim amach trí fhuinneog mo shamhlaíochta féachaint an samhlódh faic dom gurbh fhiú dom sians a dhéanamh de. Bailím mo mhéireanta le chéile i bpóca mo bhríste bréidín i bhfoirm doirn a fháiscfeadh an chuimhne amach as phaca peacach m'intinne, mar go mbraithim mé ciontach agam féin de bhrí gur ciotach an duine mé agus cur chuige sin a cuireadh ar an saol mé. Nó, sin é a síltear anois dom, n'fheadar an b'in é a sílfear fós dom? Bhuel cuirimis i gcás nach é agus murab é is leor dom san mar chúis chun cur suas le mo chinniúint mar bhrí chun brí éigin a bhaint as mo shaol de bhrí gur minic áitithe orm san a dhéanamh. Is minic gur leasc liom súd a dhéanamh mar ná feadar an fiú é mar bhonn a chur le brat machnaimh nó mar bhonn le babhta dioscúrsála a dhéanamh le héinne do mo chairde. Bhuel le héinne amháin acu mar ná fuil ann ach an t-éinne amháin go réitíonn liom amhlaidh a dhéanamh leis. Agus sin é Georges. Dar ndóigh is mise Artúr.

Is duine é Georges a ghéilleann i mbrí na háiféise, rud ná fágann gur duine áiféiseach é, dar liom, ach a mhalairt. Taibhsítear dom gur duine daingean é ar bheagán dúire mar nuair a chuimhním ar dhaoine, ar a lán daoine ar m'aithne agus ar m'eolas, is í an dúire iontu is túisce a chítear dom má chítear faic. N'fheadar. Tá Georges oscailte, gealgháireach, mórchroíoch gan spléachas le héinne bíodh is gur baisteadh é sin leis. Dá ainneoin. Dá m'ainneoinse.

2

'A Airt,' arsa é sin liom lá amháin. Suite síos ar bhinse páirce a bhíomar. Loichín taobh linn, lachain ag snámh inti gan faic againn le caitheamh chucu. Grágaíl ocrais ar bun acu. Scolnótaí, scalladh orthu, ag scóladh an chroí ann mar gur duine é a thugann lán paca pleaistic dá mhangaisíní do Chumann Naomh Uinsinn de Pól dhá uair nó trí so mbliain. Bacla t-léinte, seans, a bheadh imithe a bheag nó a mhór as faisean b'fhéidir. A bheag a déarfainnse ach a mhór a shílfeadh Georges mar ná lú leis an sioc ná a bheith taobh thiar de pé ní a bhraithfeadh sé a bheadh sa rás roimis amach nó go mbéarfadh sé air. T-léine agus ainm an ghrúpa roc-cheoil neamhspleáigh Inspiral Carpets a bhí á chaitheamh inniu aige.

'Ní lú liom an diabhal ná an ainm sin,' a deirim leis, 'ach i dtaobh go gcaithfir lipéad éigin a chur orm glacfad leis.'

'I dtaobh gur baisteadh tú?'

'I dtaobh gur baisteadh mé.'

'Ná cíonn tú an ainm áiféiseach a baisteadh ormsa?'

'N'fheadar. Is maith liom Georges. Tá sé cool. Blas na Fraincise agus mar sin de.'

'Ná maith nár thugadar Fleure ar mo dheirfiúr?'

'Á luífeadh san rómhór le réasún, a dhuine. Cad a thugadar uirthi? Ní raibh fhios agam a leithéid riamh a bheith agat.'

Ní agamsa a bhí sí ach acu san. Thugadar Ava uirthi.'

'Ava? Ava Gardiner? Ava Maria?'

'Ní hea. Níl agat. É abhá. Mar sin a fhuaimníonn siad é. Gairdín Pharthais, a dhuine, sular shloig sí an t-úll.'

'Tuigim.'

Ní thuigeann tú ná é. Ach deireann tú é sin féachaint an éisteoinn agus labhairt ar rud éigin eile. Agus is agat atá an ceart mar nach éinne den dtriúr againn is ciontach leis na hainmneacha áiféiseacha atá tugtha orainn. Ach féach fós go bhfuil a gceacht féin le múineadh acu. Tugadh Georges ormsa i ndiaidh Georges Pompidou. Níor leor an foirgneamh úd i bPáras a bheith curtha in airde ina onóir. Ní i ndiaidh Arthur Guinness a baisteadh tú?'

'Dhóbair dom gurb ea mar mhairbh an pórtar m'athair. Dóite amach idir dhubháin agus chac is trócaire. D'ól sé an braon anuas agus an sop as an srathar agus a oiread eile ina theannta. Ach níorbh ea. Baisteadh mé i ndiaidh Arthur Rimbaud file, fáidh faghartha Francach. Bhí an-shuim ag mo mháthair ina chuid stuife ina mac léinn di bíodh is nár dhóigh leat san anois ó ghaibh an saol lastuas di.'

'Ifreann ar talamh gan dabht?'

'Ar ghéilleadh dhuit in ifreann agus ina bhfuil ar talamh a thógaint chomh dáiríre sin, chomh dáiríre is a dhein sí, sea.'

Le fonn agus le feis go fonnmhar dúinn is béas linn fogha a thabhairt fén ndínit ionainn agus inár gcomhdhaoine ar an gcuma san. Mar go mbraithim go bhfuil sé de cheart agamsa leis m'ifreann a agairt orm féin.

'Ar mhachnamh dom cruthaím agus múnlaím domhan nó teorannaím an domhan atá curtha ar fáil dom. Agus nach mar a chéile an dá dhomhan acu ar deireadh mar go gcuirfeadsa ar fáil trí m'fhianaise bíodh san scríte nó díreach ráite dona thuilleadh é?'

'Eh . . . ?'

'M'ifreann ar talamh nó mo pharthas ar talamh. Ceann nó cruit?'

'Toghfadsa séasúr in ifreann.'

'Mar gur ainmníodh tú i ndiaidh Arthur Rimbaud?'

'Seans ar shmut den gceart a bheith agat. Nó díreach de bhrí gur fearr liom an t-ord san, an t-eagar san a chur ar chúrsaí – ifreann roimis na flaithis. Fulaingt ar dtús, an dtuigeann tú? Tosach áite a thabhairt don bpionós agus ansan an mhaith a thuilleamh. Nach mar sin is dual dúinne Críostaithe cuimhneamh? Ní mór dom m'ifreann as mo chuid fraochmhaireachta.'

'Ní mór liom duit an méid sin. Sin í an chonair chun na honóra. Sin é mar a chaithimidne Gaeil an bheatha nuair a chaithimid mar is cóir í.'

MICK MACCONNELL
THE RED-HEADED ANNE

All the wee birds were lining the bleak autumn branches
preparing to fly to a faraway shore
when the tinkers made camp at the bend in the river
coming back from the horsefair in Ballinasloe.
The harvest being over the farmer came walking
along the Feale river that bordered his land
and 'twas there he first saw her twixt firelight and water
the Tinkerman's daughter, the Red-Headed Anne.

Next morning he rose from a night without resting
went straight to her father and made his case known.
In a pub in Listowel they worked out the bargain
for the tinker a pony – for the daughter a home.
Where the trees peg their shadows along the Feale river
the tinker and farmer inspected the land
and a white gelding pony was the price they agreed on
for the Tinkerman's daughter, the Red-Headed Anne.

The wedding soon over the tinkers departed
eager to travel on south down the road
but the crunch of the iron-shod wheels on the gravel
was as bitter to her as the way she'd been sold.
Yet she tried hard to please him, she did all his biddin'
She slept in his bed and she worked on his land
but the walls of that cabin pressed tighter and tighter
on the Tinkerman's daughter, the Red-Headed Anne.

As white as the hands of the priest of the hangman
the snow spread its blanket the next Christmas 'round
when the Tinkerman's daughter slipped out from the bedside
turned her back to the land and her face to the town.
'Twas said someone saw her ere dusk that same evening
she was making her way out o'er Lyreacrompane
and that was the last time the settled folk saw her
the Tinkerman's daughter, the Red-Headed Anne.

Where the North Kerry hills cup the Feale near Listowel
in a farm on its banks lives a bitter old man
and he swears by the shotgun he keeps by his bedside
that he'll kill any tinker who camps on his land.
But whenever he hears iron-shod wheels crunch on gravel
or a horse in the shafts of a bright caravan
then his day's work's tormented, his night's sleep demented
by the Tinkerman's daughter, the Red-Headed Anne.

SIGERSON CLIFFORD
THE SPANISH WAISTCOAT

John Dan's house looked upon Kersey village, and Kersey looked
on the sea. It was a small, neat house with walls white as fresh
milk and laced by wires anchored to heavy stones to keep the
thatch from flying over the mountain when the great winds blew
from the sea. John Dan lived alone in the house.

He was a tall, clumsy man, high over sixty, with huge hairy
hands and the biggest pair of boots in the parish. He smoked
a pipe continuously. It was a stubby, evil-smelling briar and it

bubbled furiously when smoked. In the chapel on Sundays people avoided kneeling beside John Dan because the pipe, tucked carefully at the bottom of his coat-pocket, was no less offensive to the nose than if it had been gripped between the last four decaying teeth in the left corner of John Dan's mouth. That's the kind of pipe it was.

One fine midday John Dan, smoking and bubbling merrily against his western gable, saw a knot of people leave the wide road and walk urgently up the boreen towards him. He recognised Murthy the Post by reason of his dark blue uniform, with the polished brass buttons winking on it like little yellow eyes, and the glossy peak of his cap flashing like a mirror in the sun. 'There's strangeness here,' said John Dan to himself, and he waited and wondered.

The only time in the year Murthy called to a house so far removed from the main road as John Dan's was at Christmas, when he got a half-crown and a drop of whiskey to tide him over till that bountiful season came again. At all other times he stopped on the wide road, draped himself across his bicycle, whistled shrilly three times and waited patiently until the house disgorged somebody to collect the letter. So it was strange indeed to see him straining his heart climbing the mountain in the high heat of noon, when three shrill whistles would have brought John Dan down to the wide road to gather his mail. And Christmas so far off, and all.

As they drew nearer John Dan saw a parcel in Murthy's hand. 'Maybe 'tis a case of pipes from Nora,' he told himself.

John Dan had two daughters in America, and a brother, Denny, living ten miles across the Sound in Beglin. Nora, who was married to an Italian café owner, often sent him a few dollars. She also posted him the money to buy the green punt from Michael John Shea when he decided to take one of the farms in County Meath that the government were giving to mountainy people. The little boat was handy to John Dan for the bit of pollack-fishing he did, and it enabled him to keep his eye on the dozen lobster-pots he had anchored in his own special patch of sea beynd Lamb's Point. His other daughter, Gobnait, still unmarried and, in John Dan's opinion, likely to remain so, never sent anything except highly-coloured Christmas cards plastered with highly-coloured sentiments and signed 'To dearest

Pop from Netta.' One year in America had taught Gobnait to change John Dan's name and her own in one fell swoop . . .

He went across the yard to meet the men, his eyes curious.

'Tis from America,' said Murthy, giving him the parcel, 'and there's twenty-five shillings tax on it.'

'May the devil sweep 'em with their twenty-five shillings tax,' fumed John Dan, turning the parcel over in his hands. He carefully read the labels attached to the parcel.

'Tis wearing apparel,' he told the crowd, 'and, be the hokey, 'tis from Gobnait.'

'We know that,' said Paddy the Black Bog honestly and easily. 'We only want to see what's in it.'

'Tisn't every day you pay twenty-five shillings tax on a biteen of a garment,' said William Red Sails. 'There must be powerful stuff in it.'

They all went into the house and John Dan sawed the cords asunder with a gapped breadknife. He unwound enough tissue-paper to make a sail for a boat and then the garment in all its glory lay before them.

It was a curious piece of work, to say the least of it. It was more like a waistcoat than a coat only it had long sleeves. It was beautifully embroidered in gold and silver with a buffalo grazing on the left breast and a puma snarling on the right.

'What devil's curio is this?' asked John Dan, turning a bewildered eye on Murthy, who was feeling quite bewildered himself.

'Let me see now,' said Murthy, fingering the garment while the others waited expectantly for his decision.

Before he graduated into a whistling postman, Murthy had been a sailor. He had crossed the line, rounded Cape Horn, had been shipwrecked a few times and had had a knife stuck into him by an unfriendly Arab in a brawl in Cairo. In consequence of these varied and almost disastrous experiences Murthy's words carried some weight in the parish of Kersey.

Murthy examined the garment inside and out and felt his pedestal trembling for a fall beneath him.

'If Murthy doesn't know, nobody knows,' said John Dan earnestly to Paddy Black Bog, 'and him after ringing the world a score of times.'

Murthy's eyes gleamed and his words came slow and ponderous

like well-fed cows through a gap in a drowsy June dusk.

'I seen the likes of it in Spain. The bullfighters in Madrid used to wear its equal. 'Tis a Spanish waistcoat.'

The others emitted their breath in little whistles of appreciation and fingered the waistcoat with renewed interest. There was no country in the world so near to the minds of the people of Kersey as Spain. They knew their history and were well aware that she sent them ships round about 1600 which is only the day before yesterday to a Kersey man. And wasn't she still sending ships? To be sure the great gilded galleons had now become swift, well-designed, if ill-designing, trawlers which left their fishing-grounds as bare as the palm of your hand, but they were still ships and showed that Spain had not forgotten them entirely. So one can imagine the tidal wave of excitement that swept over John Dan's house when it was revealed by the wise Murthy that the richly-embroidered garment was nothing less than a Spanish waistcoat as worn by the bullfighters of Spain who are, as every mother's son should know, the real aristocracy of that orange-blessed land.

Paddy Black Bog smote John Dan heartily between the shoulder blades. 'You'll dazzle the parish with this,' said Paddy. 'I can see you sitting snug in the Widow Breheny's place a month from today.'

William Red Sails winced visibly at the dire prophecy. William, who was, fortunately in the circumstances, a widower, had an interest in the Widow himself and had dreamed dreams and seen visions. And the Widow had twenty acres of the best land in Kersey and a black box which she always kept locked. Locked black boxes in any other part of Ireland are not as intriguing as those in Kersey. For in Kersey a locked black box means that its owner does not appreciate the fact that banks are run at enormous expense for the sole purpose of helping those who deem it necessary to get a lock for a black box. And William Red Sails never counted John Dan much of a rival. But now all was changed, changed utterly.

'You'll wear the Spanish waistcoat on Sunday going to Mass,' commanded Paddy Black Bog, 'and I'll speak a few words to the Widow about you in the meantime.'

'Is it a grey or a black trousers I'll wear with it?' asked John Dan.

''Tis a red trousers they used wear in Madrid,' said Murthy, scratching his chin. 'But, of course, Kersey isn't Madrid,' he confided, 'and you could wear the black.'

'The black it is,' said John Dan.

On Saturday John Dan walked into Kersey and looked in on Jackie Walsh, the draper.

'I'm after a good hat, Jackie,' he said.

'How good?' asked Jackie.

'One fit to go with my Spanish waistcoat,' said John Dan proudly.

On Sunday morning all Kersey collected at the western end of the village to await the triumphant entry of John Dan. The fame of the Spanish waistcoat had gone through the parish with the speed of a mackerel-shoal evading the nets of a fishing boat down to its last tin of condensed milk. The Widow Breheny was there, too, her fifteen stone swathed in a fur coat that had cost her a pony, though the shop assistant in Tralee town assured her 'twas a squirrel had worn it before her, and sporting a hat whose twin was never beheld on land or sea.

At last John Dan arrived, guarded on either side by Murthy the Post and Paddy Black Bog. He was coatless and the Spanish waistcoat, wooed by an appreciating sun, sparkled like the toga of an archangel. He wore his new black hat at an angle that lifted ten years of his total of three score and seven, and the crease on his trousers was razor-sharp. His face had the frightened, exalted look of a man, wrongly condemned, on his way to the guillotine, in sharp contrast to the countenances of his benevolent executioners, Murthy and Paddy, which were wreathed in smiles.

A hush fell on the villagers and on the Widow Breheny's fur coat and the eyes of the multitude watched with mingled awe and admiration the progress of the new John Dan. Caesar entering Rome after dividing all Gaul into three parts didn't command half as much respect as John Dan did in his triumphant Spanish-waistcoated entry into Kersey.

The three men were halfway down the line before someone thought of raising a cheer. In a moment it had swelled to a mighty roar that shook the windows of Kersey and gave the wondering collectors at the chapel some inkling as to why their boxes were still bare of pennies.

Father Dermot, affectionately contemplating his bed of prize wallflowers and thinking how much they resembled little children dressed in old-fashioned velvet dresses, heard the cheering and lifted his head to find John Dan and all his parishioners bearing down on him.

'Bless my soul,' exclaimed Father Dermot when the luxuriance of John Dan's waistcoat impressed itself upon him. He turned to Paddy Black Bog.

'Is there a name for this – ?' he waved his hand feebly in the direction of John Dan's embroidered chest.

'It's a Spanish waistcoat, Father,' explained Paddy. ''Twas worn by a bullfighter in Madrid.'

'A bullfighter. Bless my soul,' said Father Dermot. 'Well, well, let ye march into Mass now. 'Tis getting late.' He watched them till they disappeared through the wide door.

'Bless my soul!' he exclaimed again. 'A bullfighter in Kersey! What will they think of next?'

In the parish of Kersey and indeed beyond it, John Dan's name was on everybody's lips. People who had formerly barely tolerated him now engaged him in lengthy conversations and got his opinions on the correct way to rear bonhams, catch lobsters, where the best fishing grounds for pollack were, and how to divine water with the help of a hazel-rod. They remembered the doughty deeds of his youth, his great skill as a weight-thrower, his prowess on the football field and as an oarsman.

John Dan's suit with the Widow Breheny was being pressed assiduously by Paddy Black Bog. Because of his great, though newfound fame one would imagine it to be roses, roses all the way for him, but the Widow wasn't young any longer, and William Red Sails owned the best fishing-boat in the harbour. So she decided to wait a while, and Paddy conveyed the news to John Dan.

'The ould wreck is putting it on the long finger, but I'll bate her into it yet.'

It was unfortunate that the fame of the Spanish waistcoat crossed the ten miles of sea to John Dan's brother, Denny, who was married in Beglin. He wrote to John Dan, inviting him over for a weekend, with a PS not to forget the famous waistcoat.

John Dan decided to go. He went down to the pier one evening when it was dusk and found a boatload of the young bucks setting out for Beglin with a box of lobsters, there being a better price offered in that village than in Kersey.

'Are you coming with us, John Dan?' called out Billy, son to William Red Sails, a lean stringy youth, who was eyeing the Spanish waistcoat as a weasel might eye a month-old rabbit.

They fussed around him, half of them hindering, and the rest helped him into the boat.

'Make way there for the grand Spanish gentleman,' they shouted with unholy glee.

John Dan took the tiller and they pushed off.

'Let ye go by Lamb's Point, boys, I want to haul my pots and bring a few lobsters to Denny,' said John Dan.

'Lamb's Point it is, captain,' they chorused, and their six oars rose and fell cleanly like knife blades.

John Dan ran his experienced eye from stroke to bow.

'Bow oar, pick-up,' he called out.

Billy Red Sails held up his right hand.

'It's my wrist, John Dan, I hurt it this morning hauling the pots.'

John Dan took off his Spanish waistcoat, folded it carefully, and placed it on the stern.

'There's no sense in sending a boy on a man's errand,' he said. 'Give me the oar.'

'Give the Spanish gentleman the oar,' the bloods shouted. 'Get astern, Red Sails, and mind the gentleman's waistcoat.'

The boat leaped forwards again, the oars biting triamgles of phosphorescent fire out of the heaving breast of the sea. Soon they were at Lamb's Point and while John Dan rested the others crowded about the stern, hauling his pots and shouting loudly when one contained a lobster.

'Here's one, John Dan, with tusks on him like an elephant.'

'Here's a fellow must be drawing a pension. Give him a shaugh of the pipe, John Dan.'

'This chap has a face on him like a head-constable.'

'Rogues and blackguards,' murmured John Dan. 'I wonder is every parish cursed with the likes of ye?'

They sunk the pots again, sat under their oars and pulled quickly to where the village of Beglin huddled about its score of lights. When they glided into the harbour the pier was deserted. They stood up in the boat and stretched their cramped legs. John Dan made his way to the stern while they were arguing as to who should carry the box of lobsters to the buyer. He put his hand down on the stern-seat and felt along it. Nothing but wood, wet in parts where the sea had spilled on it. He felt again to make sure. No sign of it. A dreadful fear gripped him. He cracked a match, cupped it in his hands, and flashed it on the bottom of the boat. He saw his own three lobsters watching him coldly, their long black feelers waving briskly, and a baling-tin carrying an advertisement for somebody's cream toffees. There was no trace of the Spanish waistcoat.

He turned on the crew in a rage.

'What did ye do with it, ye limbs of Satan? Where did ye put my waistcoat?'

They looked at him open-mouthed.

'He lost the Spanish waistcoat.'

'Find it for him; he'll freeze in his shirt.'

'We'll keel-haul the man that took it.'

''Tis overboard it went. Some mermaid is decking herself out in it now.'

They cracked a score of jokes and matches and searched the boat from stem to stern but there was no sign of it.

They went up on the pier carrying their box of lobsters and John Dan remained in the boat.

'Aren't you going to visit Denny, John Dan?' they asked.

'How can a decent Christian walk through a strange village in his shirt?' said John Dan.

They went along the pier, loudly discussing the mysterious disappearance of the Spanish waistcoat, and vanished into the night.

John Dan wrapped himself in a piece of sail and sat in the stern. He decided to fill his pipe and then remembered that his plug of tobacco was in the pocket of the waistcoat. He grunted loudly. He felt lost and lonely and cold.

'Would to God,' sorrowed John Dan to himself. 'Would to God, we had died in Egypt!'

With the disappearance of the Spanish waistcoat John Dan's fall from glory was swifter than his rise to it. Paddy Black Bog washed his hands of his matrimonial affairs and the Widow Breheny was married to William Red Sails within a month. However, the Widow gave William such a time of it, that he was able to repent at leisure the haste and extreme indiscretion of his second voyage into matrimonial waters. Murthy the Post whistled John Dan down to the wide road whenever he had a letter for him, and never mentioned the waistcoat any more.

John Dan took his loss hard. It was a fortnight before he ventured into Kersey village. It was a month before he decided to visit his lobster-pots.

He rowed out to them in the green punt, his pipe rising poisonous clouds in the still evening air and gurgling like a June turkey. He hauled up eleven of the pots, found them empty, baited them and let them slide down to the green depths again. The twelfth pot was heavy and he knew it had something in it.

'Must be a devil of a conger,' muttered John Dan, opening his big pocket-knife and placing it beside him.

When the pot came to the surface his eyes goggled. There, nestling among the thin rods was his Spanish waistcoat, its grand embroidery ruined forever, with a big patch of slime whitening where a conger-eel had slept on it.

John Dan drew forth the shabby sodden garment tenderly and looked at it thoughtfully. He felt in the pocket and pulled out the plug of tobacco. He then flung the Spanish waistcoat back into the sea. It floated a while and slipped slowly to the bottom. John Dan watched it wistfully till it disappeared.

JOHN B. KEANE
from THE FIELD (1965)

Bishop   Do not be afraid of those who kill the body but cannot kill the soul. But rather be afraid of him who is able to destroy both body and soul in Hell.'

In the name of the Father and of the Son and of the Holy Ghost, Amen.

Dearly beloved brethren, these are the words of Christ Himself. He was speaking about truth. How many of you would deny Christ? How many of you, like Peter, would stand up and say: 'I know not the Man!' but you can lie without saying a word; you can lie without opening your lips; you can lie by silence.

Five weeks ago in this parish, a man was murdered – he was brutally beaten to death. For five weeks the police have investigated and not one single person has come forward to assist them. Everywhere they turned, they were met by silence, a silence of the most frightful and diabolical kind – the silence of the lie. In God's name, I beg you, I implore you, if any of you knows anything, to come forward and to speak without fear.

This is a parish in which you understand hunger. But there are many hungers. There is a hunger for food – a natural hunger. There is the hunger of the flesh – a natural understandable hunger. There is a hunger for home, for love, for children. These things are good – they are good because they are necessary. But there is also the hunger for land. And in this parish, you, and your fathers before you knew what it was to starve because you did not own your own land – and that has increased; this unappeasable hunger for land. But how far are you prepared to go to satisfy this hunger. Are you prepared to go to the point of murder? Are you prepared to kill for land? Was this man killed for land? Did he give his life's blood for a field? If so, that field will be a field of blood and it will be paid for in thirty pieces of silver – the price of Christ's betrayal – and you, by your silence will share in that betrayal.

Among you there is a murderer! You may even know his name, you may even have seen him commit this terrible crime – through your silence, you share his guilt, your innocent children will grow up under the shadow of this terrible crime, and you will carry this guilt with you until you face your Maker at the moment of judgement . . .

If you are afraid to go to the police, then come to your priests, or come to me. And if there is one man among you – one man made after Christ's likeness – he will stand up and say: 'There! There he is! There is the murderer!'

And that man will have acknowledged Christ before men and Christ will acknowledge him before his Father in Heaven. But if you, by your silence, deny

Christ before men, He will disown you in Heaven, and I, as His representative, will have a solemn duty to perform. I will place this parish under interdict and then there will be a silence more terrible than the first. The church bell will be silent; the mass bell will not be heard; the voice of the confessional will be stilled and in your last moment will be the most dreadful silence of all for you will go to face your Maker without the last sacrament on your lips . . . and all because of your silence now. In God's name, I beg of you to speak before it is too late. 'I am the way, says Christ, and the truth. Do not be afraid of those who can kill the body but cannot kill the soul. But rather, be afraid of him who can destroy both body and soul in hell.'

In the name of the Father and of the Son and of the Holy Ghost, Amen.

PÁDRAIG Ó HÉIGEARTAIGH
OCHÓN! A DHONNCHA

Ochón! a Dhonncha, mo mhíle cogarach, fén bhfód so sínte;
fód an doichill 'na luí ar do cholainn bhig, mo loma-sceimhle!
Dá mbeadh an codladh so i gCill na Dromad ort nó in uaigh
    san Iarthar
mo bhrón do bhogfadh, cé gur mhór mo dhochar, is ní
    bheinn id' dhiaidh air.

Is feoite caite 'tá na blátha scaipeadh ar do leaba chaoilse;
ba bhreá iad tamall ach thréig a dtaitneamh, níl snas ná brí
    iontu
'S tá an bláth ba ghile liom dár fhás ar ithir riamh ná a
    fhásfaidh choíche
ag dreo sa talamh, is go deo ní thaofaidh ag cur éirí croí orm.

Och, a chumannaigh! nár mhór an scrupall é an t-uisce dod'
    luascadh,
gan neart id' chuisleannaibh ná éinne i ngaire duit a
    thabharfadh fuarthan.

Scéal níor tugadh chúgham ar bhaol mo linbh ná ar dhéine
    a chruatain –
ó! 's go raghainn go fonnmhar ar dhoimhin-lic Ifrinn chun
    tú a fhuascailt.

Tá an ré go dorcha, ní fhéadaim codladh, do shéan gach só
    mé.
Garbh doilbh liom an Ghaeilge oscailte – is olc an comhartha
    é.
Fuath liom sealad i gcomhluadar carad, bíonn a ngreann dom'
    chiapadh.
Ón lá go bhfacasa go tláith ar an ngaineamh thú níor gheal
    an ghrian dom.

Och, mo mhairg! cad a dhéanfad feasta 's an saol dom'
    shuathadh,
gan do láimhín chailce mar leoithne i gcrannaibh ar mo
    mhalainn ghruama,
do bhéilín meala mar cheol na n-aingeal go binn im' chluasaibh
á rá go cneasta liom: 'Mo ghraidhn m'athair bocht, ná bíodh
    buairt ort!'

Ó, mo chaithis é! is beag do cheapas-sa i dtráth mo dhóchais
ná beadh an leanbh so 'na laoch mhear chalma i lár na fóirne,
a ghníomhartha gaisce 's a smaointe meanman ar son na
    Fódla –
ach an Té do dhealbhaigh de chré ar an dtalamh sinn, ní mar
    sin d'ordaigh.

CON SHANAHAN
from ACROSS THE YEARS

In 1916 I was five years old when my father died. He was an intelligent and well-educated man, powerfully built, with a great temper. I missed him very much and used to cry myself to sleep to think I would not meet him any more.

My father inherited our house from his father. It stood, a

two-storeyed stone dwelling, where I was born along with my two brothers and three sisters. After his death, my mother was always grumbling and bemoaning his loss, how hard life was for her. She continued like this for years, though I could not see any merit in it. She was a strange woman who always found fault with her children, though she was very pious. Her family background had taught her to live from day to day.

She always managed that we had good clothes for church on Sundays and for going to school. She made shirts for my brothers and I, by hand as she did not possess a machine. She knitted socks and stockings and would remain up late at night mending and darning tears and holes and sewing patches to our trousers and jackets.

We had plenty of milk, cream and butter, and enough vegetables, for we had our own small farm a little distance beyond the village. We would kill a pig and have plenty of bacon. I remember when I was about five years old, walking up the street and seeing calves outside the butcher's shop, bellowing. It was a warm summer's day. I pushed open the half-door and saw, hanging by their hind legs, calves of different colours, twisting and kicking in all directions. Some were dead. Some were dying and one was being stuck with a knife by the butcher while his wife, Nellie, sharpened another with a round stone. The butcher sold veal for 1/3 and 1/6 a quarter and a sheep's head for sixpence. His shop was the rendezvous for children in the village, where we would see the killing of fat cows and also those that were so old they were hardly able to stand or walk.

Old Tom Nash and his wife, Ellen, who were past eighty, had a cow they were not able to look after or milk. The villagers persuaded old Tom and Ellen to have the cow killed and salted, that it would be good meat and that they would have the advantage of knowing it was their own produce. They agreed and the butcher killed the cow, helped by the neighbours. It was cut in pieces and salted and put in barrels. The elderly couple thought it would be a generous token to send pieces to their friends. Those neighbours who received it mostly buried the meat, for it could not be eaten.

After a few weeks, Tom took the rest of the meat out of the barrels and slung it up in the loft above the kitchen. It had only been used for odds and ends. Tom hurled the pieces up into the tapestry of cobwebs. He could not understand why his friends were refusing to take more of the meat. It seemed a waste but he had to get rid of the pieces. He kept a small amount for himself to last through the coming months.

He had a sound constitution and ate with relish. After a couple of months he told his neighbours that his bowels had not moved for some time. They were surprised that anyone could live in that condition. One of the smart boys suggested he try using dynamite. He would not go to a doctor, but he got Epsom salts at the dispensary. Old Tom's predicament aroused the interest of the village lads and they set to watch Tom's garden to see if there was any movement of his bowels. One morning they were surprised to see that the salts had worked.

My home was situated between a public house and a post office. The pub was noted for its great quality of porter, especialy in the winter months. It was believed by shrewd drinkers that the firkins or barrels of porter, kept against the wall that was the back of our fire, used to keep the drink at a mild temperature. Everyone used the public house, the carpenter, the mason, the thatcher, the cooper, the blacksmith, farmers and labourers, travelling people, gypsies, tinkers, the tailor, Jack the postman and Jimmy the process server.

Jimmy was a great man. He was small in stature and always wearing a hat, I think to give him a bit of height. When I met him, he stood looking at me and said:

If I were as tall to reach the pole,
I would be measured by height,
The mind is the measure of the man.

He never served a process or a summons until late at night. He would not disclose to anybody in the pub where he was going afterwards.

I often went into the pub, especially when there was singing, and that was almost every other day. The landlord, Mick Dan, and I were great friends. He was a big man, weighing I should think about twenty stone. He sat by the big peat fire with the kettle hanging in the hob ready to make the hot punch. His wife served drinks, helped by an assistant. I thought then that Mick Dan did not serve because of his bulky body, that he could not fit behind the bar. When a fight commenced the rich voices singing ceased, especially if there had been a fair that day in Listowel. Swearing and cursing would reach a height. Mick Dan would clear the house quickly and the fight would continue in the street. The other children and I would follow at a safe distance. It was very common to hear, 'Hold me back, man, or I will kill the bastard.'

I thought in my childish way how silly it was, if the man was going to kill or fight, to ask his drunken friends to hold him back. On my way home when everything was quiet, I met Mick Dan. He placed a hand on my shoulders and said, 'Those sons of bitches that cannot take their porter. Those sons of whores.'

I did not know what he meant and thought he was talking about the bores of guns, for it was at that time the country folk used to drill and parade, carrying guns on their shoulders.

Mick Dan, still resting his hand on me while I twisted and turned, trying to ease off the pressure so that he did not notice, continued, 'If your father and myself were squeezed together, nothing would have come out of us but good Irish whiskey.'

AOGÁN Ó RATHAILLE
VAILINTÍN BRÚN

Do leathnaigh an ciach diachrach fám sheana-chroí dúr
ar thaisteal na ndiabhal n-iasachta i bhfearann Choinn
        chughainn;
scamall ar ghriain iarthair dár cheartas ríocht Mumhan
fá deara dhom triall riamh ort, a Vailintín Brún.

Caiseal gan cliar, fiailteach ná macraí ar dtúis
is beanna-bhruig Bhriain ciarthuilte, 'mhadraibh úisc,
Ealla gan triar triaithe de mhacaibh rí Mumhan
fá deara dhom triall riamh ort, a Vailintín Brún.

D'aistrigh fia an fialchruth do chleachtadh sí ar dtúis
– neadaigh an fiach iasachta i ndaingeanchoill Rúis,
seachnaid iaisc griantsruth is caise caoin ciúin,
fá deara dhom triall riamh ort, a Vailintín Brún.

Dairinis thiar, iarla níl aici 'en chlainn úir,
i Hamburg, mo chiach! iarla na seabhach síoch subhach –
seana-rosc liath ag dianghol fá cheachtar díobh súd
fá deara dhom triall riamh ort, a Vailintín Brún.

Clúmh na n-ealtan meara snámhas le gaoith
mar lúireach dealbh cait ar fásach fraoigh,
diúltaid ceathra a lacht a thál dá laoigh,
ó shiúil Sir Val i gceart na gCárthach gcaoin.

Do stiúraigh Pan a dhearca in arda críoch
ag tnúth cár ghabh an Mars do bhásaigh sinn;
músclaid athaigh ghearra lann an trír
ag brú na marbh trasna ó sháil go rinn.

SIGERSON CLIFFORD
THE CAHERCIVEEN RACES

'Twas a day in September that I'll always remember,
I went with my father to Carhan's old school
And there on the racecourse were gathered in great force
Rich man and poor man, wild boy and tame fool.
There were tinkers from Galway as brown as a ha'penny,
A beggar with whiskers the longest I've seen,
The three-card trick Johnny and the four-shots-a-penny
On the day of the races in Caherciveen.

'Twas a rich Tower of Babel beside the school gable
Where the bookies were shouting and laying the odds,
'Twould take Atlas so hairy or our own Crusher Casey
To push through the crowds packed like peas in their pods.
There were tents like umbrellas where all sorts of fellows
Sold dilisc and shellfish and the juicy crubeen,
And penny Peg's legs the size of a peeler
On the day of the races in Caherciveen.
The jockeys they sat on their horses like statues,
Their fame shall remain while the Fertha still flows;
'Tis my hero, Padgen, I'd pin a bright badge on,

With the two gallant Griffins, Jimmie and John Joe.
Denis Donovan, too, from high Barr na Sráide,
And Courtney, Saint Brendan's, were sporting and keen,
While Jack Rock's spurs a-jingle would make your blood
       tingle
On the days of the races in Caherciveen.

The horses, God bless them, in my dreams I caress them,
The wild-things of beauty stole the heart from my side,
As I watched them fly over the grass and red clover
And sweep like the wind east by Reenrushen tide.
They skimmed the hawbushes, they dashed through the
       rushes,
Their jockeys arrayed in blue, scarlet and green:
'Twas the world's eighth wonder to hear their hooves thunder
On the day of the races in Caherciveen.

O that night men did gather, hearts light like a feather,
Round a meegum in Bawner's or a pint at the Plow,
They toasted the horses that won out their courses
And shouted their praises while time did allow.
'Here's a health to you, Terry, and O'Neill's Pride of Kerry,
Likewise Lass from Sussa, the westland's swift queen:
May they graze in high heaven and have comfort for ever,
They're the pride of the races in Caherciveen.'

My father is gone now, God's peace to his ashes,
The boys are young men and the old men are dead,
There is many a mile between me and the racecourse,
But the hooves of the horses beat loud in my head.
I give you my oath now I'd swap the wide world
To call back the bright days when proud I had been
A lad with his dad on the white road to Carhan,
And the splendid horse races in Caherciveen.

Briain Ó hUiginn
Haute Cuisine in Cathair Saidhbhín

Och! Éist liom, a chairde, is brónach mo scéal;
That vulgar invention called *Teanga na nGaedheal*
Has ruffled the temper and altered the mien
Of a charming young lady in *Cathair Saidhbhín*.

Ochón, 'sé mo bhrón, olagón alleliú!
The fat's in the fire and we're all in a stew;
If you call yourself Máire or Cáit or Eibhlín
You can't boil potatoes in *Cathair Saidhbhín*.

Such names should be kept in their places, you know,
On the hills and the bogs with the vulgar and low;
They should never be spoken or written or seen
In a cookery classroom in *Cathair Saidhbhín*.

Ochón, 'sé mo bhrón, olagón alleliú!
The fat's in the fire and we're all in a stew;
If you call yourself Máire or Cáit or Eibhlín
You can't bake a pancake in *Cathair Saidhbhín*.

'Tis foolish, ridiculous, childish, absurd
(And something else too, though I can't find the word)
To talk about Irish or anything mean
In the presence of gentry in *Cathair Saidhbhín*.

Ochón, 'sé mo bhrón, olagón alleliú!
The fat's in the fire and we're all in a stew;
If you call yourself Máire or Cáit or Eibhlín
You can't scour saucepans in *Cathair Saidhbhín*.

Those rude Gaelic Leaguers alone have the cheek
(Although they seem gentle enough till they speak)
To drag in philology flavoured with spleen
And mix it with pastry in *Cathair Saidhbhín*.

Ochón, 'sé mo bhrón, olagón alleliú!
The fat's in the fire and we're all in a stew;
If you call yourself Máire or Cáit or Eibhlín
You won't find a husband in *Cathair Saidhbhín*.

The Irish Revival is growing too strong
Spite of Bryce and of Birrell and Starkie and Long
And I hear for a fact that a Kerry *cailín*
Can cook without English in *Cathair Saidhbhín*.

Ochón, 'sé mo bhrón, olagón alleliú!
There's one thing I almost forgot to tell you:
If you call yourself Máire or Cáit or Eibhlín
You can frizzle a *Seoinín* in *Cathair Saidhbhín*.

J. J. BARRETT
CON BROSNAN

Of Con Brosnan, the great John Joe 'Purty Landers' said: 'Con
Brosnan was the political Bridge Builder of our time. And
remember it wasn't always popular to try breaking moulds in
those days. But Con had incredible guts and, regardless of
pressure from within his own side of the divide, or from our side,
he did what he believed had to be done to bring about peace
and healing. He was the ultimate peacemaker in Kerry football
after the Civil War.'

Con Brosnan gave a lifetime to the GAA in many capacities,
as successful Kerry player, captain and trainer. He loved his
country and the game of Gaelic football. He won six All Ireland
medals in his own career and his son Jim, now a doctor in
Dingle, was one of the most effective forwards in Kerry football
of the 1950s, winning two All Irelands, '53 and '55. Jim also
served as Kerry County Board Chairman and trainer of Kerry
teams in the 1960s. Another son, Mick, was in the panel in the
1953 All Ireland win against Armagh.

Revered in North Kerry after the War of Independence and
eventually the Civil War, Con Brosnan was above reproach in
his credentials as a leader of men, and as one who had laid his

own life on the line in the fight for freedom from Britain.

On January 19th 1921 on the Big Fair Day, in Listowel, Con Brosnan and another Moyvane man, Jack Aherne, had confronted and shot dead District Inspector O'Sullivan of the Royal Irish Constabulary, only fifty yards from the well fortified Listowel RIC Barracks and 300 yards from the British Army Garrison.

District Inspector O'Sullivan had been promoted to Listowel after, on May 28th 1920, bravely defending Kilmallock RIC Barracks against attack from some of the most lethal IRA units from the South Tipperary Brigade, the East Limerick Brigade and the East Clare Brigade. The East Limerick Brigade Vice OC, Tomas O'Maoileoin (also known as Sean Forde), listed Dan Breen, Sean Treacy, Mick Sheehan, Mike Brennan and Sean Carroll amongst the raiding party. There were some Cork and Kerry Volunteers also in the sixty-strong IRA attacking force but the one to fall on that occasion was a young Kerry schoolteacher, Captain Liam Scully of Glencar.

He had been teaching in Strand Road National School, Tralee, a stone's throw from where Charlie Kerins was born in 1918. Scully had been shot dead as an open target from inside the RIC Barracks and the two RIC Sergeants, one of them O'Sullivan, were regarded as responsible. There was a garrison of twenty-two constables accompanying O'Sullivan and he was credited with saving the lives of the seven survivors. The rest were reported to have been either burned in the blazing barracks or shot in the battle. It was generally accepted in Kerry that DI O'Sullivan was shot in Listowel as a reprisal for Scully's killing in Kilmallock. However, O'Maoileoin's account of this incident gave a much different reason for O'Sullivan's death. O'Maoileoin believed it was as a result of an interception by Liam Lynch's command of an order to bring O'Sullivan to Spike Island Prison to identify the then incarcerated O'Maoileoin as Sean Forde. It would have meant certain execution for O'Maoileoin (Forde) as he was wanted for a string of attacks on the occupying forces. And so, accordingly, two crack IRA men, Volunteer Matt Ryan and another were sent to Listowel to shoot DI Tobias O'Sullivan. O'Maoileoin's account could be correct up to the actual reason for the killing of O'Sullivan, but he was totally incorrect in thinking Ryan carried out the action. Con Brosnan, Jack Aherne and Danny O'Grady were the trio who killed DI O'Sullivan, in

Listowel, and not in Moyvane as stated by O'Maoileoin. Liam Scully's death had been avenged one way or the other.

As a reprisal for the killing of DI O'Sullivan, the village of Moyvane was ransacked and Con Brosnan's home was burned to the ground by the Black and Tans.

Con Brosnan became a household name in Kerry's fighting story. He was one who had been tested and not found wanting in the heat of battle, either on or off the pitch. Brosnan became a Captain in the Free State Army during the Civil War, as an ardent supporter of Michael Collins. Of course, he and his eventual lifelong friend, Joe Barrett, fought on the opposite sides during that bloody Civil War in Kerry. Captain Brosnan would later put his political activity behind him in the ensuing years as he pursued a glittering career as one of Kerry's greatest ever midfielders, going on to win six All Ireland Senior medals from 1924 to 1932.

The period after the Civil War was the most crucial to the future of Kerry football as the county had not played in Croke Park for nine years and in fact had not won an All Ireland title since 1914. It is remarkable therefore what was achieved by this band of political opposites in those years after the terrible conflict. When Kerry collected their sixth All Ireland title, the '24 crown, in April 1925 it had been eleven years since they had tasted success.

Brosnan played with Kerry in the losing 1923 All Ireland Final, which was actually played on 28 September 1924. Dublin won that clash but Kerry were to halt the four-in-a-row effort by Dublin in the 1924 championship played in April 1925. Brosnan kicked the winning point from a free in an exceptionally low scoring 0-4 to 0-3 Final.

Carbery's glowing tribute to Con Brosnan in the 1947 Annual is worth recapturing for the current reader:

'Con Brosnan of North Kerry, reckoned by many critics as the best centre-field man that ever played, was the man whose partnership with Bob Stack of Ballybunion made football history. They were the ideal blend and their dominance at midfield kept Kerry in the limelight from 1922 to 1932 and beyond, winning six All Irelands – the last four, 1929 - 1932 in a row to equal Wexford's record. Con Brosnan was a strong, handsome, 5'10' man, 12 stone, beautifully moulded. Like Bob Stack, "He could hold going all day". Con was a polished footballer, grand fielder, clever anticipation, kicks perfectly placed. He could "lace" home a point from 50 yards on demand, drop kick, break, pass cleverly, race through in long solo runs, fast rising ground shots for goals or points, grand feeder of forwards, he reminded me at times of another Con – the great Killarney man – Connie Murphy. Con Brosnan played a man's part in our National Struggle. He suffered much and his health suffered.'

from IN THE NAME OF THE GAME (1997)

BERNARD O'DONOGHUE
MUNSTER FINAL

in memory of Tom Creedon, died 21 August 1983

The jarveys to the west side of the town
Are robbers to a man, and if you tried
To drive through the Gap, they'd nearly strike you
With their whips. So we parked facing for home
And joined the long troop down the meadowsweet-
And woodbine-scented road into the town.
By blue Killarney's lakes and glens to see
The white posts on the green! To be deafened
By the muzzy megaphone of Jimmy Shand
And the testy bray to keep the gangways clear.

As for Tom Creedon, I can see him still,
His back arching casually to field and clear.
'Glory Macroom! Good boy, Tom Creedom!'
We'd be back next year to try our luck in Cork.

We will be back next year, roaring ourselves
Hoarse, praying for better luck. After first Mass
We'll get there early; that's our only hope.
Keep clear of the car parks so we're not hemmed in,
And we'll be home, God willing, for the cows.

EIBHLÍN DHUBH NÍ CHONAILL
as CAOINEADH AIRT UÍ LAOGHAIRE

1

B'fheidir gur aithris Eibhlín na dréachtaí seo os cionn an choirp i gCarraig an Ime.

Mo ghrá go daingean tu!
Lá dá bhfaca thu
ag ceann tí an mhargaidh,
thug mo shúil aire duit,
thug mo chroí taitneamh duit,
d'éalaíos óm charaid leat
i bhfad ó bhaile leat.

Is domhsa nárbh aithreach:
Chuiris parlús á ghealadh dhom,
rúmanna á mbreacadh dhom,
bácús á dheargadh dhom,
brící á gceapadh dhom
rósta ar bhearaibh dom,
mairt á leagadh dhom;
codladh i gclúmh lachan dom
go dtíodh an t-eadartha
nó thairis dá dtaitneadh liom.

Mo chara go daingean tu!
is cuimhin lem aigne
an lá breá earraigh úd,
gur bhreá thíodh hata dhuit
faoi bhanda óir tarraingthe;
claíomh cinn airgid,
lámh dheas chalma,
rompsáil bhagarthach –
fír-chritheagla
ar námhaid chealgach –
tú i gcóir chun falaracht
is each caol ceannann fút.

D'umhlaídís Sasanaigh
síos go talamh duit,
is ní ar mhaithe leat
ach le haon-chorp eagla,
cé gur leo a cailleadh tu,
a mhuirnín mh'anama . . .

Mo chara thu go daingean!
is nuair thiocfaidh chugham abhaile
Conchúr beag an cheana
is Fear Ó Laoghaire, an leanbh,
fiafróid d'om go tapaidh
cár fhágas féin a n-athair.
'Neosad dóibh faoi mhairg
gur fhágas i gCill na Martar.
Glaofaid siad ar a n-athair,
is n' bheidh sé acu le freagairt . . .

Mo chara thu go daingean!
is níor chreideas riamh dod mharbh
gur tháinig chugham do chapall
is a srianta léi go talamh,
is fuil do chroí ar a leacain
siar go t'iallait ghreanta
mar a mbítheá id shuí 's id sheasamh.
Thugas léim go tairsigh,
an dara léim go geata,
an triú léim ar do chapall.

Do bhuaileas go luath mo bhasa
is do bhaineas as na reathaibh
chomh maith is bhí sé agam,
go bhfuaras romham tu marbh
cois toirín ísil aitinn,
gan Pápa gan easpag,
gan cléireach gan sagart
do léifeadh ort an tsailm,
ach seanbhean chríonna chaite
do leath ort binn dá fallaing –
do chuid fola leat 'na sraithibh;

is níor fhanas le hí ghlanadh
ach í ól suas lem basaibh.

Mo ghrá thu go daingean!
is éirigh suas id sheasamh
is tar liom féin abhaile,
go gcuirfeam mairt á leagadh,
go nglaofam ar chóisir fhairsing,
go mbeidh againn ceol á spreagadh,
go gcóireod duitse leaba
faoi bhairlíní geala,
faoi chuilteanna breátha breaca,
a bhainfidh asat allas
in ionad an fhuachta a ghlacais.

2
*Nuair a shroich deirfiúr Airt (ó Chorcaigh) teach an tórraimh in aice
Mhaigh Chromtha, fuair sí, de réir an tseanchais, Eibhlín roimpi sa
leaba. Seo roinnt den bhriatharchath a bhí eatarthu*

Deirfiúr Airt
Mo chara is mo stór tú!
is mó bean chumtha chórach
ó Chorcaigh na seolta
go Droichead na Tóime,
do tabharfadh macha mór bó dhuit
agus dorn buí-óir duit,
ná raghadh a chodladh 'na seomra
oíche do thórraimh.

Eibhlín Dhubh
Mo chara is m'uan tú!
is ná creid sin uathu,
ná an cogar a fuarais,
ná an scéal fir fuatha,
gur a chodladh a chuas-sa.
Níor throm suan dom:
ach bhí do linbh ró-bhuartha,
's do theastaigh sé uathu
iad a chur chun suaimhnis.

A dhaoine na n-ae istigh,
'bhfuil aon bhean in Éirinn,
ó luí na gréine,
a shínfeadh a taobh leis,
do bhéarfadh trí lao dho,
ná raghadh le craobhacha
i ndiaidh Airt Uí Laoghaire
atá anso traochta
ó mhaidin inné agam? . . .

M'fhada-chreach léan-ghoirt
ná rabhas-sa taobh leat
nuair lámhadh an piléar leat,
go ngeobhainn é im thaobh dheas
nó i mbinn mo léine,
is go léigfinn cead slé' leat
a mharcaigh na ré-ghlac.

Deirfiúr Airt
Mo chreach ghéarchúiseach
ná rabhas ar do chúlaibh
nuair lámhadh an púdar,
go ngeobhainn é im chom dheas
nó i mbinn mo ghúna,
is go léigfinn cead siúil leat
a mharcaigh na súl nglas,
ós tú b'fhearr léigean chucu.

PAUL DURCAN
LOOSESTRIFE IN BALLYFERRITER

to Brian Friel on his sixtieth birthday

I

Dear Master – Homesick for Athens
In this summer of rain, I prayed to the Mother
Of God but she did not appear to answer
And the Loosestrife in Ballyferriter near broke my heart.

II

But then I came to the Gallarus Oratory.
Its small black doorspace was a Mount of Venus.
Within the womb of that miniature iconostasis
What I saw was a haven white as salt.

III

An Trá Bhán, an Trá Bhán,
Cá bhfuil m'athair, cá bhuil mo mháthair?
An Trá Bhán, an Trá Bhán,
Cá bhuil m'athair, cá bhuil mo mháthair?

IV

I stood in a delivery ward outside the Gallarus Oratory,
Surprised by coachload after coachload of tourists
From Celtic, from Medieval, from Modern times,
Expiring, only to be given birth to, in that small black
        doorspace.

V

The embryonic majority were from the Heel of Italy.
There were French, Swedish, German, Dutch.

[126]

There were siblings also from North America
To whom Ireland is an odyssey odder than Iowa.

VI

('Iowa' – she keened from behind a drystone wall –
'Iowa – I don't want to have to go to Iowa.
Iowa doesn't want me and I don't want Iowa.
Why must I forsake Ireland for Iowa?')

VII

There was a traffic snarl-up at the Gallarus Oratory,
All of the newly born vying to find parking space
In a gauntlet of fuchsia. In the small black doorspace
I gave vent to my grief for my foreign mother.

VIII

What is the nature of Loosestrife in Ballyferriter?
What class of a massacre occurred on the Great Blasket?
Who burned the islanders out of their island homes?
Was it the Irish who burned us out of our island homes?

IX

What we did not know as we scurried out over the waves
In the rain-laden sunlight to feed our eyes on the corpse of
the Blasket
Was that we were being observed from a small black
doorspace
By a small old man darker than his own doorspace.

X

Only the small old man living alone in his own black
doorspace,
Counting us swooping in and out of the corpse of the Blasket
In the showdown, saluted me and he whistled in the cosmos,
His eyes peering out of the sheep's carcass of his skull.

XI

His larynx thinned by the white sand of his eyes:
'It was the Irish who burned us out of our island homes',
And his smile was moist so that it stuck on the breeze:
'It was the Irish who burned us out of our island homes'.

XII

An Trá Bhán, an Trá Bhán,
Cá bhuil m'athair, cá bhfuil mo mháthair?
An Trá Bhán, an Trá Bhán,
Cá bhfuil m'athair, cá bhfuil mo mháthair?
XIII

Dear Master – Homesick for Athens
In this summer of rain, my closest grief
Lies in Tyrone dust. There is no man
Who would not murder his brother. Joy of all who grieve.

XIV

There is no God – only his Mother;
There is no God – only his Mother and;
There is no God – only his Mother and Loosestrife;
There is no God – only his Mother and Loosestrife in
    Ballyferriter.

PAUL MULDOON
from KERRY SLIDES

On a night when a hay-stack, silver-wet,
bulges out from under a fishing net
so I can barely tell sea from land
I remember the wreckers of Inch Strand

who would gather there on a stormy night
and tie a lantern or hurricane-light
to some wild-eyed pony's mane or tail
that it might flash and flare and flick and flail

like a lantern tied to a storm-tossed mast,
till the captain who'd hoped to escape
Dingle Bay's insidious shallows and shoals

now suddenly found himself foundering, fast,
surrounded by wild-eyed men in capes
wielding pikes and pitchforks and heavy poles.

At the South Pole Inn
(once owned by Tom Crean)
the ice in your gin
still grumbles and groans.

You still hear the yelps
of phantoms – men, dogs –
crying out for help
through tobacco-fog.

When he shot the gun-running sequence
in *Ryan's Daughter*
David Lean had two fire-engines
trained on his actors.

By which time Nature
must have had enough to being 'enhanced'
at the whim of every film director:
it's been raining ever since.

Six sods of turf fell out of Peig's basket.
She bent to gather them up. The Blaskets.

From the fort at Caherconree, in which she was immured,
Blathnaid dumped a gallon
of milk in the river, an urgent
signal to Cuchulainn

that the coast was clear and victory
all but assured.
We live downstream from a milk-factory
from which they run off a mangle of milk and detergent.

MÍCHEÁL Ó CONCHUBHAIR
AITHRÍ GHUISTÍ

Cois na trá so lámh le barra taoide,
An fhaid a bheidh féar ag fás go bráth 'sea bhead-sa sínte,
Nach cloíte an cás fear dán do cheapadh is laoithe,
Do chur síos sáite ins an áit ná casfaidh choíche.

'Sí dlí na reilige go ligeann gach éinne isteach,
'Sí riail na cille ná ligeann éinne amach,
Cách mar imigh ní thiocfaidh go deo thar n-ais,
Is nach trua é an duine ná tuigeann gur crua é an smacht.

Beidh mo thaise san úir go cúng faoi luí na leac,
'Gé deargadaoil dhubha om shiúl, gan riail, gan smacht,
Mar bharr ar mo [phudhair] bead ansúd go deo im' dhrab,
Gan solas im' shúil is gan fúm ach amháin cré agus grean.

Beidh mo chnámha ar an dtulaigh is mo chloigeann ansúd
        faoin spéir,
Beidh mo chroí istigh lofa is mo chosa gan lúth, gan léim,
Beidh an tsúil is an teanga 'na bpraisigh ar fud na cré,
Agus nach trua é mise nár thuigeas riamh grásta Dé.

Do bhíos-sa mear, mallaithe, aithiseach, ceanndána,
Agus puinn den mhaitheas níos chleachtas ach míghrásta,
I dtaobh rá na sagart níor dheineas díobh ach dídádum,
Is do dhéanfadh súgán sneachta mé tharrac i gcúis náireach.

Níor thugas mám ná fuascailt do na boicht ná déirc fós riamh,
Is níor chuireas cré ná paidir lem anam, faraoir géar!
Do thréigeas an tAifreann do ghlanfadh mé i láthair Dé,
Is dá dtabharfainn aire dhó dob fhearra dhom é ná an saol.

Do bhínn ag spalpadh na mionn is do dhein an drúis go léir
    mé lot,
Ní rabhas mar a dúrt ach ciontach riamh ina leath,
Ach, a Athair na Rún, glac chugat mé féin isteach,
Is cuir le hais do ghlún mé id' chúirt bhreá aolmhach gheal.

A Dhia dhil bheannaithe is a Athair Mhic Dé na ngrást,
Agus a Mhaighdean Bheannaithe rug barra léi riamh thar
    mná,
Ná cuirigí bhur dteachtaire 'om thachtadh, is tugaigí dom
    spás,
Go ndéanfaidh mé maithiúnas do m'anam sara bhfaighidh
    mé bás.

A dhia Urramaigh, a shocraigh na súile im' phlaosc,
A thug solas dom' cholainn is do chuir cíor im' bhéal,
Nach deacair dom a bheith ag lorg ort is nár dheineas riamh
    do réir,
Ach gur duine bocht gan doicheall mé, is go mbeire tú mé
    chugat féin.

A Dhia ghléigil, Aonmhic Mhuire agus Íosa,
A lig tú 'chéasadh chun sinn do shaoradh ó pheaca an tsinsir;
Ní ag fáil scéil é in aon chor ná seanchaíochta,
Ach ná lig mé féin go dtí Bateman ná isteach go Gíldean.

Michael Davitt
Faobhar na Faille Siar
in Anglia Sheáin Uí Ríordáin

Dhein Joe Daly amach
gur tú an tarna tiománaí ba mheasa
a tháinig go Corca Dhuibhne riamh
(don Athair Tadhg a thug an chraobh).

Ní fuadar 'bhíodh fút sa tsean–Anglia
ach siléig agus ansan gan choinne
seápanna beaga reatha ó thaobh taobh.

[131]

Nuair a thugais síob dom lá i seasca seacht
ón mBuailtín siar ar an gCeathrúin
bhís leathdhrugaithe agus tú ag iarraidh
meafar an bhóthair a shlánú
ag gliúcaíocht ar éigean duit amach thar stiúir.

Ach bhí 'Adhlacadh mo Mháthar'
de ghlanmheabhair agam
is ba tú mo laoch,
mo ghile, m'fhear.

BRYAN MACMAHON
from THE STORYMAN (1994)

Dialect is it? blank verse? I wrote down the following from an old tinker/travellin' woman who often camped on the country roadside and who was also a Market friend. It takes a Kerry tongue to get around its music. She told me her tale of woe only; as I have a good memory I brought it clean and correct. Here she goes:

What the Tinker Woman Said to Me

Ah, may Jesus relieve you in your hardesht hoult,
my lovely man, Like myself you are
Black hair, brown eyes, yalla shkin –
That's your beauty and my beauty;
It's the trademark of the Wards.
Buried above here I'll be, right appusit the yew tree,
First turn to the left, first turn to the right,
Twenty, maybe thirty paces, halt, black Bridgie Ward!
I love you, sir.
I love you for your hair, your eyes, your shkin.
It's in four of me grand sons.
I got four after meself and four after their foxy father –
(I can't shtick foxy people!)
As sure as Christ was nelt, sir, I suffered my share.
But I have my health.

Indeed I have, sir!
[Genuflects] That I may be sainted to the Almighty God,
I shtarts thinkin' of my son Timothy - Thigeen we calls him
(whispers) That's in the sannytorium above here, sir,
An' the minute I shtarts thinkin' of him,
A batterin' ram sir,
couldn't come bethune me an' my lovely boy.
I sat into my daughter's car, sir, and covered the
Fourteen Irish mile o' ground.
I went in above.
'Hello, Ma!' says he, laughin'.
He's my son, sir, my lawful-got son!
The heart ruz up in me but I held it back.
'Oh yeah,' says I, 'isn't it full o' funnin' you are?'
'Where are ye now, Ma?' says he.
In Ballyheigue,' says I.
I had my daughter's daughter with me – a bit of a childeen
            barely beginnin' to walk
'Cuckoo!' says he, gamin' for the benefit of the child.
The child was class of shy: We commenced laughin'.
'You're a godfather, Thady,' says I,
'Unknownsht to yourself.
Bridgie, your sister, had two more since you left.'
(That's his sister's children, sir!)
With that he fell laughin' on account of he bein' a godfather
            unknownsht to him.
I left him there, sir,
Shtandin' at the winda' advanced in his disease
And we takin' to the road.
I re'ched up my hand in his direction, sir, and I sittin'
Into my daughter's green car.
He stood there till we rounded the gateposht.
I'll tell you no word of a lie. That's a mother!
Waster Saturday that was.
At Chrussmass we were up in Newtown.
'Christmas is it,' I said, 'an' no Timothy.'

It came to Saint Patrick's Day.
In the middle o' my carousin' I shtopped an' said:
'Patrick's Day an' no Thigeen.

Listowel Races and no Timothy.
Puck Fair an' no Timothy.'
Shtandin' at the winda he was,
Black hair,
Brown eyes,
yalla shkin.
Buried above here, appusit the yew tree he'll be
First turn to the left
First turn to the right
Twenty, maybe thirty paces
Halt, BLACK THADY WARD!

AOGÁN Ó MUIRCHEARTAIGH
AMHRÁN NÁISIÚNTA

Nuair ba mhian leis na máistrí
An daoscar a spreagadh don chogadh
Achtaíodh go seinnfí an ceol
I ndeireadh oíche ar gach ócáid
D'eagla go gceapfaí
Gur oíche chuileachtan í
Gan cornasc stáit
God Save the King!
God Save the Queen!
An clabhsúr ar oíche rangáis

Tháinig ann don stát nár phoblacht
Tráth ghéill na máistrí nua
Do bhagairt na Sasanach
Leanadh de nós a n-airm
Ach gur casadh focail Pheadair Uí Cheárna
Le ceol a ceannaíodh
Ósna Stáit!

THOMAS MACGREEVY
HOMAGE TO MARCEL PROUST

to Jean Thomas

The sea gleamed deep blue in the sunlight
Through the different greens of the trees.
And the talk was of singing.
My mother, dressed in black, recalled a bright image from
      a song,
Those endearing young charms,
Miss Holly, wearing heliotrope, had a sad line,
The waves are still singing to the shore.
Then, as we came out from the edge of the wood,
The island lay dreaming in the sun across the bridge,
Even the white coastguard station had gone quietly to sleep
      – it was Sunday,
A chain on a ship at the pier
Rattled to silence,
Cries of children, playing, sounded faintly
And, musically, somewhere,
A young sailor of the island –

    He was tall
    And slim
    And curled, to the moustaches,
    And he wore earrings
    But often he was too ill to be at sea –

Was singing,
Maid of Athens, ere we part . . .
Looking suddenly like a goddess
Miss Holly said, half-smiling,
'Listen . . . '
And we stopped
In the sunlight
Listening . . .
The young sailor is dead now.

Miss Holly also is dead.
And Byron . . .
Home they've gone and

And the waves still are singing.

CON HOULIHAN
A GREAT WRITER IN CROKE PARK

I have written elsewhere about Robert Lynd, the great journalist, whose life seemed a putting of flesh on the philosophy of Wolfe Tone.

Once when consigned to a hospital conducted by Catholic nuns, he was asked his religion – and declared himself a Presbyterian, kind of; it was a fair enough description of one who was marvellously free from prejudice, probably because he grew up in Belfast.

Lynd was a great lover of many games and an aficionado of several; rugby seems to have been his favourite; hurling might have superseded it if he had known more about it.

He was in his fifties when he witnessed his first sample of the ancient game; he was in Dublin to write a piece about an early edition of the Hospitals' Sweepstakes – and made the pilgrimage to Croke Park.

He might not have been in Dublin at all but for a bitter debate on sweepstakes that had erupted in the Houses of Parliament; he was dispatched to see at first hand this demonic lottery that was causing such emotional distress in Britain.

On the way he pondered whether it is more demoralising to win £30,000 or to lose ten shillings and decided that it is better to have loved money and lost than never to have loved money at all.

As soon as he was settled in Dublin, he took a walk in Stephen's Green; 'Birds were singing above the children at play and the world was in flower in the still evening.'

The next day was the Sabbath; that didn't inhibit the Presbyterian (kind of) from going to Croke Park to watch a joust between Dublin and Limerick.

'How charming the teams looked in the brilliant green of Limerick and the brilliant blue of Dublin!'

And, of course, there was a band – 'pipers . . . dressed in green kilts and with flowing saffron robes, many wearing feathers in their caps.'

The players walked two by two, 'a green-shirted man beside a blue-shirted man, each carrying a hurley, the weapon used in the game.'

The use of the word 'weapon' is interesting; Lynd seemingly saw the game as a substitute for battle – which to some degree it is.

The use of the word 'shirt' is also interesting; it isn't long since a Catholic priest in this country objected to that word in the context of Gaelic games.

Seemingly it smacked too much of soccer. How culturally exclusive can we be?

Anyhow, whether 'shirt' or 'jersey' was the more appropriate, the game went on – and both alarmed and enthralled our visitor.

It didn't start, of course, without a building up of a head of steam; the pipers rendered 'ancient, warlike airs,' including The Bold Fenian Men'. Times haven't changed much.

Lynd goes on to say: 'One could not help regretting that no Irish painter has ever arisen to perpetuate on canvas the colours of the hurling field as Degas perpetuated the colours of the racecourse and the ballet.'

I second his lament; most of our painters, alas, look on sport as unworthy of their art.

The game begins. Lynd writes: 'I do not know the rules of hurling but, as a moral equivalent to war, it seems to me to be about the only rival of Rugby football.'

He goes on: 'It is said to be the original form of hockey; some people have described it as hockey without rules.'

I know of a Cockney who calls it 'a kind of wild 'ockey.'

Let us listen to Lynd: 'Hurleys . . . rise into the air like weapons of war and the player is allowed to do almost anything he likes with his hurley except deliberately hit a player on the other side.'

Of course, Lynd was apprehensive; almost everyone watching his first game of hurling cannot but be.

'Hurleys meet in the air with a wild crashing of wood; one of them is broken into two pieces, and small boys rush into the field in a struggle to retrieve a broken blade as a memento.

'The casualties to sticks certainly went into double figures. The casualties to players were less numerous, but the ambulance men must have been on the field about eight times.'

Robert Lynd couldn't help feeling glad that there was no international hurling.

'Imagine a game . . . played between France and Scotland.' Indeed . . . the soul boggles.

The truth, of course, is that when hurling is well played and well refereed, it is a far less dangerous game than rugby.

Lynd goes on: 'It is certainly a swift and beautiful game, calling into play all the skills of eye and hand and foot.'

He says that it is worth crossing the Irish Sea to see a man catching the ball amidst a frenzy of hurley-wielding opponents and sending it up the field into the goalmouth.

It is a pity that he didn't live to see Tony Doran plucking the ball from a forest of ash and palming it over the bar or into the net.

Lynd doesn't tell us who won the game but I suspect that it was the men in brilliant green.

'On the whole the Limerick men seemed to be about a quarter of a second faster than the Dublin men in everything they did and it looked at half-time as if they would run through them . . . '

It didn't prove to be as simple as he foresaw; Dublin had a man who was inspired and inspiring.

'There was a Dublin back who played like a demi-god and who was always a quarter of a second faster than any Limerick man who was near him.'

He goes on: 'Even when a game is one-sided, an invincible player can keep it exciting to the end.'

As Lynd walked away from Croke Park, a friend says: 'After this, I don't think you need feel nervous about going to a bullfight.'

from WINDFALLS (1996)

DAN KEANE
THE KERRYMAN

He came across from Denny Street,
A boy about fourteen.
I felt a beauty in his voice
That filled the passing scene.
He kept his course with solemn step
He neither rushed nor ran,
But advertised the ware he sold:
'*The Kerryman, The Kerryman.*'

I heard and watched with eager eyes
As down the Mall he went
His eyes ne'er wandered left nor right
From his avowed intent.
He sold and thanked, he thanked and sold
But still maintained the song
That drew the customers to him:
'*The Kerryman, The Kerryman.*'

The voice was round and strong yet sweet
And rich in every tone;
There in that crowded busy street
He just shone out alone.
A few wee imitators
He did not even scan,
But kept his course with dignity:
'*The Kerryman, The Kerryman.*'

I heard him quicken up his pace
As customers came nigh
'*Kerryman*, sir! *Kerryman*, sir!'
Was his appealing cry.
But that was many years ago
I wonder where he is gone
Who thrilled my heart to hear him shout
'*The Kerryman, The Kerryman.*'

Thomas Kinsella
Ballydavid Pier

Noon. The luminous tide
Climbs through the heat, covering
Grey shingle. A film of scum
Searches first among litter,
Cloudy with (I remember)
Life; then crystal-clear shallows
Cool on the stones, silent
With shells and claws, white fish bones;
Farther out a bag of flesh,
Foetus of goat or sheep,
Wavers below the surface.

Allegory forms of itself:
The line of life creeps upward
Replacing one world with another,
The welter of its advance
Sinks down into clarity,
Slowly the more foul
Monsters of loss digest . . .

Small monster of true flesh
Brought forth somewhere
In bloody confusion and error
And flung into bitterness,
Blood washed white:
Does that structure satisfy?

The ghost tissue hangs unresisting
In allegorical waters,
Lost in self-search
– A swollen blind brow
Humbly crumpled over
Budding limbs, unshaken
By the spasms of birth or death.

The Angelus. Faint bell-notes
From some church in the distance
Tremble over the water.
It is nothing. The vacant harbour
Is filling; it will empty.
The misbirth touches the surface
And glistens like quicksilver.

PAUL DURCAN
DÚN CHAOIN

for Bob, Angela and Rachel, in Nigeria

I was standing at the counter
In a bar at the world's end.
The large weathered man behind it
Was more native to the place than the place itself.
His father's fathers . . .
A big blue man like that, I thought, could not be strange
With a stranger:
So when he did not speak
An old fear whistled through me:
I am not welcome in this place.
I kept a grip on my pint glass
And my eyes to the left of me
Gripping the bay-window and outside
The red sun at nightfall
In the same place as the bar room
Descending the window pane.
Its going down took about as long
As it takes a boy or girl to climb down a tree.
Gone and not long after
I thought I could hear
A longlost music long lost from the earth
And as I looked up from the counter shaking my head
The big man too was shaking his, birds and tears
Falling out of the rafters of his eyes. The both of us
Laughed and he turned up the volume

Of his openly concealed battered old wireless,
Telefunken,
And when we were going out he said: Good night
And may God bless you on the road.
I went out willing to sleep on mountainsides anywhere
Fearing no man or beast, machine or mist.

AOGÁN Ó RATHAILLE
GILE NA GILE

Gile na gile do chonnarc ar slí in uaigneas,
criostal an chriostail a goirmroisc rinn-uaine,
binneas an bhinnis a friotal nár chríonghruama,
deirge is finne do fhionnadh 'na gríosghruannaibh.

Caise na caise i ngach ribe dá buí-chuachaibh,
bhaineas an cruinneac den rinneac le rinnscuabadh,
iorra ba ghlaine ná glione ar a broinn bhuacaigh,
do gineadh ar ghineamhain di-se san tír uachtraigh.

Fios fiosach dom d'inis, is ise go fíor-uaigneach,
fios filleadh don duine don ionad ba rí-dhualgas,
fios milleadh na droinge chuir eisean ar rinnruagairt,
's fios eile ná cuirfead im laoithibh le fíor-uamhan.

Leimhe na leimhe dom druidim 'na cruinntuairim,
im chime ag an gcime do snaighmeadh go fíorchrua mé;
ar ghoirm Mhic Mhuire dom fhortacht, do bhíog uaimse,
is d'imigh an bhruinneal 'na luisne go bruín Luachra.

Rithim le rith mire im rithibh go croí-luaimneach,
trí imeallaibh corraigh, trí mhongaibh, trí shlímruaitigh;
don tinne-bhrugh tigim − ní thuigim cén tslí fuaras −
go hionad na n-ionad do cumadh le draíocht dhruaga.

Brisid fá scige go scigeamhail buíon ghruagach
is foireann do bhruinnealaibh sioscaithe dlaoi-chuachach;
i ngeimhealaibh geimheal me cuirid gan puinn suaimhnis,

's mo bhruinneal ar broinnibh ag broinnire broinnstuacach.

D'iniseas di-se, san bhfriotal dob fhíor uaimse,
nár chuibhe di snaidhmeadh le slibire slímbhuartha
's an duine ba ghile ar shliocht chine Scoit trí huaire
ag feitheamh ar ise bheith aige mar chaoin-nuachar.

Ar chloistin mo ghutha di goileann go fíor-uaibhreach
is sileadh ag an bhfliche go life as a gríosghruannaibh;
cuireann liom giolla dom choimirc ón mbruín uaithi –
's í gile na gile do chonnarc ar slí in uaigneas.

An Ceangal
Mo threighid, mo thubaist, mo thurainn, mo bhrón, mo
       dhíth!
an soilseach muirneach miochairgheal beoltais caoin
ag adharcach foireanndubh mioscaiseach cóirneach buí,
's gan leigheas 'na goire go bhfillid na leoin tar toinn.

DESMOND EGAN
from PENINSULA

EPILOGUE

out the window of my study
Papel rasgado de um intento
a leaden March morning gives
and blue tatters show
there's a crow gawking from a bare tree
a volley from an unseeable blackbird

and for no reason I remember Kerry
the long road of stillness
An Fheóthanach shivering with daylight
the perspective to the Sisters
mist heights a view of abandoned ocean
somebody's voice coming a long way

life draining from a hill

landscape of tragic faces
where time fades to eternity

that great grey movement
over us all

*Papel . . . : 'The torn paper of a draft', from a poem by Fernando
Pessoa
An Fheóthanach: place name, Feohanagh*

FARMER NEAR SYBIL POINT

folded-in on himself like the peninsula
unlonely although
full of an unreachable gloom
he heads through a gate under

mountains of no illusion

COOSAKNOCKAUN

utter stillness
of one small boat glimpsed out
off the cliffs
on top of the incomprehensible sea

I am an outsider

GALLARUS

an upturned boat no Parthenon but
this temple in the local gritstone
also adheres with faith for mortar

stoop under its heavy lintel step
into an age of illumination

light from the eighth century still
splays from the east into our gloom

take time enough to be there
this is a serious place

an idea moulded along
Platonic lines coaxed out of masonry
when it and the fingers the hope cohered

watertight
Kerry

as little in need of music
(a fiddle flailing through noise)
as Sicily
not for lovers either
its grin middleaged

but sustained by its own truth
some continuum

a recession of peaks

BALLYFERRITER

Piarras Ferriter's town!   *Irish in the supermarket*
and the vowels still have the sea   *but there's a feel of absence*
the consonants rock in them
the sentences a ghost of the rhythm
of a civilisation   *and Fáilte Abhaile on a streamer*
                    over the fire in O Muircheartaigh's bar
that old wonderful resistance
                              the songs are of exile

has there been a pining
since Piaras died and Sybil
and the 600 at Dún an Oir

with no sea or river
to lighten the loss?

sad Ballyferriter where it always rains

*Piaras Ferriter, an important Irish poet, was the last of the
seventeenth-century chieftains to hold out against the English; he was
hanged in Killarney in 1653. Sybil Lynch eloped with one of the
Ferriter family and drowned accidentally while hiding in a cave
beneath the castle; Fáilte Abhaile: welcome home*

THE GREAT BLASKET

its authority   *mist islands*
slowly drew us in   *a feel of the tremendous*
                                            sea through the currach's skin

but the slipway was in moss
those proud cottages sagging   *the imaginary crash of surf*
inwards like Irish and   *whitening in the distance*

the winds of Europe   *cold of a summer morning*
blew through blank windows
                                            and nothing but elements
O Criomhthain   *to add to a quarter century*
Peig
Muirís O Súilleabháin

I waited on a cliff-height for
some sign from mainland Ireland

began to understand why mediocrity
never became the norm out here
where existence is an exile

past *An Tráth Bhán* icy waters
still coursed through the Sound and
over the ships of history
dear dear place
empty in the last mild collapse

of a once-great Gaelic vision
which persisted into our time

CUAS

the surge into this fissure
is brimming with weed from deep waters

a currach bucks at its rope
and there are cables of foam in contrails
across the mouth of the creek

where St Brendan launched
his leather boat to discover some
new world for Christ

the same massive swell
brings fear in its spread and
rush around the pier

the kind of inlet you
might remember dying
as you could the crimson hedgerows
dripping with fuchsia up the road
the montbretia incandescent in orange

and go consoled

NOIRIN

she's well able for the men
and nods to an order
while pulling another pint

her eyes whip about with
the same mix of motives
that raises her arm and she

hardly notices the tumbling stout
though with a woman's exciting clearness

she knows her own know
would never confuse
shrewdness with intelli
gence

and is more than willing to hunt change
lead a visitor upstairs to
the phone that isn't out of order
talking in Irish to herself

NEAR ANASCAUL

there comes a stillness
where the route moves upward
and the skyline begins to brighten

PÁDRAIG Ó MAOILEOIN
as NA hAIRD Ó THUAIDH (1966)

Labhras cheana tamall siar anso ar na 'Laethanta Breátha,' mar a thugaimíst orthu, a bhíodh ag teacht dhon Chom chughainn sa tsamhradh ag foghlaim na Gaeilge agus ag cur aithne ar na daoine. Cuairteoirí aonlae ab ea iad so, mar a dúrt, a thugadh geábh ar maidin agus a bhíodh imithe arís tráthnóna. Ach do bhí daoine eile bunoscionn leo so ag déanamh orainn leis, daoine a thugadh coicíos nó mí, nó, b'fhéidir, cúpla mí inár bhfochair, agus iad ag cur fúthu ar lóistín i dtithe na ndaoine. Is í an Ghaeilge a thugadh na daoine seo dhon áit comh maith, agus is maith blasta mar a thugadh cuid acu leo í. Gaeilge ar a son féin, a bhí uathu agus ní labharfaidís leat ach í, rud a dh'fhág meas orthu féin agus ar an dteangain san áit. Is le saolú Chonradh na Gaeilge a thosnaíodar so ag teacht ar dtúis, agus dob shidé an chéad chomhartha a chonaiceamairne go raibh aon mheas ag éinne uirthi. Dob é an chéad léas amach as an ndoircheacht é do dhaoine bochta ná raibh aon taithí ar an solas acu. Rud ab ea é a thug ardú meanman duinn, agus a mhúscail ár meas ar an oidhreacht uasal a bhí fágtha againn. Do bhí an dúthracht agus an sprid a shíolraigh as so in airde láin agus mise im shlataire ag dul ar scoil ann.

Do bhí dream eile daoine a thagadh inár measc comh maith leo so, ollúin agus boic mhóra eile ó chéin agus ó chomhgar; ach is é a mhalairt a thugadh iad súd ann. Ní hé taoide rabharta na hathbheochana a chuir iad so chughainn, ar shlí – b'fhéidir eile gurb é – ach is é is mó a thug ann iad cúrsaí teangeolaíochta agus béaloideasa. Ní har oilithreacht a thánadar san ann, ach ar chúrsa staidéir, Marie Sjoestedt, Kenneth Jackson, Robin Flower agus Karl Marstrander, agus a leithéidí eile. Ina dhiaidh san agus uile, do thánadar so isteach comh mór san ar shlí agus ar mheon na ndaoine nuair a fuaireadar greim ceart ar an gcanúint gur thiteadar i ngrá leis an áit agus leis na daoine, agus go bhfillidíst ann bliain i ndiaidh a chéile tar éis a gcúraim a bheith críochnaithe acu ann. Marie Sjoestedt bhocht féin, go dtugaimís Máire Franncach uirthi, agus gur dh'imigh droch-íde uirthi blianta ina dhiaidh san i bPáras, do scríbh sise dhá leabhar ar fhoghraíocht agus ar dheilbh na canúna so againne. (Ní maith liom an focal 'deilbhíocht' atá in úsaid inniu air seo, toisc ár mbrí féin a bheith againne le 'deilbhíocht'; an saol a bheith ag dul chun deilbhíochta, a deirimíd, leis an saol a bheith ag dul in olcas – is ón bhfocal 'dealbh' a thagann sé.) Do scríbh sí an dá leabhar so i gcomhar le Séan a' Chóta – Séan Óg Mac Murchadha Caomhánach, mar a thugadh sé féin air féin, teideal ardnósach a bhí ag gabháil le spridna haimsire, agus a dhá oiread tuillte aige mar shaothraí náisiúnta agus mar scoláire Gaeilge, ach nach de shliocht na gCaomhánach é, rud a dhein ainm cúl le cine dhe, mar ná fuil a leithéidí ann ach Cíobhánaigh ar fad. Is i bhFrainncis atá an dá leabhar so scríte, agus is é an trua go deo san. Bean ab ea Máire a bhí álainn ina pearsain agus uasal ina méin, agus do thug gach éinne gean di.

Is cuimhin liom an chéad lá riamh a cuireadh Jackson in aithne dhi istigh i dtigh an Phrincess, iníon Rí an Oileáin, lá éigin. Ansan a bhí sí ag cur fúithi i mBaile an Teampaill i nDún Chaoin, lámh leis an sáipéal, díreach. Bhí Jackson tar éis seacht seachtaine fada díreach a bheith tugtha istigh san Oileán aige an uair sin, agus é imithe comh fiain le gabhar ann. Do bhíos féin istigh lena linn mar is minic a thugainn an samhradh ann comh maith le héinne. Bhí sé ar bheagán Gaeilge nuair a tháinig sé ann ar dtúis, ach eolas na leabhar a bheith aige uirthi, ach mise fé dhuit gur aige a bhí sí ina sruth agus é ag fágaint na háite.

Maidean Domhnaigh ab ea í seo gur thug sé geábh amach i gceann des na naomhóga a bhí ag teacht amach chun an Aifrinn, agus, ar nós ár dtí féin, do bhíodh gnáthmhuintir an Oileáin ar thigh an Phrincess, toisc buannaíocht istigh a bheith acu ann ar an gcuma chéanna. Soir leo, agus Jackson in éineacht leo. Bhí Máire Franncach istigh rómpu, agus do chuir bean mhaith an tí an bheirt stróinséirí in aithne dhá chéile. Bhí cur amach aige uirthi, gan dabht, agus súilaithne, b'fhéidir, comh maith. Do bheannaigh sé dhi, i bhFrainncis líofa; dar ndóigh is aige a bhí sí, agus teangacha eile mar an gcéanna. Tar éis iad a bheith scaitheamh beag le chéile ar an dteangain sin, áfach, cad déarfá le Máire ná gur dh'fhéach ina tímpeall agus go ndúirt leis: 'Nár chórtaí dhuinn, an measann tú, iompú ar theangain na ndaoine galánta so inár dtímpeall, agus gan é a bheith le casadh linn gur ag cúlchainnt orthu atáimíd?'

As Gaeilge a chaith sí an carúl so leis, ionas go dtuigfimíst í: Ar an nGaeilge a bhíodar le chéile as san amach go dtí aimsir Aifrinn, agus sinn ag éisteacht leo. 'Ar mh'anam féin,' a dúirt duine den ndream a bhí ar an láthair, 'gur maith í, a bhuachaill.' Bhí meas uirthi mar gheall ar an méid sin a rá, mar bhí a fhios acu gur le barr tuisceana a dúirt sí é.

Comh fada le Flower de, nó 'Bláithín' mar a thugaimíst air mar ná freagródh sé d'aon ainm eile, do dhein seisean a tharna baile den áit ón gcéad lá a chuir sé aithne air. Do bhíodh a bhean agus a chlann ina theannta ag teacht ann aon uair a dh'fhéadadh sé é, agus Gaeilge i gcónaí á labhairt acu leis na daoine agus eatarthu féin. 'An duine uasal ó Londain,' mar a thug Tomás Criothain air, agus dob é a ainm é. Dob é an tOileán Tiar an focal deireanach a bhí ar a bhéal aige, de réir dealraimh, agus é ag fáil bháis i Londain, nuair a bhí an t-eolas go léir a bhí bailithe as na leabhra móra aige imithe as a cheann. D'fhág sé le huacht go scaipfí a chuid luaithrí ós cionn an Oileáin, rud a deineadh. Más ea, ní gan deoir ar ghruannaibh seandaoine é a thug laethanta fada meala ina chuibhreann agus a bhain pléisiúr agus taitneamh as a chomhluadar.

B'fhuiriste dhom dul a thuilleadh leis an liosta so, ach cáb áil liom. Do dheimhnigh na daoine galánta so dhuinn gur thuigeadar sinn agus gur thuigeadar duinn. Chun é seo a dhéanamh, do thánadar ar aon leibhéal linn féin. D'imíodar amach as a mian féin agus d'itheadar an deargán anuas den dtlú díreach mar a dh'ithimís féin é, gan aon nuaíocht ná aon tsólaistí eile, ach an ailp a dh'ithe díreach mar leagtaí ós a gcomhair í. Is mar seo a thánadar isteach ar gach aon ní, gan aon acht á dhéanamh ná aon acht á bhriseadh acu ach luí isteach le nósa na ndaoine agus a gcuid féin a dhéanamh dhíobh. Tá a rian air, do thógadar a leacht cuimhne féin in mbéal agus in aigne na muintire.

Dob shin iad an dá dhream daoine a bhíodh ag teacht go Gaeltacht Chorca Dhuibhne agus mise ag éirí suas ann. D'osclaíodar so fuinneoga ar shaol eile dhuinn ná raibh a fhios againn a bheith ann in aon chor nó go dtánadar inár measc, saol Gaelach, saol a chuir suim san oidhreacht a bhí fágtha againn agus a roinneamair go fonnmhar leo. Ba mhór linne mar dhí-umhaltacht ar na daoine séimhe seo aon chuid den oidhreacht so a cheilt orthu, agus níor cheileamair.

Lasmuigh den dá chleas so, dob é an duine fánach eile a thabharfadh turas orainn. Ní mar sin atá inniu, áfach, tá atharrach scéil ann ná tuigim cén bhrí atá leis. Ní hé ná go bhfuil an Gaeilgeoir dúthrachtach ag teacht ann fós, agus tá súil agam gura fada bheidh; ach tá dream eile ag teacht nach aon mhaith dhon áit. Béarlóirí críochnaithe iad so ná fuil uathu ach Béarla, agus nach aon mhairg leo an loitiméireacht atá á dhéanamh acu. Tagann siad ann ó Bhaile Átha Cliath comh maith le Sasana, agus gan aon fhuadar fúthu ach, mar a déarfá, *intellectual slumming*, rud nach féidir dóibh a dhéanamh in nDún Chaoin ná i mBaile an Fhirtéaraigh ná i mBaile na nGall, dá dtuigfidís féin, ná an dream a thugann ann iad, i gceart iad féin. 'Generi-tex-i-u-m,' mar a dúirt fear an Choma.

'Tair i measc na n-asal ar feadh tamaill go bhfeicfidh tú á n-iomlasc féin i smúit an mhóinteáin iad; tair go gcloisfidh tú an patois teangan atá fágtha ages na natives. Sea, tair go Corca Dhuibhne agus tabharfaimídne Béarla dhuit a chabhróidh leat chun an phictiúra a bhreith abhaile in iomlán leat . . . Trufais agus cacamas dá leithéid seo, agus ní haon ní eile, a sméideann ar na daoine saonta so. Dá mbeadh a fhios acu é, tá cleas foghlamanta go maith istigh leo ansúd thiar ná ligfidh puinn den dtéid leo; dá mbeadh is gurb iad na 'róinte' féin iad – ach cad ab áil liom á rá, nach iad san lucht na foghlama ar fad gan fhios d'éinne?

Tagann na Béarlóirí seo go Dún Chaoin díreach mar a théadh an Sasanach ina lá féin, agus mar a théann an Meiriceánach sa

lá tá inniu ann ar an Mór-roinn agus gur éirim d'aon teangain
acu ach dá n-allagar tráchtála féin; gan aon tuiscint acu don
gcultúr ársa atá san áit rómpu, ná don gcneastacht agus don
síbhialtacht a shíolraigh as an gcultúr san leis na mílte blian. Is
é an chuid is measa dhe so, comh fada lenár muintir féin de, go
bhfuil giollaí agus scraistí aimhleasta ina measc a dheininn
tláithínteacht leis na stróinséirí seo sa teangain iasachta, agus gan
í sin acu ach go breallach, rud a thugann blas den *local colour* dom
dhuine agus gur fiú leis nóta a dhéanamh ina dhialainn de.
Móraíocht is cúis leis seo, gan dabht, ach is móraíocht bhréige
í ná fuil bunús ná dealramh léi.

Ní fadó shoin in aon chor agus mé ar mo chamchuarta trí
Chorca Dhuibhne gur bhuaileas isteach aon oíche amháin go
tigh óil mar an raibh lán an tí de chuideachtain. Níor rófhada
istigh dom gur thugas fé ndeara gurb iad lucht an Bhéarla a bhí
i gceannas an chomhluadair cé go rabhadar ar an gcaolchuid go
maith ann, ní hamháin in iomadúlacht ach i ngaois agus i
bhfoghlaim, dá dtuigfidís féin é. Bhíos féin caite fúm ar bhairille
i bhfochair na 'róinte' agus sinn ag cur an tsaoil trí chéile. Ba
ghairid a bhíos im shuí, ambaic, gur dh'eirigh an stróinséir agus gur
dhein ceann de féin láithreach ar an gcomhluadar. Do sméid sé air
seo agus do ghlaoigh uirthi siúd chun duain nó scéal nó amhrán
a rá, agus is ann a chuala an píosa aithriseoireachta Béarla is
slachtmhaire dár chuala le fada de bhlianta, an té a thuigfeadh é.

'Tuigeann tusa go maith í seo, a Phaidí,' arsa an chéad rón
liom féin.

'Tuigim dáb aon mhaith dhom é,' arsa mé féin.

'Ambaiste, sea agus maitheas,' ars an tarna rón.

'N'fheadar,' ars an chéad rón.

'N'fheadaraís, a bhuachaill,' arsa dhá rón, trí cinn.

'An diabhal an bhfeadar, mhuis,' ar seisean arís. 'Ní haon áit
dá leithéid é agus gan aon tuiscint ag éinne air ach acu féin.'

'Tása Dia go bhfuil an ceart aige,' arsa rón eile go raibh a
cheann fé loch aige go dtí so. 'Dob fhearr liom féin stéibh den
g*Cnoicín Garbh Fraoigh* nó de *Bhá na Scalg* dá mbeadh sí ag
éinne.

'Féach an bhfuil,' arsa mé féin, ag séideadh fúthu.

'Tá, ar mh'anam mhuis,' arsa rón eile a bhí ag teacht agus
trí chiota móra pórtair lán go barra féna gcúrán buí ag
déanamh orainn trís na Béarlóirí.

'Más ea, éiríodh,' a dúrt féin.

'Éireoidh nuair a bheidh an t-ionú ann,' arsa fear na gciotaí.

'Rabharta í seo, a bhuachaill, agus bíodh 'fhios agat nach fada a bheadh a leithéid ag líonadh in aon chor.' Dob fhíor do.

Do tháinig an *Cnoicín* leis an ionú; do tháinig agus *Bá na Scealg*, agus an *Clár Bog Déil*, agus an *Binnsín Luachra*. Do thóg fear veidhlín amach agus thairg an bogha ar a sreanga trí huaire féachaint an raibh sí i dtiúin. Ansan do lig sé síos óna smigín ar a bhrollach í, agus dob shiúd leis ag taoscadh cheoil amach aisti. Bhí gach aon phreab aici istigh ina dhorn agus ba dhóigh leat ná raibh aon phutóg ina corp ná raibh ag rinne istigh inti fé chnagarnaigh na cruaríleach a bhí á fháscadh aige aisti.

Do bhuail fear buille ar an úrlár, ag freagairt ceoil. Ansan do thug sé aon léim amháin as a chorp agus do bhí sé in lár an úrláir. Do deineadh fáinne dho, agus d'éirigh sé le casadh na ríleach agus do shatail an dá nóta deireanach den gcasadh féna dhá sháil. 'Way leis as san agus é fé mar bheadh sé ag rince ar phláta dhuit. Pramsach á bhaint anois agus arís as leacacha an úrláir aige chun deimhniú a dhéanamh ar nóta áirithe den gceol, ach é go triopallach cos-éadrom seolta tríd an gcuid eile den gceol. Bhí sé ina chuid den gceol é féin agus a chuid rinnce, díreach fé mar do bheidís fuaite isteach ina chéile. Nuair a dh'éadromaíodh an ceol do chífeá ina chois é. Nuair a thagadh an casadh agus an t-uaibhreas d'éiríodh air féin mar an gcéanna. Ní raibh an rinnceoir críochnaithe i gceart in aon chor nuair a bhí fear eile ar a shálaibh, agus fear eile díreach ar a shálaibh sin, sa tslí 's gur ag baint na gcos dá chéile a bhíodar fé dheireadh, gach éinne agus a steip shuaithinseach féin aige, nó crans dá chuid féin ar steipeanna a bhí rinncithe roimis age fear eile.

Duine neamheontach críochnaithe a dhéanfadh ceann de féin in áit mar seo ina bhfuil saibhreas teangan agus filíochta agus ceoil i measc daoine nár léigh aon leabhar riamh, cuid acu, ach ná ligfeadh an tsíbhialtacht agus an tuiscint dóibh iad féin a chur in iúl ann go dtí go n-éireodh an fhuil in uachtar acu agus ná féadfaidíst é a bhrú ar a gcroí a thuilleadh. Do cuireadh an teitheadh ar an mBéarla an oíche úd ach go háirithe, pé faid gairid a sheasóidh lucht an 'éirí amach'.

N'fheadarsa an dtuigeann Dún Chaoin agus Baile an Fhirtéaraigh, agus as san ó thuaidh go Béal an Chuasa, conas mar do bheadh acu dá mbeadh an saibhreas so bailithe uathu.

An dóigh leo go mbeadh daoine ag taisteal orthu ina gcéadtaibh gach samhradh mar a bhíonn? An measann siad go meallfadh an radharc iad? Tá, gan dabht, an radharc ann comh breá agus comh scópúil agus atá in Éirinn. Sáraíodh éinne, cuirim i gcás, an radharc atá le feiscint ó Cheann Sratha ag duine ag féachaint uaidh trí riascaibh agus trí thránna geala gainnimhe ó thuaidh isteach go barra an Dúinín agus go slinneán Chnoc Bhréanainn. Agus nuair a bheidh a riocht den radharc san fachta aige, iompú go mall righin ar a sháil, agus a shúil a leagadh ar íoghar na spéireach thiar agus theas. Ansúd a chífidh sé na línéirí móra ó Southampton agus ó Chóbh Corcaí, agus dá mbeadh a shúil agus a chluas i dtiúin i gceart aige go gcloisfeadh sé osna agus go gcífeadh sé deoir ar ghruannaibh daoine atá ag amharc go tromachroíoch ar an gcúinne beag deireanach dá bhfóidín dúchais. Sea, tá an radharc ann agus an tógaint croí, an t-uaibhreas agus an oscailt scairte. Ach tá rud is tábhachtaí fós ann, daoine go bhfuil rud acu a chaithfear a roinnt le daoine eile go bhfuil suim acu ann agus gur fiú é a roinnt leo.

MÁIRE MHAC AN tSAOI
JACK

Strapaire fionn sé troithe ar airde,
Mac feirmeora ó iarthar tíre,
Ná cuimhneoidh feasta go rabhas-sa oíche
Ar úrlar soimint aige ag rince,

Ach ní dhearúdfad a ghéaga im thimpeall,
A gháire ciúin ná a chaint shibhialta –
Ina léine bhán, is a ghruaig nuachíortha
Buí fén lampa ar bheagán íle . . .

Fágfaidh a athair talamh ina dhiaidh aige,
Pósfaidh bean agus tógfaidh síolbhach,
Ach mar conacthas domhsa é arís ní cífear,
Beagbheann ar chách mar 'gheal lem chroí é.

Barr dá réir go raibh air choíche!
Rath is séan san áit ina mbíonn sé!
Mar atá tréitheach go dté crích air –
Dob é an samhradh so mo rogha 'pháirtí é

JOHN B. KEANE
from BIG MAGGIE (1969)

[Maggie closes the door after her and walks down to the front of the stage. The light closes in behind her]

Maggie I'm alone now but I'm free and not too many women can say that. But I need not be alone and that's the beauty. A woman need never be alone as long as men crave what she has, and that never gives out. When I married, God help me, I was only a slip of a thing. I hadn't an idea what I was facing. You think someone would have warned me but they all stood back and let me go ahead. Marriage was the only safe place for a young girl they said. You'll have a home, you'll have security. My marriage was a lifelong battle with me always on the defensive and my husband trying to bend my will right from the beginning. Oh there were words of love. Blandishments. Didn't he call me a fair mare one time and he drunk. 'You're a fair oul' mare,' he said and he spent after being astride me for the one bare minute.

You know the first time, indeed the only time, I saw a penis, before I was married, was on a young garsún and he bathing in the river. It was a harmless little tassle of a thing and sure me, poor innocent me, didn't I think that they were all like that till the first night of our honeymoon. You'd think my love-life already trimmed and stunted to the marrow would have to endure no more but the awful truth was that my sex-life, my morals, my thought, word, and deed were dominated by a musty old man with a black suit and a roman collar and a smell of snuff. I was suffocated by the presence of that old man. He sat in his confession-box, withering and me not knowing which way to turn for guidance. Do you know my husband never saw me naked? He never saw me white and shiny and shivering without one blemish on me from head to heel. I must have seemed as frigid and cold to him as a frozen lake. How could I thaw with my upbringing and my faith, my holy, holy faith.

Maybe that's what drove him into the arms of Moll Sonders and God knows how many others. My body might say one thing but my faith always said another and my instincts were no match for that faith.

Oh I curse the stifling, smothering breath of the religion that withered my loving and my living and my womanhood. I should have been springing like a shoot of corn. I should have been singing with love, tingling, but my love never grew. 'Tis a wonder that I didn't surrender entirely to insanity in a country where it was a mortal sin to even think about another man. And there was another man. He was dark-eyed and quiet and he passed me a hundred times on the road and he'd say 'How ya there, Maggie?' and he'd give one of the cows he was driving a little tip in the back with his ashplant and I'd say 'Fine thank you, Martin,' and he'd pass on. I saw him blush once but he never uttered one word of love to me in all those years and I longed for him. I craved him in my dreams and I thinking how lovely it would be to walk with him through the dewy fields. But he did blush.

And yet I never beamed at that man or set my cap for him or held his hand or winked at him or even gave him the faintest clue as to the names I called him and we cuddled together in those dreams. My curly ram, my sugar stick, my darling.

He's dead now that easy-going man and my husband is dead and all too soon I'll be dead but I can have anything I want for a while anyway. By God I can have any man in Ireland if there's a man I fancy and who fancies me. There's still time to fulfil myself. From now on I'll confess my fantasies to a lusty, lanky man who'll be a real match for Big Maggie Polpin.

The weal of the chastity cord is still around my belly and the incense is in my nostrils. I'm too long a prisoner but I'll savour what I can, while I can and let the last hour be the sorest.

MICHAEL DAVITT
AONACH NA SÚL

I

Tá ina bhiaiste na mbrístí gearra
na gcíocha gan chíochbheart
ó d'ardaigh an ceo.
Tá an Daingean ag déanamh
súilíní
ag faire féachaint
an bhfeicfí:
    súile circe
    súile sprice
    súile bric
    súile cait
    súile bodhra
    súile balbha
    súile margaidh
    súile folaigh
    súile buinní
    súile an tsaoil
    súile a mháthar
    súile gael
    súile gall
    súile gallghael
    súile gaelghall
    súile na háite
    súile snáthaide
    súile bóna
    súile tóna
    súile siúil
    súile súl

II

Táimid ag glinniúint
trí spéaclaí 3D
ar Iníon Uí Shúilleabháin
súilín óir a Mamaí.
A Mhuire!
péire breá malaí
aon mhac imrisc amháin.
Táimid ag piocadaíl
ar Double Club Burger
a bhfuil Keep America Beautiful
scríofa ar chúl an pháipéir shnasta
atá fáiscthe air.
Tá seanbhrocaire truamhéileach
ag féachaint
mar a bheadh tincéir
ag iarraidh déirce.
In ainm Dé
canathaobh go bhfuilimid
ag ithe Double Club Burger
anyway?
Thiar, thiar, goid diogaí.
Seo dhuit. Píosa Double Club Burger.

III

Tá an milltéan mic
ina chulaith check
ag baile ó Springfield Mass.
maraon lena bhudragár mná
ar gor faoina folt gorm.
Conas a sheasann sé an teas
ina chulaith check?
Conas a sheasann sé ise?
Cén saghas áit é Springfield Mass.?
Bhfuil páirc phoiblí ann
bláthanna

faichí bearrtha
jagaeirí?
Dá mbaileoimis céad míle páipéar snasta
Double Club Burger
sea agus iad a ligint le gaoth ag
Féile Bhrúscair Pháirc an Earraigh.
Bheadh stáitse againn
agus P.A.
fiche míle grúbhaer,
is ní cheadófaí Béarla!

IV

Ní chímid faic ach taobh bus.
Anois Eorpaigh
sean-Eorpaigh is Eorpaigh óga órga
ar nós Gearmánaigh ó Chalifornia
fiacle bána
craiceann buí
glan,
conas a choimeádann siad chomh
glan?
Bhan bheanaíle aghscraoim plíos.
Sainc iú
Eant fitch bhé íos
De Cleevawn Guest House?
De Cliabhán Geist Heabhas?
Abhait de róid ababhait tiú myles.
Sainc iú . . .

V

Tá iascairí ag teacht i dtír ag ól beer.
Tá an brocaire ag iarraidh dul in airde
ar phúidil ó Ghlasthule (trua).
Tá budragár an mhillteán mic
ag glacadh pic (peck check click).
Tá bus ag iarraidh dul soir.
Tá bus eile ag iarraidh dul siar.
Tá Merc an Mhinistir stiuc sa trácht.
Tá súil Dé ar maos sa bhá.
Faigh deontú eacs thim ababhait
dait Galetuct Greint?
   Gaid úr raight.
Faidhl híos daor laighc.
   Faidhl aighim thiar.

SISTER STANISLAUS KENNEDY
A TIME FOR SOLITUDE

I am a person who lives a very full and hectic life. Often I wish
it were not so hectic. People who know me and know how I am
always flying around from one thing to another laugh when I
tell them that my ambition is to be more contemplative, to
withdraw from the bustle of the world and spend more time in
prayer and meditation. Maybe they are right to laugh. Maybe
I would miss my busy lifestyle more than I think I would, but what
I do know for sure is that it is in the time I spend in solitude and
quiet that I discover who I am and what my life's journey is all about.
It is in solitude that I find I can forget about the things that bother
me, that I can learn to see those things as essentially small things,
and that I can allow myself to be opened up to wonder.

Silence
In his lovely poem where he writes in the first person as silence,
Brendan Kennelly says, 'Once I was the heartbeat of the world/
But am an outcast now.' Silence is indeed a stranger to people
who live in today's busy and noisy world. When I look back on

the lives my parents and neighbours lived, I can see that they lived and worked for long stretches in silence and often also in solitude. My father worked in the fields, on the hillside and in the boglands, making and saving hay, cutting and saving turf, sowing and reaping corn, walking with sheep and cattle, horses and ponies, often in complete silence and solitude. Others worked out at sea, fishing in the light and in the dark, totally engrossed in the task at hand, sometimes with mates but also often in a solitude and silence that can only be appreciated by the experienced. Women like my mother worked in their kitchens, preparing food, making bread, churning butter, tending to and caring for flocks of chickens and ducks and milking the cows, feeding the calves. Many of these activities were carried out in silence and solitude, which gave the people an opportunity to lose themselves in thought, as they worked in tune with the things around them. As a child I roamed barefoot through the fields and bogs and along the streams and rivers. Often I sat in silence for hours, day after day, on a riverbank, alone or with my brothers and sisters or neighbour children, fishing for trout. Silence was part of the rhythm of our lives: we knew the sound of silence and we lived it.

The people I grew up among, many of whom were writers and storytellers, would not have thought of themselves as mystics, but they had a breadth of understanding and a true wisdom that I am sure came from a combination of the life they lived so close to the earth and their long hours of silence as they worked. They had a sense of the sacred and that they located not just in church but in the solitude of their own hearts.

Hildegard of Bingen

In early medieval times, around the eleventh and twelfth centuries, there was a group of holy men and women living as hermits in Germany, who were known as the Rhineland mystics. They lived in silence and solitude, and the writings they have left us have shown us a depth of understanding that came not from books or learning, but from their experience of solitude, silence and deep contemplation.

Perhaps the best-known today of these mystics is Hildegard of Bingen (Bingen is a little town on the banks of the Rhine, not far from Cologne), who lived between 1098 and 1179 and may have been Germany's first mystic. She is renowned not only for her sanctity and her writings but especially for the extraordinary religious music she wrote for women's voices, a remarkable achievement for a woman in those times. As well as being a mystic, a visionary, a prophet, a composer and dramatist, she was a great healer and social reformer and a scientist. Her book of simple medicine is an encyclopedia of natural science. She also wrote four books on animals, two on herbs and trees, and three on gems and metals, books that are enjoying a new interest in today's world, where we are regaining an interest in natural medicine and holistic healing. She is now recognised for the extraordinary woman she was, with accomplishments in an astonishing range of areas.

Hildegard was particularly close to nature, and acutely aware of the mystery of God's presence in all things. One of my favourite sayings of hers is, 'All creation is a symphony of joy and jubilation.' She wrote extensively about the contrast between night and day, light and darkness, and she was conscious that in the face of our darkness we can touch into our own greatness – the wonder of our own being and the wonder of God.

Hildegard coined the term 'veriditas' (green-ness), which was an expression of nature's power to birth and nurture life. Growing up as she did with the lush verdancy of Rhineland Germany, Hildegard saw a divine presence in her surroundings, and through her contemplation in solitude, she was able to deepen her awareness of the divine presence everywhere. From that verdant landscape in which she lived and contemplated came the metaphors that filled her writing: 'the verdancy of justice', 'the greening power of faith', the 'vigour that hugs the world', phrases that bring to mind Dylan Thomas's poem about the essential unity of humanity and nature: 'The force that through the green fuse drives the flower/Drives my green age'. One of the particular gifts of Hildegard's solitude was the acute perception it gave her of our inter-connectedness with the natural world, and that is a gift that solitude can give anyone who is prepared to receive it.

Social Solitude
Solitude, which by definition depends on being alone, withdrawing from the company of others, is nevertheless distinct

from isolation. By enabling us to be more tuned in to ourselves, solitude in fact allows us to relate to the world around us. Monks and hermits, mystics like Hildegard, live a life of almost total solitude, yet in their way are vitally linked to the world, although living apart from it. Thomas Merton, a great spiritual thinker and writer, who after an active life in other spheres became a Trappist monk, explained in his writings that the contemplative only withdraws from the world in order to listen more intently to the most neglected voices which proceed from its inner depths. A monk, he said, is 'a marginal person who withdraws deliberately, with a view to deepening fundamental human experience.'

Solitude is not a form of running away or a refusal to become involved with the world. Rather, solitude helps to create communion, because we take others with us in our hearts into our solitude and there relationships deepen. In solitude we may experience a deep bonding with others, even though we are not present with them at that time. Solitude and silence make us wise, because in solitude we come to know ourselves, and through this experience we learn to deal more kindly with ourselves and so also with others. Knowing our own struggles, we can recognise the struggles of other people, knowing our own frailty and fragility we are less quick to condemn, less certain of our convictions and more open to the goodness in other people.

Finding Ourselves in Solitude

A time for solitude is a time for intimacy with ourselves, a time to befriend ourselves and embrace ourselves. Intimacy with ourselves is impossible if solitude is not a habit of our lives. Solitude creates the conditions for us to be at home with ourselves, and only through being at home with ourselves, and it is only through being at home with ourselves that we can learn how to be at home with others and with our God.

'The unhappiness of a person resides in one thing: to be unable to remain peacefully in a room', wrote the seventeenth-century scientist and philosopher, Blaise Pascal. But it is not easy to be alone with ourselves, to rest with ourselves in solitude. One reason we tend to shy away from solitude is that we don't want to meet ourselves, we are afraid of who we really are. Solitude brings us face to face with ourselves and we may not like what we see. In solitude, if we are honest with ourselves, we can see what we could be but are not, what we want to be and have failed to become, and there we find a new depth of emptiness in ourselves.

And yet it is also in solitude that we can learn to see beyond those frailties of ours, that emptiness within, to a new depth of potential and a new self-awareness, which leads to self-acceptance. If we reject ourselves, if we refuse to say yes to who we are, then we are impoverishing ourselves. If on the other hand we accept ourselves as we are, with our faults and inadequacies and in the silence and solitude of our own hearts embrace who it is we are, then we can make room for the transforming power of love to begin within us and to radiate through us.

Being alone with ourselves is demanding, yet if we do not learn to face ourselves we will live a life of shallowness. It is in solitude that we can discover the true beauty of ourselves. In solitude we find, deep down inside ourselves, a microcosm of all the hopes and fears, joys and sorrows, pain and delight of the whole universe. Silence and solitude enable us to listen beyond the chaos that is inside us and around us and to hear our own unasked questions.

In solitude we can tune ourselves in to the true source of our being, the true source of our identity and security, which we may call God. It is in solitude that we can face without fear our own inner poverty and our brokenness – our faults, our frailties, our inadequacies – knowing that in God's embrace we are transformed by a love that has no requirements and no limits.

A Sacred Space
All cultures have had their sacred places and spaces: places in the wild, gardens, cemeteries, cathedrals, monasteries, mosques. Today's people too are seeking space and sanctuary for the sake of their own sanity. We all need this space for solitude and we can all find time for it if we make it a priority, if we value it. We can only value it if we experience it, but once we have experienced it, we will prize the opportunity to stop, reflect, be quiet and feed our spirit, alone and at rest with ourselves.

from NOW IS THE TIME (1998)

JOHN B. KEANE
CERTAINTY

This is the place, I was told
See the tall grass lie low.
They rested here and made bold.
Now for a certainty I know.

Take note of the bluebell broken,
The fern mangled and dead,
And look at this for a token –
Here's a hair from her head!

BEARNARD Ó LUBHAING
AR MUIR IS AR TÍR

Cé gó raibh cuid mhaith dár gcomharsain a thaistil an domhán agus cuid eile acu a chaith seal i Meiriceá, bhí cuid eile gur ar éigean a chuadar thar bhaile an Daingin i gcaitheamh a saoil. Ní raibh ach taxi amháin sa Daingean sna triochaidí agus ní raibh oiread is carr amháin príobháideach i bParóiste Fionntrá ar fad. Bhí carranna ag na sagairt agus ag na dochtúirí agus b'shin eile go dtí tar éis an Chogaidh. Ní raibh ach gléas amháin raidió ar an mbaile, i dtigh James Curran, agus gan fáil air ach i gcomhair an chluiche ceannais peile; ní raibh aon leictreachas ná córas séarachais; ní raibh aon iar-bhunoideachas ach don mbeagán a chuaigh go dtí Scoil na mBráthar sa Daingean nó go dtí na Coláistí Ullmhúcháin. Ach, dar ndóigh, níor bhraitheamar uainn na hacmhainní sin mar go rabhamar aineolach orthu. Bhí sé intuigthe go gcaithfeá do chaitheamh aimsire féin a chur ar fáil agus úsáid a bhaint as do chuid seifteachais agus do chuid samhlaíochta féin, agus ní raibh aon easnamh orainn sna cáilíochtaí sin.

Bhíomar ar bharr na farraige agus tráigh bhán Fionntrá fúinn thíos mar pháirc imeartha. Measaim ná fuil éinne gearrtha amach ón saol mór má tá cónaí air in aice na farraige. Bhí teagmháil rialta againn leis an Mór-Roinn nuair a thagadh báid iascaigh ón mBriotáin agus ón Spáinn isteach sa chuan i gcomhair foscaidh agus, uaireanta, chun a stóras bídh agus uisce a athnuachaint. Bhíodh an-ghliondar orainn nuair a thagaidís in dtír – bróga adhmaid orthu, éadach gorm cadáis agus berets dubha an iascaire. Bhí boladh láidir na Gauloises ar an dtobac a dheinidís a fhilleadh ina dtoitíní, go haiclí, cliste agus iad ag comhrá i dteanga iasachta.

Dheinidís branda dearg ón Spáinn a mhalartú ar phaca prátaí nó bulóga builín gan cur isteach ó fhear an chustaim. Is cuimhin liom uair amháin gur tháinig an Cléireach anall ó Bhaile na nGall chun last buidéal branda a bhreith abhaile leis go dtína thigh tábhairne le cabhair m'athar. Dar ndóigh is i gcoinn na hoíche a tharla an gnó san agus ní raibh d'eolas againne inár stócaigh air ach an méid a d'fhoghlaimíomar ag cúléisteacht leis an gcogarnaíl ar maidin. Col ceathrar do mo mháthair ab ea an Cléireach agus muna mbeadh an ceangal gaoil ní gheobhadh sé aon chabhair inár dtighne sa droch-obair mar a chonacthas di é!

Le teacht agus imeacht na taoide, dhá uair sa ló, tá an radharc tíre in aice na farraige ag athrú do shíor. Nuair a thráigh sí d'fhág sí loganna i measc na bhfochaisí ina bhféadfaí mionscrúdú a dhéanamh ar an saol fóthoinn. Is sna loganna seo leis a dheinimis ár gcuid bád a dheargadh sa tine chun poll a chur ann don gcrann agus píosa de cheirt mar sheol. Bhí uirlisí an chúipéara a bhí imithe as úsáid um an dtaca seo an-úsáideach sa ghnó seo. Dá mbrisfeadh cogadh amach ar an 'bhfarraige' ní bheadh aon easpa seileanna chun an cath a riar, clocha á raideadh go tiubh ar fhlít an namhad agus buamaí ag pléascadh i ngach treo le barr díograise. Bhíomar go mór faoi thionchar an Chéad Chogaidh Dhomhanda agus na cathanna fuilteacha sna trinsí – scéalta a tháinig chugainn ar chuma éigin ó bhéal go béal. Bhí an buachaillín mánla Eoin Curran agus mo dheartháir Maidho an-eolach ar na cúrsaí sin óna gcuid léitheoireachta agus dheinimis na cathanna sa *Western Front* a aththroid ar na leacacha soir ó Thobar na hAille. Bhíodh miongáin mar shaighdiúirí, ardáin agus ísleáin agus loganna ar na leacacha mar thrínsí, clocha beaga don mbuamáil mharfach, agus leis an scrios agus an bascadh a deintí ar na miongáin d'fhéadfá páirc an áir i bPasschendaele nó i bhFlóndras a shamhlú i ndeireadh an chatha.

Théimis siar ar an dtráigh chun cathanna níos dáiríre a

throid. D'fhéadfá trinsí a athchruthú ar an ngainimh ansin le sluaiste agus píosaí móna mar lón cogaidh á chrústáil ar a chéile le fuinneamh. Bhí an mhóin seo le fáil go flúirseach nuair a bheadh sé ina lagtrá mar portach a bhí ann le cuimhne na ndaoine ach é ite anois ag an bhfarraige. Níorbh chás leat úsáid a bhaint as clocha anois is arís dá mbeadh an mhóin imithe i ndísc agus an cath á riar. Nuair a scoilteadh ceann mo dhearthár de thoradh ceann des na cathanna sin agus go mb'éigean don ndochtúir greim a chur ann, chuir san deireadh leis an réalaíochas. Ag an am gcéanna is iomdha luíochán a bheadh againn ar dhaoine neamhurchóideacha ag gabháil an bhóthair, á gcrústáil le scraithíní.

Bhíomar an-thógtha le héachtaí Tom Barry agus a ghníomhartha gaile is gaisce in iarthar Chorcaí. D'éirigh linn pléascáin neamhdhíobhálacha a dhéanamh le cúpla seile a chaitheamh ar roinnt gráinní *carbide* istigh i stán chócó a mbeadh poll curtha ina thóin. Tar éis cúpla nóimeat, nuair a líonadh an stán leis an ngás, dá gcuirfeá cipín solais leis an bpoll bheadh pléascadh glórach a shéideadh an clúdach den stán le fórsa, i dtreo go gceapfadh an duine a bhí ag dul thar bráid ar an rothar go raibh an bonn pollta ar a laghad. Bhí an *carbide* seo i úsáid ag Gardaí agus ag m'athair ag an am chun solas a sholáthar do lampaí rothar agus bhí teacht againn air gan dua.

Nuair a tháinig na *Fitups* leis na céad pictiúirí reatha, agus as na comics a bhí ag teacht sna beartáin ó Mheiriceá, chuireamar aithne ar na buachaillí bó agus na Rua-Indiaigh. Le cabhair scéalta Zane Grey, leis an nduí mar *phrairie* agus *six-guns* ó shiopa Maggie Devane sa Daingean bhíomar feistithe chun lá a mheilt mar *Riders of the Purple Sage* nó dul ar thóir na *Apaches* nó na *Cherokee* i measc na ndumhach gainimhe.

Ó Shamhain go Bealtaine ní raibh aon Domhnach breá ná beimis ar an gcnoc ag fiach an ghiorria nó an mhadarua le coin agus iliomad gadhar neamhaitheanta. Anois is arís san earrach chuirfí tine leis an aiteann tirim, agus is ansan a bheadh tiomáint ar iarraidh an tine a smachtú – lasarnach agus deatach agus teas ár gcoimeád siar.

Thugaimis cuairt amháin in aghaidh na bliana ar bharr Shliabh an Iolair a bhí laistiar agus lastuas dínn mar shaghas Everest nó Kilmanjaro. Bhí Sliabh an Iolair mar thuar na haimsire againn; dá mbeadh sé glan bheadh an aimsir breá ach ba mhinicí é ag scamhaíl anuas orainn faoi scamall is faoi cheo. Bhí sé ann i gcónaí go dtéach an ghrian faoi laistiar de, mar áit dhiamhair, dhraíochta agus ba mhór an lá é inár saol nuair a d'éirigh linn an rúna bhriseadh.

Domhnach breá i lár an tSamhraidh thugamar faoi, suas ó Chill a Ruith, feadh an locha agus an fhaill laistiar de go dtí an mbarra bog slím ina ndeintí móin a bhaint. Chuir mo chéad radharc ar an loch a bhí i gcom an tsléibhe uafás agus alltacht orm – é dorcha, diamhair agus i bhfad níos fairsinge ná a mbeadh súil agat leis. Ó bharr an tsléibhe bhí an radharc dhochuimsithe ag síneadh amach ar an bhfarraige mhór, bád gaile in íoghar na spéire, Sceilg Mhichíl agus Dairbhre agus Uíbh Ráthach uait ó dheas, agus ó thuaidh go Béal na Sionainne. Bhíomar ar aon dul leis an mbuachaillín ón mBlascaod a dúirt gur fada fairsing í Éire nuair a leag sé a shúil ar an radharc chéanna ó bharr an Chlasaigh agus é ag dul go Ráiseanna Fionntrá.

Théimis go rialta go dtí Leaba an Fhir Mhuimhnigh – dolmán i measc na sléibhte os cionn Chathair Ard; lá eile go dtí an dTuairín Bán i mBaile an Ghóilín in aice béal chuain an Daingin; lá i gcomhair Cé an Chuain agus fothrach Stáisiún na nGardaí Cósta a loisceadh i gCogadh na Saoirse agus gach Domhnach Cásca bheimis ar an dturas go dtí Teampall Mhancháin i mBaile Riabhach le turas a thabhairt ar an dTobar beannaithe i gcomhair an phátrúin. Bhíomar ag brath romhainn, de shiúl cos, go dtí teorainn ár ndomhain bhig féin, agus ár dtuiscint ar an stair as ar fáisceadh sinn ag leathnú dá réir.

D'imrímis ár gcuid caide le díograis ar an nduí laistiar den Halla Rince agus ba mhinicí sinn ag iarraidh an liathróid peile a bhreith amach as poll portaigh nó tor aitinn ná aon rud eile.

Nuair a bhí an brothall ann théimis ag snámh ón slip go dtí an dtráigh, uaireanta go dtí Cé an Bháid ag brath ar an dtaoide agus níos déanaí go dtí Poll na Caorach mar a raibh doimhneas uisce i gcónaí. Bhímis cosúil le róinte, lomnocht agus bolg le gréin go dtí gur ghearán Mrs McDonnell sinn. Ní fhéadfadh sí dul ag bailiú duilisc gan aghaidh a thabhairt ar Dinny Sugrue agus a chlann mac farainn agus sinn ag tabhair scanaill don gcomharsanacht! Dia idir sinn agus an t-olc!

I rith an tsamhraidh leis is minic a chaithimis smut de lá b'fhéidir ag iascach ballach ón gcarraig síos ó Fhaill na Mná, báirnigh mar bhaoite agus slat iascaigh déanta as bambú ó Bhaile an Ghóilín. Bhí an-shásamh le baint as an iascach seo nuair a bheadh an taoide ag líonadh agus na ballaigh ag priocadh go cíocrach. Bhíodh an-éileamh ar an iasc garbh seo le cur i mbairille goirt i gcomhair an gheimhridh.

Nuair a bheadh an uain ann chuige, ba bhreá é siúl ar an dtráigh le buicéad agus é a líonadh le cnuasacht trá, mar a tugtaí air. Bheadh miongáin, muiríní, duileasc, carraigín, portáin, iascáin agus iliomad sliogán anaithid agat ag teacht abhaile. Bhí leaba mhór diúilicíní i gCuas na Feamnaí, ach, toisc go raibh cáil na buinní orthu, is ar éigean a raghadh éinne sa tseans orthu ach fophótaire a mbíodh dúil acu iontu.

Tríd is tríd is deacair a shamhlú conas a gheobhadh éinne bás den ocras agus an saibhreas bídh seo ar fáil faoinár gcosa. I mbéaloideas na ndaoine bhí an fhlúirse bídh seo snadhmtha ina n-aigne leis an ndrochshaol agus drochmheas acu air dá réir, go mór mhór i measc na bhfeirmeoirí beaga. Sa lá atá inniu ann tá an 'cnuasacht trá' ar an mbéile is blasta agus is daoire i mbialanna galánta an Daingin.

Nuair a thagadh dúluachair na bliana chúlaímis go dtí Cistin Uí Churráin atá luaite cheana agam. Oícheanta geimhridh bhíodh tine mhór adhmaid ón gcoill i mBaile an Ghóilín ag lasarnaigh ar an ngráta oscailte. Bhí bord mór trom déanta as cláracha tiubha *pitch pine* a tháinig isteach leis an dtaoide agus is air a d'imrímis ár gcluichí achrannacha cártaí, lúdó agus fichille. Chaith Mícheál Ó Curráin agus a bhean chéile, Nóirín, go lách, fáilteach linn – ní raibh aon rialacha dochta agus bhíomar saor ón smacht inár dtigh féin. Ní raibh aon chosc ar chaitheamh tobac agus is ann a chuireamar aithne ar na cailíní don chéad uair.

Bean álainn ina meon agus a pearsanacht ab ea Bean Uí Churráin, iníon feirmeora ó oirthear Luimnigh, machaire méith na Mumhan. Dála muintir an taobh sin tíre bhí an-luí aici leis an gceol agus na rincí Gaelacha agus dheineadh sí tréaniarracht ar na steipeanna a mhúineadh dúinn le ceol an chonsairtín. Bhí leabhair sa tigh a bhain lena seanathair, an Máistir Ó Curráin, agus roinntí go fial linn iad. In Éire na linne sin do b'é an easpa leabhar ba mhó a ghoill ormsa ach go háirithe. Is sa tigh sin a chuir mé aithne ar na scéalta cosúil le *Coral Island, Treasure Island, The Magic Wand*, Scéalta *Just William, Kickham*, agus a lán eile a chothaigh ionam an dúil sa léitheoireacht atá ina chrann taca agam riamh ó shin. Beidh mé i gcónaí i bhfiacha mhuintir Uí Churráin as an aoibhneas, as an gcraic agus as an oideachas a bhí le fáil againn sa chúlchistin theolaí sin nuair a bhíomar go léir óg.

as CEANN TRÁ A HAON (1998)

THE KERRY RECRUIT

About four years ago I was digging the land,
With my brogues on my feet and my spade in my hand.
Says I to myself, 'What a pity to see
Such a fine strapping lad footing turf in Tralee.'

So I buttered my brogues and shook hands with my spade,
And I went to the fair like a dashing young blade,
When up comes a sergeant and asks me to 'list,
'Arra, sergeant *a grá*, put the bob in my fist.'

'O! then here is the shilling, as we've got no more,
When you get to headquarters you'll get half a score.'
'Arra, quit your *kimeens*,' ses I, 'sergeant, goodbye,
You'd not wish to be quartered, and neither would I.'

And the first thing they gave me it was a red coat,
With a wide strap of leather to tie around my throat,
They gave me a quare thing I asked what was that,
And they told me it was a cockade for my hat.

The next thing they gave me they called it a gun,
With powder and shot and a place for my thumb;
And first she spit fire and then she spit smoke,
Lord, she gave a great lep and my shoulder near broke.

The next place they sent me was down to the sea,
On board of a warship bound for the Crimea.
Three sticks in the middle all rowled round with sheets,
Faith, she walked thro' the water without any feet.

Whan at Balaklava we landed quite sound,
Both cold wet and hungry we lay on the ground.
Next morning for action the bugle did call,
And we got a hot breakfast of powder and ball.

Sure it's often I thought of my name and my home
And the days that I spent cutting turf, och *mavrone*,
The balls were so quick and the fire was so hot,
I lay down in the ditch, boys, for fear I'd be shot.

We fought at the Alma, likewise Inkermann,
But the Russians they whaled us at the Redan.
In scaling the walls there myself lost an eye,
And a big Russian bullet ran off with my thigh.

It was there I lay bleeding, stretched on the cold ground,
Heads, legs and arms were scattered all around.
Says I, if my mam or my *cleaveens* were were nigh
They'd bury me decent and raise a loud cry.

They brought me the doctor, who soon staunched my blood
And he gave me an elegant leg made of wood,
They gave me a medal and tenpence a day,
Contented with Sheela, I'll live on half-pay.

ANONYMOUS

SEAN O'FAOLAIN
from KING OF THE BEGGARS
A LIFE OF DANIEL O'CONNELL (1938)

He had at least a million members enrolled in his army of beggars by the end of 1825. That is measurable from the weekly contributions, which amounted at times to £2,000. Had that been evenly maintained, and no large contributions given, as they were, the total would have been £100,000 every year, or, counting each shilling as a member, two million members. It seems more than reasonable to halve that in order to arrive at his total of active followers among the poor.

Once more, as we realise how little we can know about those millions, we suffer the old exasperation of ignorance. How they lived we know; it has all been gathered again and again from travellers' notebooks, from the pages of Lecky – it has been excellently repieced in Daniel Corkery's *The Hidden Ireland*. But of what use are these externals of poverty, mud, lice, hunger, when what we want is to get inside the minds and hearts of these people? They are a blank page to us, for there was no novelist, no dramatist, who thought them worth his sympathetic attention, they lived, themselves, in a condition the nearest imaginable to illiteracy; and they seem – because of our ignorance – to be in such a morass of non-personality that they never emerge as critical, individual human beings. One pitiful ballad will do – written in this year, just after his arrest for his reference to 'a new Bolivar', its references arcane, half of it insensible to annotation – to suggest the intellectual slough into which the people had fallen during the Penal Days. It is worth giving, however wretched, in full. It was printed in broadsheet at Newry, and is called 'O'Connell's Garland':

Ye true sons of Erin give ear to my fiction
Which I now dictate in the year '25,
The enemy's schemes, their plans and their fictions,
Thanks to kind heaven with them did not thrive,
To get under arms they raised the alarm
That on New Year's night we'd rise up in arms

With mischief well fraught they taught to harm
The true sons of Erin and Tarra's old halls.
See how they endeavour to snare O'Connell
By false accusations and flaming lies.
May heaven defend you, our friend, dearest Dan,
From machinations they daily devise.
On Catholic Rent they vent their whole malice
Saying they are rebels that respects the chalice.
But who stained Whitehall with the blood of Royal Charles?
Sure it was not done by the sons of the hall.
My boys, be advised, be obedient and study
To your king most gracious, evading all plots.
Let them be accursed that would touch the blood royal,
We ne'er killed the lady Mary Queen of Scots.
Though we lost our estates, court-gates, and towers
When the renegade he defied royal power
Defending our king in an ill-fated hour
That surely undone the true sons of the hall.
Is not all persuasions our neighbours and brothers,
The man of Samaria the argument proves.
I think it is right in the sight of our Maker,
And is not practised by Swadler and Quaker
Though we are condemned in each villainous paper
Because we belong to the sons of the hall . . .

To interrupt this wretched fair-day ballad-singer, it may be as
well to say that by comparison with any score of political
broadsheet ballads of the day it is not unduly illiterate; it is
average. We note, however, that it repeats several of Dan's
teachings: his hatred of sectarianism; his loyalty to the throne;
his dating of Irish history from its true beginning – the defeat
of the Stuarts at Limerick; and his horror of illegal societies.
Even in this rude ballad-singer by the kerbs of Newry the
essentials of his teaching are evident. Hear the bard to the end:

O Tara my country I love thee 'tis certain
Beyond any place on the face of the globe,
And does not men love the place they gets birth in.
Must we love the nation that did us disrobe?

Five spacious roads to your door was completed,
Your turrets were high and your stairs elevated,
But now low in ruins, my jewel, you're prostrated
Where the proud Dane he was slain in your hall.
Without fee or reward the bard that composes
For you dear O'Connell I'd ransack my brain
To present you this as a garland of roses
Mixed with the white lily and shamrock so green.
If I would get leave to range I would rather
To gather wild flowers in the bower of our faith
Around the bleak ruins of our courts and fine gardens
Before the sweet bloom was consumed in the halls.

It was such folk, so defenceless, so without tradition – the crude
repeated reference to the 'sons of the hall' is the mark of an already
decayed race-memory – that O'Connell, in 1826, asked to vote for
his nominees in several parliamentary elections, so daring a thing
to ask that it was like flinging them to the wolves. It meant that
for the first time in history they must defy their landlords who held
power of life and death over them, who had for generations bought
and sold their votes as if they were cattle. O'Connell showed that
he knew what he asked of these people when he organised a New
Catholic Rent to defend victimised voters.

The poor illiterate wretches rose to his fall. In Monaghan,
in Louth, and above all in Waterford they threw out the
nominees of their masters. Their defeat of Lord George Beresford
in Waterford was particularly gallant. Lord George had held the
seat for twenty years; he was one of a family of the greatest power
and influence not only in the South but in Government circles
in Ireland and Great Britain; he was one of a line that had been
a bulwark of Anglo-Irish domination all through the eighteenth
century. The Beresfords could not believe it when they heard
that a rival had been nominated; he was, of course, a Liberal
Protestant, a Mr Villiers Stuart, for the people could not by law
elect one of their own. They stormed and raged, declared it was
'a palpable insurrection', abused Stuart in the most insolent
terms, said his action was 'ungentlemanlike', and not only felt
but had the folly to declare that his nomination was an
interference with the rights of property – the property being the
votes of the Beresford serfs and the emoluments and honours

of a rotten borough. Wyse, the historian of the Catholic Association, declares that O'Connell himself was incredulous as to the chances of a victory, and threw himself into the election only when he saw with his own eyes the fever of enthusiasm that had risen in the country. It may be so. Once in the fight his voice roused that enthusiasm to frenzy, and his work as agent for Villiers Stuart was as priceless as it was ruthless. The real credit, however, for the victory goes to the tenants who so bravely stood up to the Beresfords and defied their power, to the priests who organised and encouraged them, to Wyse and the other lieutenants of O'Connell who had for a long while previous been preparing the way – mainly middle-class people, for this class had begun to back O'Connell now, though chiefly in private. He may have resented so much autonomous activity – he was never a man to prefer colleagues to agents. He may well have felt that the power he had engendered was rising in a flood about him and was already passing out of his control, the common fate of the popular leader, whose only hope then is to keep ahead of his army or be lost in its dust. O'Connell may not have originated Waterford. He was soon so much the head and fount of the fight that he was, nominally, proposed as a suitable member himself, availed himself of the proposal to make a tremendous speech, and withdrew in favour of the candidate already decided on.

As agent for the candidate there was not a move by his opponents that he did not blast. When the Duke of Devonshire chartered a special steamboat to take his serfs from Lismore to the polls ('these degraded serfs,' says Sheil, 'are driven to the hustings as beasts that perish to the shambles'), O'Connell terrified the women by giving them the most outlandish accounts of the dangers attaching to sea-voyages in such boats as the 'Tay Kettle' – his nickname for the ducal steamer.

A story of a different kind tells how the old Marquess of Waterford, then almost dying, was brought regular bulletins of the defections of his tenants, some sullenly and silently holding themselves against his agent, some boldly holding up in the courts their bribe-money. He bore it all until he was told that the bugle of his huntsman, Manton, was no longer being heard at Lord George's meetings. He sent for the old retainer.

'Are you, too, abandoning me?' he asked from his bed.

The old huntsman stuttered, and stumbled, his red cap

twisting in his hands, almost crying to have to say it, yet resisting even this powerful appeal to his feudal loyalty:

'Long life to yer honour,' he said, 'I'd go to the world's end for yer honour. But sure, please your lordship, I can't go agin my country and my religion.'

One would like to believe that the rest of the story lies when it records that Manton and his family were evicted after Lord George withdrew, in chagrin, leaving the field to his resurgent serfs. It is probably only too true, since after the election they were flung on the wayside by the hundreds. 'Obey or starve!' had been the rule, and they had not obeyed.

MÍCHEÁL FANNING
DANIEL O'CONNELL AT TARA

for Desmond O'Grady

Thirteen hundred vehicles roll
from Dublin
towns in green and white.
A mist – a sea of banners –
descends on Tara.
Forty bands march,
ten thousand horsemen,
multitude countless
as the bearded grain.
I parade on horseback
apparelled in my green uniform
and green repeal cap,
horsemen to my left and right.
The sound of mass is on the wind.
I speak with the gale,
give a stirring repeal oratory.
Afterwards I, Daniel O'Connell,
partook of tea, yellow meal bread
and herrings
in Maguire's teahouse.

PÁDRAIG Ó CONCUBHAIR
THE GREEN FLAG RAISED

The following letter was received by the Earl of Clarendon, Lord Lieutenant of Ireland, on 7 August 1848.

5 Dawson Street
Dublin
May it please Your Excellency
I have this day received a letter from the county of Kerry and avail myself of the earliest moment of laying an extract from it before your Lordship. The writer, Richard FitzGerald of Listowel Castle lives within four miles from Duagh and I fear if immediate assistance be not rendered that the town of Listowel will be in the possession of O'Gorman and his rebel crew. Listowel is near the village of Abbeyfeale where the rebels muster under O'Gorman's command. Fully relying upon your Excellency's prompt protection for the unprotected neighbourhood and town of Listowel, I have the honour to remain your Lordship's most obedient servant,
    John St John Barry

Listowel
5 August 1848
My dear Barry
What will your stay in Dublin be? I have just now heard from the Rev John O'Connor, Co-adjutor to the Rev Mr O'Mahony that the Rev Mr Harnett, P.P. of Duagh came into Mr O'Mahony just now and told him that in the parish of Duagh thousands of armed men have taken the field and that they were to join the Abbeyfeale people and march into Listowel, possessing themselves of the arms in it and killing everyone who does not join them. Are the Government fast asleep? I request you will forthwith give information to His Excellency to the foregoing effect.
    Yours sincerely
    Richard FitzGerald

The Kerry Evening Post, Tralee, Saturday 5 August 1848
ALARMING INTELLIGENCE! ROBBERY OF THE UP AND DOWN
LIMERICK AND TRALEE MAILS BY THE INSURGENTS

By accounts received last night (which will be found below), we
learned that indications of an insurrectionary spirit had extended
themselves to Abbeyfeale, a town just outside the borders of this
county, following in the track of Mr Richard O'Gorman, one
of the insurgent leaders. Accounts from that locality were looked
for with much anxiety by this evening's mail.

The Limerick coach arrived an hour late, and to the general
alarm of the well-affected it was soon known that the insurrection
had already broken out there – an armed party of peasantry
having stopped the mail coaches just at the point where they
meet, and robbed them of both the up and down mails, taking
away the bags, but without injuring any of the persons on either
coach.

The intelligence is not only alarming in itself, but that alarm
is considerably increased when we take into account the manner
in which this outrageous act was committed. As we could learn
from the Guard and Coachman, the particulars of this attack are
as follows: When the two coaches drove within about six perches
of each other, an armed body of near two hundred men called
upon them with levelled guns to pull up. Having done so, there
was among the attacking party a discussion as to whether they
would cut the traces and poles or not: finally, it was agreed not
to do so, and the people contented themselves with taking all
the mail bags, and warning the Coachmen and Guards not to
come again there tomorrow, allowed the coaches to proceed to
their destinations – the Limerick first, and shortly the Tralee.
The insurgents then, sounding horns, leisurely walked off the
road through the mountains in the direction of the village of
Brosna in this county.

The party was armed with guns and a few carried pikes: some
the common pitchfork. They appeared to be well dressed men,
generally wearing tweed coats, cut in the shooting jacket fashion;
and although the scene of attack was just close to the house of
a wealthy farmer they did not make the least attempt at
concealment.

The Listowel Resident Magistrate, Patrick Cheevers, wrote:

> An armed party of peasantry this day assembled in Abbeyfeale and stopped the mail. The said party intend to plunder the town of Listowel of firearms and some alarm prevails. Because of the fear of this attack I have deemed it proper to send at once for the police of the outskirts of the district.
>
> The one main cause of all those serious and alarming proceedings seems to have been a meeting held by Mr O'Gorman a few miles from Abbeyfeale at which he is alleged to have used very strong and exciting language. This meeting took place on Thursday 3 August, on Friday 4, arms were taken from many respectable persons and on Saturday 5, the Mail Coaches were attacked and robbed.

The *Tralee Chronicle* reported:

> About one hundred and thirty men armed with guns, pistols, pitchforks and crooks leapt from their ambush and possessed themselves of the mails and the arms of the Guard.
>
> Being remonstrated with by the Guard, John Purcell, their answer was 'We want to free our country and stop the communications.'
>
> The party consisted mostly of young lads bare-footed, numbering however a great many respectable middle-aged countrymen. They threatened to saw through the coach-shafts if their demands were not met and one of them actually produced a saw and set to work with it.

The postmaster in Abbeyfeale confirmed the attack:

Post Office
Abbeyfeale
5 August 1848

If this letter arrives safely I beg to inform you of the occurrence which took place here this day. The Tralee and Limerick coaches were met by a considerable party of rebels. They took away all the mailbags to and from Kerry including mine. In the course of a couple of hours a person came to me saying that one of the leaders wanted to see me to give me back the bags. I at once went to Mr Galway, the R.M. and told him, asking his advice. He hesitated and then sent for Mr Coppinger, Chief of Police, who, I believe, with fifty men, arrived here on last evening.

Both said they would consider and send me an account. Mr Galway sent his man to me saying he would send an escort with me which I declined in dread that I would lose my life. I said I would go alone which I accordingly did. I went to one of the leaders, I suppose, who began opening the bags and also all official letters and also letters to and from Policemen. Some of the official letters they kept and they returned some more after reading them. They also met one letter which was registered, and asked what was the green cover for. I said it may be that it contained money.

They said they did not mean to deprive any man of his property but as the government had suppressed the papers on which they should depend for political information they would take care that their means of communication should be obstructed also. They put all the bags into both sacks – whether they are in the proper ones I cannot say till I see the guards, and I shall give them up in the same way I got them. I procured a horse and car from a farmer hard by, who was kind enough to bring them in to town. The Rising here is attributed to a detective who came in coloured clothes (i.e. in disguise) to arrest or trace out Mr

O'Gorman. The detective was detected – it was a miracle he did not lose his life.

Mr Galway then thought it was his duty to bring police from Newcastle which added to the excitement and from then to the attack in the coaches.

That, sir, is the fateful statement: The country is in a dreadful state. God only knows what will happen tomorrow, Sunday, as the rebels told me it was their firm intention to enter this town with a view to attacking the police, and all this, I am convinced of, happened on account of the detective as I heard the people say had he come in his proper uniform he would not be molested. This locality was very peaceful heretofore, nor had they any thoughts of an outbreak, at least so soon.

I have the honour to be
Your faithful servant
John Fitzgerald

Afterwards a large assembly of persons gathered on the hills of Duagh on the opposite side of the River Feale. Gavin Duffy writes:

That night the watch fires of a rebel encampment burned on the hills round Abbeyfeale.

The attack on the coaches caused a sensation and Mr Bianconi himself wrote to the Lord Lieutenant informing him that it was the first time that the mails had been taken from any of his vehicles since he founded his transport service in 1815.

The Castle was not unaware of what was going forward and, as the Postmaster stated, Head-Constable Hogben was on his way through Abbeyfeale to arrest O'Gorman when, 'dressed in coloured clothes, he was taken by the peasantry and deprived of his warrant, his six barrelled pistol, his wallet with £10 and his watch. He was marched in triumph to Athea amidst the booing and every other insult of the women and children, to know how the General would dispose of him, though some recommended shooting him at once.'

Richard O'Gorman however ordered that he be released. 'No person in Abbeyfeale would give him a lodging. At last he was taken to a cabin out of town where he lay until morning. He was later taken to Newcastlewest where his wallet and watch were restored to him.' There was good in Head-Constable Hogben. When Richard Twomey, one of the local leaders, was finally arrested on 30 August Magistrate Galway reported: 'Head-Constable Hogben says he owns his life to him and is disinclined to prosecute him unless specifically directed to do so.'

Richard O'Gorman continued to raise the people on the Limerick-Kerry border. He sent messages to Smith O'Brien but some were arrested and no news was received. He then travelled to Tipperary Town and communicated with O'Brien in Ballingarry. He was instructed to return to Limerick and await developments. On 9 August, 15 men with blackened faces 'believed to be from County Limerick' stole five guns in the parish of Knockanure. Magistrate Cheevers reported: 'They received no willing encouragement from the peasantry of the district.'

When it became clear that no more could be achieved O'Gorman ordered his men to disperse. Some were later arrested, many of them 'kept the hills of County Kerry' for the remainder of the year.

from THEY KEPT THE HILLS OF KERRY
1848 BY THE FEALESID*E* (1998)

PADDY BUSHE
POETS AT SMERWICK

In November 1580 an expeditionary force of 600 Italian and Spanish soldiers landed at Smerwick, County Kerry, to aid the Irish Geraldine rebellion against Queen Elizabeth. They fortified the site of an older fort called Dún an Óir, or Fort del Oro. The fort was besieged and captured by English troops under Lord Grey. On his orders, the expeditionary force was massacred, and their bodies thrown over the cliffs. Some Irish soldiers and camp followers were tortured and hanged. Elizabeth commended Grey for his actions, regretting only that he had spared some officers.

I POSITIONS

'Then put I certyn bandes who straight fell to execution.
            There were 600 slayne'
Lord Grey's report to Elizabeth

This is the bare statement.
Details lingering in other gleanings.
How the weapons were dented
From an excess of hacking.
How, at the forge, two men,
Bones hammered on an anvil,
Died for three days. Such details
In flat prose can be swallowed
Until the prose throws up two names
That had before been castled gracefully
Among the trees of the Blackwater,
Silver poets of a golden age:
Ralegh snug in anthologies, Spenser ingenuously
Singing the praises of his Faerie Queene.
But at Smerwick, Edmund Spenser, secretary,
Scripted beautifully Lord Grey's report,
And Walter Ralegh, captain, organised the kill.

II ECHOES

Smerwick. A hard Norse ring to it.
Fire and ice beat out the shape.
Raiders with reddened eyes and salt lips
Named it, leaving echoes

Among cliffs like sharp, arbitrary edges.
These heights, those angular consonants,
Echo no woods, frame no soft vowels. Here
Is no Blackwater Valley. Here the bones lie out.

III   SONNET

The prisoners were penned inside the fort,
An open challenge to Elizabeth.
So Grey, as Spenser wrote in his report,
Thought her best served by their exemplary death.

Thus Walter Ralegh, captain, part-time poet,
Was drafted in to organise the work.
To gut six hundred men was heavy-going,
But Ralegh thought it out like any clerk

Compiling figures. Every man must kill
His share. In order that there'd be no doubt,
He'd have to show the carcasses to fill
The quota Walter Ralegh figured out.

The body count worked out at five per man.
That tidy mind would make a sonnet scan.

IV   THE LIE

When Ralegh came out of Ireland,
Did poetry also demand a cloak
To spread over those bloodier pools
He had waded to this more courtly siege
Of his impregnable, capricious queen?
Did any simile leer from the caked
Whiteness of Elizabeth's face,
Or the red gash of her mouth?
Was there, in the surges of the dance,
In those energetic sweating lines,
A sudden dizziness that transformed
The expert forking of sweetmeats
Into the apt, the vital image?
Or did the poet's mind retreat
Into itself, and give him both,
Butterfly and butcher, the lie?

V   FOOL'S GOLD

Dún an Óir. Fort del Oro.
Named for gold that wasn't there.
Strange how Ralegh blundered
Towards the scaffold, a lifetime later,
Sailing up the Orinoco for gold, no gold,
For El Dorado. Fort del Oro.
Dún an Óir. Beginning
Towards an end. Blood and gold
Like the slashed crimson trunks
Of a courtier dancing in
And out of favour.

VI   SPENSER'S NOTES FOR THE MUTABILITIE CANTOS
        (NOV. 1580)

Of Gentilnesse:
How in its servise, it seemeth necessarie to forget what
it did whilom signifie, so that it perishe not despite
itselfe. How this enforceth him who serveth politie to
considre all things in a double fashione.

Of the Breaking Wave:
How it changeth by th'effecte of all the brokene
bodies, from being as newe milke to a sauvage redde,
as if there hath bene a butcherie of the greate Leviathan.

Of Courtesie:
How it changeth constantlie its dresse, from the
soldier's stained cloake to the silke of the Courte.

Of Fortune:
How, as men do say, it resembleth a greate wheele which
can bringe men up and down by turne. How chieflie,
howevre, it doth brake them as doth the racke.

Of Visionne:
How it can be in the same houre the blindnesse of
poesie and a view towards advauncement.

VII   QUESTION

A question, Edmund Spenser:
What's the difference between an allegory
And a massacre? Between
A gentil knight was pricking on the plaine
And the grating of a pile against a pelvis?
Between a marriage hymn on the Thames
And pregnant women hanged at Smerwick?
Between your knight's iambic horror at
A donghill of dead carkases he spide
And the copperplate acount you sealed and signed?

VIII   AN APOLOGY FOR POETRY

At Smerwick, I watch the gannets
Circle over the unseen shoal,
Staring down the long clarity.

Sunflashes on their white wings
Dazzle. I barely see the black tips
Flick them on course, as they twist

On the instant
(Of scales' panic, too late)
Of silver sacrifice.

Watching from the cliffs, I see
Necessary angels. I admire
The ordained patterns, their grace.

This is an apology for poetry.

JOHN MORIARTY
from TURTLE WAS GONE A LONG TIME
VOL. 1 CROSSING THE KEDRON (1996)

It was after closing time and Martin was proud of God.

'That's the long and the short of it now,' he declared, 'I'm proud of God.'

I managed him up the steps. We were almost at the door when he stopped, elaborately, not going a foot farther.

'Give me your hand,' he said.

'Lave it there,' he said.

'My besht friend,' he said.

'The coldesht day in winter,' he said, 'and the hottest day in summer.'

Knowing that I wasn't appeased, he looked up at me forlornly:

'No use hangn a man without a head, John. No use hangn a man without a head.'

'No, Martin, no.'

No.

I managed him through the hall door, out into the night.

Even in the dark he was proud of God. 'Thanks be to God and his Blessed Mother, we had a hishtoric booze. Thanks be to dh'Almighty Redeemer we had a brave drink, in brave company, and John! do you know John, I'd shtand naked in the shnow lishtnen to that one. A lovely girl she was, John. A lovely girl and a grand girl and sure tishnt from the wind she took it, dont I know all belongn to her for four generations back.'

'The song she sang, John, sing that song.'

I sang one verse:

And how proud was I of my girl so tall,
I was envied mostly by young men all
When I brought her blushing, with bashful pride,
To my cottage home by Loch Shileann side.

'Lave it there,' he said, shaking my hand.

'Twasa hishtoric booze, wazhnt it, John?'

'Twas Martin, twas.'

Shaking my hand, he assured me again, whatever the weather, he would be with me. On the coldesht day in winter he'd be with me. With me, if I needed him, on the hottesht day of summer.

We made it as far as the stand of trees. He wanted a smoke. We sat down.

Holding the lighted match vertically for a moment, it bloomed into an unflickering, perfect flame. It didn't illuminate the dark. Making way for it, the darkness of this dark December night withdrew from a brief distraction it had no need of.

And I wondered: would the universe be a brief distraction to it also?

Drawing hard on his pipe, having with difficulty put the lid on it, he retrieved, as much from his suddenly beneficent memory as from his overcoat pocket, the half bottle of whiskey he had bought.

I knew we'd be here for a long time.

Having oilskins on, I lay back on the leaf-strewn, twig-strewn earth under the trees, lime trees and chestnuts.

Come next April, this will be a sea of daffodils, I thought. A sea, it will sometimes seem, of yellow consciousness. In comparison, the consciousness with which we run the world, the consciousness we have settled for, will seem dull and grey. Can we believe Hindus and Buddhists? I wondered. Deep down in our own inner soil, in our thought-strewn, dream-strewn, desire-strewn soil − are there, deep down in us, bulbs of other kinds of consciousness? Bulbs that, given a chance, would bloom like Martin's match? Bloom in our darkness? Lotuses of other kinds of consciousness, crimson consciousness, sapphire-blue conscious-ness, blooming in the aqueous and vitreous humours of our eyes. I thought of the water lilies in the lake above at Lisnabrucka, their roots in the mud, their stems reaching up through the water, their blossoms in sunlight. Is it possible, I wondered, that I've never risen above the mud? When will my chakras open?

'You ha' me kilt, John,' Martin said. 'You ha' me kilt. Never once have I seen you at the holy mass in Roundstone, and you a grand man and a fine man and a great neighbour. You ha' me kilt, not believn in God, man or the divel.'

'All whom it may concern,' he said. 'All whom it may concern . . . '

I knew that whatever it was it was intended to particularly concern me.

'There was a man down Carna way one day, John, sittn on the seawall he was, smokn his pipe. A tourisht came along and shtopt and the man who was drivn rolled down the window and ashkt, 'Am I on the right road to Carna?' The Carna man took his pipe out of his mouth, he looked up the road and down the road and then, lookn at your man in the car, he said, 'You are, yeh, you're on the right road to Carna, but you're turnt the wrong way.'

'I'm on the right road alright, Martin. That's what you're telling me isn't it? I'm on the right road to heaven but, and tis a big "but", isn't it Martin, I'm turnt the wrong way.'

'Tis against your own feet you're walking, Martin.' I was trying to manage him across the cattle trap at the end of the avenue.

'Whisht,' he said. 'Whisht, John. God bless you, John, you're one way is one way but I can't help it can I if my one way wants to be every way?'

Awkwardly, all ways, we crossed over.

'I'm as drunk as a nine-wheel cart, John.'

'I know, Martin.'

Eyesight in this kind of darkness was a bad habit. Wholly ineffective though it was, it nonetheless distracted attention from hearing and touch – from information coming to us through our feet.

'Where are we, John?'

'On the back road.'

Where's that?

'At Ballynahinch.'

'Ballynahinch!'

'Yeh.'

'The corns is killn me.'

Knowing what this meant, I ignored the remark.

'Not long now till Christmas, Martin.'

'Christmas!'

'Yes.'

'I'm lamed, John.'

Having pity for him, but against my will, I groped my way, groping the air, to the side of the road and I sat him down on a low wall. I sat down myself.

'Where are we?'

'At the stable.'

'The shtables.'

'Yes.'

'God be with dh'oul shtables. God be with dh'oul shtables. Many and many and many is the fine bucket of fine cow's milk Ted and mesel milked in them oul shtables. Ted and mesel. Ted and mesel. The Lord have mercy on Ted, the Lord have mercy on Ted, the Lord have mercy on Ted – Say it, you son of a bitch, say it.'

'The Lord have mercy on Ted,' I said promptly.

The thought of it, Ted dead and buried below in Carna, it was all too much for him. He took to the bottle.

Given how the mood had changed, it was a sob of light that bloomed from his matchstick now. Briefly perfect, it died on its way to the bowl of his pipe.

And the whiskey wasn't helping.

'Wings I thought twould give me, John. But no. Fins it gave me. The fins of an eel it gave me. I'm an eel in a boghole, John.'

Is there, I wondered, thinking of Martin and me sitting there on a low wall in front of the old stables, is there a desolation that is independent of us? A desolation of the time or of the place. A desolation of the night. Up the road it had come and here we were, our mood inexplicably changed. We had a pipe, a sob of light, and a whiskey bottle. And we had two antiphons, the first being, the coldesht day in winter and the hottesht day in summer, the second being, no use hangn a man without a head.

It was our midnight mass. Our mass for the dead.

It was our mass for all that was dead in ourselves.

It was our mass for the bulbs that never sprouted in us.

It was our mass for the sea of yellow consciousness that never bloomed is us.

Kyrie eleison

Kyrie eleison

Kyrie eleison

No use hangn a man without a head.
No use hangn a man without a head.
No use hangn a man without a head.

No, not on a night as dark as this.

And yet it wasn't a destitute dark. Or a bereaved dark.

It didn't yearn to be sown with stars. A sense I had, walking beside the most silent reach of the Owenmore River, is that the metaphysical is sensuous, so sensuous that, its presence once felt, hearing, seeing, touch, taste and smell swoon away, knowing themselves to be empty distractions.

It occurred to me, crossing Lowry's Bridge, that we needed a hymn tonight. But I didn't give it much thought, because, here in Connemara tonight, Night was having its Easter. We were walking in an Easter of darkness. An Easter of Divine Darkness. The Dark as it was before it was trivialised by starlight and sunlight.

'Happy Easter, Martin.'

'Are you there, John?'

'I am, Martin.'

'Where are we?'

'At Lowry's Bridge.'

'I'm as drunk as a nine-wheel cart, John.'

'Me too, Martin. Me too. I'm as drunk as the nine-wheel cart that has come for to carry us home.'

Coming out onto the road to Derrada, Martin wanted to go left.

'No, Martin, no,' I said. 'That's the way to Ballinafad.'

He erupted. No whorin Kerryman would tell him the way home.

'Don't I know the place like the back of my hand. Washnt it here, right here at six o'clock one morning, that I met my father and mother, me comin from a wedding or a wake in Emlaghmore, and them, the two of them, drivn two cows before them to the auld cow's fair in Clifden. John! God bless you John, the random is on you . . .'

It was a long argument.

In the end, taking command, I stood him in the middle of the road and said, 'Now, Martin, that's your right ear, isn't it? And in it you can hear the sound of the Owenmore River, can't

you? And knowing this place as well as you do, knowing it like
the back of your own hand, you know that the road along the
river is the road to Derrada, you know that, don't your Martin?'

Having won the argument, I felt sorry for him. Hoping it
would mollify him, I reminded him of the song the young
woman had sung. I knew he would ask me to sing it. I sang it.

> Fare thee well old Ireland, a long farewell,
> My bitter anguish no tongue can tell,
> For I'm going to cross the ocean wide
> From my cottage home by Loch Shileann side.

> At the village dance by the Shannon stream
> Where Blind O'Leary enchantments played,
> No harp like his could so cheerily play
> And no one could smile like my Eileen gay.

> And how proud was I of my girl so tall,
> I was envied mostly by young men all,
> When I brought her blushing with bashful pride
> To my cottage home by Loch Shileann side.

> But alas! our joy twas not meant to last,
> The landlord came our sweet home to blast
> And he to us would no mercy show
> And he turned us out in the blinding snow.

> And no one to us would then open their door,
> O God! your justice, it was rich and sore,
> For my Eileen fainted in my arms and died
> As the snow fell down by Lock Shileann side.

> Then I raised my hands to the heavens above,
> I said a prayer for my life's lost love,
> O God of Justice, I loudly cried,
> Revenge the death of my murdered bride.

> Then I laid her down in the churchyard low
> Where in the springtime sweet daisies grow;

I shed no tears, for my eyes were dry
As the snow fell down by the graveyard side.

So fare thee well, old Ireland, fare thee well, adieu,
My ship is taking me away from you,
But where e'er I wander my thoughts will bide
At my Eileen's grave by Loch Shileann side.

'Enchantments played,' Martin said, lingering as though he were himself enchanted by every syllable.

We had a new antiphon:

en-chant-ments played!
en-chant-ments played!

Our midnight mass was growing.

We had already crossed Dervikrune Bridge when a sheep coughed on the side of Derrada Hill.

'What ails you?'

'Nothing, Martin. Nothing. Twasa sheep that coughed.'

'One of Petey's sheep?'

'Yes.'

'Hooze, I suppose.'

'Or fluke?'

'Fluke. Musht be fluke.'

He stopped, his head bowed. 'The Lord have mercy on Petey,' he said. 'The Lord have mercy on Petey.'

'Yes,' I said, instantly, 'the Lord have mercy on Petey.'

'Petey Welsh!' he said. 'A great neighbour was Petey. Petey was up there on Derrada Hill one day, a hill he walked every day, after sheep, but this day, no matter how hard he tried, he couldn't come down out of it. Thinkn that he had maybe stepped on a foidin mearai, he took off his coat, turned it inside out, put it back on, and now, with the greatest ease in the world, he found his bearings, walked down the hill, and in his own door.'

'*Foidín mearaí*, you call it, Martin?'

'That's what it's called, the sod of confusion, the sod of bewilderment. Tis well known they are out there, such sods. Shtep on one of them and you'll wander around bewildered and confused all night till the moon comes up, or you'll wander around, the random on you, till you take off your coat and put it back on, inside out.'

'Even if we take off our natures, and put them back on inside out I don't think we'll reach home tonight, not at the rate we're going, Martin.'

He didn't answer.

'How are you, Martin?'

'Never better. And yourself?'

'Fine, Martin, fine.'

'My besht friend, John. Lave it there,' he said, breaking free from me. 'Lave it there,' he said, shaking my hand. 'The coldesht day in winter and the hottesht day in summer.'

'That's right, Martin.'

''Tis, John, tis.'

'The river has a lovely name, hasn't it Martin?'

'The river?'

'Yes.'

'You mean the Owenmore?'

'Yes. The long, long flowings and the little falls of the Owenmore.'

'The Owenmore?'

'Yes, Martin. The long, long flowings and the little falls of the Owenmore would be soul to someone who came here having no soul at all.'

'No soul at all?'

'I had no soul at all, none that I was aware of, when I came here, Martin.'

'What was that?'

'A salmon, Martin. A salmon leaped.'

'A salmon?'

'Yes.'

'Salmon is whores, John. Ted and Mickey and Josey and mesel was up here poachin one night. We set the nets but then the thunder came, three or four big rolls of it and that was it. We knew that was it. We went home without a shcale. You know that, don't you? Salmon sink to the bottom when there's thunder. On a night of thunder twould take an otter to frighten them out of their lie, into the nets.'

'How are you, Martin?'

'Not good. To tell you the Chrisht's truth I'm not good. I'm by no means good. Tis like being blind.'

'Should we turn our coats inside out?'

'No.'

'No.'

'No. No use. Where are we?'

'At the quarry.'

'I don't believe it.'

'We're at the quarry, Martin.'

'I'll not believe it.'

'It's alright, Martin.'

'We could be somewhere awful.'

'We could be, Martin, but we aren't. We are passing the quarry.'

'You're shtubborn.'

"Tis you that's shtubborn, Martin.'

'We'll sit down.'

'No, Martin, no, we won't.'

'We'll wait for mornin.'

'We won't, Martin. God bless you, Martin, God bless you and spare you, but try to keep walking. We'll make it, Martin.'

'We're losht!'

'We aren't.'

'Where are we?'

'We're at the quarry.'

'I see no quarry.'

'Alright, Martin, alright,' I said. I stood him now again in the middle of the road. 'Can you hear the river, Martin? Can you hear the near roaring? That's the roaring at the eel weir. And the roaring farther on, can you hear that farther roaring, that's the roaring at Ted's place. Below Ted's place is Lynne's place. Below Lynne's place is my place. Round the corner from my place is Petey Welse's place. And up the bohreen from Petey Welsh's place is your place.'

'Places! Places! Places! You have me mezhmerizhed with places! Where are we?'

I faced him towards the quarry wall, or what I presumed was the quarry wall, and I told him to look straight ahead.

Staggering forward a little, he stood there, his hands resting on his knees, peering into the void. He was looking hard. I could sense how hard he was looking. He looked for a long while. At last, recognising something, he half called, half wailed, 'John! Are you there, John? Are you there, John? Oh John, sure I know well where we're now, John. I know well where we're now, John. But where the fuck are we?'

Sitting by my revived fire, having left Martin home, I attempted, if only initially, to come to terms with Martin's answer.

Is the whole world, I wondered, a *foídín mearaí?* Is every lobe of the human mind, dreaming and waking, a *foídín mearai?* And the easy assurance we almost always have of knowing where we are in terms of our whereabouts, is that, because it is so unsuspected, the most serious of all our bewilderments? I imagined it this way: asleep one night, here in my house in Derrada West, I slip into a dream. In the dream I experience myself to be in Iran, walking in arid country south of Isfahan. A man who comes towards me asks me, where am I? A few miles from Isfahan in Iran, I say, pointing to the blue dome of the Majis-I-Shah mosque. While my hand is still pointing I wake up and to my astonishment I'm not in Iran at all but in my room in Derrada West.

Waking up from dreaming. Waking up for waking.

Waking up from waking I realise that I'm not in a universe at all. I'm in the void. The void that is void of worldly reality. Cartographers of the universe are cartographers of that void. And so it is that I imagine myself talking to a modern astronomer, Carl Sagan, say.

'Astronomers have been looking at the universe for a long time now, Carl. During the last three centuries ye have been looking at it through optical telescopes and, more recently, ye have been listening to it through radio telescopes. Could you tell me, where are we?'

'Well,' I imagine Carl saying, 'the universe is composed of galaxies. Some of these galaxies are in clusters called megagalaxies. One of these galaxies is called the Milky Way. It is a spiral galaxy. It has a hundred million stars in it. On the outer arm of the spiral there is a star that we call the sun. Circling about that sun are nine planets. The fifth planet out is called the earth. That's where we are.'

To which I reply, 'Are you there, Carl? Are you there, Carl? Oh! sure I know well where we're now Carl. I know well where we're now, but, knowing where we are in terms of our whereabouts, what kind of knowing is that? One day, waking up from waking, you will find yourself pointing at the void.'

The only antiphons I was left with going to bed were:

enchantments played,
enchantments played,
foídín mearaí,
foídín mearaí.

Lying there, too frightened to fall asleep, I calmed and consoled myself with a Hindu parable:

Narada was a solitary. So altruistically motivated was he in his long and perilous quest for the Truth, that one day it was Vishnu, the Great God, the Great Mayin himself, who was standing in his door.

'Conscious of all that you have endured on behalf of all things,' Vishnu said, 'I have come to grant you the boon of your choice.'

'The only boon I have ever wished for,' Narada replied, 'is to understand the secret of your maya. It will please me, Holy One, if you show me the source, and the power over us, of the World illusion.'

As if to dissuade him, Vishnu smiled, strangely. But, having named his boon, Narada remained silent.

'Come with me,' Vishnu said, his strange smile not fading. Before long the arid land they were walking in had turned into a terrible, red desert. Moisture in their mouths was turning to ashes. Like the cracked rocks their minds were cracking.

Claiming he could go no farther, Vishnu sat down.

Seeking water for his God, Narada struggled on. To his great delight, the desert gave way to scrubland, the scrubland gave way to sown land and then, in a valley below him, there it was, a lovely green village.

He knocked on the first door. So enchantingly beautiful was the young woman who opened it that he instantly and entirely forgot what it was he had come for. It was strange. As if this house had always been his home, he sat and ate with the family. Early next morning he was working in their fields with them. At seed-sowing he worked. At harvest he worked. In the quiet time between seasons, he asked her father if he might have the young woman's hand in marriage. Three children were born to them, and when the old man died Narada became head of the household.

One year the monsoon rains were like the rains at the end of the world. Night and day there was no let-up. The river burst its banks and, struggling one night to reach the safety of higher ground, Narada's wife was swept away. Wailings in the chaos of waters was the last he heard of his three children. He was swept away himself but, miraculously, not to drowning. He was sitting on a hill. So terrible and red was the glare he couldn't open his eyes. Moisture in his mouth was turning to ashes. Like the cracked rocks, his sanity was cracking. Then, from behind him, he heard a voice, familiar but enigmatic: 'I've been waiting for almost a half an hour now, did you bring the water?'

Our Hindu parable.

Our Hindu

Ite, missa est.

Go, you are sent forth.

From O'Leary's enchantments and from Vishnu's enchantments.

From Loch Shileann side and the Green Village.

From Ireland and the World-Illusion.

From the *foidín mearaí*.

Too disturbed to sleep, I retrieved *The Dark Night of the Soul* by St John of the Cross from beneath my pillow:

In what fear and danger then must man be living, seeing that the very light of his natural eyes, by which he directs his steps, is the very first to bewilder and deceive him when he would draw near unto God. If he wishes to be sure of the road he travels on, he must close his eyes and walk in the dark, if he is to journey in safety from his domestic foes, which are his own senses and faculties.

Like Narada, I had stepped off the *foidín mearaí* and that was as dangerous as it was when, innumerable incarnations earlier, I had first set foot on it.

'No use hangn a man without a head, Martin.'
'No.'
'No use hangn a man without a head.'
The spell was broken and now, like the skull at the foot of the cross, I could hear the God, himself crucified, asking the question:
'I thirst. Did you bring the water?'

STEVE MACDONOGH
BY DINGLE BAY AND BLASKET SOUND

In Ballyferriter in Corca Dhuibhne
the Three Sisters rear their heads to look
out over the endless expanse of the sea.
In Ballyferriter in Corca Dhuibhne
cohorts of German boy scouts
shade their eyes towards Atlantic sunset;
beside them a gaggle of girls from Dublin
pile into the bus for the Dún an Óir.
No one grows up in Ballyferriter
without having one eye on the horizon
where sky meets sea and clouds roll in.
No one looks at the outline of the 'Dead Man';
no one watches the light change in the west
of an evening that moves from blue to yellow,
from yellow to gold, to pink, red and purple;
no one watches or looks without knowing
that on the far distant shore of the ocean
lies a new destination, a life and a home
in a place that will never be home.
In Daniel Keane's a Corkman plays fiddle,
a Yank talks folklore and a Dub sings;
at the bar three local men in their sixties,
their eyes sinking misty into pints.
There are Spaniards in the Blasket Sound,
seized by the great mouth of the sea
from ships of the Armada;
Blasket and mainland fishermen too,

pulled to death before their time.
And now it is the air that plucks
the young of Ballyferriter
not to death but to exile
from the gateways of farewell
at Shannon, Cork and Dublin.
No one grows up in Ballyferriter
without having one eye on the horizon,
or an ear to the phone for news from beyond
from sisters, brothers, friends . . .
And in the lands of opportunity
young emigrants dream
of becoming anything they wish,
yet know the reality of the possible.
But 'home', they say, 'is the only place
you can just be yourself.'
Home is the deep and healing well
to which they return; and here
they pay the round and dance
like pilgrims at an old pattern.
Few see the reasons for their exile,
few want to know, it being enough
to learn a new place in a new world.
At home it is only brochures
and bureaucrats that brag
about the wonders of deep ploughs;
the rest register vegetables
rotting on the dump or ploughed back,
register an industry of excuses
for management expenses.
The confident promontory forts
express a proud, developed past,
but their ruins watch over
seas whose produce is stolen
and fields where buachalláin buí
is the only crop.
The people of Duibhne are scattering
while wide-boys and apparatchiks
bray like satisfied donkeys,
reaping funds in the name

of heritage and co-operation.
Language is turned on its head:
money gives power to liars,
makes fools of true women and men.
No one grows up in Ballyferriter
without having one eye on the horizon
where sky meets sea and clouds roll in.

ROBIN FLOWER
from THE WESTERN ISLE (1944)

Seán Ó Duínnlé, though he lived to be an old man, had a shorter life than his coeval tower. He was not born on the Island, but came in, as did most of the ancestors of the present inhabitants, from the mainland. Of his early life before he commenced poetry nothing is recorded. It was in the years of the Great Famine that the vein of poetry first pulsed in him, and the story goes that indignation made him a poet. He was a great *spailpín* , a wandering harvester, who in the season would sling his reaping-hook over his shoulder and go *síos amach*, northwards into Kerry and Cork and even to County Limerick. On these wanderings he acquired an immense store of knowledge, tales and poems and sayings, all that vast flood of popular tradition which remained while Irish was still a living power, and of which we painfully collect the flotsam on the ebb today. In Ireland, as in medieval Europe, the tales spread among the people of the roads, the wandering harvesters, the tramping men and the beggars, the poor scholars and poets and migratory schoolmasters. Seán had graduated in this university of the road; and if we find, as I have found on the Island, a tale which can be traced back, through the jest-books of the Middle Ages and the sermon-books of the preaching friars to the Arabs of Africa, and through Persian books to ancient India, it is by such men that it has been carried from extremest East to farthest West, to die at last by a turf fire within hearing of the Atlantic wave.

He came back from one of his pilgrimages with money in his pocket, and, going into the Dingle sheep-market on his way through, saw a fine sheep that he fancied there. He had no sheep

at home, and he thought that this would make a fine beginning
for a flock. So he bought it, conveyed it to Dunquin, tied its
legs together, and threw it into a boat which carried them both
home to the Island. There he set it free on the hill, and settled
down in his house, at the top of the village where now is only
a bare space with no vestige of a human dwelling, and took his
ease after his wanderings, dreaming of the fine flock that was
to grow out of this single sheep. But he reckoned without his
neighbours. There were some evil characters in the village, and
before long news came to him that the sheep was killed and
eaten. Anger came upon him, to think of the wicked folk who
had eaten his dream of prosperity, and he swore he would have
the law of them at the court of Tralee.

There was another case pending over the unfortunate islanders.
In those days the Tiaracht was owned by a rich lady of the
Dingle neighbourhood named Betty Rice. The puffins used to
come from overseas at the beginning of spring to nest in that
solitary pyramid of the sea, and, when their young had come to
a certain stage in their growth they were fine fat birds, the best
eating in the world, and the best kitchen to potatoes that the
heart could desire. Betty Rice used to send a boat to the Island
at this season to kill the young of the puffins—*fuipíní* they were
called—for the servants on her farm to eat. The islanders held
that there was no property in the birds of the air; and, acting
on this excellent theory, they were wont to anticipate Betty's boat
and kill the *fuipíní* for themselves, for their potatoes were dry
eating without something to take the monotony off them. In the
year of Seán's misfortune, a boat had set out and spent a great
day among the birds; but when they were coming back to the
harbour in the evening, who should they see on shore but Betty's
steward, who had come to muster a boat's crew for the morrow's
expedition. They were caught red-handed; the steward went
home in a passion and told his mistress that there would be
nothing for her servants that year, for the islanders had made
a ruin of the rock and had left nothing behind them. She was
fit to be tied with rage, and swore that they should go to prison
for their robbery.

The time of the court came, and half the Island set out for
Tralee, some of them to argue the case with Betty Rice, and
others to meet the charge of the stolen sheep. Betty's prisoners

went to friends in Dingle, who appealed to her mercy, but she would not listen to them, and by her manner so angered them that they swore they would do their best to procure the failure of her cause. They went to Tralee with the islanders and spoke overnight to Daniel O'Connell.

On the next day, when the court was opened, the Counsellor, as the people called him, was there, sitting half asleep while Betty's man of law detailed the wrong that had been done to her and her servants. When he had finished, the Counsellor woke up and craved the hearing of the court. It was a case of something near to starvation, he said; the islanders had never done such a thing before, and would never do it again, but sheer need and the monotony of their potato diet had so afflicted them and their children that they had to go after the birds; but if they were set free this time the court might be assured that it would be long enough before they would set foot on that fatal rock again.

The eloquence of the great advocate prevailed on the court, and the islanders were liberated with a warning. Betty flung out of the court in a rage, and in her disgust never sent for the birds again, so that they were free game ever after.

BRENDAN KENNELLY
BABY

I find it interesting to be dead.
I drift out here, released, looking down
At men and women passing judgement
In the streets of that moneymad little town.
I enjoy the jokes about me, scribbled in the Gents,
I like the lads in suits, their smart legal faces,
I follow them through every argument,
I note their gas antics at the Listowel Races.
There was a hope of love at the back of it all
And in spite of clever men making money
That small hope still survives.
Will I name the clever men for you? Yerra, no.
I smile to watch them prospering to their ends
But thanks be to Jesus I won't have to live their lives.

They're trying to find out who killed me,
A fascinating exercise.
If I were water I'd let them spill me
And I'd run out of their eyes.
If I were fire I'd burn books of law
And half-burn the men who study them.
If I were air I'd slip into their lungs
And out of pity revive them.
If I were earth – O now that I think of it
That's what I am or am becoming
A little more quickly than you, and painlessly.
Tell me what you think it means to be alive,
I'd love you on that topic, expounding.
Being dead, I must find out, you see.

And yet, being dead, I may grow
To be a small, cheeky flower
Peeping through a veil of snow
On the scarred face of the earth
That never grows ashamed;
Or I may be
A blade of grass to nourish you;
Or a book
Wherein the nosey world may read
Of lovers' luck
And what it means to bleed.

When I was being formed in her body
I could tell she was kind.
My toes my fingers my eyes
My hands my bum my tiny mind
Knew that.
She carried me everywhere.
I couldn't see where I was going.
She did.

Streets, roads, fields, kitchens,
Bedrooms, chapels, small hotels, fish and chip places,
Glances of men in cars, glances
Of women both barren and fulfilled –
I'm buried now under the strong feet
Of money. I'm dead. I hope my mother
Sings and dances.

ÉAMON KELLY
THE PARISH CLERK

Now, Father MacGillacuddy's parish clerk was a tall graceful
man falling slightly into flesh, with a soft serene countenance
like you'd see on a tomcat after drinking a lot of milk. He was
slow and stately in his gait as he walked the road, a straight back
on him – you'd swear he'd swallowed a crowbar – and a long black
coat buttoned up to the chin. Ideas above his station! You could
forgive passing strangers for tipping the hat to him. Only for
he keeping out of the bishop's way people said he'd have got a
parish, for he was very devout.

When the bishop was coming for confirmation, Father Mac
put the parish clerk whitewashing the dry wall in front of the
house. The parish clerk got his bucket and set into work, making
short, lazy brush strokes in time with the slow air of a hymn –
you'd know by him that he'd love to give out benediction!

Hail Queen of Heaven the ocean star,
Guide of the wanderer here below,
Thrown on life's surge, we claim thy care,
Save us from peril and from woe!

Along came Father Mac. 'Very nice,' he said, 'singing at your
work and a hymn too. Very laudable, but show me the brush.
Don't you think this would be more suitable,' he said as he
changed the tempo to:

Father O'Flynn you've a wonderful way with you,
All the old ladies are longing to pray with you.
All the young women are longing to play with you,
You have a way with you Father O'Flynn!

The bishop was very old and didn't even notice the whitewash
when he came. The confirmation was held that year in the
outside chapel, five miles away from the presbytery, and the
bishop, because of his age, was short-taken during the ceremony,
and the parish clerk brought him out the sacristy door and
ducked into Hannah Maroya's. She had a contraption in the
yard; the missioners used to stay there. Hannah Maroya's man
that made it. He threw his hat down on the bottom of a tay chest,
drew the pencil around it, cut out the hole and propped the chest
over the stream in the back garden. But Hannah Maroya thought
that a bit draughty for a bishop, so she said, 'Wait a minute, my
Lord.'

She wasn't long away but the bishop thought it was an
eternity.

'This way, your Lordship.' she said and she took him down
in the parlour and there, with a good sup of hot water at the
bottom to knock the sting out of it, was a big chinaware pot and
a blessed candle lighting at each side of it! That was respect!

from Ireland's Master Storyteller (1998)

Bryan MacMahon
The Valley of Knockanure

You may sing and speak about Easter Week or the heroes of
    'Ninety-eight;
Of the Fenian men who roamed the glen in victory or defeat.
Their names are placed on History's page, their memory will
    endure;
Not a song is sung for our darling sons in the Valley of
    Knockanure.

Our hero boys they were brave and true, no counsel would
  they take;
They rambled to a lonely spot where the Black and Tans did
  wait.
The Republic bold they did uphold, though outlawed on the
  moor,
And, side by side, they bravely died, in the Valley of
  Knockanure.

There was Walsh, and Lyons, and Dalton, boys, they were
  young and in their prime;
In every house, in every town, they were always side by side.
The Republic bold they did uphold, though outlawed on the
  moor,
And side by side they bravely died in the Valley of Knockanure.

In Gortaglanna's lovely glen three gallant men took shade,
While in young wheat, full soft and sweet, the summer
  breezes played.
But 'twas not long till Lyons came on, saying, 'Time's not
  mine nor your'
But, alas! 'twas late and they met their fate in the Valley of
  Knockanure.

They took them thence beside a fence, to where the furze
  did bloom;
Like brothers so, they faced the foe, for to meet their dreadful
  doom.
When Dalton spoke, his voice it broke with a passion proud
  and pure;
'For our land we die, as we face the sky, in the Valley of
  Knockanure.'

'Twas on a neighbouring hillside we listened in calm dismay;
In every house, in every town, a maiden knelt to pray.
They're closing in around them now with rifle fire so sure,
And Dalton's dead and Lyons is down in the Valley of
  Knockanure.

But ere the guns could seal his fate, Con Doe had broken
through;
With a prayer to God, he spurned the sod, and against the
hill he flew,
The bullets tore his flesh in two yet he cried with passion
pure:
'For my comrades' death revenge I'll get in the Valley of
Knockanure!'

There they lay, on the hillside clay, for the love of Ireland's
cause,
Where the cowardly clan of the Black and Tan had shown
them England's laws.
No more they'll feel the soft winds steal o'er uplands fair and
sure,
For side by side, our heroes died, in the Valley of Knockanure.

I met with Dalton's mother, and she to me did say:
'May God have mercy on his soul who fell in the Glen today.
Could I but kiss his cold, cold lips, my aching heart 'twould
cure,
And I'd gladly lay him down to rest in the Valley of
Knockanure.'

The golden sun it is sinking now, behind the Feale and Lee;
The pale, pale moon is rising far out beyond Tralee.
The dismal star and clouds afar are darkened o'er the moor,
And the Banshee cried, where our heroes died, in the Valley
of Knockanure.

Oh! Walsh and Lyons and Dalton brave, although your
hearts are clay,
Yet in your stead we have true men yet to guard the gap today.
While grass is found on Ireland's ground your memory will
endure,
So God guard and keep the place you sleep and the Valley
of Knockanure.

LONELY BANNA STRAND

'Twas on Good Friday morning all in the month of May
A German ship was signalling beyond there in the bay,
'We've twenty thousand rifles here, all ready for to land,'
But no answering signal came from the lonely Banna Strand.

A motor-car was dashing through the early-morning gloom,
A sudden crash, and in the sea they went to meet their doom,
Two Irish lads lay dying there just like their hopes so grand,
They could not give the signal now from lonely Banna
    Strand.

'No signal answers from the shore,' Sir Roger sadly said,
'No comrades here to welcome me, alas! they must be dead;
But I must do my duty and at once I mean to land,'
So in a boat he pulled ashore to lonely Banna Strand.

The German ships were lying there with rifles in galore.
Up came a British ship and spoke, 'No Germans reach the
    shore;
You are our Empire's enemy, and so we bid you stand.
No German foot shall e'er pollute the lonely Banna Strand.'

They sailed for Queenstown Harbour. Said the Germans:
    'We're undone,
The British are our masters man for man and gun for gun.
We've twenty thousand rifles here, but they never will reach
    land.
We'll sink them all and bid farewell to lonely Banna Strand.'

They took Sir Roger prisoner and sailed for London Town,
And in the Tower they laid him as a traitor to the Crown.
Said he: 'I'm no traitor,' but his trial he had to stand
For bringing German rifles to the lonely Banna Strand.

'Twas in an English prison that they led him to his death.
'I'm dying for my country,' he said with his last breath.
He's buried in a prison yard far from his native land,
The wild waves sing his Requiem on the lonely Banna
  Strand.

Anonymous

Joseph O'Connor
from Hostage to Fortune (1952)

The civil war was on in Father Tim's time. It poisoned the air
and put an end to the friendly intercourse of neighbours.
Careless talk brought armed men to your floor in the night to
put a bridle on your tongue. The chance sight of an armed band
passing through the trees in the dark got you a tip on the
shoulder and an escort to take you in custody a long way from
the scene of operations. If you were not a combatant, you were
not to be seen or heard after sunset. You had better go to bed
and pull the blankets over your ears. Even Father Tim observed
the unwritten curfew, and went home before dusk.

One evening in February, one of those gloomy evenings of
low sky and unending rain we get in Killarney, he sat silent in
the armchair waiting for the rain to ease off to go home. He had
been jumpy all day, taking more snuff than usual and losing the
drift of his own stories. Katie had suggested a glass of bread soda
in warm milk to put him right.

'Me tummy is all right, ma'am; thanks, all the same.' He
stretched his arms high. 'Aw-aw-haw! I guess I'm tired. I had
a busy day. I better be going; that rain will never stop.'

A knock at the back door startled us all. Unexpected knocks,
or rather, unidentifiable knocks, were bad news for someone.
Katie got up and went out to the back kitchen to investigate.
Women have always intervened between their men and the
unknown in times of hot blood and strained friendships. Father
Tim and I sat listening to place the strange voice that mingled
with Katie's in a muffled undertone. Then we heard her say,
'Come on into the kitchen. There's no one here but friends.

Come on; you'll be all right.'

A young fellow, watchful and holding a heavy Springfield rifle at the ready, followed her into the kitchen. He was wet through and through. Water ran through his sodden hair and down his boyish face; it was already forming a pool at his feet where he stood inside the door, eyeing us suspiciously. He looked wretchedly woebegone in spite of the bold front he tried to present to us.

'Put away that rifle, young fella-me-lad,' said Father Tim. 'It might go off and kill someone. Sure, you wouldn't want that to happen. Would you now?'

The friendly words and Father Tim's disarming smile broke through the false front. The boy's tension dissolved. He slouched in his weariness and looked around for a corner in which to put the heavy rifle out of sight.

'Give it to me,' said Katie, 'and sit down there at the table. Give me your topcoat, too. It'll be drying at the fire while you are having a bite to eat. 'Tis easy seen you had no dinner today.'

'Why then, I hadn't, ma'am,' he admitted with a shamefaced grin. 'Nor breakfast, but as little. But a cup o' tay 'ill do me. I'm in a bit of a hurry.'

He wolfed the cold meat and mixed bread he got with the tea and gradually became the nice, wholesome lad he was by nature. At last he pushed his empty plate away, and looked at me.

'What place is this, if you pl'ase, sir? I'm a stranger to these parts.' Father Tim answered him. It was safer, he thought, for a priest to talk to strange gunmen than for me, an ordinary layman.

'You're in Fossa, my boy, and that is the boss of this house, Joe O'Connor by name. And may I ask you who you are and where you're from? You needn't tell me, o' course. That's up to yourself.'

'I'm Paddy Ahern, Father, from Glencar,' he said cautiously, as if on his guard.

'You're Paddy Astray-in-the-Rain, so,' said the priest in fun to put the lad more at his ease. The questions were putting him on guard again. 'But I think I can put you on the way you want to go.'

Paddy said nothing, but I noticed that he grasped the fingers of his left hand in his right and squeezed them, as pupils do under unwelcome questioning. Father Tim turned towards Katie.

'Could we go down in the room awhile, Paddy and myself? I want to have a talk with him, all by our two selves.' He threw an arm around the boy's shoulder to take him into the sitting room, but was taken aback when Paddy went to the corner for his rifle.

'Beg pardon, Father, but I swore an oath never to let the gun out of my sight as long as the sight was alive in me eyes to see it.'

'Bring it along, by all means. It can't hear what I have to say, but make sure it is harmless, while 'tis in the house.'

Katie drew the topcoat back from the fire and went off to put the younger children to bed, leaving me standing with my back to the hob and wondering what brought a Glencar volunteer so far off his own fighting ground. Was he straight or crooked, a real combatant on a mission to our fellows or a spy working through our area for our fellows to locate a leak? He looked honest and acted just as one would expect a straggler to act in a strange house. But you could never tell. He might have been chosen for the job on his ingenuous face. Better say nothing and ask no questions while he was in the house. He might be dynamite, that a loose word would detonate.

When he and Father Tim came back into the kitchen, all my doubts vanished. The boy was transfigured. His face radiated happiness; his voice trilled with it.

'God bless you, Father. I'm as happy as Larry now that I have my soul made, and I know where to find the lads.' He turned to me. 'Where's herself, sir? I'd like to shake hands an' thank her for the grand feed she gave me.'

'I'll call her down,' I told him, 'but before she comes I'd like to know if you can find your way from here in the dark. 'Tis no joke, even for ourselves, to poke our way through the woods and the bogs after nightfall. Mind I'm not asking you where you're bound for. I'd rather not know.'

'Ach! I'll manage all right, sir.'

'I don't think you will, Paddy,' said Father Tim. 'A strange fox wouldn't find his way to where you're going, through brambles and furze and swamps. You'll need a pilot. Won't he, Joe?'

A high-pitched noise caught our ears. The faint roar of armoured cars racing through the dark on a bloody mission, full of nervous, amateur soldiers ready to fire at shadows. Too well he knew the rumbling roar and the sudden, promiscuous shooting into hedgerows that might conceal an ambush. Paddy knew it too.

'Staters!' he rasped out. He tensed like a setter at point, his teeth showing and his head outstretched to listen. He tiptoed to the front door and waited at the crouch as the oncoming roar grew louder. When it zoomed past, shaking the house and the ground under it to the foundations, we all let loose the breath we had held imprisoned in our excitement and loosed our joints. Paddy came back into the kitchen and slung the strap of the Springfield over his shoulder.

'They're going *west*, Father. I must be going, if... ' He stopped short, lest he say too much for my ears. It was clear, from the stress he had put on the direction, that he and the priest understood what that implied. Katie had joined us while the cars were passing and had brought Seán with her from the bedroom. Seán is our second boy. I was glad. I wanted to offer him as a guide, but one never knows how a mother will take a suggestion which puts her son's life in peril. Rather than risk the humiliation of her refusal, I had decided to go part of the way with the Glencar boy, though I knew Seán knew the woods much better than I did. I helped Paddy into his topcoat.

'Seán here will go with you till you're clear of the rough ground.' I told him as soon as I saw Katie getting Seán's raincoat from the kitchen rack. Paddy shook his head and said he'd make no more trouble for us; he had upset us enough as it was. Katie pushed a paper pack of bread and meat into his pocket and tapped him on the cheek.

'You go first, Seán,' I said. 'Keep to the fence till you get up into the wood and wait in the trees till Paddy joins you. He'll tell you then where he wants to go. We don't want to know. It'll be better for us if we are raided and questioned afterwards. Off with you.'

The young rascal was delighted with his importance. He winked at the young partisan and went out the back way into the dead rain and dark, as gay as if the sun was shining and he was off on the hunt with the terriers. When I thought he had reached the wood I said, 'Well, Paddy, we may as well be going,' and took him by the hand. He shook mine warmly and went across to Father Tim and bent his knee for a blessing. Katie took his two hands in hers and said:

'Give me your mother's address and I'll write to her for you.'

'My mother is dead, Ma'am,' he said and added when he saw the tears well up in Katie's eyes, 'But you could write to my sister. Ahern, Glanbehe, will find her. There's but the one family of Aherns in Glanbehe.'

I led him out past the cowhouses to the field gate and showed the way along the hedge up the hill to the wood where Seán was waiting.

MÁIRE MHAC AN TSAOI
OÍCHE NOLLAG

Le coinnle na n-aingeal tá an spéir amuigh breactha,
Tá fiacail an tseaca sa ghaoith ón gcnoc,
Adaigh an tine is téir chun na leapan,
Luífidh Mac Dé ins an tigh seo anocht.

Fágaidh an doras ar leathadh ina coinne,
An mhaighdean a thiocfaidh is a naí ar a hucht,
Deonaigh do shuaimhneas a ligint, a Mhuire,
Luíodh Mac Dé ins an tigh seo anocht.
Bhí soilse ar lasadh i dtigh sin na haíochta,
Cóiriú gan caoile, bia agus deoch,
Do cheannaithe olla, do cheannaithe síoda,
Ach luífidh Mac Dé ins an tigh seo anocht.

COLLETTE NUNAN KENNY
WEEKLY SMILE

I cried inside and out
When our teacher's cane struck knuckles.
Giggled when she hoisted
Her crumpled tweed skirt
To heat her backside,
Showing her sky-blue bloomers –
To fearful gaping eyes.
Beside her a milk bottle exploded,

Her sleeping dog yelped
Scattering shocked rats
Like furry splinters
Across a bare room.
Even window panes shuddered
At her volcanic sneeze.
Every Friday 'Black Babies'
Were given pennies under her
Haughty watchful gaze.
When he nodded his thanks
We saw her weekly smile.

DONAL HICKEY
FR DINNEEN: THE DICTIONARY MAN

One of the most brilliant scholars to emerge from Sliabh Luachra in the past two hundred years was, indisputably, Fr Patrick Stephen Dinneen. Because of his utter commitment to the revival of the Irish language, he became known as an tAthair Ua Duinnín and is best remembered for his famous Irish–English dictionary which was first published in 1904, with the larger edition coming in 1927.

But he was much more than a lexicographer. He was also a writer, a poet, a mathematician, a controversialist and a complex, eccentric personality – to say the least. The son of struggling tenant farmers, Matthew and Mary Dinneen, who had about ten hungry acres at Corran, four miles south-west of Rathmore, he was born on Christmas Day 1860. One of ten children, Patrick attended Meentogues national school where his uncle, Michael O'Donoghue (Mick the Master), was teaching. A reserved boy, he was a dedicated pupil and a lover of books and learning – traits in keeping with the traditions of the Dinneen clan. He remained a pupil in Meentogues until he became a monitor whilst in his teens.

Irish was still spoken in the area and was the main language of the Dinneen household. In his youth, Patrick, growing up in the aftermath of the Great Famine, personally experienced hardship and eviction and the family was forced to move house on a few occasions. His father was a sheep dealer who travelled widely to fairs in the south and was a shrewd, intelligent man of the world. Mary Dinneen was a hard-working, deeply religious woman and, according to folk tradition, was regarded by many people as a saint.

Having shown obvious potential as a student, Patrick was tutored in Latin by Fr Cornelius O'Sullivan, Rathmore, and entered the Jesuit (Society of Jesus) Novitiate at Milltown, Dublin, in September 1880. He took an honours BA degree in modern literature and mathematics at the Royal University and was conferred with an honours MA in maths in 1889. He then studied theology at Milltown and was ordained a priest by Archbishop Walsh at the Jesuit Church of St Francis Xavier, Gardiner Street, Dublin, in July 1894. For a few years after he taught at Jesuit colleges including Clongowes and Mungret, often making the journey on foot from Clongowes to Maynooth college where he would copy the work of Kerry poets from manuscripts.

An tAthair Ua Duinnín's first poem and novel were published around the turn of the century and he began collecting the poems of Aodhagán Ó Rathaille at that time. The year 1900 marked a turning point in his life for he left the Jesuit order. The reasons he did so remain unclear. The order has strongly rejected claims that he went his own way because of differences over the dictionary, or a dispute about royalties from his varied literary activities. The more likely reason is that Ua Duinnín, who was strong-headed, a loner and sometimes difficult to get on with, found it hard to accept the discipline of the order. Nor would he be able to give the high level of commitment he desired to the revival of Irish whilst a member of the order.

According to the superior of the order, an tAthair John J. Coyne:

De réir mar a bhí se ag dul in aois, mhothaigh an tAthair O Duinnín saol an Chumainn rud beag dian air, toisc é bheith aonaorach ón nádúr agus toisc e bheith beagáinín corr ann fein freisin. Thaobhaigh a chuid uachtarán leis an rud a rinne se, óir chonachtas dóibh gurbh fhearr an úsáid a d'fhéadfaí a bhaint as a chuid talanna taobh amuigh d'ord crábhaidh.

[As he was growing older, Fr Dinneen felt the life of
the Society a little difficult because he was detached
by nature and also because he was a little unusual in
personality. His superiors agreed with what he did
because it was clear to them that greater use could be
made of his talents outside a religious order.]

As Fr Coyne remarked in that last sentence, an tAthair Ua
Duinnín made the best of use of his freedom to develop his
talents outside the order. As well as his first dictionary, he
produced fifteen books in Irish, gave Irish classes and visited the
Gaeltacht early in the century. He became a leading figure with
Conradh na Gaeilge in the national revival and was active in that
body's publications committee with Pádraig Pearse. He continued
to turn out scholarly works and was a prolific contributor to
Gaelic magazines, newspapers and periodicals of the day.

This love of the language shines through in his writings as
the following extract, published in the period between 1902 and
1904, illustrates:

The language is the root on which all the other
elements are grafted and it is the language in its living
state, and not the language as found in books and
manuscripts, that is the true basis of this general
national revival . . . The national language is the poor
man's literature and folklore, it is his history and
tradition, it reflects what he knows of his own country
and the outer world, it is his fund of music and
song . . . I for one, had I to choose, as I hope I never
shall have to choose, between the ruins of Tara and
the living Irish tongue, would not hesitate to say,
perish Tara, but leave me the language of the Gael in
its living state.

Other people worked with him on the Irish–English dictionary,
among them J. J. O'Kelly (Sceilg), who was a prominent
journalist and author in Dublin at the time. and a leading
collaborator in the production of the dictionary. A native of
Valentia, County Kerry, O'Kelly was Minister for Education in
the Republican government of 1921. O'Kelly reported that Ua

Duinnín was in poor health at the time, looking gaunt and anaemic and acting very moodily – the weight of the undertaking was taking its toll. But the completion of the dictionary brought much mental relief and, according to O'Kelly, 'there was an instant improvement in his general health which, to our general delight, was maintained until he became quite robust.'

Most of Ua Duinnín's time was spent in the National Library in Dublin and he was also involved in the establishment of Coláiste na Mhumhan, the first training college for teachers of Irish. He had several rows with other members of Conradh na Gaeilge, until finally he left the organisation in 1909, following the controversy over the attitude of some bishops to compulsory Irish in universities.

The scholarly priest has many achievements to his name, including what was regarded as the first novel in Irish, *Cormac Ua Conaill* (1901). From a Sliabh Luachra viewpoint he gets the kudos for focusing attention on the work of the Munster poets, notably Ó Rathaille and Ó Súilleabháin, about whom he would have heard a great deal in his youth when they would still have been very much alive in the folk memory. Stones from Eoghan Rua's house were, according to local tradition, used in the building of the school which the priest had attended as a child in Meentogues.

The priest did invaluable work in collating, editing and publishing collections of poems of the poets from his area. He also went to endless lengths to get his hands on the manuscripts which were then available.

An tAthair Ua Duinnín wrote several school textbooks, plays and essays, and a number of poems. Though not generally known as a poet – his talents were channelled in other directions – he could have held his own with the best of them had he devoted more of his time to writing poetry. The following is the first verse of his 'Looking Out For The Spaniards':

> Sorrow darkens Desmond's valleys, sorrow muffles Desmond's
> hills,
> Sorrow's voice in plaintive cadence sounds through Desmond's
> thousand rills;

For the spoiler's hand has cursed her, from the Galtees to the
    sea,
Where all shattered and dismantled smokes in ruins proud
    Dunbuidhe.

From the time he left the Jesuits, an tAthair Ua Duinnín's status
as a priest was *suspensus a divinis*, which in effect meant that he
could not say Mass or administer the sacraments. The Jesuit
order stressed, however, that he left with full permission and that
later in his life he rejected an offer to allow him celebrate Mass
again. For more than thirty years, he was a personality on the
streets of Dublin and made friends with people of every station,
including the poor. He was also known as a priest who loved
children and enjoyed quizzing them and passing on his knowledge
of Irish to them. Sceilg recalled how he would visit his home
on Sunday afternoons, rarely calling without chocolate for his
children, with whom he felt as much at home as their elders.
Sceilg said he was excellent company, quite at ease in all circles,
sparking with repartee and punning with all the abandon and
sprightliness of youth.

Towards the end of his life, he lived in lodgings at
Portmarnock, a seaside suburb to the north of Dublin, and took
the train each morning to the City centre, with the National
Library his usual destination. A distinctive figure, he used to
wear an old-style top hat, a long black coat, baggy pants and
good strong boots, and carried a bundle of books and papers in
his arms.

Whenever he returned to his old home at Corran, he would
work in a little room attached to the house (which is no longer
there). But he didn't spend all his time in the room and there
are people who can still picture in the mind's eye the solitary
figure in black walking along the road westwards towards
Killarney.

He died on 29 September 1934 in St Vincent's Hospital in
Dublin, having collapsed a few days before in the National
Library. The last rites were given to him by a Jesuit. Whatever
about his split from the Jesuits, an tAthair Ua Duinnín remained
a regular churchgoer throughout his life, had conservative views
and often defended the position of the Church in public
controversies.

His funeral was a noteworthy occasion in Dublin. Solemn requiem Mass was celebrated in the Jesuit church in Gardiner Street, and amongst the huge attendance were Éamon de Valera and Seán T. O'Kelly, both of whom went on to become presidents of Ireland, as well as leading academics and literary personalities of the day.

He was laid to rest in the poets' corner of Glasnevin cemetery.

A monument in Killarney bears testimony to this day to the achievements of Ua Duinnín. He was responsible for getting the statue of a *spéirbhean* erected close to the spot on Martyr's Hill in the town where the west Kerry poet, Piaras Feiritéar, was hanged by Cromwellian forces in 1653. The monument also honours the Glenflesk poet Seafraidh Ó Donnchadha as well as Sliabh Luachra's Aodhagán Ó Rathaille and Eoghan Rua Ó Súilleabháin. Ua Duinnín is also credited with having had erected a plaque commemorating the poets at Muckross Abbey in Killarney.

from STONE MAD FOR MUSIC
THE SLIABH LUACHRA STORY (1999)

SÉAFRAIDH Ó DONNCHADHA AN GHLEANNA
DO CHUALA SCÉAL DO CHÉAS GACH LÓ MÉ

'*Ciarraíoch cráite áirithe éigin*'
Do chuala scéal do chéas gach ló mé
is do chuir san oíche i ndaoirse bhróin mé,
do lag mo chreat gan neart mná seólta,
gan bhrí gan mheabhair gan ghreann gan fhónamh.
Adhbhar maoithe scaoileadh an sceóil sin,
cás gan leigheas is adhnadh tóirse,
athnuachadh loit is oilc is eólchair',
gríosadh teadhma is treighde móire
díothú buíne chríche Fódla,
lagú grinn is gnaoi na cóige,

mar do díogadh ár ndaoine móra
as a bhfearann cairte is córa.
Mór na scéil, ní héidir d'fhólang,
ár ndíth do ríomh lem ló-sa;
fuair an fhéile léim a dóthain
is tá an daonnacht gach lae dá leónadh.
Ní bhfuil cliar in iathaibh Fódla,
ní bhfuilid aifrinn againn ná orda,
ní bhfuil baiste ar ár leanabaibh óga
's ní bhfuil neach le maith dá mhórdhacht.
Créad do-ghéanaid ár n-aos ónna
gan fear seasaimh ná tagartha a gcóra? –
atáid gan triath ach Dia na glóire
is priosáil dá ngriosáil tar bóchna.
Greadán maidne dearbhadh an sceóil sin,
gabháil gharbh na n-eachtrann oirne;
maith 'fhios agamsa a t-adhbhar fár ordaigh –
d'aithle ár bpeaca an tAthair do dheónaigh.
Dá mbeith Tuathal fuadrach beó againn,
nó Féidhlimidh do thréigeadh tóra,
nó Conn, fear na gcath do róchur,
ní bhiadh teann an nGall dár bhfógra.
Ní mhaireann Art do char an chródhacht
na Mac Con ba docht i gcomhlainn
ler scanrnadh clann Oilealla Ólaim –
is séan do Ghallaibh ná mairid na treóin sin.
Is léan do Bhanba marbhadh Eóghain,
an tréanfhear fa céile don bheódhacht.
Ní bhiadh neart gan cheart ar fhódaibh
ag na Gallaibh meara móra;
do bhiadh neart is ceart is cródhacht,
do bhiadh smacht is reacht fá róchion,
do bhiadh rath ar ar san bhfómhar,
dá mbeith Dia le hiathaibh Fódla.
D'imigh Brian na dtriath ón Bhóirmhe
do bhí tréimhse ag Éirinn pósta;
ní bhfuil Murcha cumasach cródha,
i gcath Chluain Tarbh ba taca re comhlann.
An tráth fa láidir na treóin sin,
Clann Chárthaigh 's an Tálfhuil treórach,

Níor shaoileadar Gaill dá bhfógra
tar toinn nó gach laoi thar teórainn.
Atáid na danair i leabaidh na leóghan
go seascair sámh, go sádhail slómhar,
bríomhar biamhar briathrach bordach,
coimtheach cainteach sainteach srónach.
'S is é rún is fonn na foirne,
dá mhéid síth do-níd rér bpórne,
an drong bhíos ag ríteach leó againn,
súgradh an chleasaí, an chaitín chródha.
Is trua le chroí 's is tinn, dar Ólainn,
nuachar Chríomhthainn, Chuinn is Eóghain
suas gach oíche ag luí le deóraibh,
gan lua ar an gclainn do bhí aici pósta.
Teagh Tuathail, mo-nuar! do toirneadh,
cró Chuinn gan chuimhne ar nósaibh,
fonn Fhéidhlimidh tréithlag tóirseach,
iath Iúghaine brúite brónach,
Achadh Airt fá cheas gan sóchas,
críoch Chobhthaigh fá oghaim ag slóitibh,
clár Chormaic, fáidh foirtil na gcomhfhocal,
fá orchra, lean d'fhothram deóra.
Mo léan! ní hé tréine an tslóigh sin
ná buirbe na fuirinne ó Dhóbhar
ní neart naimhad do chaill ár ndóchas
acht díoltas Dé atá i ndéidh a chóra:
peaca an tsinsir, claoine an tsóisir,
aithne Chríost gan suim 'na cómhaill,
éigean bhruinneall briseadh pósta,
craos is goid is iomad móide;
neamhchion gnáth is táir ar ordaibh,
réabadh ceall is feall is fórsa,
éamh na bhfann gan chabhair gan chómhthrom
ag saobhlucht sainte is caillte ar chomharsain;
tréigean Dé le séada is seódaibh,
gléas le séantar gaol is cóngas
géill don neart 's an lag do leónadh,
claonadh breath 's an ceart fá cheó a chur.
Cé tá an eangsa go teann ag tórmach
fá láimh leabhair na nGallsa nó againn,

áilim Aonmhac tréan an hÓighe
go dtí an ceart san alt 'nar chóir dhó.
Is bíogadh báis liom cás mo chomharsan
na saoithe sámhdha sásta seólta,
i dtír ba ghnáthach lán de thóbhacht
Ite, vade dá rá leósan
is gan acht cairde ó lá go ló acu;
dár gcur uile i dtuilleadh dóchais
dá mbeith fábhar dá fháil dóibhsin
's gan ansoin acht *till further order.*
Galar gan téarma is maothchás mór liom,
greamanna géarbháis cé táim glórach
scaipeadh ar an bhféin dár ghéill clár Fódla
is Eaglais Dé dá claochlá is ordaibh.
Atá scéimh na gréine go nóna
fá éiclips ó éirgheas ló dhi;
atáid na spéire i ngné dá fhógra
nach fuil téarma ár saoghail fófhada.
Fuair an cairdeas bás a dhóthain –
le lucht séad ní géar an sceólsoin;
ní léir dhom éinneach ar mh'eolas
noch do-bhéaradh réal chum bróg dhom.
Fágaim sin ar chur an Chomhachtaigh
Aonmhac Muire gile mhóire
as a bhfuil ár n-uile dhóchas,
go bhfaghaidh sinne is sibhse cómhthrom.
Aicím Áosa rí na glóire,
mar is fíor gur tríonas fhónas,
soilse laoi agus oíche d'ordaigh,
do dtí an ní mar shaoilim dhóibhsin.
Amen
                    [Ceangal
            Gríosú cnead, laghdú ar neart,
                síorú ar cheas bhrónach,
            fíorú ár bhfear do gheimhliú i nglas,
                foilsiú a n-acht oirne,
        críochnú ár bhflaith do dhíorú amach
                ar dhroim tonn tar bóchna,
        do mhínbhrúigh iag mo chroí dúr leasc
            re maothú ár ndearc ndeórach.]

BRENDAN KENNELLY
MY DARK FATHERS

My dark fathers lived the intolerable day
Committed always to the night of wrong,
Stiffened at the hearthstone, the woman lay,
Perished feet nailed to her man's breastbone.
Grim houses beckoned in the swelling gloom
Of Munster fields where the Atlantic night
Fettered the child within the pit of doom,
And everywhere a going down of light.

And yet upon the sandy Kerry shore
The woman once had danced at ebbing tide
Because she loved flute music – and still more
Because a lady wondered at the pride
Of one so humble. That was long before
The green plant withered by an evil chance;
When winds of hunger howled at every door
She heard the music dwindle and forgot the dance.

Such mercy as the wolf receives was hers
Whose dance became a rhythm in a grave,
Achieved beneath the thorny savage furze
That yellowed fiercely in a mountain cave.
Immune to pity, she, whose crime was love,
Crouched, shivered, searched the threatening sky,
Discovered ready signs, compelled to move
Her to her innocent appalling cry.

Skeletoned in darkness, my dark fathers lay
Unknown, and could not understand
The giant grief that trampled night and day,
The awful absence moping through the land.
Upon the headland, the encroaching sea
Left sand that hardened after tides of spring,
No dancing feet disturbed its symmetry
And those who loved good music ceased to sing.

Since every moment of the clock
Accumulates to form a final name,
Since I am come of Kerry clay and rock,
I celebrate the darkness and the shame
That compel a man to turn his face
Against the wall, withdrawn from light so strong
And undeceiving, spancelled in a place
Of unapplauding hands and broken song.

A Note to 'My Dark Fathers'
In 'My Dark Fathers' I tried to define my own relationship with
Irish history. One day I attended a talk given by Frank O'Connor
about the famine that happened in Ireland in the nineteenth
century and had such harrowing effects on the Irish character.
I was trying, at the time, to write a poem about that history
which I had lived with since childhood. During his talk,
O'Connor spoke of a traveller's (Mrs Asenoth Nicholson's)
description of a woman dancing on the Kerry shore:

> This woman, who danced before me, was more than
> fifty, and I do not believe that the daughter of
> Herodias herself was more graceful in her movements,
> more beautiful in her complexion or symmetry, than
> was this dark-haired matron of the mountains of
> Kerry.

This image struck me immediately. The woman was the entire
people, capable of spontaneous artistic expression; capable of it,
that is, before the famine. But then came the terrible desolation.
O'Connor made me aware of Peader O'Laoghaire's *Mo Sgéal
Féin*, where there is the following description of the dead and
the dying:

> You saw them there every morning after the night out,
> stretched in rows, some moving and some very still,
> with no stir from them. Later people came and lifted
> those who no longer moved and heaved them into
> carts and carried them up to a place near Carrigstyra,
> where a big pit was open for them, and thrust them
> into the pit.

[225]

This is the 'pit of doom' in my poem. There is a description of a man named Paddy bringing his wife, Kate, from the workhouse back to his hut:

> Next day a neighbour came to the hut. He saw the two of them dead and his wife's feet clasped in Paddy's bosom as though he were trying to warm them. It would seem that he felt the death agony come on to Kate and her legs grow cold, so he put them inside his own shirt to take the chill from them.

In the poem I identify this woman, dead from famine disease, her 'perished feet nailed to her man's breastbone', with the woman comparable to the daughter of Herodias, dancing on the shore in Kerry. Perhaps the most frightening consequence of famine is described in George Petrie's collection of *The Ancient Music of Ireland* – the terrible, unbearable silence. To my mind, this meant not only the silence that followed racial suffering akin to what Hitler inflicted on the Jews, but it meant that Ireland became the grave of song. I was witnessing the death of the dance:

> This awful, unwanted silence in which, during the famine and subsequent years, almost everywhere prevailed, struck more fearfully upon their imaginations, as many Irish gentlemen informed me, and gave them a deeper feeling of the desolation with which the country had been visited, than any other circumstance which had forced itself upon their attention.

These images of the pit, the woman, the rows of dead, the terrible silence, were in my mind after hearing O'Connor talk. Shortly afterwards, I was at a wedding and a boy was asked to sing. He did so, but during the song he turned his back on the wedding party. In his averted figure I saw the woman who forgot the dance, the land that rejected its own singers. I think I understood then the sad farce of Irish censorship, the modern middle-class commitment to complacency and swinish apathy,

Joyce's nightmare, the ferocious bitterness of many Irish poets and artists I have met, the contemporary fear of the silence of the self (a grotesque parody of song is preferable to no song at all), and behind it all, the responsibility of the poet to explore and celebrate the entire thing. If 'My Dark Fathers' achieves the clarity I hoped it would, that is what it means. Or at least, that is part of its significance, because no human being can say exactly what a poem means. Only the poem can say that.

CLAIRR O'CONNOR
DREAM OF MY FATHER

It was his hand, a giant hand.
I was sitting in it, his thumb
my armrest. Market day;
smell of fresh dung,
cows jostling with cars in the Square,
farmers in wellington boots and caps,
tomato complexions bruised from the wind.
The Protestant clock stuck at a quarter past ten.
He put me down among the stamping horses.
I did not cry.
Their hooves blocked out the sky.

DICK SPRING

My earliest memories are of Strand Road, Tralee. I was always conscious of being in a political household. It was a relatively small house and my parents had lived there since 1944, about a year after they got married. It was the centre of activity in that street and the door was always open. In those days one could keep the key in the door without worrying too much about it. My father, Dan, had a great expression on Sundays when we went for a family drive. He would ask, who was going to mind the house? What he meant was, who would be around if anybody came looking for the TD?

I particularly remember evening times doing lessons around the table. Three or four of us fighting for space with our school books and my father would be doing his constituency work at the top of the same table. It was never a quiet house as there were always people coming and going. People would just walk in at any time of the day.

We lived next to a nursing home and in those days we had no phone, so when my father would need to make a call, he would do it from the nursing home. There was a famous Nurse Regan who used to take telephone messages from him. In those days also there was no such thing as free postage for TDs, so another memory was being sent off at night for twenty threepenny stamps and if you couldn't get them at the local shop we often had to go out to Blennerville with my father in the car where there was a small post office which stayed open late.

You ask how I opted for the law. Well one thing I decided at an early stage in secondary school in Roscrea was that I was not going to do anything related to the sciences. Boyle's Law was enough for me. I felt more comfortable with the humanities, English, history and commerce subjects.

From early days the idea of law and politics looked like a natural pattern. In those days lawyers seemed to dominate the Dáil. I think my father was keen that, if any of us was going into politics, we would have a legal training. I did not decide for a long while which side of the profession I would go for, solicitors or barristers, but I chose the latter.

I believe my brother Donal could have been equally as effective a politician as I. But it was timing and where I was at a particular time that led me into politics. I found myself free to help in elections in my teens when I was on platforms at a very early age. I can recall speaking in Eileen Desmond's campaign when I was a student in Trinity. I'm not sure that my Trinity speeches won her many votes in mid-Cork, I must confess.

My first memory of canvassing was in Dingle in the 1957 campaign when I was seven years of age. I distinctly remember walking around Dingle, which was in North Kerry in that election. It became part of the South Kerry constituency for subsequent elections. Politics was in the blood even then, but that didn't stop me from attempting to go away from it. In my twenties I wanted to be as far away from Ireland as I could be.

I went off to the States for a few years and that was to get away from living life in what I thought was a fish bowl. You were always conscious of being a TD's son. He was going before the public and he would not want us to do anything, as anything which we might do would be a reflection on him and he would ask us to mind ourselves. There was that sort of pressure. You would be conscious. It wouldn't be a fear of the law, but it was your father as he would take anything personally. He expected not to get any reports on us that might reflect on him as a public representative. This meant we were more restricted.

There wasn't a minister in Kerry since the thirties until my appointment to cabinet in the eighties. There is an expectation in Kerry and people are very conscious of that. People, irrespective of their political affiliations in Kerry, are very proud to have somebody from the country at the cabinet table and that has come back to me very strongly, particularly in the past twelve months. People are entitled to believe that Kerry should get its share of the action and a reasonable share of the national cake. I am conscious of that. There is a question of balance. What you want to ensure is that you get your share and not to be forgotten and that you don't get it at the expense of others.

I have set goals in relation to certain services: hospital services, education services, the whole question of roads. I am not talking just about potholes but about the whole road network, as all these services have a very important bearing on people's lives. Jobs is probably the key question. If you provide jobs, a lot will follow from that. As Minister for Foreign Affairs I am obliged to travel a good deal, but on any of my trips I am always looking out for potential investors to help in our fight against unemployment.

Irrespective of politics, if you were to offer me a choice in the morning about where I would like to live, I would still opt for Kerry, probably a site overlooking Tralee Bay.

The quality of life in Kerry is as good as you will find anywhere, particularly in relation to facilities and in terms of resources. I wouldn't say to my children, you must live in Kerry. They have a great affinity with the United States, where their grandparents live. They are very much half Irish and half

American. Kristi and the children enjoy living in Kerry. Tralee has great amenities, is close to the beaches and is a great town to live in. My eldest, Aaron, is thirteen, Laura is eleven, and Adam is seven. Aaron shows a flair for art and writing; maybe he should have a law degree as well just in case.

I went away to boarding school in Roscrea when I was twelve and I then went on to Trinity. I then went on to America; then I came back to Dublin; then back to Tralee. So here in Tralee they have always been used to me coming and going. People know I have to move at a very fast pace. Maybe on a Thursday night, the odd time, I might go down for a drink, people would see me on the television news giving an interview in Brussels or somewhere earlier that day. People know that I work hard and I enjoy working hard.

When I have a night off, I prefer to have a night at home. If I was allowed to relax I think I might enjoy two pints in one of my local pubs. If I finish early, say eight or nine at night, I really like to put my feet up and enjoy a good book. I usually read a book about the country I have just returned from, not having had the time to get to it before travelling to that country. I was in the Gulf recently and I am still reading *Arabian Sands*. I like reading political and travel books.

But for real relaxation I find nothing better than a good walk on Banna Strand, which I associate with my childhood. We probably had the only car in Strand Road for a long time and my father would often take a carload of us and the neighbours' children to Banna. He would often go by the bog in Kilflynn, where we would do a few hours' work. The big treat on getting to Banna would be Nash's lemonade and Marietta biscuits. Banna Strand still has a great magic for me.

People ask me if my bad car accident had any effect on my outlook. It didn't have the same effect Augustus John experienced when he dived into the Rover and banged his head and started producing better-quality material after it. Initially it didn't affect me, but at times you stand back and just realise that it was a close call. Even in the tightest of political adversity, it puts things in perspective. There are times in my business when you feel the world is coming down on top of your head, and you think to yourself: what if the lights had gone out in 1981 when I had that accident as I was being driven to Dublin? I think my philosophical approach is that any morning you can get out of bed is a good morning as there are many people who have been in lesser accidents and suffered smaller injuries who cannot.

Being in that kind of situation gives you a resilience; now I am not sure if that resilience had been there prior to the accident, but I feel sure it is there now. I can use it to my advantage. It is probably one of those shattering experiences which you can turn to your own benefit.

Getting back to the Dáil, the Dáil is not responsive to the demands of Irish life. For a long time in the seventies and eighties, the courts were the main legislative dynamo in this country. People were making constitutional advances through the courts rather than through the Dáil. For a period the legislators were behind the people, but I think that has changed in recent years. I think we need a more open and tolerant society, rather than a confessional society, and to let people run their own lives with as little interference as possible. I think the Dáil has improved. You wonder if a system set up and modelled on the Westmionster model is the best way to get things done in an age of confrontation and mass communications. I would put a question mark there as I don't have an answer – what is the alternative? I think politicians work within the constraints of the day. If somebody came along and said, 'Look, tailor your work to the needs of the people on a day-to-day basis', I think politicians would go with that. You operate within a system. Overall I feel that many changes are still necessary in relation to how we get things done and how government works on a day-to-day basis.

There is a huge workload and rural politicians have a totally disjointed life, some of the week in Dublin and the weekend in your constituency, working in both places. Kerry is distant from Dublin, but thanks to Kerry Airport I can travel more easily than when I was previously in government. Then I had to spend eight to ten hours on a road trip to Dublin. Nowadays I can get up in an hour and a half without the pressure of being on the road.

Kerry is the premier tourism county, but we have to be careful to keep industrial employment and maintain the balance between industry and services. We are holding that balance. The Regional Technical College in Tralee is making a tremendous impact. Apart from employing 170 staff and having thousands of students, it is giving Kerry a training base for prospective employers. We can't compete totally with the universities, but it does give a skills base. I would like to see a high-quality tourism industry in Kerry. We will never get the mass market. The quality of the facilities will remain high. There is scope for cultural tourism in Kerry, ranging from Skellig Rock to the literary traditions of the county. FÁS in Tralee is also a very important asset.

You ask me to compare working as Tánaiste with Garret Fitzgerald and Albert Reynolds. Well, you will have to wait for me to write my own book to find the answer to that one. It is well known that they are men of totally different styles, backgrounds and political interests. It is important that the Taoiseach and the Tánaiste work well together – this involves cabinet cohesion and effective decision-making. I had a good working relationship with Garret Fitzgerald and have a good one with Albert Reynolds. Never forget that you are talking about two leaders of two different parties.

In the day-to-day working relationship we have exchanges every day. Our offices are only fifty yards apart down the corridor. Our staff are in close contact. Given my portfolio in Foreign Affairs, there is obviously a huge link with the Taoiseach's office. It is working. It's two people who try to get the chemistry right. But it is strictly business.

I don't see us ever going back to the single-party government. I think there is a certain irony in what is happening at the moment. If we can maintain the momentum we have attained now in May 1994 and build on the achievements to date, it will ironically be Fianna Fáil who will have proven that coalitions work, despite fifty years of campaigning that coalitions couldn't work.

I think the norm is going to be parties cooperating. One of my main aspirations in politics is to get Ireland away from the traditional divide of the Civil War. If we can work with Fianna Fáil, that may also throw up the prospect of Fine Gael working with Fianna Fáil. That may well happen in the future. I'd like to get rid of that divide. Let the parties be able to work with one another and bury what basically was the division of the Civil War.

It is still in the background. At local level there would be some enmity between Fianna Fáil and Fine Gael. Our generation has no association with it, wants to move on from that and look to the future rather than the past.

My real frustration in politics is the fact that the violence in Northern Ireland isn't stopping and that those living in Northern Ireland cannot get out of bed some morning and say we must settle this conflict, we must compromise before another person dies.

Why is Ireland on the world map? Because of the conflict in Northern Ireland. There are a lot of other reasons why Ireland should be on the world map in terms of what we are producing, not just in terms of commercial goods, but also in the arts. There is an artistic explosion taking place in this country in all forms of drama, art and film-making. That is why we should be on the world stage. For example, somebody who has just returned from Yugoslavia was telling me that all they knew about Ireland in Yugoslavia was U2 and the IRA.

Getting back to Kerry, I think the fact that we are so far from Dublin means there is this strong pride that we can do it ourselves. That is best reflected on the football field. And if you look at the administration of the State, Kerry has always had a very strong Kerry component. Numerous secretaries of government departments are Kerry born and educated. There has always been a very strong tradition in education in Kerry, looking for quality education as the key to progress.

I often talk to pupils in local schools and I tell them they are living in a country where the quality of life is as good as you will find in any other country in the world. The opportunities are limited, but if you are prepared to put in the work and get the qualifications, you can be an achiever here. But one has to have the discipline to make the effort. Why are so many Irish people successful abroad? If we could keep that energy here and get stuck into producing the goods in Ireland, it could be a much better place.

I have no problem about people going abroad to see the wider world. But be prepared to come back. Kristi has come from Virginia to live here and I am fortunate in that she happens to be a very strong woman. I don't wish to sound condescending, but I don't think you could bring your average American woman into a North Kerry political family and expect that it would be plain sailing. But I am fortunate in being married to a strong woman who has made a career out of ensuring that our kids have at least one parent around as much as possible. She has made many sacrifices.

Ongoing innovation has marked out Tralee's annual International Rose Festival. They're a great core of people. They will have internal difficulties, but without a split. There is enormous commitment and the festival is now well supported by the town. It puts the town on the national and the international map. The Rose selection is a great show and very professional. It is a fair reflection of how things in Kerry are done, when people set out to do things. The Aquadome is a £4.4 million project and it will probably be the most modern facility of its kind in Europe. It will be open twelve months of the year. There is no future in eight-week tourism.

Europe is not going to be a paymaster indefinitely, and the Structural Funds we are getting this time won't be there again. We have a chance between now and 1999 to build our road structure, to develop our education base. I think this is the last big round-up and what we have to make sure is that when it is over we can stand on our own two feet.

It is serious business to make sure we can compete with the best. There is a great opportunity there. We will be spending over the six-year period £7.2 billion, which we wouldn't have otherwise.

Dick Spring was Tánaiste at the time this article was written.

from VOICES OF KERRY (1994)
EDITED BY JIMMY WOULFE

Tomás Rua Ó Suilleabháin
Amhrán na Leabhar

Tomás Rua, schoolteacher and poet had been transferred from Derrynane Bridge to Portmagee. He placed his huge and valuable library of books – both printed and in manuscript form, all leather bound – and his clothes on a boat which was travelling from Derrynane Bay to Valentia Harbour. He himself travelled by road. Unfortunately, the boat overturned near Carraig Eibhlín Ní Rathaille just outside Derrynane Bay and his priceless library was lost. 'Amhrán na Leabhar' also known as 'Cuan Bhéil Inse' was his poetic response and is probably his best known song which is also very popular with pipers as a slow air.

Go Cuan Bhéil Inse casadh mé
Cois Góilín aoibhinn Dairbhre
Mar a seoltar flít na farraige
Thar sáile i gcéin.
I Portmagee do stadas seal,
Faoi thuairim intinn maitheasa
D'fhonn bheith sealad eatharthu
Mar mháistir léinn.
Is gearr gur chuala an eachtara
Ag cách mo léan!
Gur i mBord Eoghain Fhinn do chailleathas.
An t-árthach tréan.
Do phreab mo chroí le hatuirse
I dtaobh loinge an taoisigh chalma
Go mb'fhearrde an tír í 'sheasamh seal
Do ráib an tséin.

Mo chiach, mo chumha is m'atuirse!
Mé im iarsma dubhach ag ainnise
Is mé síoraí 'déanamh marana,
Ar mo chás bhocht féin!
Mo chuid éadaigh chumhdaigh scaipithe,
Bhí déanta cumtha, ceapaithe,
Is do thriaill thar thriúcha Banban

Mar bhláth faoi me dhéin.
Iad bheith imithe san fharraige
Ar bharr an scéil,
Is a thuilleach acu sa lasair
Is mé go támach trém néal;
Ba thrua le cách ar maidin mé
Go buartha, cásmhar, ceasnaithe,
Is an fuacht a chráigh im bhalla mé
Gan snáth ón spéir!

Ní hé sin a chealg me
Ná chráigh mé arís im aigne,
Ach nuair chínn féin fuadar fearthainne
Gach lá faoin spéir;
Neart gaoithe aduaigh is anaithe
Is síon rómhór gan aga ar bith,
Tinte luatha lasrach,
Is scáil na gcaor.
Chrom an uain ar shneachta 'chur
Le gála tréan
Ar feadh deich n-uair gan amharca
Le fáil ar ghréin.
Na doitheanna cruadha peannaide
A líon rómhór den ghalar mé,
D'fhág suim gan suan ar leaba mé
Go tláth i bpéin!

Dá shiúlfainn Éire is Alba
An Fhrainc, an Spáinn is Sasana,
Agua fós arís dá n-abrainn
Gach aird faoin ré,
Ní bhfaighinnse an oiread leabhartha
B'fhearr eolas agus tairbhe
Ná is mó bhí chum mo mhaigheasa
Cé táid ar strae.
Mo chreach! Mo chumha ina n-easamh súd
Do fágadh mé!
Is mór an cúrsa marana
Agus cás liom é
Mallacht Dé is na hEaglaise

Ar an gcarraig ghránna mhallaithe,
A bháigh an long gan anaithe
Gan ghála, gan ghaoth.

Bhí mórán Éireann leabhartha,
Nár áiríos díbh im labhartha,
Leabhar na Laighneach beannaithe
Ba bhreátha faoin spéir.
An 'Feirmeoir' álainn, gasta, deas,
A chuireadh a shíol go blasta ceart,
Thug ruachnoich fraoigh is aitinn ghlais
Go gealbhánta féir.
Scoirim as mo labhartha
Cé chrádar mé,
Is ná cuirfeadsa aon ní ar fharraige
Go brách lem ré;
Moladh le Rí an nAingeal ngeal,
Mo shláinte arís a chasadh orm,
Is an Fhoireann úd ón anaithe
Gan bá 'theacht saor!

EOGHAN CORRY
PÁIDÍ Ó SÉ: THE VENTRY SENTRY

They call him 'Pee-Oh'. Ó Sé was a determined and stubborn young fellow, typical of Ventry, renowned as the longest-lasting stronghold of the Vikings in Ireland. Páidí was fitness-proud when he was first hailed as a fine football prospect at the age of 15. He was to be found running along the beach, again and again. He keeps it up. Páidí Ó Sé's Ventry pub has pictures of Páidí, facing the Atlantic on cliff-faces and beaches, wild surf all around him, sometimes a ball in hand.

In 1974 South Kerry played West Kerry in a championship match. Mick O'Dwyer, the veteran footballer was marked by one of the under-21s who was not long out of St Brendan's College and a contender for the county team. Páid Ó Sé was born on May 16th 1955, when O'Dwyer was already winning medals with South Kerry. Mick O'Dwyer was so impressed by Páidí's determination, aggression, and skill that he earmarked him for future reference.

A minor for three years – 1971, 1972 and 1973 – Páidí was on the fringes of the under-21 team that won the All-Ireland championship, and made his senior inter-county debut when he came on as a sub in the drawn National League final in 1974. He played in the replay against Roscommon in the familiar right-half-back position. The *Kerryman* hailed the arrival of Ó Sé as a badly needed 'attacking wing-back'. Trying to stop him attacking so much was to become a key to Kerry's strategy in future years. Their first move was to put him in at corner-back against the new All-Ireland champions, Dublin, in a Killarney league match in November 1974. Páidí Ó Sé turned on his best display so far. But being corner-back in the championship against Tipperary did not keep him out of the action. A long Páid Ó Sé delivery out of defence led to a John Egan punched pass in the second half.

He was one of three successes against Meath in the league quarter-final. When Kerry trailed Tipperary in the 1975 championship, Páidí launched the kick that was punched over the bar for the equaliser. He was moved to wing-back in the Munster final, and marked David Hickey successfully in the 1975 All-Ireland final.

Páidí was a character at the young team's training sessions. He had no time for conventional medicine, he told masseur Owen McCrohan, and pinned all his recovery chances from injury on a drop of seal oil.

In 1977 Páidí had a good year and was man of the match against Cork, setting up Ger Power for the first goal in the Munster final. But at mid-field against Dublin he went adrift, picking up a booking on the way. His solo runs against Roscommon in 1978 and a great performance on David Hickey enhanced a growing reputation. In 1980 Ó Sé was to make his most significant block. Ten minutes from the end of a stormy All-Ireland final against Roscommon, Charlie Nelligan blocked down a great shot from Michael Finneran, Aidan Dooley drove the rebound back along the ground, but there was Páidí, full of grit and tenacity, to fling himself headlong, land and manage to keep the ball off the ground to avoid a certain penalty. He stood the battleground on the goal-line, and put the ball out for a 45.

It earned him an overdue All-Star in 1981.

Páidí was a warrior, responsible for the foul that almost gave Sligo a penalty goal in his first All-Ireland semi-final, responsible for an occasional hard knock on bruised Corkmen and Dubliners down through the years. In 1979 he was booked for a personal foul in the semi-final, and although he was best of the backs in the All-Ireland final he was booked in the first half and sent off in the second for clutching Anton O'Toole around the neck. A dozen Dublin players said the decision was wrong in the dressing room afterwards. But one or two of them were nursing bruises with Ó Sé initials on them. In 1981 he was to complain that his reputation begat a spot of hard-mannery on the part of opponents: 'I'm a marked man.' Marked man or not, the crowd loved it. Before the 1984 All-Ireland final even got under way Joe McNally gave Páidí Ó Sé a shove. Ó Sé pushed him back. The crowd looked on in amazement at the two men psyching each other to the strains of 'Amhrán na bhFiann': *'Anocht a théam sa bhearna baoil . . . '*

Páidí loved to solo forward in quest of scores. He scored after 11 minutes in the All-Ireland final, and had a good last quarter against Offaly in 1982. When Sheehy missed the penalty that day, Ó Sé began to fear the worst.

It was as captain that he put in his best displays for Kerry. When West Kerry ended a 35-year famine by winning the 1984 county championship, their first since 1949, the chance of a captaincy loomed up.

Lispole won the West Kerry championship, and the club nominated Páidí as county captain. It fulfilled an ambition. O'Dwyer, on the brink of retirement after his success in the Centenary final, said he was not going to let down his old colleague. O'Dwyer stayed on, for Páidí's sake.

In the 1985 championship he held Dave Barry scoreless from play, held O'Hanlon and Nudie Hughes scoreless in the twice-played semi-final against Monaghan (winning an RTÉ man-of-the-match award in the replay), and held Joe McNally scoreless in the All-Ireland final. At the end of 1985 he was back on the victory rostrum with West Kerry after the county final.

He was influenced by those county championship matches with West Kerry, especially matches against Austin Stacks. They taught him a lot about the passion of championship football.

When the West played the Stacks there was a great town-versus-country conflict involved: a miniature Dublin versus Kerry; the championship system in Kerry blooding its hounds.

Ó Sé trained West Kerry in later years on his nights off. But his relations with his club, Gaeltacht, were stormy from his youth. He felt they did not allow him the leeway he deserved for the county team; they wanted him for matches they desperately needed to win to avoid relegation; he needed time off after the near-total commitment that the county team, never mind West Kerry, demanded. Ó Sé has his detractors in the local club, but they are languishing in the third division of the league and are crying for his talents to help them escape.

Ó Sé was finding the prospect of getting fit more and more difficult as the years went by. As early as 1979 O'Dwyer paid tribute to his efforts: 'Páidí was in a state of near-collapse, but he never tries to dodge it.' In winter-time Páidí would do his stints of running along the cliffs and beaches near his home, puffing and panting to the backdrop of some of Ireland's most spectacular scenery. Church Cross is just a hundred yards from three long miles of golden Ventry beach, the ancient site of Cath Fhionntrá, where Fionn mac Cumhaill defeated the King of the World. 'Páidí rowing to the Blaskets' was an ideal photo opportunity for photographers in All-Ireland week.

He was also tempted to try his hand at other sports. While he was based in Limerick, he played rugby with Young Munster. But in Ventry there are no other sports.

Páidí Ó Sé was once described by Con Houlihan as 'as happy at corner-back as a shepherd dog with a block tied to his neck.' He was also unhappy at centre-field in 1977. His happiest position was at wing-back, roaming forward to pick off an occasional point. In 1985 he served as long-range free-taker for a time and even took a penalty in an open draw championship match against Cork.

Having started out life as a garda, Páidí eventually took the lease on the famous Kruger Kavanagh's pub in Dún Chaoin in 1981, and learned that being a famous footballer can pay off. Kruger had been a tireless Dún Chaoin man who held a commission in the American army and counted boxers, gangsters and politicians among his friends. The guesthouse was already famous as a stopping point, Ireland's most westerly spot. The lease was highly successful, as Páidí felt the pub and his own reputation helped complement each other. It was always a short-term arrangement, until Kruger's nephew returned to take the reins.

In 1985, at the third attempt, he used his reputation from Kruger's to get a licence for a new pub at Church Cross. In May he started building it. In July it was finished, a violent white apparition in the 'bungalow bliss' mould, opposite the family grocery shop.

Ó Sé wanted Charlie Haughey or Matt Connor to open the place. Haughey did the honours eventually. The end of the counter is reserved for trophies, the right-hand wall for the proprietor's Bank of Ireland All-Star portrait. The video machine was reserved for All-Ireland final re-runs with the publican's express wish: 'I hope there won't be any more horror movies.'

Páidí entertains there. Players call round on the day after matches. Four or five would always rent out a caravan in Ventry for the week after the All-Ireland and enjoy themselves after the abstemious summer. Football visitors, many from the north, would call. They do the round of pubs: Pat Spillane's in Templenoe, O'Dwyer's in Waterville, Doyle's in Tralee, Páidí's in Ventry. You have to be in residence or the visitors will be disappointed.

Páidí was captain in 1985. Before the match against Cork in the 1985 Munster final, he was bubbling with rage in the dressing-room, bouncing the ball from his hand to the floor: 'Let's get these Corkmen.' He finished with a massive bounce. The ball rebounded into the ceiling, smashed the light bulb and plunged the place into darkness. The fearsome Kerry 15 burst into laughter.

'The years flew past. I suppose it was easy when you were winning All-Irelands or Munster championships, and getting trips and medals every year. If we had won one medal in 1975 and another ten years later, it would probably seem like a very long time.'

from KINGDOM COME (1989)

SIGERSON CLIFFORD
THE GHOST TRAIN FOR CROKE PARK

*Trains left the more distant parts of Ireland at midnight on Saturday
for the Gaelic Football Cup Final in Dublin on Sunday. Kerry and
Kildare were popular rivals.*

I'm living here in London not as young then as I was,
And the poor skull neatly tonsured at the top
And the crow's feet at the corners kicking strongly for my
              ears,
I'll be lucky if 'tis at my ears they stop.
But this London that I mentioned, though 'tis fair enough
              by day,
Can be as lonely as a fiddle after dark;
Ah, the old town beneath the mountain, 'tisn't poor I was
              but rich
On the night we took the ghost train for Croke Park.

Wisha, God be with you, Kerry, where they never lock the
              fire,
With the kettle singing on the sooty crane,
And my mother – 'Will you hurry now and leave the mirror
              sound,
Myko Lairy's passing Hurley's with the train.'
Then the quick run out the half-door of that houseen down
              the lane,
And I dressed as neat as any Excise clerk
With the blue suit and the brown boots and the medal on
              its chain,
The night we took the ghost train for Croke Park.

Ah, I mind it all so clearly when the stars danced on the hills
With their faces scrubbed and shiny, and the powder in their
              hair,
And the tide across the sandbanks turning lazy in its sleep,
And a lonesome curlew, bubbling here and there.

We all met at Keating's corner when 'twas midnight by the
        clock –
Casey's mouth-organ made music like a lark –
And we gave the Kerry warcry as we marched north two by two
To lep aboard the ghost train for Croke Park.

And the ree-raw at the station, faith, 'twas better than Puck
        Fair
With the shouldering, and shouting, and the din;
We had bottles full of lemonade, and biscuits, for the boys,
And a brew beagawneen stronger for the men.
Dan Keeffe blew on his whistler and he waved the green flag
        high,
Beyond by Foxy Jack's place I could hear a shepherd bark,
And we shouted 'Goal for Kerry!' at the inoffending sky
As the ghost train left the station for Croke Park.

We spread a coat between us and we handed out the cards,
Sure we always brought the deck for thirty-wan,
But 'tis talk we did, not gamble, for with football in our brain
The card game closed as soon as it began.
'Twas Kildare that we were playing, and we gave them little
        chance,
As the cards lay face-down, idle on our laps,
And 'twas Kerry, Kerry, Kerry while the stars kept up their
        dance;
All you'd see on the Kildare side was our caps.

Bob Doyle, who knew his football, swore that we'd win by
        a goal,
The Tailor felt we'd get there by a street,
And myself, may God forgive me, thought by twenty points
        or so,
'Wisha, five or six is plenty,' said John Pete.
'Their backs will never hold us if they lepped up to the
        moon,'
And Dave Hanley nodded wisely at Pat Clarke.
All the experts had the scoreboard chalked up ere the ball
        was thrown,
In the ghost train steaming proudly for Croke Park.

Then the soft grass and the sunshine and the marching of
    the bands,
With the green and gold flag fluttering over all,
There's Con Brosnan running swiftly and our Sheehy shooting
    low,
And Larry Stanley jumping skyhigh for the ball.
It put the heart across me when the leather grazed our goal,
And my throat with shouting tattered like a scraw;
There was never sweeter music than that final whistle blown,
And the board said, let me whisper, 'twas a draw.

Loud and long we held the inquest steaming home from
    Dublin town,
And we wrote down who kicked well and who played poor,
But John Pete agreed with me that all the luck was with
    Kildare,
And Bob Doyle maintained we'd win the next time sure.
We still chalked up the scoreboard, and the chalk was green
    and gold;
Said the Tailor, white teeth grinning like a shark,
'Sure, we only took their measure and we'll cut the cloth to
    scale
When we take the Ghost Train three weeks for Croke Park.'

DEIRDRE SHANAHAN
THE BEACH ON SILHOUETTE ISLAND

After the nurse had been in, she went up to her father, in the
nursing home. How many times she had climbed the stairs to
his room overlooking the sea, chosen because he liked to hear
the gulls and have the smell of salt.

He lay against the pillow with his glasses off and teeth on
the locker at the side, so that she noticed his unwrinkled, soft
skin. One of the few things he was proud about.

He turned away in a hurry, as if hiding something.

'Ah . . . Catherine.'

'Yes.'

'I thought it was the old girl, Maguire.'

'What were you doing?'

'Nothin'. Have ye bought me any baccy?'

'You know you're not allowed any.'

'Ah, I'll never have a puff again. And there's nothing to do here.'

'You could listen to the radio.'

'Me left ear's going deaf.'

'Read the papers then.'

'I hate them, The old ink comes off on me hands. Haven't you any little thing of yer own to show me? Have ye any sketches?'

He shifted around in the bed, as if he would give anything to be out of it.

'I forgot. I'll bring them next time.'

The pad of drawings lay on her sofa in the flat, where she had just been looking at them and where she wanted them to stay, not have to carry them aournd like old memoirs, rough sketches of Carson before he left. She was trying to capture those difficult dark skin tones, the places on his cheeks where his skin became almost milky, those times when his jet eyes could look fearful and sad at the same moment. She spent hours smoothing lines on the creamy thick paper paler than skin, letting her crayon follow the grain. If it could come to a kind of life, if she could seize and capture that head as she once had, holding it in her arms, cradling it in her arms, stroking his rough pad of hair after they made love, when she was slow and dizzy with excitement. She smoothed her index finger over his wide cheekbones, defining his face.

'A shame ye mother can't see them.' He coughed, jerking up against the sheets. She would've liked to.'

'Yes. I suppose so.'

The word hung between them and he lay back with his left cheek on the pillow, like a baby in a great calm with the faint bellow of the waves below. Him, her and the waves, this was all that was left of the summer before, when she had turned to them, as a kind of refuge after the break with Carson and joined them at a cottage on the coast of Kerry.

She walked along the shore, up and down on the rocks after a breakfast of thick bread and butter salt rich as sea spray. She wanted to be alone to find company in the rocks. In a pool there was a clump of oyster shells with their deep silver interiors like fish scales or mother of pearl brooches. The sea crinkled in to a blister, rare for that time of year. Waves pounded and fell away with open arms.

'Where've you been, dear?'

Her mother came up, hot and out of breath, her face strained. She raised an arm to her hair and caught the trails of flour in her curls.

'Won't you come in now for your breakfast, dear. It's chilly and you haven't a cardigan on. You'll get a cold like your father.'

Her voice rose and sank in the waves.

Catherine stayed on the rock till the wind was cold. Dammit she would get this ridge of outcrop and the peculiar kind of light, the way she wanted it. Being by the sea was exhilarating and had opened up her senses like a first rush of pleasure. The demands of her mother irritated. Why couldn't she go away and let her work. There must be plenty to occupy her in the house or the small village, after all it had been her idea to visit the place of her girlhood seeking out old friends from over fifty years before. She had never understood her daughter sketching, 'scribbling' as she called it even on holiday.

'But I have to. To keep alert, alive to what's around me.' Her mother stopped in the midst of a field and nodded.

'Yes dear, I suppose so. But can't you have a rest for a day or so. All that close work can't be good for your eyes.'

'I can't. I can't.' Catherine yelled.

'What's that?'

'Nothing.'

'You want to be careful. You'll be washed away.'

She patted down her long flowery apron and returned to the house.

Catherine rose a little from her chair. Yes, his watery grey eyes were open.

'You never came to see her much.

'I did.'

'Not when she needed you.'

'Oh Dad . . .'

'She asked for you, at the end. You were all she had, not like her sister with the half dozen of them running around.'

'I was travelling.'

'You were always off.'

'I'm back now.'

'You'll be off again soon. Why did you go that long way?'

'Carson . . . wanted to see the part of Africa his family came from.'

'It's a shame you weren't at that place when I rang, like you said you would be.'

'I couldn't help it . . . he wanted to go somewhere different.'

'Which one was he anyway?'

'The one who had the studio next to me.'

'Ah that fella. The black one.'

'Dad.'

'Wasn't it him?'

'Yes.'

'And what happened? How is it ye didn't make a match?'

'He . . . went away . . . we . . . just broke up.'

'Ah well, you're old enough to know your own mind. We can't keep tabs on you any more.'

And they couldn't. Somehow she was never around, she knew last Christmas she had been in India, Easter it had been Senegal. She spent her father's last birthday in Mexico driving through scrubby villages with shacks and chickens and women in black who looked for all the world, except for their tan, as if they might have belonged in the extreme west of the Kerry she remembered from her youth. She was always travelling from one place to another, always away, at one end of the earth when she should have been at the other. Travelling and art was the attraction with Carson. He managed to combine a love of both and in himself was like the two, either on the move, quick, agile and fleet or quiet and at rest, totally absorbed in his work.

She walked through the woodyard with him, in London, as he told her about the varieties of wood, veneers, grains of wood he was considering for his next piece. He had got to know the manager and had worked out good deals with him for off cuts, odds and ends they would not sell. She liked him better this way, when he wasn't working and obsessive about time, never wanting to go out. In the winter he had stayed many nights in the studio, not even going home to her, but grabbing a few hours sleep between two and six am before setting to work.

'Slaves,' he told her. 'But different from Michaelangelo.'

When he finished, it was he who suggested they go away.
'I need to live a bit so I have something else to put into my work.'
'Okay.'
'What about a week in Brittany?'
'I can't.'
'Why not?'
'My mother.'
'Yeah.'
'She's not well. I haven't seen her for a while. I'd like to go over.'
'You don't usually bother.'
'That's the trouble.'
'So . . .'
'I can't come.'
'Why don't you go this week when I'm in Birmingham.'
'She'll be out of hospital later and that's when she needs me.'
'Go if you want to,' he added in a hurt, childlike voice.
'She is my mother.'
'Okay, Okay.' He strolled off into the next aisle of wood, with his hands in his pockets.

Damn him, she thought. Why does he have to be like that, just when I need him.

It's all right We can put it off for another time. It's only France. We can go somewhere else. Somewhere really exotic. Would you like that?'

You left in June for Morocco, Egypt and on to Kenya. At the east coast he wanted to go, changing their plans on to Silhouette Island. They had been there six days but she would always know on which one her father had phoned, because she would never forget the day she saw the dogs.

Carson lay in the whiteness of the fine sand.
'The shoreline's so straight? It just goes on and on,' she said.
'Crazy isn't it?'
He moved close.
'Uhhhmm. You smell nice. The sea.'
'No. Diorissima.'
'Oh.'
He encircled her with his arms, flecks of sand on his legs and the pinky brown soles of this feet.

'What's the matter? Don't you want to?'

'Eh . . . no.'

'I feel . . . '

'What?'

'Nothing . . . just . . . not now.'

'Please yourself.'

He rolled off.

A gutful emptiness rose in her. Usually she loved the secrets and tricks his hands played on her, but that day she felt different. He stood up.

'I'm going for a walk.'

She watched Carson stride off, a tall dark shape like an arrow piercing the horizon. She watched as if she could not run after him. For moments afterwards, as she turned the pages of her book it felt as if he was still there. As if he was the quietness. She looked again and there he was way out near the crush of waves gazing out, as if the future was on the horizon, and one that was not with her.

'You'll strain your eyes, Catherine.'

'I want to get this before it changes.'

Her mother came up close, looking over her shoulder. She took off her glasses.

'What is it?

'A man.'

'Oh.'

'What part of him is it? He has no eyes?'

'His back.'

'He's a big bulk of a fella and isn't it dark?'

She looked up to see her mother topple side to side.

'Ma, are you all right?'

'I'll just sit down.'

'What's wrong?'

'I don't know. The heat I expect. There hasn't been a good summer like this in years.' She fell exhausted into a chair holding her glassed in her hand. Frayed and tired, her skin was thin and loose. In that instant Catherine wanted to hold her, hug her into rejuvenation, make her into the woman she had known when growing up, strong, resilient, constant as the stars.

'I think I'll have a lie down.'

'Yes ma. That's the best thing.' She held her round the waist and took her upstairs, going slowly so that she did not falter, until she stopped.

'But you father will be back at lunchtime and he'll want something.'

'Never mind, lie down, while you have the chance.'

'I must get him a sandwich.'

'He can do that.'

'No he can't. He could never manage without me.'

'I have. But what's the use of thinking on it now. He's a good man and he likes his food.'

'Where was I?'

'You were saying you would lie down. Come on.'

She got her into the room, on top of the eiderdown. So that the once pretty face was now painfully visible with all its strains and creases.

'I wish . . . '

'What?'

'I wish you were married . . . settled down.'

'God, don't start that again.'

'What, dear?'

'I'd like to be. It just hasn't happened, that's all.'

'Oh.'

'Are you all right?' She was trying to get up from the bed, the hem of her dress rising to show the tops of her stockings and her pink slip.

'Call me if he comes in.'

Catherine sat by the bed for a few minutes while her mother settled. Her hair was thinner and her dress sagged around her waist where it had once fallen from a full bosom. Her breath barely audible as she slept, she moved ever so slightly as if in a difficult dream.

'Catherine?'

'Yes.'

'Ah you're there.'

'Of course. How do you feel?'

'I've still the pain. What's the noise?'

'The wind.'

'Are you sure?'

'It's only the wind.'

'I feel as if this place will be blown away.'

'Of course not, how could it?'

'Didn't they have hurricanes in America last year?'

'They always do.'

'Ah but those ones were worse than ever. Those poor people having their homes swept away. In the end that's all a person has, in his home.'

On the white beach of the island a yelp broke the silence. A lean grey dog trotted up to another straggly black haired one, a few yards ahead of her.

Glaring. A shift from foot to foot. The dark one moved. Glassy eyed with deep brown fear. His stocky legs slipped and collapsed. The grey dog leapt on to his back. Catherine watched in strange fascination. The grey dog's paws strangled his opponent. He gripped its sides, hurling himself over with spirited kicks. Tufts of hair flew. The graze of muscle and feet. Ears sharpening. Blood trickled down the leg of the black dog. The grey one ran off up the beach into stray grasses.

She felt sick, seeing the short dog stumbling away, dragging its leg behind, the thick of it splashed with scarlet spots. She wanted to rush and pick it up. But knew it was no good. It trailed back to the main road.

When it was out of sight she sat waiting for Carson to come back. He seemed brighter and she was pleased.

'Are you all right?' He asked. 'Not sick?'

'No, I was just . . . thinking about my mother. How time passes.'

'You worry about her too much. There's no point. She's had her life now you've got yours. Just live it. I'm sorry about earlier on. I was a bit of an arsehole. Do you want to go in now?'

So they did and when they made love it felt easier and she wanted to hold him close for hours. Alarmed with the sense of loss, with lingering images of the dogs' violence, she hungered for and consumed his comfort.

But when they got home to a rainy November he mooched around the flat for hours.

'This place is too quiet, I need a buzz. Might go stateside. Find out the scene there.'

'Go to America?'

'Yes. Aren't you gonna come? Or do you like being cooped up in this chicken run of a city?'

'I can't just get up and go. It's too far. And I'd have no job. I know I don't earn much at the college teaching, but at least it's money coming in.'

'But this place is so drab. And look at the weather. You could easily find a job. We could go skiing in Vermont. I've got friends there. And San Francisco down by the water. Someone else I know has a house.'

'It's not as easy as that. At least not for me.'

'Okay. Let's discuss it later. We can arrange something.'

They walked and they talked for hours in the flat, staying up late at night while the rest of the city slept and there were just pin points of street lights for company in the rows of terraced houses.

He went to New York on business. He went again and came back. The third time, it was for good. He phoned once but didn't write. In the growing weeks everything between them was as wide as the Atlantic.

'Are you there?'

'Yes.'

'Martha?'

'It's me . . . dad.'

'Ah . . . Is there a cup of water?'

'Here.'

She helped him up on to the pillows. Frail wisps of hair shimmered. He drank before falling back to sleep with his mouth open. She replaced the three kinds of tablets to the back of his locker, ruffling up the lacy doiley under the vase of daffodils. The nurse would have done that, just as her mother had years ago.

He slept with breaths coming easily, his face familiar yet different, the sagging neck like a chicken's. She went over to the large window, careful not to wake him. Three boys were kicking a ball and she remembered Carson had liked football and often went to matches, though he never had the time, when she knew him. Perhaps, she thought, he liked me better. And now it's probably baseball. She wondered how he was, how successful he had become; it was either exceedingly or very. He would not have let any opportunities slip under his grasp.

A woman walked with a dog across the beach. Her headscarf fluttered in the wind. She could have used this scene if she had her pad. She could have sketched this woman. She realised how few she had made of her mother. Except ones done the previous year, fresh after the break with Carson.

'You're still there?'

She turned away from the window. 'Yes.'

'What time is it? Have you a watch?'

'Ten to four.'

'Ah . . . she'll be on with the tea. She makes me drink it, though it's terrible weak.'

'I've got to be going now, Dad.'

'You'll be along tomorrow?'

'Of course.'

'Would you get me a little thing?'

'How little?'

'Some Players.'

'I certainly won't. If Nurse Maguire catches you, or I do . . . '

'It wasn't anything. Just a thought.'

'Well you can forget it, Dad.'

She bent to kiss him on the forehead. The old devil, she thought. Trying to kill himself. Run out on me.

Before the nurse came, Catherine went downstairs. Each step resounding like waves and she thought of her mother standing on the rough part of the beach. You can't hang on to anyone, not in thoughts, or scents or sketches. You have to let go, or they go. They evade. Sometimes a brooch is left, old jewellery passed down or a few Blues records, but nothing real, nothing you can carry or hold on to. 'Washed away, washed away' echoed in her head, in the tone of her mother's voice in prayer, at one of her evening rosaries, an invocation to the beach, to all the beaches she had ever known, from there to Silhouette Island.

PAUL DURCAN
A VISION OF AFRICA ON THE COAST OF KERRY

On the coast at Meenogahane,
Near Causeway,
Nellie presides in the kitchen of her cottage,
At eighty-five, exchanging the time of day
With tourists, educating us:
Nellie who has never in her life
Been out of her townland
Except 'the wanst'.
Five years ago at eighty,
When she had a stroke,
She was transported
By county ambulance
To the Regional Hospital in Cork.
Do you know what I saw there?
No, Nellie, what did you see?
I saw a black man.
A black man?
A black man – you should have seen his neck!
His neck?
Oh the neck of him – the lovely neck of him!
The lovely, wet, shiny, rubbery neck of him!
I asked him if he would let me put my hand on it
And he did, he let me –
And it was all black, do you know?
Oh it was lovely, I tell you, lovely!

DONAL HICKEY
PÁDRAIG O'KEEFFE
LAST OF THE FIDDLE MASTERS

The belief in some quarters that real artists often find greater glory in death is certainly true of Pádraig O'Keeffe, who died in 1963. He has posthumously earned a level of fame that he could never have dreamed of in his heyday as a musician. His professional career would have been close to the bottom of the points table in today's terms.

His talents notwithstanding, he was a poor man, often despised by the respectability. He lost his job as a primary school teacher quite early in life; was a social outcast in the eyes of some; a man who spent many of his days and nights in pubs and someone who generally led a bohemian existence.

Unfortunately for Pádraig (he was locally known as Patrick Keeffe), he lived at a time when traditional music was not in vogue and he was scarcely known outside his native County Kerry. He missed out on the television era and also to a large extent on radio, which recorded his music when he was past his best. Ironically, however, it has been largely through radio that the music of O'Keeffe and of his many distinguished pupils has come to be recognised and appreciated. He has passed on a huge legacy in the form of hundreds of very old tunes, neatly written out by himself for pupils on now yellowing pages of copybooks and even on the back of cigarette packets. He is the most renowned of the many music teachers in the area and he also had more pupils than anybody else.

Whilst undoubtedly a superb fiddle player, his greatest achievement has been the manner in which he handed on the music. This gives him the leading position in the pantheon of Sliabh Luachra musicians and also a major place on the national scene. O'Keeffe is an outstanding figure in an era when traditional music is enjoying popularity that he could never have envisaged. There is a tendency amongst some musicians to hold back tunes from one another, but those who knew the fiddle master are adamant that that could not be said of him.

A bronze bust of O'Keeffe, which proudly dominates the

village green in Scartaglen, a place in which he spent much of his time playing music, is evidence that the wheel has come full circle for a sad and tragic figure in many respects. He is now amongst the immortals of music.

Any available photographs depict an ageing, world-weary and wrinkled face that had seen a hard life, but the facial features on the memorial are of a younger, sharper man. His cap is tilted sideways towards his right ear and he gazes westward over rolling farmland towards Killarney. The bow is held in his right hand and the fiddle stands erect pointing towards his left shoulder. Beneath, an inscription in Irish and in English says simply, 'Last of the fiddle masters of Sliabh Luachra.'

Pádraig O'Keeffe was born in Glounthane – a highland district between Ballydesmond and Castleisland, in 1887 – the eldest of nine children. His father, John O'Keeffe, was principal teacher in the nearby primary school and a man with a stern reputation; his mother was Margaret O'Callaghan, who hailed from Doon, Kiskeam, over the border in County Cork. It was from his mother's side of the family that he brought the music and he once claimed to be able to tune a fiddle when he was only four years of age. The O'Callaghans were a well known musical and dancing family and Margaret's brother, Cal, was a very good fiddle player who had a strong influence on Pádraig. The O'Callaghans got much of their music from Corney Drew, a blind fiddler in their area, and unusual tunes which Pádraig played in later life came from Drew, who had inherited music from the late eighteenth and early nineteenth centuries.

Pádraig spent a lot of his youth in Doon, where he learnt a great deal of music. At the prompting of his parents, he reluctantly went on to train as a primary teacher in Dublin, and took up a number of temporary posts in Kerry before succeeding his father as principal teacher in Glounthane, in May 1915, where he was to remain until his dismissal from the job five years later.

Some of his pupils have described him as a first-class teacher, but the discipline of having to teach them every day and spend his time within the walls of a school was too much for his free, artistic spirit to bear. He was in trouble with the Department of Education for not turning up in school regularly, for not keeping records and for showing a lack of enthusiasm for the job. It is said that he was rarely, if ever, in school on the day after receiving his salary cheque, which would be spent on a drinking spree. He kept a fiddle hanging on the wall in school and would play at lunchtime.

After getting at least five chances from the school authorities he was eventually replaced by another teacher, in 1920. That was the end of his life in the classroom and he devoted his remaining forty-three years to teaching and playing music – his true vocation. His audiences were small and they could be found in country pubs or remote farmhouses where a boy or girl with an ear for music eagerly awaited the arrival of the master.

In his hands a fiddle became an instrument of enchantment. He could keep audiences spellbound for instance with his playing of 'The Old Man Rocking the Cradle' in which he made the fiddle intone 'mama, mama'. For this novel tune which is based on a lullaby, he would put a large door key in his mouth and use it to mute the fiddle: the 'mama' sound, like that of a baby crying, would result.

Pádraig never owned a car. He cycled occasionally but he nearly always travelled on foot, walking the roads of Sliabh Luachra with a distinctive stride, frequently covering twenty or twenty-five miles a day in all kinds of weather. He stood at around six feet in height and was a strongly-built man with a fine mop of curling hair under a tightly-fitting peaked cap. He smoked Woodbine cigarettes.

He is remembered from his younger days as being well-spoken, clean, tidy and having a pleasant manner. He was very gentle and kind in his approach and people would remark on his unusual, fast walking style.

According to one of his most accomplished surviving pupils, Paddy Cronin, O'Keeffe was the best music teacher of his generation and he gave endless time to pupils in his efforts to ensure that they got the tunes right. When it came to imparting music, he was never in a hurry, even though a visit to a pub might be the next thing on his mind. An emphatic instruction to play slowly is something that has remained firmly etched on Paddy's mind.

Pádraig had an easily understood, ingenious system of writing music, with the figures 0, 1, 2, 3, 4 denoting the fingers of the left hand. The spaces between the five lines were used to show where the four strings of the fiddle were. This system, which he may have devised himself, was also used for teaching other instruments. He charged sixpence (2.5p) per tune and it is estimated that he handed on up to a thousand tunes in this manner though former pupils such as Johnny O'Leary believe that he took at least as many more tunes to the grave.

Some pupils went to great lengths to receive lessons from Pádraig and there is one story of a pupil from the Taur area who used to ride a chainless bike all the way to Glounthane: given the uphill, downhill nature of the road, it was a practice that made perfect sense.

In order to meet popular local demand from dancers, Pádraig played plenty of slides and polkas, but his preference was for reels and his specialty – slow airs. Although he was known for the sweetness of his playing, there was a haunting, lonesome quality to his airs – some of which are in the RTÉ archives. They can also be heard on a very worthwhile cassette produced by Peter Browne, of RTÉ radio. His style of playing airs such as 'O'Rahilly's Grave' (most likely a lament for the poet Aodhagán Ó Rathaille) reflected the hardship of his own life.

Peter Browne says that the recordings on the tape are the best available of O'Keeffe and even if they come from the later part of his life there's reason to be grateful that the light of his rare genius shines through from an earlier and outstanding period in traditional music.

West Limerick musician Dónal de Barra believes that the ups and downs of O'Keeffe's life influenced his music and made it all the better. 'People sometimes ask what is the difference between the music of O'Keeffe and that of other musicians. I think it's like the difference between prose and poetry. In O'Keeffe's music there was poetry,' maintains de Barra, a former president of CCÉ.

Pádraig remained single and he used to call the fiddle 'the missus', declaring that it gave no bit of trouble at all. 'Just one stroke across the belly and she purrs,' he would say. In his younger days, he had a long-running romance with a neighbouring girl, Abbie Scollard, who, despite his heavy drinking, remained loyal to him and did her best to persuade him to keep his drinking to moderate levels. When the subject of marriage was raised with the O'Keeffes by a member of Abbie's family, the question was apparently ruled out by Pádraig's mother, who felt he shouldn't marry below his station. In any case Abbie emigrated to America, where she later married and had a family.

Pádraig was a private man who didn't discuss deeply intimate matters such as his broken relationship and the loss of his teaching job, but there are people who believe that Abbie Scollard's departure from Glounthane affected him traumatically, even if he didn't let on in public. However, he never indicated any regrets about having to leave Glounthane school, except perhaps with regard to the financial loss.

Throughout his life he had very little money, but always liked to have the price of a pint of stout in his pocket as he faced into a pub. He looked on that as a 'seed' and once he had money for the first one his listeners and friends would keep him supplied with pints and halves of whiskey for the remainder of an evening.

Always cracking jokes, he loved company and being in pubs. Fiddler Mikey Duggan has unforgettable memories of Sunday evenings spent in Lyons's pub, Scartaglen, with him and other musicians. Tunes would be interspersed with stories and conversation: there was nobody as good as Pádraig for keeping a group of musicians together and savouring the craic.

He shared the family home with his mother, who died in 1938, and thereafter he lived alone. He appears to have been reasonably domesticated, having a reputation of being a good baker and keeping a fairly decent table. Nor was he troubled too much by church laws of fast and abstinence. 'There are only two kinds of fast days – the day that you haven't it and the day you can't eat it,' he observed once when told that he shouldn't be eating sausages on a fast day. His brother, Cal, lived in Castleisland and was devoted to him, often paying his household bills.

With the passage of time the legend of this remarkable personality continues to grow and countless anecdotes still circulate with Pádraig as the central figure. It's hard to believe that so many sayings could be attributed to one person and so many yarns told about him. In reality it is not possible that all these stories and sayings could involve him, but it can be taken that a goodly number are very much his own.

An example is the story of the parish priest who upbraided him for not being a regular attender at Sunday Mass, something which also made him a rarity in his time. ''Tis like this, father,' he is reputed to have said to the priest, 'five minutes in a church is like an hour, but an hour in a pub is like five minutes.'

Also renowned as a mimic, he could distort his face to fit another character and could change his voice to sound like a dog yelping or a lion roaring. An intelligent man, he read the newspapers and did his best to keep abreast of what was happening in the world. Though he mixed mainly with people who had far less education than himself, he also enjoyed the company of those with whom he could discuss subjects on a higher plane.

He liked to show off his command of the English language and one of the classic stories featured Pádraig responding to visits by a neighbour's trespassing donkey. Unable to sleep because of the animal's nocturnal activities, Pádraig sent the following humorous note to the owner: 'The pilfering propensities of this decrepit old animal of yours and his nightly wanderings around my residence have completely deprived me of my sleep. Therefore, if you don't remove the cause of the aforesaid disturbance, I am very reluctantly obliged to take more dramatic legal and immediate proceedings.' The owner returned the note to Pádraig forthwith with five shillings saying, 'He's worth it for that language.'

Strange to relate, Pádraig didn't have a fiddle to call his own for a long period of his life, but favourite pubs, such as Lyons's and Charlie Horan's, of Castleisland, always had fiddles for him whenever he wished to play.

As he grew older, Pádraig's appearance disimproved. People who met him for the first time in the late forties and early fifties described him as being slightly stooped, dishevelled and the worse for drink. Sadly, all available photographs of him are from that period and they graphically help tell the story of his life. Musically, he was well past his prime and wasn't as interested in playing as before. He was sixty when in 1947 he made his first radio recording with Séamus Ennis, with whom he became very friendly.

Some of the broadcasters who met him found it practically impossible to converse with him and interviews were out of the question, though he did offer a few cryptic answers to Ciarán Mac Mathúna on one occasion.

One of his best pupils, the late Jerry McCarthy, of Scartaglen, who died only a few years ago, found it hard to understand how Pádraig had become such a popular figure in the modern era:

There were times when certain pubs were closed against him. They (the pubs) didn't want him because he was short of money and customers might feel he was looking for drink from them. There were people who looked down on him and others would leave a pub if they saw him there. But I never heard him saying anything about those people and it didn't seem to worry him.

Pádraig, however, still commanded the esteem of his friends in Sliabh Luachra who were always prepared to stand him a drink, or give him some money when they knew he needed it.

The harsh winter of 1962–3 was the death of Pádraig. Snow lay frozen on the ground and the steep roads around Glounthane were impassable for up to seven weeks. Those close to him had seen his appearance deteriorate for about a year before he passed away. That winter he was a virtual prisoner in his own home, but he spent a week with Tom and Mary McCarthy in their pub, at Main Street, Castleisland, in February. He was very ill and took only his usual liquid nourishment.

He made a final visit to Glounthane, driven by a neighbour, Paddy Jones. After a few days, however, his brother Cal was sent for and a doctor advised that he should be admitted to St Catherine's Hospital in Tralee. There was a brief stop at Cordal post office for his pension and a packet of Woodbines, and also at McCarthy's, where, ominously he shook hands with and bade farewell to Tom and Mary. That was unusual for him.

The feeling in the locality was that he would recover and be home again soon, but such was not to be and he died peacefully of pneumonia, on 22 February 1963, aged 75. His funeral was one of the biggest ever seen in the area and he was laid to rest in the family plot in Kilmurry graveyard.

And so one of the famous, colourful artists of Sliabh Luachra, a man who in the tradition of the poet Eoghan Rua Ó Súilleabháin lived like an artist, had passed on. Regrettably, he was not fully acknowledged in his own lifetime. Were he to return he would surely be surprised to find that all has been put right and that he is being accorded the honour that is his due.

The music of Sliabh Luachra is now far more popular than it was in his time and it will be passed on to the future generations.

from STONE MAD FOR MUSIC:
THE SLIABH LUACHRA STORY (1999)

BERNARD O'DONOGHUE
THE UVULAR R

The City on Sunday morning: turf briquettes
And Calor-gas rounded up in network compounds,
And the mist so dense you can hardly see
The ochres and light greens of Sunday's Well
Across the river. We were the Cork crowd;
We always lacked the definition
Of the more western voice and land in Kerry.
The south Cork coast, kind and all as it was,
Wasn't Dingle. Our gaeltacht was speckled,
Consonants that compromised and faded
On the mouth's roof like Communion wafers.
That our bruachs were riverbanks; that our local names
Took the English word for it: Newquarter,
Watergrasshill and Coalpits and Halfway.

MARY CUMMINS
MY FATHER, THE SERGEANT

*This reflective piece probably grew out of the awful things now
commonplace in Irish life. It must have said things to a huge number
of people since I got more response to this than to anything previously
written. Warmly favourable letters and calls came from all over the
country from people who had grown up in similar surroundings –
partly thanks to Gay Byrne, who read some of the piece on his radio
programme and reached listeners who are not normally Irish Times
readers.*

The paraphernalia of coming from a garda household littered my
childhood and continues to pervade the various ways I view life
and people. The barracks (where we lived in 'the quarters') was
a powerhouse of activity. We were at the centre of things. Even
in winter when it appeared there was nothing much happening,

the County Kerry barracks hummed along, fuelled by an energy of its own and the things it dealt with.

Even when the summer tourists had gone, the schools had reopened, the emigrants had returned to Harlesden, Camden Town or New York, and the extra guards drafted in for the season were scattered, there was a new, but no less exacting, routine for my father and three or four guards who were there all year round.

The barracks in Ballybunion is in a commanding position, taking up one side of the square. From its windows you can look down the Main Street, up Church Road and see all the incoming traffic from Tralee, Listowel or Limerick. It is a big rambling house with a long landing upstairs and wide window-seats everywhere. You could sit reading, hidden behind the curtains. We had no inside bathroom for a couple of years. Then a small bedroom was turned into one, leaving me with an abiding yearning for bathrooms that are real rooms. In the 1950s, 1960s and into the 1970s, the barracks was a caravanserai at the centre of things. The guards did the census and much else of an official nature. People came to get passports, references, requests to find missing relatives in England, to look for advice if they were thinking of taking a civil case to court – often over land – or to get a young man to marry the girl he had got into trouble.

There was little or no welfare and I remember my father sending women, widowed or deserted, or men with problems to Dan Spring, our local Labour TD. My parents never discussed politics but it was taken as read that it was Dan Spring who got things done.

You could set your watch by my father. He went out our back door, crossed the yard and went in the back door of the barracks at 9.20 am precisely every weekday except Mondays. On Mondays, they had a special inspection and drill in the day-room at 9 am sharp. His uniform, which was always spick-and-span, got a special damp-ironing that day. He polished his shoes until you could see yourself in them. He Silvo-ed his buttons, using a special gadget that fitted around the buttons, so that the liquid did not get on the material. My mother would brush down the back of his jacket. His hat was put on with a little more care on Mondays and court days.

At one minute to 1 pm he recrossed the yard and came back into the kitchen for dinner. Afterwards, he sat in the enormous armchair near the range and read the paper. Sometimes he closed his eyes and appeared to doze. After the Topical Talk on the radio, he would ruffle his paper again. He was always gone by ten to two. At twenty to four, he came back again for a cup of tea and a couple of plain biscuits. Then he donned a gaberdine coat in winter, or a light tweed sports jacket in summer, called the dog and often one of us, and set off down the Main Street. At five to four exactly he dropped a bundle of official brown envelopes with a harp on them into the letterbox outside the post-office – the post was collected at 4 pm. There was never a day when he did not have a decent handful of letters to send off.

In summer, we went to the strand for a swim. In winter (after the Listowel Races until Easter or Whit) we (or he on his own) would go for a long, brisk walk back the Long Strand, or up and down the now-eroded path on the sandhills that skirted the golf course. Sometimes he would go all the way to the Cashen River, and come back by the road, calling in at the graveyard to inspect new graves – about six or seven miles in all. He like walking but he and the guards also often cycled out the country. They were sometimes on official business but nonetheless stopped to talk to farmers working in fields or in their haggards. There were regular houses where they would have a cup of tea or a drink of water.

A few times a year we would go on a really long walk to the Hill and down the other side. In that flat part of north Kerry, the Hill is simplistically named but it has a heroic past. Its real name is Cnoc an Áir (massacre), and it is where Fionn and the Fianna are supposed to have fought a bloody battle with invaders. You went up past Doon Church, to Rahavannig and Derra – the dividing line between us and Ballylongford. Lahasreagh, Ballynoneen and down by Moohane and Ahafona and back up the village by East End. On this walk, the townlands merged into one another. My father knew them all. He knew where each one started and finished. He knew who was in every house, who had died there, who had emigrated and who had troubles. He might tell you things, but not much. He was compulsively, obsessively secretive – or perhaps it was just discretion. Sometimes he would spell things backwards for my mother and we would try to guess a word here and there. Sometimes they would talk in Irish. We would try to keep up.

But there was an implicit, unspoken rule that we never repeated anything outside the house. Usually we had little interest.

This undefined discretion permeated to the wives of the guards. They had a special relationship. While they were part of the general life of the town – the ICA, cleaning the brasses in the church or whatever, they also had a particular friendship with each other. Often it was only the jobs of their spouses they had in common but that close, almost familial thing existed between, like a mantle of responsibility. This clannish rapport between garda families was a universal thing. When someone got promoted or someone else's child did particularly well in any field, it was almost as good as if it had been one of us. We picked things up by chance and stored them away. For example, there was no bank in Ballybunion for much of my childhood. A lending agency in Cork used to ring my father to find out about people's creditworthiness. If he took the call on the phone extension in our hall, we would overhear the conversation by staying very quiet on the landing upstairs or opening the door of the back kitchen a fraction. 'Yes, he's fine,' he would say. 'A good farm of land there. They're an industrious family.' Or he would urge caution. 'Well, I wouldn't give him that much. Maybe half. They say she is bringing a good dowry with her, but nothing definite is settled yet.'

Sometimes, late at night, women would ring, their voices shrill with bitterness and anger. They wouldn't give their names but demanded that such-and-such a pub or hotel be raided. Usually it was because their husbands were holed up, drinking after hours, unwilling to go home.

My father was famous for his strictness, his authority and his sense of duty. He came from that generation of sergeants and guards who were never off duty. If the barracks was closed, people just came round to our door. The phone was always turned over. He never took days off and had only minimal holidays to visit relations. The shelves in the pantry off the kitchen were laden with bottles of whiskey, brandy and sherry which the publicans and hoteliers delivered faithfully every Christmas Eve. I used to wonder why they bothered since he continued to raid them all with assiduous regularity. Brendan Kenelly says he and his pals always had to give duty dances to the sergeant's daughters, feeling it might lessen the penalty if they were caught without a light on their bikes going home.

My father used quaint language when talking about some 'clients' as he described them in a withering tone. He would call some of them 'blackguards' or 'real blackguards'. A rogue or a rascal was a lesser evil.

We often went to sleep to the howls and rich, roaring language of the drunks in the lock-up, which face on to the back yard. They would bang the door, curse and swear until they passed out, exhausted, in the tiny cell.

My father was a tall, tidy, meticulous man with neat, distinctive writing. His own father had been in the RIC and had died young, leaving my grandmother with five young boys to rear on a small pension. My father's pride in the Garda Síochana or 'the force' as he usually referred to it, was cosmic. There was no other body of men like it, no better members, no higher standards. He died the year after he retired in 1975 – twenty-one years ago tomorrow.

from THE BEST OF ABOUT WOMEN (1996)

ALFRED, LORD TENNYSON
THE SPLENDOUR FALLS

This poem was inspired by a visit to Killarney and the poet tries to describe the wonderful effect of bugle notes re-echoed from the Eagle's Nest Rock as he stands in the midst of romantic scenery in the splendour of the declining sun which lights up Ross Castle, sets aglow the summits of the surrounding mountain peaks, flashes along the surface of the lakes and sparkles on the waters of the O'Sullivan Cascade as they tumble down the slopes of the Tomies Mountains.

The splendour falls on castle walls
And snowy summits old in story:
The long light shakes across the lakes,
And the wild cataract leaps in glory.
Blow, bugle; blow, set the wild echoes flying,
Blow, bugle; answer, echoes, dying, dying, dying.

O hark, O hear! how thin and clear,
And thinner, clearer, farther going!
O sweet and far from cliff and scar
The horns of Elfland faintly blowing!
Blow, let us hear the purple glens replying:
Blow, bugle; answer, echoes, dying, dying, dying.

O love, they die in yon rich sky,
They faint on hill or field or river:
Our echoes roll from soul to soul,
And grow for ever and for ever.
Blow, bugle; blow, set the wild echoes flying,
And answer, echoes, answer, dying, dying, dying.

An Seabhac (Pádraig Ó Siochfhradha)
Jimín agus an Gandal

Maidin Lá Nollag chuaigh Cáit agus mo mháthair go dtí an chéad Aifreann. Bhí mé féin agus Daid i mbun an tí. A fhad a bhí Daid ag crú na mbó chuaigh mé féin ag féachaint ar na rudaí go léir a bhí sa chupard. Thóg mé úll agus líon mé póca liom de rísíní, agus bhí smut den mbairín breac ann gearrtha agus chuir mé chugam é sin, leis.

Nuair a bhí mé ag dúnadh an chupaird arís, bhuail smaoineamh mé; rug mé ar an mbuidéal buí agus leath-líon mé cupán as. Bhlais mé é, ach a bhuachaill ó! dá olcas é an stuif dhubh aréir roimhe sin ba sheacht measa an rud buí. Dhófadh sé thú, a dhuine! Ansin ní fheadar cad a dhéanfainn leis. Ghlaoigh mé ar an madra agus chuir mé faoina phus an cupán, ach ní fhéachfadh sé air, a mhic ó. Níor dhein sé ach sraoth a chur as.

Ansin chuimhnigh mé ar sheift eile. Fuair mé dorn mine buí agus fhliuch mé leis an stuif as an mbuidéal é agus chuir mé so bhuaile amuigh é ar phláta. Siúd chuige an gandal mór agus d'alp sé a raibh ann.

Níor bhraith mé faic air go ceann tamaill. Ansin chrom sé ar ghogalaigh. I gceann tamaill d'éirigh sé as sin agus chrom sé ar shiúl timpeall agus leathcheann air. Fáinne bhí sé a dhéanamh agus é ag siúl. Ansin stad sé agus leath sé a dhá chois amach ó chéile agus bhí sé á shuaitheadh féin anonn is anall. Chuirfeadh sé na cait ag gáire.

Ansin luigh sé agus dhún sé na súile agus ní fhaca aon oighre riamh ach é ar shean-Diarmaid chríona anseo amuigh nuair a bhíonn sé ag titim dá chodladh sa chathaoir mhór os comhair na tine agus é ag míogarnaigh.

Sa deireadh luigh sé ar fad anuas ar an talamh, shín sé a phíopán uaidh amach agus leath sé a dhá sciathán, agus níor fhan anam ná brí ann ach chomh beag agus dá mbeadh sé marbh.

Am baice bhí mé ag breith chugam ar eagla go gcaillfí é, agus níorbh fhios dom cad a dhéanfainn. Chuala mé Daid ag teacht ó chró na mbó agus chuir mé díom isteach. Nuair a chonaic Daid an gandal stad sé agus bhí sé ag caint leis féin.

'Dar mo bhriathar ach go bhfuil sé seo ina "chocstí!"' ar seisean. 'A Jimín,' ar seisean ag gloach.

Bhí mé féin ag scuabadh an urláir ar séirse. Tháinig mé don doras.

'Cad a dhein tú leis an ngandal seo?' arsa Daid.

Tháinig stad ionam féin. Níor mhaith liom bheith ag ceilt na fírinne maidin Lá Nollag. D'inis mé an scéal ina chodanna beaga do Dhaid. Chonaic mé air go raibh sé míshásta liom.

'Díolfaidh tú as na cleasa lá éigin, a bhuachaill,' ar seisean. 'Is dócha gur tú a chuir deireadh leis an gcat seo againne, leis, i bPoll a' Lín thíos.'

Cheap mé go dtitfinn as mo sheasamh. Mheas mé nach raibh 'fhios ag aon duine beirthe é. Bhí mé maol-chluasach go maith ansin a deirim leat. Mheas mé dar ndóigh go n-inseodh Daid an scéal do Mham. D'imigh mé liom go dtí an tAifreann. Le linn an Aifrinn d'iarr mé ar Dhia mé bheith saor ón olc a bhí ag bagairt orm.

Nuair a tháinig mé abhaile ón Aifreann bhí an gandal in aice na tine ag Mam agus an t-anam ag teacht arís ann.

Ní bhfuair Mam amach riamh cad d'imigh air mar nuair tháinig Daid abhaile bhí sí ag iarraidh fios a fháil uaidh cé tháinig isteach ar maidin gur thug sé an fuisce as an mbuidéal dó.

Bhí Daid ag déanamh grinn den scéal agus ní inseodh sé di. Thug sé súil orm féin, uair, a d'fhag mé mí-chompórdach go leor.

Is maith é Daid mar sin féin.

as JIMÍN MHÁIRE THAIDHG (1921)

EILEEN SHEEHAN
KISS

He came to me

his voice in my head
like a white flame licking

his hands through my hair
like a sweet breeze blooming

my name on his tongue
like a snowflake melting

his mouth on my mouth
like the warm earth yielding

Death is a seriously sexy man.

LUAÍ Ó MURCHÚ
COME, PIPER, PLAY

Stark Pipers shall blow
Stout drummers shall beat
And the shout of the North
Shall be heard in the Street

Joseph Campbell, '*A Prophesy*'

All that Sunday morning the boy had worked indoors and around
the yard at the jobs his mother had laid out for him. When she
had hurried from the house he had watched her as far as the first
turn in the lane and had seen her disappear around the bend
alongside the glen where the land began its fall to the road. His
mother had gone before he had noticed her wedding and engagement
rings hanging from a cup hook on the dresser. In her hurried
preparations for Mass she had forgotten the rings. He knew that
if she missed the rings before she reached the road she would stand

in the lane, as she had so often done before and would call to him
in the hope that he would hear her and would bring them out to
her. But she would not return for the rings or retrace her steps under
any circumstances. That would be unlucky. The boy washed the
breakfast things and replaced them on the dresser.

As he washed the potatoes for the dinner in the wooden tub
in the stream behind the house, a flock of tiny ducklings came
around the corner and made for the water with joyous peeps. The
boy smiled and paused in his work to watch the ducklings
followed by the bewildered hen which had hatched them. Of all
the young things around the place the boy loved the young ducks
best of all. He never tired watching their buoyant movements
on the pool at the top of the haggard, how they spun and
frolicked on the surface of the water, splashing and paddling and
ducking underneath to beshot upwards again like rubber balls.
He loved the feel of their tiny golden bodies, fluffy and palpitant
when he lifted them and pressed them against his cheek. They
would lie, passive and unafraid, in his hand, unlike the chickens
that would struggle and chirp hysterically till sometimes the old
hen would fly up at him in defence of her young ones and he
would have to let it go. The boy laughed with delight at the way
the ducklings waggled their scutty little tails when frightened
and how earnestly they guzzled with tiny bills in puddles and
sinkholes. Soon the ducks would grow fat and portly and his
would be the task of escorting them in the evenings as they
waddled heavily home, replete with juicy slugs, from the damp
grass of the fields that sloped to the river.

The boy carried the potatoes into the kitchen. He was
curiously aware of the empty sound of his boots on the
floorboards as he moved with the pot to the stove.

By noon he had most of the tasks done. His mother should
soon be home. The boy went to the door again and listened. His
movements were restless and tense. It suddenly occurred to him
that if he hurried he would still have time to clean out the byre.
Quickly the boy removed his boots and stockings, ran to the byre
and began to fork the pile of manure and straw through the
opening in the wall at the end of the byre and into the dung
hill. Half-way through the job he paused suddenly, went to the
door and listened.

And then he heard it. Faint it came at first, borne on the April breeze that stirred the fresh green of the beeches along the edge of the distant wood. Far away and fading at times as the wind veered momentarily, then thin and clear came the music again. Stronger now, and with the blurred support of thudding drums, yet still wavering and uncertain, came the music. Dropping the pike, the boy shot from the byre and ran towards the music.

All morning the boy had been watching for the band. Now as he caught the stirring music of the pipes he ran with urgency, determined to be in his usual place when the band passed. As he sped along by the hedge where the chicken coops were ranged at intervals he saw his mother returning up the lane. Luckily she had not seen him. If she saw him she would give him more jobs to do and he's miss the band. He knew she would be coming from the house immediately afterwards to feed the chickens clamouring behind the wire. The boy ran for the old lime-kiln near the gap that led into an upper land. Quickly he pushed his way through the whins that grew in and around the lime-kiln. He saw his mother come up the field carrying a bucket of food for the chickens. As he pushed further into the whins he was suddenly aware that he had forgotten his boots. The spines of the whins bit viciously into his chest and thighs. He heard his mother call him, 'Kevin, where are you?' The boy pushed his way still further through the whins and into the very middle of the lime-kiln.

He peeped from the whins and saw the chickens rushing frenziedly for the food his mother had scattered on the grass. Hither and thither ran the birds – White Whyandottes, Black Minorcas, Light Sussex, Rhode Island Reds. Clutch after clutch spilled out over the grass as his mother moved from coop to coop till all the chickens were fed. She stood watching the birds feeding for a time before returning towards the house. She was a small woman, intent and anxious. As she moved slowly down the field she pulled dry sticks for kindling from the hedge.

Now the boy wriggled from among the whins and raced effortlessly against the hill. His bare feet thudded on the trodden grass of the path and he leaped the stile that led into the lane. He stopped again to listen. No doubt of it this time! The band was really coming. Now the music was unmistakable though still muffled by the shoulder of the hill that rose beyond the road.

The boy raced down the sloping field, jumped the ditch that edged the small bog beyond and pushed through the hedge on to the roadside.

The people were coming home from church now. Some greeted him where he stood as they trotted past in traps and spring cars. He answered them shyly. One woman called to him, 'Hi, Kevin, where's your boots?' The raillery irritated him. He knew he should have been wearing his boots on a Sunday. But his mother had always warned him to take them off when he went cleaning the byre. And this time the music had come before he had time to finish the work and put his boots on again. Two men cycled past, thrusting strongly at the pedals. Each had a pair of football boots, wrapped in a jersey and tied to his handlebars. Three girls of about the boy's age came past as he waited. They walked primly, conscious of their Sunday finery. He disliked girls, they were so cool and scornful. The boy looked down furtively at the spots of dung on his bare legs. The girls walked past shouldering each other and giggling.

And then as if suddenly freed from the restraint of the hill, the band rounded the corner. Haloed in sound it came. The boy tensed as he heard again the high notes of the chanters blend with the sustained roar of the drones. Pinpoints of light lanced from the shimmering drums. A whole riot of colour and sound engulfed the boy – green tassels looping the drones and swinging opulent and free as the pipers strode; carven ebony of the drones and chanters ending in creamy circles of ivory with the motif repeated in the pipeclayed cordage and leathers of the drums; saffron fringes falling from the distended bags nudged by the black sleeved pipers; silvery circles relieving the dark wood of the drones; green and saffron of kilt and cloak; green, orange and red of streaming ribbons; slanted feathers, jaunty and crisp in each man's cap; the whole a web of vibrant colour stitched by the staccato rattle of the drums.

With rigid correctness the men marched, pipers and drummers, intent and absorbed. Their green stockinged legs recalled to the boy the linked wheels of the Newry train. As the band approached, the three tenor drummers swept their sticks from off their drumheads with an upward flourish and instantly the three drums fell silent. Now the leading side-drummer of the four alone maintained the tempo. The rattle of his drumsticks rose with a dry sharpness over the music of the pipes. The leader knew he was good and pride in his artistry was clear in the tilt of his jaw. Poised and assured, the other three side-drummers, sticks held rigidly over their drums, waited for their cue as they marched. Then, just as they came level with the boy, they came in again on the score with a simultaneous crash that sent the music on a higher flight. The rhythm made the boy hold his breath. Soft came the beat of the tenor drums, giving mass and depth to the lighter instruments. The boy watched, aloof and absorbed, as the whirling tenor drumsticks rose and fell, twirling in the air, one rising, one falling, with ever the side-drums throbbing ceaselessly. Tremors shook him in the intensity of his delight and his skin rose in gooseflesh. No thoughts came to him. He was receptive only. Back from the pipes streamed the ribbons, whipping and tautening as the breeze caught them. Resolute and confident the bandsmen strode. Each man seemed to be listening.

He thrilled again, as he so often had before, to the precision of the marching men as the band approached the corner of the road where, barefooted on the grass margin, he eagerly awaited the drill and change of tempo that would mark the passing of the band along this particular part of its route. Here it seemed to the boy as if he himself was, for the time being, the pivot on which each rank turned the corner, the bandsmen nearest to him marking time as he came abreast for five or six steps while the remainder of the bandsmen in that particular rank each took a slightly longer step than his companion on his left to complete the arc of movement until the whole rank was again in line when the band as a unit took up the rhythm and pace of the march and he saw again the swing of the kilts in time to the steps of the marching men and the longer sway of the fringed shawls from their shoulders.

But it was the flag that in a sense symbolised to the boy all that the band stood for. On the white background of the band's standard, the Hound of Ulster rose, rampant and questing, with glaring eyes and tensed forefeet. Ravening jaws seemed to howl a challenge to every enemy. Upwards and outwards he sprang over the marching men and as the breeze caught the folds of the flag the Hound seemed to come alive and to writhe in convulsive fury. The boy tingled. There were tears in his eyes and his heart thumped.

Now the bank was nearly past and the boy became aware of the sullen rumble of the drones as their sound surged backwards towards him, dominating the music of the chanters. Under the trees the metallic echo of the drums seemed to reach him half a note late. But the pipers and drummers, sure of their timing, strode with confidence to the rhythm of the drums. He watched the line of brown shoes rising and falling, rising and falling, as they bore the music away from him.

Faint and more faint came the music. At regular intervals the three side drummers fell silent, then came in again to reinforce the ceaseless rhythm of their leader. Yet it was as one they drummed, ending always with crisp precision. And over all came the rattling roll of the leader. The music came still, swelling and falling in waves to where the boy stood motionless on the grass by the roadside. Now the intensity of his feelings was passing and he drew a deep breath, almost a sob. The band had cleared the rise of the road ahead and for a while he caught again the wavering gleams of the golden pikeheads where the Hound of Ulster moved in the van. A last flirt of streaming ribbons on the crest of the brae, a thin far call from the pipes, a fading rattle from the drums and the band had passed.

The boy moved his bare feet reluctantly and was suddenly aware of the coldness of the grass. The countryside seemed empty and the sun had gone in. From the edge of the wood the wind breathed in the beeches emphasising the hush and the emptiness of the fields. He heard his mother call again and now he saw her on the hill where she stood by the stile. Slowly he turned to go. There would be another time. The band would pass again. And again he would be waiting. And then he began to run. He remembered the cans of water he had still to carry from the well.

Seán Ó Ríordáin
Ceol Ceantair

Chuala sé an ceol i gcainteanna Dhún Chaoin,
Ní hiad na focail ach an fonn
A ghabhann trí bhlas is fuaimeanna na Mumhan,
An ceol a chloiseann an strainséir;
Ceol ceantair
Ná cloiseann lucht a labhartha,
Ceol nár chualasa riamh,
Toisc a ghiorracht dom is bhí,
Is mé bheith ar adhastar ag an mbrí.

Ceol a cloistear fós sa Mhumhain,
Fiú in áiteanna 'nar tréigeadh an chanúint.

George Thomson
The Prose Poems

The Blasket books have certain features in common with the
Homeric poems. Those poems took shape out of shorter lays
which had been transmitted orally over many centuries; and, thanks
to an exceptionally favourable combination of historical conditions,
the transition from speech to writing was effected so skilfully that
many characteristics of oral recitation were carried over into written
literature. Among these were the use of ornamental epithets,
conventional phrases and set passages, repeated without variation,
to describe certain recurrent situations, such as starting out on a
journey, preparing for battle, partaking of a meal, and so on.

There are also, of course, important differences. In the
historical period the Homeric poems were recited, not sung. In
earlier times they had been changed by a minstrel accompanying
himself on the lyre. The Gaelic tales were in prose, but it was
a special kind of prose with many poetical features, including
those just noted in the Homeric poems; and it had been
customary at an earlier period for the narrator to insert into his
story from time to time a short lyrical poem appropriate to the

situation. All these features can be traced in the Blasket books.

A typical example of these conventional formulas, regularly employed both in the traditional and in the autobiographical tales, is the following:

We turned stern to land and prow to sea, hoisted our sails and set out for the west with a fair breeze behind us.

We took oars and sails aboard and set prow to sea and stern to land, as they did in the old tales long ago.

Soon we had turned our faces to the island and our backs to the Wild Bank.

In the last instance the formula is inverted, because the men are rowing and therefore facing the other way. Other examples (not easy to translate, because they depend largely on alliteration):

If it be no better, let it be no worse.
They made neither stop nor stay.
Without care, concern or complaint.
We were discussing and debating the ways of the world.
He received the choicest and finest of food and drink.

In addition, there were many phrases alluding to incidents in the heroic tales:

They were scattered like the children of Lir.
As hard on her subjects as Queen Maeve in Connacht long ago.
The black curses that Fionn put on the limpets.

These formulas were all part of the storyteller's stock-in-trade, and were often to be heard even in ordinary conversation. They show how deeply the forms of popular speech had been influenced by the storyteller's art.

Nor is that all. The Islanders delighted in conversation, which they liked to adorn with couplets or quatrains taken from their repertory of traditional poetry ('as the poet said long ago'); or they might reproduce some image or idea from the same source as though it were their own. This was all the easier, because the thoughts embodied in their poetry were their thoughts.

Maurice is chatting idly with his grandfather on a sunny morning in the hills:

My grandfather and I were lying on the Castle Summit. It was a fine sunny day in July. The sun was splitting the stones with its heat and the grass burnt to the roots. I could see, far away to the south, Iveragh painted in many colours by the sun. South-west were the Skelligs, glistening white, and the sea around them dotted with fishing boats from England.

'Isn't it a fine healthy life those fishermen have, daddo?' said I.

I got no answer. Turning round I saw the old man was asleep. I looked at him, thinking. You were once in the flower of youth, said I in my own mind, but, my sorrow, the skin of your brow is wrinkled now, and the hair on your head is grey. You are without suppleness in your limbs, and without interest in the grand view to be seen from this hill. But, alas, if I live, I will be one day as you are now. (TYA 75).

The Islanders had a quatrain, which they attributed to Pierce Ferriter. It ran as follows:

Look at this head agape with holes for eyes,
And look how bare this toothless jawbone is!
Look too, for all your strength and beauty now,
The day will come when yours shall be like this!

The boy's thoughts have been moulded, in form and content, by the quatrain.

In addition to such echoes of popular poetry, which are characteristic of all the Gaelic dialects, the Blasket books contain a large number of extended passages descriptive of natural phenomena, all constructed on similar lines, with nothing to distinguish them from poetry proper except the lack of metrical form. Examples of these 'prose poems', as they may be called, are to be found in Tomás, Maurice and Peig. In *Twenty Years* they are skilfully integrated into the narrative so as to display the ever-changing panorama of nature as a background to the activities of man.

Let us begin with an example from Tomás, which is here translated for the first time. (The captions have been supplied by the present writer).

A Winter's Day

It is a winter's day, and looks like it. The blast of the great wind is driving the waves over everything that it can reach. The rocks out to sea are hidden from sight by the squalls of white surf bursting over them. The grass that was green yesterday is withered today. Even the people's skins are changing in the bad weather. Sheep that have been blown out of their resting-places in the hills are trying to force their way into the houses. The fish that lay all summer sunning himself on the surface of the water, has vanished in the storm. The young woman who was as spruce as the swan on the lake, when she comes in with a bucket of water, the comb has been snatched from the back of her head by the wind, her hair is straying into her mouth, there is mud on her clothes, the water is half-spilt, and she is as cross as someone who is out of tobacco. Of the old people, whose bones had been so fine and soft in the warmth of the sun, one has a shrivelled leg, another complains of his arm, and another is dozing over the fire, and they are keeping an eye on him lest he fall into it.

There are many cures in fine weather, and much harm in hard.

There follow three examples from Maurice:

Nightfall

It was growing late. The sun was sinking on the horizon, the dew falling heavily as the air cooled, the dock leaves closing up for the night, the birds crying as they came back to their young, rabbits rushing through the fern as they left their warrens, the sparkle gone out of the Kerry diamonds, and a lonesome look coming over the ravines. 'It is night, Tomás.'

A Stormy Day

I had now spent a month on the sea, as happy as a prince returning home in the evening and setting out with the chirp of the sparrow. But one day, when we were out as usual, I noticed a difference. The fine view was not to be seen, there was no gladness in my heart, the birds were not singing nor the seal sunning himself on the ledge, no heron, ring-plover nor sea-pie was at the water's edge picking the limpets, no path of gold in the Bay of Dingle nor ripples glittering in the sunshine, no sultry haze in the bosom of the hills, no rabbits to be seated with ears cocked on the clumps of thrift. A gale was blowing from the south, and where the water lapped before, the waves were now hurling themselves with a roar against the rocks, not a bird's cry to be heard but all of them cowering in their holes, big clouds sweeping across the sky ready to burst with the weight of the rain, the wind howling through the covers, the bright flowers above me twisted together in the storm, and no delight in my heart but cold and distress.

Greeting the Sun

It was a beautiful morning, a streak of light across Cnocachoma in the east and life coming into everything. The sheep which had been sitting in the furrow in the run of the night rose and stretched itself. The folded leaf was opening. The hen which had hidden her head under her wings was crying gob-gob-gob to be let out into the fields. Bird, beast and man were awaking to pay homage to the sun. A moment before not a sound was to be heard but now the birds were singing, the cow, the sheep, the ass, and even man himself throwing up their snatches of song.

These passages embody the primitive belief in the kinship of man and nature, both subject to the same cycle of day and night, summer and winter, birth and death. This is a prominent feature of Gaelic poetry.

from THE BLASKET THAT WAS (1982)

JOHN MCAULIFFE
AFTER GOETHE'S FIFTH ROMAN ELEGY

The presence of the past almost suffocates.
Walking, the streets are like a graveyard.
I turn to my books to make some sense
Of its proximities, spending the days
Reading in the garden at my leisure.

But at night I am called to endeavours
That are two-sided, only half mine,
And twice more pleasure – it is then
That I am truly escaped. I step
Over the blue pool of our clothes on the floor
And gaze at the white breast and down the hip
Where I'm now guiding my hand.
Though my beloved keeps me from the dawn
She makes up for those hours in the dark.
But we are not only kissing, we talk
Wisely, and if she sleeps, breathing steadily
(She shakes for one instant first), I gently
Count out a pentameter on her warm back.

Then, a fire's lit in my heart – the old gods
Look on us as they've looked for millennia
At the clear margin of disaster and confusion.

BRYAN MACMAHON
A WOMAN'S HAIR

On Sunday afternoons when the bar was closed and my father
had gone off to a football match my mother would take the
opportunity offered by the quiet house to wash her beautiful hair.
There were times when she would do so, I realised later, solely
to gratify me, her only daughter – and indeed, her only child.

When my mother's hair was washed, rinsed and had almost dried, I would insist on her sitting on a rocking-chair. I would then stand on a stool beside her to catch the cascading hair above the point where it had gently tangled and would resolutely force the comb through it. As accurately as I recall the texture of my mother's hair, I also remember my stolid father's uncomprehension of it as a bond between between me and her: all he seemed to understand was the filling of spill-over pint-glasses for the cartmen and countrymen who made the vacant lot at our gable on the town's edge a stopping place on their way to the market.

But always between my mother and me, and complementary to the bond of flesh and blood, was the shining spancel of hair. I had combed it and plaited it and piled it and experimented with it until my father bustling in and out of the kitchen scarcely know whether to laugh or scowl at such tomfoolery which – to him – was of a piece with my mother's obsession with music and the incomprehensible tock-tock of the metronome on the top of our piano. And when, as ladylike as she had lived, my mother died, I was left with the memory of her hair spread out like a fan on the white linen pillow on either side of her waxen face.

After my mother's death – I was then ten years of age – I was packed off to a boarding school. I pined for home and after two months was brought back and sent to the local convent day-school, where I was an irregular attender, being kept home on slight pretexts.

At this time I was something of a day-dreamer: washing ware at the window of the scullery, I would look out on the vacant lot beside our house and watch the carters unyoke their horses and tie hissing nosebags of oats about their animals' necks. I recall seeing a thunder shower fall on an unprotected box-cart of unslaked lime so that later the rocks of lime bubbled like molten lava. At certain times, too, the site grew still more interesting for it was a halting-place for the restless of the Irish roads—umbrella-menders, ballad singers, knife-grinders, men and women subject to the compulsion and tyranny of movement.

One Saturday evening in early June, as dusk fell, a tramp and his wife – more likely his 'woman' – pitched a crude shelter just below our scullery window. The ice-cold air and the early evening stars had already given warning that a night of heavy frost would follow. The shelter was a crude one – a dirty canvas sheet slung over a ridge-pole held three feet above the ground by a few curved sally rods with limestones fallen from our yard wall to keep the soiled skirt of the camp in place. The shelter could be entered at either end, simply by groping back the flaps.

The tramp was black-bearded and was sixty if he was a day; the woman seemed to be in her early twenties. She had clear-cut features with a weather-worn complexion and there was in her stare a vacancy that seemed to offer a clue to such an odd pairing.

But it was her luxuriant dark hair that, despite its tangled and even filthy nature, attracted my attention. It appeared to be of a finer texture than my own hair, or indeed that of my mother, but the wind and the sun played havoc with it. I grimaced at the thought that such hair seemed a waste on the young woman's head.

As darkness fell, the tramp and his woman entered our bar, squatted on the floor in a corner, and began to drink stolidly, now and again muttering gutturally at each other. My father kept growling half-refusals to their requests for more drink, but the tramp and the woman kept blackmailing him and begging for more. I felt that my father continued to serve them simply because my mother had always pleaded for the 'travellers': 'Don't judge them, Tom – their life is hard. If they get drunk itself,' she would say, 'what harm is it? And they haven't far to go when they leave us – only from the bar to the gable outside.'

So, aloof and alone, the oddly-matched pair drank and muttered and growled and lisped and never spared an upward glance for the other customers.

When closing-time was called, and overcalled, with my father hanging threateningly above them, they at last staggered to their feet, bundled themselves out the door and moved towards their shelter. There, swaying giddily, they groped at the flaps and at last fumbled in, and down, almost bringing the canvas about their ears with their blundering movements. Watching them from the darkness through the just-open window of the scullery, the night air icy on my face, I wondered at the mystery of the cave in which they slept, with perhaps their bodies oddly tangled up in one another. Then I looked up at the frost-polished heavens, shuddered in the cold, and finally, closing the window without a sound, eased home the brass bolt on it. Thoughtfully I made my way to bed.

In the morning I woke to find that the frost had painted palm trees on the window-pane. I prepared the Sunday breakfast, then glanced out at the now glittering canvas of the tent. The frost had made the morning air soundless so that the town seemed unusually still. My father always slept out the Sunday mornings. As I came downstairs after having given him his breakfast in bed I heard a low knocking at the side-door.

I tiptoed out into the hallway. As again the knocking came, 'Who's out?' I asked sharply. 'Me!' said a deep hoarse voice which I recognised at once as being that of the bearded tramp. 'What do you want?' I asked. 'A knife or a scissors,' he growled. I paused, a constriction of fear in my heart. 'My father is in bed', I told him. 'Can you wait till he gets up?' 'I must get it now – we have to be off!' The man's 'we have to be off' assuaged my latent fear that he meant harm, yet I asked, 'What do you want it for?' 'Something that's caught in the frost!' 'Is it the canvas?' 'Give me a knife or a scissors and I'll return it safely,' he muttered in reply.

I stood irresolute. A knife – no! But I could give him the battered black-and-silver tailor's scissors that was in the drawer of our kitchen table. With a cry of 'Wait!' I ran, rattled open the drawer and going to the door, opened it cautiously and handed out the scissors. A glimpse told me that the man was sober but his face was haggard and white-cold with traces of drink-rust about his lips. Muttering a word of thanks, he moved away.

After a time, I ran to the scullery, climbed on a chair and, leaning over the sink, looked out on the shelter. What I saw made me cry out and beat with my knuckles on the frame of the window. I unshot the bolt, swung open the window on its hinges and screamed 'No! No!' at the top of my voice.

The tramp, who was kneeling on the ground at one end of the shelter, looked upwards over his shoulder at me. His black hat was pitched back on his poll and a single lock of hair was plastered onto his white sweating forehead. 'No! No!' I screamed again, then leaping off the chair I raced through the kitchen, tore into the shop, grabbed a claw hammer from the tool-box under the counter and, opening the hall door, went pelting out.

The man, the scissors still in his hands, was on one knee at the

end of the tent. Beneath him, prone on the ground and protruding
from under the canvas of the shelter lay the woman's head and
breast. The tumult of her hair was spread out beneath her head.
I verified what I had guessed at from my first glimpse through the
window, that her hair was frostlocked in a small but comparatively
deep pool of water that lay just outside the end of the camp and
that the tramp was about to cut the hair so as to release it.

The woman's face could have been one carved in cameo on
the brooch my mother wore, but for the fact that the rust of old
drink befouled her lips about which an odd not-caring smile now
played. The white skin of her lower throat and upper breasts was
in startling contrast to her dark complexion and to the soiled
ground beneath her head. 'Wait!' I cried again, pushing the man
aside; crouching, my fingers verified that the hair was vice-
gripped in a frozen pool of animal urine.

I tilted the head sideways and with the hammer-head began
to hack at the edge of the frozen pool. Under my blows the ice
cracked brown-white at its edges. When I had reduced part of
the edge of the pool to powder, I tried with the claw of the
hammer to lever upwards on the ragged block of the frozen pool.
Try as I would, I failed to gain a purchase on the powdered ice.

The man, still in a kind of animal crouch, was directly behind
me and watching me dully. He held the scissors in his hand.
Again I attacked, seemingly as fruitlessly as before, for even the
claw of the hammer could do little more than break off futile
smithereens. Although I continued to punch and claw, releasing
the hair seemed a baffling task.

I paused; then furious and tense, I snatched the scissors from
the man's hand. Forcing its two points together to make a single
point, which I thrust deep under the ice-block, I began to lever
the ice upwards. At first I made no impression on it but, at last,
hearing the ice squeak, I again inserted the scissors at a different
place, this time with the points about an inch apart, and levering
with all my strength, brought the whole irregular frozen block
in which the spread of the woman's hair was locked, completely
free of the ground.

For a moment or two, utterly spent, I hung above the woman;
then half-dragged, half-helped her to her feet where, smiling
grotesquely, she continued to regard me sidelong with slightly
daft, slightly whimsical, wholly animal eyes. Her neck and

shoulders were white and bare and the brown dripping block of ice dangled between her shoulder blades.

Gripping the hammer and scissors. I began to push her out into the street and towards our hall-door which still stood ajar. I pushed her into the kitchen where by now the morning range was a grin of fire. Sobbing somewhat, I steered her before me into the scullery. There, standing on a chair, I made her bow her neck as I filled an enamel basin with hot water. Cupping the water in my hands, I poured it over the matted poll. I kept working furiously until the melting ice began to fall in chunks into the basin. Then I took up a bar of soap and frenziedly lathered the woman's hair. I found myself working under an odd compulsion.

Not a word passed between us. Again I changed the water in the basin until at last, as I rinsed the hair, the water poured clearly. I put a towel about her head and draped a bath-towel over a chair.

I then took out – she watched me dreamily – a large oval-shaped zinc bathtub and, setting it on the floor, affixed a length of hose to the nozzle of the hot-water tap and sent steaming water pouring into the vessel. Almost stamping my foot, I signed to the woman that she should stand in it and wash herself. Duly she began to drop her rags to the floor. I tiptoed upstairs and, opening the mahogany wardrobe on the landing, piled a skirt and blouse of my dead mother over one arm and snatched some underclothes from a drawer beside it. A pair of lizard-skin shoes, old fishnet stockings, these too I took; finally, opening a dusty trunk, I removed a clutch of hairpins and a comb inset with brilliants.

Returning to the kitchen, I peeped through the keyhole into the scullery; the woman was still standing in the steaming tub, indolently rubbing the cake of soap into her limbs. Young as I was, I realised that she had a beautiful body.

I prepared the breakfast. When I thought that she had finished washing herself I pushed open the door a little and left the clothes on the floor beside it. After a time I heard the basin clank against the trough and scrape the woman's nails as she rinsed the vessel. A little while later she came slowly out, wearing my mother's clothes.

Holding my breath, I watched her walk forward. The house was without sound. In mid-kitchen she turned and, looking at the table, indicated that she wished to eat. I placed food before her. She ate her breakfast slowly and thoughtfully, crumbs falling unheeded to the floor. When she had finished I placed the delf on a tray and pointed to the rocking chair by the fire. The woman rose slowly and then went and sat on it. I took the tray to the scullery, piled the ware into the basin, ran the hot water on it and returned to the kitchen. From a press to the left of the fire I took a towel turban and set about combing out the drying hair.

I was patient with the hair, teasing it gently where it had knotted and working diligently until at last it was a blue-black thunder-cloud about her head and shoulders. Between me and the glow of the fire its edges were rimmed with red-gold. Wholly absorbed, I kept on combing as the hair became still drier and more beautiful – more tractable too, until at last it glistened and shone and shook and floated and fell in plenitude about her waist. The woman turned her head quite sensitively to accommodate me as I worked.

At last I combed the hair back over the ears and, setting it aside the comb, began to plait and pile, twisting it this way and that, pinning it at a point that took my fancy by inserting the comb with the brilliants in it and then undoing it capriciously as if dissatisfied with the result. The hair, now wholly dry, was sensual under my fingers, so that I was reluctant to finish, and time and time again, with an exclamation of sham annoyance I let it fall. Each time I broke off, the woman smiled at my feigned disappointment. About us the house grew still more silent.

This went on for some time until I could find no excuse to continue. Then the woman's long bare arm curled intuitively around me and drew me gently down on to her lap. At first I was inclined to resist, but her implied certainty that I would obey her was so absolute that I yielded. There was a pause in which my buttocks tested the welcome seat offered by her thighs, then, reassured, I sent my arm over her shoulder and dug my fingers deep into the thicket of hair at the nape of her neck.

Almost imperceptibly at first, but with a mounting sense of rhythm, and muttering, humming and crooning as she moved, the woman began to rock backwards and forwards on the chair with a movement reminiscent of the metronome on the piano-top. I found myself nestling closer to her breasts: of its own volition my head butted against her and before I knew, or cared, my lips and teeth were on her nipples. I heard myself, as at a distance, mouthing warm and pleasant incoherencies.

So drugged were we both that the vague knocking on the hall door did not disturb us, nor a moment or two later did the sight of my father in the kitchen doorway, dressed only in his pants and shirt, with the bearded tramp standing beside him, trouble us in the least. After an uncomprehending glance at us the two men turned away and moved dully into the bar, leaving us alone to rock a solution to one of the many compulsions of our shared womanhood.

PÁDRAIG Ó FIANNACHTA
REILIG DHÚN CHAOIN

Codail, a chaora,
Is a uain ag méiligh.
Codail, a Sheanduine,
Gan sobal ná sraothairt.

Codail, a Ghaeilge
Faoi na fóda glasa.
Codail, a Pheig
Faoi do leic mhóir léith.

Tá glas ar an ngeata
Dom choimeád amach
Le heagla go bhfanfainn
Mar chloch ar do leacht.

PEIG SAYERS
PIARAS FIRTÉAR

Le lín Dochtúir Céitin a bheith a seiribhís na h-eaglaise, do mhair taoiseach calama spridiúil a n-iarthar Chiaraí a gCorca-Dhuíne. Do bhí sé 'n-a chónuí a dtig fada fairsin a ndún breá aereach go nglaoatar Dún an Fhirtéaraig 'sa lá tá aniubh ann air. Do bhí aer bog cúrha na mara múire ag séide isteach er gach taobh chuige. Isé an ainim a bhí er an dtaoiseach san, Firtéar; dá bhrí sin tá Dún an Fhirtéaraig mar ainim air, agus tá an p'róiste sluinithe do mar an gcéana. Do bhí mac ag Firtéar gurbh' ainim do Piaras. Nuari a dh'eighri' sé suas a n-aois fir, do bhí sp'rid agus misneach agus lú 'n-a chruí, 'n-a chná; is mú cath cruaig do throid sé er son a thíre agus a theangan.

Is math do theastuig a lethéid do laoch 'san amm úd, mar do bhí crá agus clipe agus géirleanúint er na Cat'licithe bochta 'san amm san. Do thug Piaras fé ndeara go gcathfuí rod éigint a dhéanamh a thúrfach curthom na Féine dosna daoine bochta. Dá bhrí sin do bhailibh sé chuige múrán d' fhearaibh troda, agus ba mhinic do bhuin sé cnead as a namhaid; ach fóraoir, ní raibh tréan buan riamh. 'Se sin an scéal céana ag Piaras é, mar do thit sé a mblá óige, agus a dtosach a shaol do crochach é er Cnucán na gCaerach a Cíl Áirne. Do crochach sagart agus easpog cráifeach diaguithe a n-aonacht leis. An lá a bhíodar á chrocha, do bhí múrán daoine bailithe ann. Isé an sagart a' chéad duine do crochach. An t-easpog a bhí le crocha 'n-a dhiaig; do riug sé er láimh er Phiaras agus dúirt sé 'Is trua san, tusa a bheith dá chrocha aniubh; ní h-aon tácht sine a chrocha, mar tá súil agum go mbeig easpuig agus sagairt a n-oileán na hÉirean go deire 'n domhain; ach ní bheig do lethéid-se do thaoiseach cró ná do chúl cosanta le fáil ansa' tir seo go deó 'ríst. Dá bhrí sin is múr an scrios agus is trua, tu chuir do d' chuis. Seo duit cloihín bheanuithe; cuir a d' bhéal í, agus ní crochfar go deó tu.' Do thug an cloihín agus do chuir sé 'n-a bhéal í. Ansan do tháinig an t-amm chuin na cnáibhe do chuir er a mhineál; nuair a bh' amm leis an gcrochtóir a ghnú a bheith déanta, do chuai' sé ag trial air chuin é thógaint leis ó'n gcroih. Nuair a buineach an córda do mhineál Phiarais ní marabh a bhí sé, ach có beó le breac. Do tháinig úna mhúr er na daoine a bhí láirtheach. Dúradar leis an gcrochtóir gur b' amhla nár dhin sé a ghnú a gceart. Ansan do cuireach an chnáibh er mhineál Phiarais an tarna h-uair, agus tugach níos mú aimmsire do mar dhe ná mar tugach ruimé sin; ach do b'é an scéal céana é—ní raibh Piaras marabh. Ach an tríú h-uair dúirt sé leis na h-uaisle do bhí 'n-a thímpal, 'Ná measaíg, a dhaoine,' er seisean 'go bhfuil córda ná gad ná cnáibh do chrochfach mise; ach anis ní bheig fuíleach na croihe le glaoch oram ná er mo shliucht a m' dhiaig.' Do thóg sé 'mach an cloihín bheanaithe as a bhéal, do bhuin sé fíor na cruise air féin lé, mar Críostaí fúnta do b'ea é; ansan do chaith sé an chloihín thara n-a ghualain, agus do labhair sé as árd, "Sea anis, a bhuachail,'

er seisean leis an gcrochtóir, 'scaoil oram é.' Ní fad' an mhuíl a
bhí an gad er a sciúch nuair a bhí sé fachta bás. Ba mhúr an tru'é,
mar fear math deirciúil grámhar a b'ea é, treóraí na mbochtán
agus cúl cosanta na cléire 'san amm san.

Deirtear, gur bean óg fé ndeár Piaras do chrocha an lá úd;
mar do bhí dlí chlaon ann 'san amm san, agus do sheasaimh sí
er fheag múráin aimmsire, measaim, go raibh sí á chuir a
bhfeidhm nú go dí go rángaig Connsiléir Ó Conail a dteideal.
Ba chruaig an dlí í, aon bhean óg a luífach a súil er ógánach 'san
amm san, a rogha aige a bheith uasal nú íseal, bocht nú saibhir,
do bh'fhéidir leis an mnaoi óig dearabhú air, agus chathfach sé í
phósa nú folag lé é chrocha. Ach mola le Dia, níl an dlí ghrána san
anis ann. Do bhí iníon Pradaistiúnaig tímpal Oileáin Ciaraí, do bhí
a muíntir anashaibhir; do fuair sí radharc súl er Phiaras cúpala uair,
agus do thit sí a ngrá leis. Ach do phósfach Piaras í mara mbách
go raibh canáile mhúr eatortha. Ní raibh sí dá chreideamh féin, agus
rod eile, do bhí sé mar namhaid aige n-a h-athir agus aige n-a locht
leanúna 'san amm san. Do thug sé scéala do Phiaras chuin í phósa,
ach b' éigeant do an dúltamh do thúirt di. Deirtear, gur b'in í-a
dhearabhuig air, agus gur b'í cúis a chrochta í an lá brónach úd a
gCíl Áirne. Tá rann a mbéalaibh daoine a dhéin sé sara crochach
é. Seo mar tá sí:

'Ní h-é marú an Dúna do dhúbhaig mo mhineál riamh,
ná a ndúrathars liúm a Siúnda an Oileáin Tiar,
ach an mhaighdean mhúinte bhúig-mhilis na gcocán gcliar
nár dheaghas 'n-a clúid a dtúis ná ndeire mo shael riamh.'

Is sara tháinig an méid seo trasna er Phiaras, do theastuig
ó n-'athir cleamhnas a dhéanamh do le cailín óg álain, do threibh
uasail go raibh coidireamh ma' aige ortha. Aon lá 'mháin do leig
an seanfhear, 'sé sin seana-Fhirtéar, chuige duine dá ghiulaí, fear
go raibh úntaoibh ma' aige as. Dúirt sé leis dol go dí n-a lethéid
sin do thig, agus gan fios a rúin ná chúirim a thúirt d' aon duine
sa teaghlach san ach don dall a bhí ann. 'Túir chúm,' erse Firtéar,
'go cruín beacht tuairisc er gach ní a bhuinean leis an dtig agus
a bhfuil ann.' D'imig an giula, agus níor dhéin sé stad ná cónuí
nú gur bhuin sé 'mach tig na mná óige. Do fáiltíoch ruimis agus
do cuireach gach cóir air, mar do bhí uirim mhúr don bhFirtéarach
'san amm úd. Do bhí mí caite aige 'sa tig, agus níor fhiarhuig
aene do cad a thug é. Ach aon lá 'mhain, do labhair an dall leis,
'A mhic mo chruí,' er seisean, 'tá fhios agum-sa cad a thug 'on

tig seo tu; anis – is údair cliste mise má táim dall féin, is údair
er gach dán Piaras Firtéar – íns do an dán beog so a déarfad leat.'
Ansan dúirt sé leis a' ngiula:

'Íns do Phiaras Firtéar an Dúin,
ó 'sé is údair leis gach dán,
go ndúirt an dall a bhí 'sa chúine
gur thit crú ó'n láir bháin.'

Có lua do tháinig an giula abhaile, d'íns sé do Phiaras cad
dúirt an dall leis. Có lua agus d'airig Piaras an dán san, do thuig
sé é go math. 'Dar fíor,' ar seisean, 'níl aon ghnú aguine di feasta.'
Níor bhac sé lé ná lé n-a muíntir as san suas; ach mo bhrón is
mo mhairig, níorbh' fhada 'n-a dhiaig sin go raibh Piaras curtha
chuin báis. Ba mhúr é cú agus brón na nGaol 'n-a dhiaig, níorbh'
aon úna, mar do bhí sé 'n-a chárta cúil agus chú chosanta a
gCiaraí er feag na mblianta a bhí sé fé bhlá.

Deirtear, gur chaith sé tamal 'san Oileán Mhúr, agus is dói
liom gur fíor e, mar tá úin dheas er a' dtaobh leastuaig don
Oileán, agus glaotar 'Scairt Phiarais' mar ainim er an bpoll san.
Deir na seandaoine, gur mú saighdiúir ma' a dh'ídig se 'sa pholl
san. Do b' fh'riste do e sin a dhéanamh; is aige a bhí an curthom
ma' ortha, mar tá an poll so isteach a gclíothán an chnuic a rín
ghéar shleamhain, agus an fharaige mhúr a' bris' isteach er na
caraigeacha fé n-a bun, agus is mú duine a shluigeach sí agus
thógfach sí as a' slí gan fisgint go brách aríst. Deirtear, gur mú
saighdiúir math do scaoil Piaras Firtéar le fánaig ansúd a n-aimmsir
an chatha agus an chruatain; ach baochas le Dia tá gach saol a' boga.
Do bhí fir mhatha a nÉirin riamh, agus do bhí fir mheata leis 'n-
a measc, ach ní bheig an saol mar sin as so suas, le cúnamh Dé.

Do chúm Piaras dán beog ag tagairt don bpoll so go raibh
sé ann 'san Oileán Mhúr. Dúirt sé:

A Dhia tá thuas, an trua leat mise mar táim
a bpríosún uaigineach, is nách múr go bhficim an lá;
an braon tá thuas a n-uachtar lice go h-árd
ag titeam a m' chluais, is fuaim na tuine lé m' sháil.

as SCÉALTA ÓN MBLASCAOD (1938)
KENNETH JACKSON A CHUIR IN EAGAR

Piaras Feiritéar
An Bhean Do B'annsa Liom Fán nGréin

An bhean dob'annsa liom fán ngréin,
Is nárbh' annsa léi mé féin ar bith,
'Na suidhe ar ghualainn a fir féin,
Ba chruaidh an chéim is mé istigh.

An guirtín branair do rinneas dom féin,
Is mé bhfad in bpéin 'na bhun,
Gan ag an bhfear a tháinig indé,
Acht a fhuirse dó féin 's a chur.

Má rinnis branar gan síol
Is fear maith den tír uait 'na bhun
A fhreagas an Mhárta san am chóir
Is a fhreastalas dóigh le n-a chur −

Is mairg do-ní branar go bráth
Is ná beir fás fada dá chuid féir,
Is an tan do chuadhas-sa in bhfad
Gur coilleadh mo nead thar m'éis.

Da mbudh duine mise raghadh i bhfad,
Is d'fhágfadh mo nead thar m'éis,
Do chuirfinn anál fá n-a bruach
Do chuirfeadh a fuath ar gach éan.

Cumann go dté a sac i sac
Ní dhéan feasta ar eagla an bháis;
Is é do bheir mo chroidhe 'na ghual
An grá fuar a bhíos ag mná.

Is mairg atá mar atáim,
Is mairg do bheir grá leamh,
Is mairg do bheas gan mnaoi
Is dhá mhairg ag ná bíonn ach bean.

MÍCHEÁL Ó RUAIRC
THE SANDWOMAN

On the Great Western Island
(or so the story goes) when
emigration had decimated
the island community and
overfamiliarity and an alien
morality had put paid
to sexual gratification

the boys from the village
would gather on the strand
on those long summer evenings
when the waves crashed
like broken dreams
on their burning need
and there on the beach

out of reach of the houses
where the tide had gone out
they would construct
a woman out of sand
fashion her with their desire
into a work of art
and with the urgency

of their fingers breathe
life into her limbs
until she lay before them
like a living woman
firm breasts rising and falling
in time with the waves crashing
along the coastline

her thighs wide apart
and the mound of Venus

full and sensuous. No longer
burdened by their shame they would
take turns in mounting her
sending the hot seed spinning
deep into the earth

and then to wander off and
play football or linger and look
as the sea took possession
of this woman of their imagination
secure in the knowledge
that somehow tomorrow would
yield up a different dream

EIBHLÍS NÍ SHUÍLLEABHÁIN
from LETTERS FROM THE GREAT BLASKET (1978)

22 March 1941
You have asked me a question in your last letter about the girls
and their husbands. You see that them girls are married outside,
love the island still and love the people they left there but could
not find enough courage to marry there as married troubles are
great ones and they could not face them inside these days with
no old women helpers or any women, you know as the people
are reducing so is their courage going . . .

25 November 1941
There will not be any candles this year, I have two since last year
which will do Christmas night and the night after. There isn't
any paraffin oil with the last two months and the old custom
which we call *slige* that is the cover of a box of shoe polish with
wick covered with seal or fish oil that is the small light, on
everybody's table these long nights. We don't complain of it, and
a good turf fire burning and nobody is hungry so far thank God
for that. Islanders feel happy amidst hard times until anybody
is sick this time of the year always.

23 February 1942

We have determined at last to leave this lovely island, I know you will be very sad to hear it, but things are not as they should be and times are changed and especially for us here with a child at school age and no school and people saying and telling us the child must go to school very soon. They may take her away somewhere when they think of it you would know, so we thought it best to go out somewhere ourselves and try and have at least one joy out of this hard life, to live with our child. So the next time you will come to this island there will be no Eibhlís but the ruins of the house, only the walls as we are taking out the head [roof] of the house there near Ballydavid as Seán's friends are living there on fishing. He will go out fishing there with them. You may be sure I'll miss the calm air of our dear island and the beautiful White Strand. You know people interested in Eibhlís and the island would not do. Visitors coming in and going out of our house talking and talking and they on their holidays and they at home having comfortable home and no worry during winter or summer, would never believe the misfortune on this island no school nor comfort, no road to success, no fishing, not five hundred of mackerel was caught when last summer it cost £3 a hundred, no lobsters last summer, very very scarce, hard times, everything so dear and so far away. Surely people could not live on air and sunshine. No not at all. There are two more families leaving also with us. I can't really say what time we are going out, April or May. I will know in my next letter.

I was very troubled when this commenced but when I am understanding and looking at it from other sides I am getting all right again, for instance girls who grew up with me and went to America years ago and made their home there, never saw their parents since nor the island, surely I have shared many I may say happy years there; whatever happens on this island I have one gifted thing to tell you of it I was always happy there. I was happy among sorrows on this island. I think I will not be interesting in life at all from this on when I am gone out on the mainland. I will be very sad to leave my parents.

4 April 1942
Yesterday Good Friday Niamh and I visited the Gravel Strand
as it is an old custom here to bring home something to eat from
this strand this holy day, also John was there picking limpets or
in Irish báirneach. He had a half-gallon tin full. I counted thirty
people there, men almost all, only five or six girls. The men were
going out to the very end out cutting seaweed and carrying in
small amount roped in through the large stones. Indeed it was
a great task, and taking them up to the field where the ass can
come for it. Before it was spread on the fields ready in the late
cold and raining evening, you may be sure they had done a good
day's work. They haven't any good hopes of good potatoes this
year without guano, which is very very scarce, they will be very
very wet but anyway they are making the best of what they have
like always and hope God to help them for the rest. You may
be sure that poor islanders work for their meals and to tell the
truth has a very poor meal after the day and is too far from some
good food or a good drink to take after their hardworking day.
They were all very wet in the strand that day.

14 April 1942
I will try and give you a full view from the air on our island at
present. We had a most glorious weather with the last three
weeks and as always islanders think they are just on the mainland
while it lasts moreover these days, then you go and buy half a
pound of coffee and no sugar is there, no soap, no tea, no tobacco
and the worst of all no flour nor bread nor biscuits nor paraffin
oil for light nor a candle. Yesterday the day being beautifully
calm two islanders went to Dunquin and walked it all the way
into town. One of these was the Queen's son Mike the Poet and
the other was Keane, who is seventy years of age, and they
walked and tramped it all the way from town more late in the
evening, this old man carrying three stones of flour on his back.
You may understand these hardships on island life and you may
be sure that there is a certain strain of body and mind and able
to age a good young man of strength and energy. And to make
matters worse these men could not light their pipes after their
hard day's ordeal after their resting at home late in the evening
as they did not get a pipe of tobacco in town. It was the same
with two younger boys before this and their families at home

were gone to bed before them without eating any bread all day save a few old potatoes, which is not worth much from now on unless you have saved the bigger ones and put them apart, but thank God we have them for indeed many the meals they make and they are too glad to have them. I am afraid they won't go far now by some of them as they are making two good meals of them during winter and then where there is a cow and also an ass asking for some potatoes are easily exhausted.

6 November 1942
Niamh was attending school for a month and it closed then as some fever broke out around. She is more happy here among a class of her own than in the island, she was missing a group of children laughing and shouting. She always likes to be writing and having a book pretending to be reading and singing. When she is asked would she prefer this place to the island, she always says, 'I would rather being in the island.' It's 9.30 and Niamh is thinking of going to bed and before Rosary is said and the fire is settled up and the table for John some bread and butter and some milk in the saucepan for to heat for him. We have a better chance here of getting our rations than on the island, my God things are difficult enough to get on the mainland and you may be sure that living on the islands is no joke at all these days. To tell you the truth I am glad (in spite of being lonely after them) of being out in the cold and dreary nights of winter.

8 January 1943
The oldest person on the island died in the middle of Christmas some days ago; his age was ninety-six. His name was John Kearney, a next-door neighbour of us in there. He was blind with the last eight or nine years and he had a miserable life there in latter years for his son married in his house died four years ago and his wife the year before. His own wife died suddenly in his best house and everything was going from bad to worse for him, no doubt he was strong and healthy, he can say it. May he rest in peace, amen. He said there lately if all went went as he would like them to go on he would live more than a hundred but unless he was all iron he had to break down. Only one canoe was in the funeral, that brought out the corpse, the day was not well and they were shocked by the bad weather and outside the

landing place in Dunquin, the quay nearly all went by the storm so it's all a wreck there unless in a very calm weather. So everyone tells us we are lucky to have come out this year. I am glad we are also for Niamh's sake and by God when the young people are leaving, sure it's no place at all then. You come out to Dunquin, then you will not get what you like to get, then after a hard day's toil going rowing out and in again you will come home without that thing you badly want. Of course it's changing from bad to worse from day to day.

10 February 1943
Well dear friend we are in the beginning of the New Year and thank God we are all well and happy so far and have enough to eat and drink as always. I think we are very lucky to have been out this winter for it is the severest winter that came with ages and even yet it is bad and very bad and such rain and snow nearly every day. In the bad weather I don't miss my lovely island so much but in the warm weather of course I think of the beautiful scenery of my island which I did not admire so much until now. Of course with God's help I will see them all again some day during the summer season, how I'd love to see my parents once again and all my friends and throw myself once more on the White Strand.

8 December 1945
Please God I will visit my island home early in the New Year if I get any chance at all and see the old parents and friends. Niamh showed me a book a few nights ago and a photograph of the old house in the island in it, I was nearly crying when I saw it, though sands of memories were running through my mind of how I used to see the old pictures of the sea so calm and the seagulls crying and the canoes coming in from the mainland and the White Strand, white with white sand, how crowds of us after school used play together on it like one family, so scattered now and not even one child on this lonely white sands. A great pity. What do you think?

2 December 1951
To tell the truth about Niamh my plans for her is to cross the ocean when the time will come and that is, that she will be strong and healthy enough to do so. To go over to America, the country

of the poor and for the poor, for the parents here in Ireland would be naked out only for their children go over in time, to send money to pay for their debts and send every stitch of clothes for bedding, curtains and human use. Everything from America.

30 December 1951

How quickly the years gallop away as you say. I was sitting here by the fireside a few nights ago and I was looking on the old clock which is in a glass-case, the one we had in the island, and it's the same glass-face that's on it. I was thinking of how often Tomás – the islandman – looked on the same clock nobody could count, and a snap of yourself was inside in a corner of the clock. Well I had so many things running through my mind, some gay and some sad memories too, I was thinking that you often too made me happy since I married, always sending parcels and things and thank God, said I, I have him again this Christmas behind me, and Niamh will be with me a few more Christmases but then I am sure I will not be happy any more then. The old folk of the island will be scattering to their graves and no more island holidays then, and such and such were coming before my eyes near the fire. I think more and more of my island home Christmas Eve than any other time and a terrible storm has just passed and Seán (my brother) will not come out at all this year and I missed him very much. Do you ever have such dreams? You do not have time to yourself to do so I suppose.

AOGÁN Ó RATHAILLE
CABHAIR NÍ GHAIRFEAD

Cabhair ní ghairfead go gcuirthear mé i gcruinn-comhrainn –
dar an leabhar dá ngairinn níor ghaire-de an ní dhomh-sa;
ár gcodhnach uile, glac-chumasach shíl Eoghain,
is tollta a chuisle, 'gus d'imigh a bhrí ar feochadh.

Do thonncrith, m'inchinn, d'imigh mo phríomhdh óchas,
poll im ionathar, biora nimhe tr'm dhrólainn,
ár bhfonn, ár bhfothain, ár monga 's ár mínchónghair
i ngeall le pinginn ag foirinn ó chrích Dhóbhair.

Do bhodhar an tSionainn, an Life, 's an Laoi cheolmhar,
abhainn an Bhiorra Dhuibh, Bruice 'gus Bríd, Bóinne,
com Loch Deirg 'na ruide 'gus Toinn Tóime
ó lom an cuireata cluiche ar an rí coróinneach.

Mo ghlam is minic, is sílimse síordheora,
is trom mo thubaist 's is duine mé ar míchomhthrom,
fonn ní thigeann im ghaire 's mé ag caoi ar bhóithre
ach foghar na Muice nach gontar le saigheadóireacht.

Goll na Rinne, na Cille 'gus chríche Eoghanacht,
do lom a ghoile le huireaspa ar díth córach;
an seabhac agá bhfuilid sin uile 's a gcíosóireacht,
fabhar ní thugann don duine, cé gaol dó-san.

Fán dtromlot d'imigh ar a chine na rí mórga
treabhann om uiseannaibh uisce go scímghlórach;
is lonnmhar chuirid mo shrutha-sa foinseoga
san abhainn do shileas ó Thruipill go caoin-Eochaill.

Stadfadsa feasta – is gar dom éag gan mhoill
ó treascradh dragain Leamhan, Léin is Laoi;
rachad 'na bhfasc le searc na laoch don chill,
na flatha fá raibh mo shean roimh éag do Chríost.

DANIEL CORKERY
EOGHAN RUADH Ó SÚILLEABHÁIN

Aodhagán Ó Rathaille, that spirit so quick with all the proud
and lonely sorrows of the Ireland of his time, had been buried
only a little more than twenty years when, almost in the same
spot of outland – one mile away, to be exact – another poet was
born who also may be said to have been quick with Ireland's
sorrows, no longer proud and lonely sorrows, however, but
reckless and wild. Ó Rathaille is a tragic figure, mournful, proud;
Eoghan Ruadh's life was even more tragic, but then he was a
wastrel with a loud laugh.

That piece of outland, in which both were born, was truly

Irish in its fortunes, and its story is full of meaning. It stretches eastward from Killarney to Rathmore, the Abhainn Ui Chriadh (the Quagmire River) running through it southwards to join the Flesk. On the north-east lies the mountain mass known as Sliabh Luachra; and the school of poets, of which Eoghan Ruadh is the greatest, is known as the Sliabh Luachra school. When the Geraldines were crushed, the piece of outland was swept and harried and left desolate – houseless and unpeopled. In time some few of the O'Sullivans came northwards from Kenmare and set up new homesteads in it, undoing with patient labouring the work of the despoiler; and from these O'Sullivans sprang the boy Eoghan Ruadh.

In another way, too, the piece of land helps us to realise history. Let us look at it: All to the west of the little river belonged then to the MacCarthy Mór; all to the east was part of the Kenmare estate. That estate was in the grip of middlemen, those 'deputies of deputies of deputies'; but the MacCarthys' tenants do not seem to have been rack-rented at all: it was probably one of those half-forgotten spots where many immemorial customs supplied the place of law; and, as compared with the rack-rented eastern riverbank, was a land flowing with milk and honey. Milk and honey may, indeed, have been actually the most plentiful of foods in it; and if it were so it was only fitting, for nowhere else in Ireland were so many sweet singers gathered together: the south-west corner of Munster was the Attica of Irish Ireland and Sliabh Luachra its Hymettus.

We are told there was a 'classical school' in it – but what we are to understand by the phrase is that the Irish tradition had somehow never been quite extinguished there; that one or more bardic schools had flourished in the district of old; that a broken-down bardic school or Court of Poetry still assembled there; that the study of Irish poetry was the chief business of that school; that among the students would be found certain 'poor scholars' who had travelled thither on foot, some of them hundreds of miles, from those places where such schools had ceased to exist; that of those students some would later enter Continental universities and become priests, while others would obtain Commissions in the armies of France, Austria or Spain.

'On Sunday evenings throughout the summer season a "patron", or dancing festival, was held at Faha, and in the plain beneath, a vigorous hurling match was carried on. The whole district on both sides of the river was permeated with the spirit of learning and the spirit of song. The O'Rahillys, the O'Scannells, the O'Sullivans and other families included men of conspicuous ability and no mean poetical talents. Between the people on either side of the river a rivalry, reminding one of the supposed derivation of that word, sprang up in hurling and in poetry. The people grew critical; each new poem or song was subject to a severe examination, and if approved, was inserted in a book specially kept for the purpose, called "Bolg an tSoláthair." In the winter evenings the neighbours assembled to see what new piece was added to the bolg, and thus a constant stimulus to poetic effort was maintained. Native music, too, was fostered with native song, and an Irish piper was an institution at Faha which the surrounding rent-crushed villages could not afford. The academy at Faha prepared students for the more advanced seminary at Killarney, where candidates were educated for Holy Orders, and was not a mere grinding establishment, but fostered poetry and music and supplied a strong stimulus to the efforts of genius. The course comprised, besides Irish, English, Latin and Greek. In Greek, Homer seems to have been a favourite, and in Latin, Virgil and Caesar and Ovid.'

'The more advanced seminary at Killarney' – yes, for the penal laws against religion were being relaxed; and the Church was just beginning to re-organise itself as an institution with a body as well as a spirit. From day to day, the passing of priests to and from the Continent was quickening; and parishes were beginning to set up regular services in buildings set apart for the purpose. But though the penal laws were becoming less rigorous the condition of the people was worsening rather than improving; they were growing poorer and poorer. The peasants, almost all Catholics, were increasing rapidly, while the whole political and social economy of the country was still working towards their extinction, a tug-of-war that led to widespread brutality and wretchedness. The Church had begun to grow active, and only in time, for the long period of social disorganisation had undoubtedly sapped some of the moral stamina of the people: in ever-growing numbers the richer Catholics were openly turning Protestant to save their estates; and the example both of these and the hard-drinking and boisterous squirearchy was

influencing the mind of the labourers: Jack would have his fling
as well as his master. The Church had not yet, however, had time
to chasten, except in the least degree, the almost melodramatic
spirit of violence that was abroad, common to both high and low,
so that the peasants still took to the cudgel as readily as the
squires to the pistol. All this we note as we turn the pages of
Arthur Young, who went through the country just when Eoghan
Ruadh was in the prime of his life; and all this we should keep
in mind if we would understand the tragic wayfaring of this child
of song.

I

Meentogues, where he was born, was a place of poor land, of
small holdings, of struggling people. Across the river was Faha,
where the school was. Over the threshold of this school, a sooty
cabin, it is likely, no boy of the place ever stepped who more
quickly won the attention of the poet-teacher, for Eoghan came
of a household where poetry was still, in the Gaelic mode,
accounted as riches and as a stay against misfortune. He quickly
learned to read in tattered and dirty manuscripts those great
Gaelic stories and poems, the outlines of which he had already
become acquainted with at home. So, too, in Latin and Greek
he made his own of the world-famous stories that he would have
heard already spoken of among his people and their visitors: ever
afterwards the bright figures of those stories were to haunt his
imagination. In English he must have learned to read with ease,
to judge by the occasional poems he wrote in it.

The 'poor scholars' caused him but little surprise, for these
were now an old institution in the place. To such a school they
were accustomed to come without books, without money, without
a way of supporting themselves; and Eoghan's people, not the
poorest in that countryside, would very likely have had, in the
traditional way, one or more of them as guests upon their
hearthstone. But he might have wondered at the differences
between their language and his own; certain poets, that he would
have little or no difficulty in understand, must have, in many
cases, needed much study from them; and beginning with this
fact, he might have learned that his native parish was not typical

of all Ireland. It took him a longer time, probably, to realise that he himself was not typical of even the boys of Sliabh Luachra.

One morning, we are told, he was late for school, and that he made his excuse in verse: *Ar dhrúcht na maidne is mé ag taisteal go ró-mhoch* – 'In the dew of the morning while journeying early.'

And the story is credible, since no day would pass over those fields about his house without impromptu verses having been made, the labourers flinging them out almost as readily as the schoolmasters. But it is not right to think of him as a studious boy. If it is true that he was intended for the priesthood, it is only fitting to imagine him as restrained and docile; but remembering what he became while still in his young manhood, and the name he left behind him, to do so is impossible. One pictures him as good-looking, with hair as golden as red – not, indeed, far different from the colour of his sun-tanned brow and cheeks – as narrow-headed, high-crowned, lithe, tall, sinewy; as carrying himself well, daring, and not easily put down; as full of life, witty, and given to laughing; yet one must also recollect that he could be very still over a book and very patient in copying a manuscript.

When he was eighteen he opened a school on his own account at Gneeveguilla, a place two miles to the north of Meentogues. A contemporary of his, out of bitter experience, had called schoolmastering an empty trade, yet all his life through, whenever his fortunes were hopeless, on this empty trade Eoghan was to fall back. This first school of his did not last long – 'an incident occurred, nothing to his credit, which led to the break-up of his establishment.' Such incidents, it may be as well to say it, were afterwards to occur frequently; and because of them, and the want of self-control they denote, we may be certain that from this time, when he had to fly Gneeveguilla, with a threatening priest behind him, he scarcely ever afterwards knew what peace was, however much he laughed or sung. He returned to his home.

The boy-schoolmaster then became a *spailpín*, a wandering farm labourer. It may not have been necessary for him to start off on such unprofitable wayfaring, but the life of itself had much in it to appeal to one of his gifts and years. It was when the turf had been brought in from the bogs and had been built into stacks, that the *spailpíní* of Kerry tied up a few oaten cakes in their handcloths, shouldered their spades, and set off for the rich lands of Limerick, of North-East and East Cork. Their wives would then lock up their cabins, and, with their children swarming about them, set off to beg along the roads until their men returned at Christmas-time. Year after year this break-up and re-union of the family took place; and one imagines those *spailpíní* as railing at their lot, and yet finding it not easy finally to give it up, as is the way with sailors and wanderers of every description; the charms of the change of skies, the change of companions, the freedom, renewing themselves in the memory the moment the home-life sinks again into dullness. But, of course, it was only rarely that the *spailpín* had any choice in the matter, no other way of living being left him; when the rich Catholic was hemmed in on every side, the poverty-stricken peasant must have had about as much freedom as a slave in choosing how he should live.

One can imagine, too, how eagerly a band of these labourers, and it was in squads that they traversed the countryside, would entice a young man of Eoghan's character to accompany them; for since the beginning of the world wit and song have not failed to shorten a lengthy road. Whatever the reason was, before he was twenty years old he shouldered his spade and set off to mow the meadows and to dig the potatoes in the County Limerick. One thinks of him as setting out with high heart and quick nostril: the roads were crowded with life; and taverns were frequent, the coaches swinging up to them in noise and dust and bustle; and in every tavern there would be new stories of highwaymen, of duelling, of kidnappings, of elopements and forced marriages, for it was the heyday of that melodramatic tragicomedy that meant life for the Anglo-Irishman. For Eoghan, moreover, there would be a Court of Poetry here and there, hidden away in quiet villages, to be discovered; and in any countryside a poet, or a group of them, with their manuscripts and their traditions, might be come upon. Yes, at least on his first round, for he was never to cease making them, what between his youth, the novelty of the roads, and the freedom, his heart must have been high and his eyes alert at this setting out for the unknown.

There remain three poems of his, with which we will

afterwards deal, that keep still fresh for us, in spite of the century and a half that has since gone by, those autumn wanderings on the roads of Munster of the young Kerryman in his knee-breeches and peaked cap. They make us certain of everything: of his wit, his daring, his way with the lasses: certain, too, that the memory of him that even today still lingers on these roads is not far astray when it recalls him as a playboy, a Mercutio, albeit a rustic one, with the same turn for fanciful and even dainty wit joined to the same fatal recklessness of spirit.

II

A little before Christmas he returned to his homeland by the little river; and it so happened that the stage was set, as if for his coming. The unmarried and the married men of the place had met in the hurling field, and the ancients had won the bout. To perpetuate the triumph, songs had been written; and these songs did not go unanswered; so that presently the hurling contest was thought of as but the cause of the greater effort in song that, before Eoghan's arrival, had, like a fever, overtaken every poet from Knocknagree to Ballyvourney. As is usual, the younger generation were being scoffed at for their having dared to knock at the door. In their extremity, it had become necessary for them to induce an aged poet, Tadhg Críonna Ó Scannail (Old Theig O'Scannell), by dosing him with whiskey, to take their side, and write them verses satirising the feebleness and the ineptness of old men (the poor poet needed but to behold himself). These verses, however, Matthew Hegarty of Glenflesk had roundly replied to, calling the writer of them a senseless renegade to deny his friends for the sake of drink; so that the married men still maintained their pride of place. The battle stood thus when Eoghan Ruadh returned from his first round on the roads of Munster.

In a poem he had previously written on his having to mind his own illegitimate child while its mother was out, he promised it, to quiet it, with a hundred other dainty and impossible gifts, the staff of Pan: to read now the poem he contributed to the contest, its assurance, its hearty gesture, its boastfulness, is to see him entering the fray armed, indeed, with that selfsame staff, wherever he, not yet twenty years of age, had come by it. He took the part of youth, and without misgiving he might well have done so, for he was never to reach middle age, not to mention old age; and his song sung, there was an end to the struggle. Indeed, there are nooks in Munster to this very day where, if an old man, forgetting his impotence, raises his voice against the young, he will find himself answered in one or another couplet from that head-long poem that the young labourer then flung disdainfully from his lips, as if to show what youth could do when it had gone afield and mixed with many men.

III

For the next ten years he wandered annually, either as *spailpín* or schoolmaster, over the roads of the South. Sometimes, it is likely that instead of returning to Sliabh Luachra when the crops were all gathered in and no further work was required in the farms, he would remain where he was, open a school, and carry it on until the coming of summer again. We know for certain that at one time he did keep school at Donoghmore, which is not more than ten miles from Cork – a countryside that was then and for long afterwards well known for Irish scholarship and poetry. In other places, of which we have now no record, he must have done the same; but again he made his way back to Meentogues, never, however, to settle down or make himself a home. His wanderings have not yet been traced on any map; perhaps they never will; and our only way of filling up this period of ten years is to think of him as travelling the autumn roads with his spade on his shoulder, or as seated in a hut or by a farmer's hearth, a group of young men about him, all of them deep in the story of Ulysses, another wanderer, while the red glow of the turves lights the pages for them and the winter's winds sweep past outside.

So went the years; but how passed the slowly trailing days of them? – those days with their tally of pain, insult, longing, sickness, fierceness, weakness; with their fits of wild love-making, drunkenness; with their dull slavery of teaching, of turf-cutting, of potato-digging, of grass-mowing; with their discovery of kindred spirits, of young poets, of Courts of Poetry; with their patient labouring upon almost indecipherable manuscripts; with their ecstasies of new songs dreamed or fashioned or sung in a triumphant voice – how those slow-trailing days passed for him, dark or bright or wild or slow or fast, we shall never be able to imagine, except dimly and, therefore, wistfully. 'Tidings of him are to be found in every county of Munster. There is no town nor stronghold nor fort from the Siuir to Beara that he did not walk there; and in them there remained the memory of him so long as even a remnant of the Irish language remained in the mouths of the people. Here he was a teacher; there a labourer. In this town he drank and took his pleasure. At fair and market he was often seen with a crowd about him, for whom he made sport or poured out verses, or retaliated on someone who had tried to put him down. Usually he was among the poets, making sport for them, answering and counter-answering them, satirising or making a laughing stock of someone who appeared too officious. Often, again, he went on foot from house to house, spending a night here, another there, letting on to be a poor, simple man that had had no rearing or schooling, putting foolish questions to the woman of the house, and failing to understand her replies, speaking out clearly at last his own opinion, and praising or dispraising the family in good verses. Sometimes, again, he made bold on some priest, in the form of a poor tramp who did not know the Commandments; only to break out, when the priest had done his best to teach him them, in impromptu verses, satirising the priesthood. He was fine company for the labourer. Neither conversation nor song nor story failed him from morning till night.'

Except in some such general terms, we cannot speak of the ten years from 1770 to 1780 – that is, from his twenty-second to his thirty-second year. It is probable that it was during these years he made the greater number of his poems, verses of pure poetry, of poet's poetry; but it is certain that it was during them he established the tradition of himself that the winds of a century and a half have not yet quite swept from the roads of Munster. In point of character, he was sinking lower and lower; and at last it became necessary for him to take refuge in the army, although every better impulse of his nature must have rebelled against the act. He was at the time schoolmaster to the children of the Nagle family, whose place was near Fermoy, and how, from being one of their farm labourers, he had come to be in this position lingers still as a legend in the Irish-speaking parts of Munster. I have had it told to myself that one day in their farmyard he heard a woman, another farmhand, complain that she had need to write a letter to the master of the house, and had failed to find anyone able to do so. 'I can do that for you,' Eoghan said, and, though misdoubting, she consented that he should. Pen and paper were brought him, and he sat down and wrote the letter in four languages – in Greek, in Latin, in English, in Irish. 'Who wrote this letter?' the master asked the woman in astonishment; and the red-headed young labourer was brought before him; questioned, and thereupon set to teach the children of the house. Other accounts vary slightly from this, but it may be taken as illustrating the legends of him that even yet survive in corners of Munster. Owing to his bad behaviour he had to fly the house, the master pursuing him with a gun. Fermoy was an important military station, and he soon put the walls of the barracks there between himself and his pursuer. From Fermoy he was sent to Cork, and from Cork he sailed almost immediately in a transport for the West Indies – and a new chapter had opened for him.

IV

To say nothing of the alien rabble of the lower decks, the scourings of English prisons, among whom he now found himself, to be thus caged in was a dismal change for one who had had whole counties for his adventurous feet. What manner of men swarmed in a man-of-war at that period, as well as what manner of men ruled over them with ruthless authority, we know from the realistic pages of Roderick Random, and Mr John Masefield has in our own days written for his countrymen these terrible words: 'Our naval glory was built up by the blood and agony of thousands of barbarously maltreated men. It cannot be too strongly insisted on that sea life in the later eighteenth century, in our navy, was brutalising, cruel, and horrible; a kind of life now happily gone for ever; a kind of life which no man today would think good enough for a criminal. There was barbarous discipline, bad pay, bad food, bad hours of work, bad company, bad prospects.' And stressing the phrase 'bad company' he quotes from the contemporary Edward Thompson: 'In a man-of-war you have the collected filths of jails: condemned criminals have the alternative of hanging or entering on board. There's not a vice committed on shore that is not practised here; the scenes of horror and infamy on board a man-of-war are so many and so great that I think they must rather disgust a good mind than allure it.'

Between these lower decks, then, Eoghan Ruadh, the landsman, the wandering minstrel, was now imprisoned, one of those thousands of barbarously maltreated seamen. His one talent was no longer of use; if in his few hours of sleeping, *aisling* poems still brightened in his brain, it was only bitterness to recall them once they had scattered in the hurry-scurry of the seaman's uprousing. In those silent night watches of his across the unfamiliar waters, he no doubt comforted himself with the quiet singing of the songs of Munster, his own and others; and also, doubtless, he would often astonish his illiterate English shipmates with his strange stories of Greece and Rome, with his amazing gift of tongues; he was not, therefore, utterly forlorn both of moments of forgetfulness and moments of triumph. Must we not also recollect, however, that as surely as it was in his nature to give way to wild fits of loud-voiced recklessness, it was also in him to sit tongue-tied, revolving his fate, and finding but little comfort in looking either backwards or forwards. In such moments he saw himself with clear eyes: in one such, the Spirit of Ireland came before him, as radiant as ever, with reproach in her eyes: 'Do not insult me, Bright Shape of the Fair Tresses,' the tortured poet cried to her; 'by the Book in my hand I swear I am not of them; but by the very hair of the head I was snatched away and sent over the floods, helping him (the English Monarch) that I do not wish to help, in the ships of the bullets on the foaming sea, I that come of the stock of the Gaels of Cashel of the Provincial Kings!'

Ná tarcuisnigh mé, a gheal-scéimh na gcúil-fhionn,
Dar an leabhar so im ghéag, níl braon dá gcrú ionnam,
Ach taistealach théid tar chaise le fraoch,
Do stracadh in gcéin ar úrla,
Ag cabhair don té nár bh-fonn liom,
I mbarcaibh na philéar ar chubhar-mhuir,
Is gur scagadh mo thréad as caise d'fhuil Ghaedheal
I gCaiseal na réacsa cúigidh!

To the longing that is so heavy a weight in every exile's heart was added in his case the pain of helping those whom he, the descendant of Provincial Kings, despised. Though it is quite certain that in the rough-and-tumble of the seaman's life, he could, as well as the next, take care of himself – the Munster of his day being no bad training ground in such arts, there was still an implacable round of circumstances leagued against him: he was one of a despised race; he was a peasant; his strange accents were an offence; his messmates, we have seen what they were; and he was a poet. Taking everything into account, among the thousands of maltreated men between the decks of Rodney's ships, perhaps there was not one more miserable than this baffled son of music and dreams.

It was his lot to assist in one of England's most famous sea-fights. 'The ship in which he sailed joined the English fleet under Rodney, then vice-admiral of Great Britain, somewhere before the West Indies were reached. On the morning of the twelfth of April in that year, 1782, Rodney, who had lately been blundering, was awakened by Sir Charles Douglas with the intelligence that God had given him the French enemy on the lee bow 'not far from old Fort Royal.' De Grasse, the French admiral, in vain tried to get to the windward. The engagement began at seven o'clock, and at close quarters. As the French line got southward under the lee of Dominica, it was gapped by varying winds. Through one of the gaps Rodney's own vessel, the 'Formidable' passed, the 'Bedford' followed, another leading vessel found also a passage. The ships astern followed. The French fleet were routed, and De Grasse's flagship, the 'Ville de Paris', surrendered to the 'Barfleur'. Rodney, whose recent manoeuvres had ended in failure, was in ecstasies of delight. He had won a victory, perhaps, hitherto unsurpassed in the annals of British naval warfare, and was fully conscious of the importance of his triumph. In an account of the fight, written by himself, we read:

> The battle began at seven in the morning and continued till sunset, nearly eleven hours, and by persons appointed to observe, there never were seven minutes' repose during the engagement, which, I believe, was the severest ever fought at sea, and the most glorious for England. We have taken five and sunk another.

V

We do not know how it came about that the poet was transferred from the navy to the army: as a soldier, however, stationed in England, we find him no less unhappy than he had been at sea. Beyond the poems that he wrote at this time, no other information either of his whereabouts or his condition, seems to have been discovered; and in these poems what we are chiefly aware of is his disgust at being mistaken for a rake from London, his bitterness at having had to undergo some term of imprisonment, and in *Ceo Draoidheachta I Gcoim Oidhche* (A fog of wizardry in the depths of night) – as good a poem as he ever wrote – we find him again visited by the Spirit of Ireland, with whom he makes equal sorrow, finishing, however, on the universal hope: 'Should our Stuart come to us from beyond the sea with a fleet from Louis and from Spain, in the sheer dint of joy I'd be mounted on a swift, stout, vigorous, nimble steed, driving out the "ospreys" at the sword's edge' – and then, with this couplet, he entirely and triumphantly shakes the trouble from his mind:

> Is ní chlaoidhfinn-se m'intinn 'na dheághaidh sin
> Chum luighe ar sheasamh gárda lem rae.

'And after that, as long as I lived, never more would I dull my mind with mounting guard' – an unforced expression that opens up for us the many-sided miseries of a soldier who is aware that he has any mind to dull.

Aching still to be at home, he blistered his shins with spearwort when all other stratagems to get free had failed him. His companions, it is said, refused to mess with him, so terrible had the sores become; and doctor after doctor having tried in vain to cure him, he was at last free to go home.

He seems to have made straight for Kerry. Arrived there, he sent a letter to Fr Ned Fitzgerald, asking him to publish from the altar that he was about to open a school at Knocknagree – a bleak, windswept hamlet, only a few miles from his birthplace. The letter, which was in verse, was written both in Irish and English, and it is strange that only the English portion has come down to us in its entirety:

Reverend Sir –
Please to publish from the altar of your holy Mass
That I will open school at Knocknagree Cross,
Where the tender babes will be well off,
For it's there I'll teach them their Criss Cross;
Reverend Sir, you will by experience find
All my endeavours to please mankind,
For it's there I will teach them how to read and write;
The Catechism I will explain
To each young nymph and noble swain,
With all young ladies I'll engage
To forward them with speed and care,
With book-keeping and mensuration,
Euclid's Elements and Navigation,
With Trigonometry and sound gauging,
And English Grammar with rhyme and reason.
With the grown-up youths I'll first agree
To instruct them well in the Rule of Three;
Such of them as are well able,
The cube root of me will learn,
Such as are of a tractable genius,
With compass and rule I will teach them,
Bills, bonds and informations,
Summons, warrants, supersedes,
Judgment tickets good,
Leases, receipts in full,
And releases, short accounts,
With rhyme and reason,
And sweet love letters for the ladies.

The school did not last long; it may be that it broke up naturally at the approach of summer, or that the ex-soldier, though not yet thirty-six years of age, had lost the power of working on steadily day after day. In either case, in the early summer of 1784, he paid a visit to Colonel Daniel Cronin, of Park, near Killarney: it was only lately that Cronin had become colonel of a body of yeomanry, and before his honours had had time to dull, the poet thought to present him with a complimentary poem in

English. The Colonel either neglected or refused to acknowledge the song in the only way that could now recompense the poet. When we learn that he thereupon blazed up and put all his wits into composing a fierce satire on the Colonel, we somehow indulge the thought that the unfortunate poet had not even yet quite come to the dregs of his self-respect; for the faculty of resentment finally ceases altogether in those whose only plan is to live on the bounty of others. Soon afterwards some of Cronin's servants and himself chanced to meet in an ale-house in Killarney and a quarrel arose between them; blows followed, and the Colonel's coachman is said to have struck the poet a sharp blow on the head with a pair of tongs – the weapon first to hand in the place. The one blow was sufficient: with his head bound, and hot with fever, he made his way back to Knocknagree.

On that windswept hilltop, 'on the eastern side of the fair field on the northern side of the road opposite the gate of the pound', was a hut for fever patients. It was about two hundred yards distant from the houses – far enough away to prevent contagion, far enough also to be as lonely and desolate to the dying man as the middle of the sea. In this hut he was laid, and some woman of the place went in and out, attending on him. He was putting the fever off him, he was convalescent, when 'an act of self-indulgence, it is said, brought on a relapse from which he never rallied.'

When his end was not far off, he sat up in bed, asked for pen and paper, and set himself to write his last verses, his poem of repentance, as the Irish fashion was; but he was weaker in limb than brain – the pen slipped from his fingers, to his own sudden enlightenment, it seems, for *Sin é an file go fann 'nuair thuiteann an peann as a láimh* – 'Weak indeed is the poet when the pen falls from his hand,' he whispered, lay back, and in silence died. *Eoghan an Bheóil Bhínn* – Eoghan of the Sweet Mouth!

'Pen', 'poet' – a poet, in his own thought, to the very end, no matter to what misguided uses the rough racket of the world had put him while he lived.

The winds still played with him: though it was mid-summer (1784), a thunderstorm broke upon the uplands as he lay in the midst of the keeners, and had not ceased when the time for burial was come. To reach Muckross Abbey, the Blackwater had to be crossed, but there being no bridge, the floods made this impossible. A temporary grave was, therefore, quickly dug, and the mourners dispersed for the night. On the following day the coffin was shouldered again, and he was carried over the river and laid with his people in the Abbey. This, though it is now generally accepted as the truth, has been always disputed, and even today some of the people of that countryside assert that the poet lies at Nohavile, where the first grave was dug.

from THE HIDDEN IRELAND (1924)

EOGHAN RUA Ó SÚILLEABHÁIN
CEO DRAÍOCHTA

Ceo draíochta i gcoim oíche do sheol mé
trí thíorthaibh mar óinmhid ar strae,
gan príomhcharaid díograis im chóngar
's mé i gcríochaibh tar m'eolas i gcéin;
do shíneas go fíorthuirseach deorach
i gcoill chluthair chnómhair liom féin,
ag guíochan chun Rí ghil na glóire
's gan ní ar bith ach trócaire im bhéal.

Bhi líonrith im chroí-se gan gó ar bith
sa choill seo gan glór duine im ghaor,
gan aoibhneas ach binnghuth na smólach
ag síorchantain ceoil ar gach géig,
lem thaoibh gur shuigh sí-bhruinneall mhómhrach
i bhfír is i gcló-chruth mar naomh;
'na gnaoi do bhí an lí gheal le rósaibh
i gcoimheascar, 's níorbh eol dom cé ghéill.

Ba trinseach tíubh buí-chasta ar órdhath
a dlaoi-fholt go bróig leis an mbé,
a braoithe gan teimheal is mar an ómra
a claonroisc do bheo-ghoin gach laoch;

ba bhinn blasta fírmhilis ceolmhar
mar shí-chruit gach nóta óna béal,
's ba mhín cailce a cí' cruinne i gcóir chirt
dar linne nár leonadh le haon.

Feacht roimhe sin cé bhíos-sa gan treoir cheart,
do bhíogas le ró-shearc don bhé
's do shíleas gurbh aoibhneas mór dom
an tsí-bhean do sheoladh faoim dhéin;
im laoithibh do scríobhfad im dheoidh duit
mar a scaoileas mo bheol seal ar strae
's gach caoinstair dár ríomhas don óig dheis
is sinn sínte ar fheorainn an tsléibhe.

'A bhrídeach na righinrosc do bhreoigh mé
le díograis dod shnó 'gus dod scéimh
an tú an aoilchnis trír dísceadh na mórthruip
mar scríobhtar i gcomhrac na Trae,
nó an rí-bhruinneall mhíolla d'fhúig comhlag
cathmhíle na Bóirmhe 's a thréad
nó an ríoghan do dhlígh ar an mórfhlaith
ón mBinn dul dá tóraíocht i gcéin?'

Is binn blasta caoin d'fhreagair domhsa
's í ag síorshileadh deora trí phéin
'Ní haoinbhean dár mhaís mise id ghlórthaibh,
's mar chímse ní heol duit mo thréad;
's mé an bhrídeach do bhí sealad pósta
fá aoibhneas i gcoróinn chirt na réx
ag rí Chaisil Chuinn agus Eoghain
fuair mírcheannas Fódla gan phlé'.

'Is dubhach bocht mo chúrsa 's is brónach
'om dhúrchreimeadh ag coirnigh gach lae
fá dhlúthsmacht ag búraibh gan sóchas,
's mo phrionsa gur seoladh i gcéin;
tá mo shúilse le hÚrMhac na glóire
go dtabharfaidh mo leoghan faoi réim
'na dhúnbhailtibh dúchais i gcóir mhaith
ag rúscadh na gcrónphoc le faobhar.'

'A chúileann tais mhúinte na n-órfholt
de chrú chirt na coróinneach gan bhréag,
do chúrsa-sa ag búraibh is brón liom
faoi smúit, cathach ceomhar gan scléip;
'na dhlúthbhrogaibh dúchais dá seoladh
Mac cúntach na glóire, do réx,
is súgach do rúscfainnse crónphoic
go humhal tapaidh scópmhar le piléir.'

'Ár Stíobhard dá dtíodh chughainn thar sáile
go críoch inis Áilge faoi réim
le *fleet* d'fhearaibh Laoisigh 's an Spáinnigh
is fíor le corp áthais go mbeinn
ar fhíor-each mhear ghroí thapa cheáfrach,
ag síorchartadh cách le neart piléar,
's ní chloífinnse m'intinn 'na dheáidh sin
chun luí ar sheasamh garda lem ré.'

MAURICE WALSH
THE QUIET MAN

The Quiet Man he sate him down, and to himself did say,
'I'll sit and look at Shannon's Mouth until my dying day:
For Shannon Mouth and Ocean-blue are pleasant things to
    see,
But Woman's mouth and sky-blue eye! – to hell with them!'
    said he.

Paddy Bawn Enright, a blithe young lad of seventeen, went
to the States to seek his fortune – like so many of his race.
And fifteen years thereafter he returned to his native Kerry,
his blitheness sobered and his youth dried to the core; and
whether he had found his fortune, or whether he had not, no
one could be knowing. For he was a quiet man, not given
much to talking about himself and the things he had done.

A quiet man, slightly under middle height with good shoulders
and deep-set steadfast blue eyes below brows darker than his
dark hair – that was Paddy Bawn Enright. Paddy Bawn means

White Patrick, and he got that ironic nickname because there was not a white hair on him. One shoulder had a trick of hunching slightly higher than the other, and some folks said that that came from a habit acquired in shielding his eyes in the glare of an open-hearth steel furnace in a place called Pittsburgh, while others said it was a way he had learned of guarding his chin that time he was some sort of sparring partner punchbag at a boxing-camp in New York State.

He came home at the age of thirty-two – young enough still for romance or for war – and found that he was the last of his line of Enrights, and that the farm of his forefathers had added its few acres to the ranch of Red Will O'Danaher of Moyvalla. Red Will – there was a tradition of redness in the Danaher men, hair and disposition – had got hold of the Enright holding meanly; and the neighbours waited with a lively curiosity to see what Paddy Bawn would do about it; for no one, in living memory, remembered an Irishman who had taken the loss of his land quietly – not since the Fenian times, at any rate. But that is exactly what Paddy Bawn did. He took no action whatever. Whereupon folks nodded their heads and said contemptuous things, often enough, where they might be relayed back to Paddy Bawn.

'Maybe the little fellow is right, too! For all the boxing tricks he is supposed to have picked up in New York, what chance would he have against Red Will?'

'That tarnation fellow would break him in three halves with his bare hands.'

But Paddy Bawn only smiled in his own quiet way. The truth was that he had had enough of fighting. All he wanted now was peace – 'a quiet, small little place on a hillside,' as he said to himself; and he quietly went out amongst the old and kindly friends and looked about him for the place and the peace he wanted. And when the place was offered, the wherewithal to acquire it was not wanting.

It was a neat, handy small croft on the first warm shelf of Knockanore Hill below the rolling curves of heather. Not a big place at all, but in sound heart, and it got all the sun that was going; and, best of all, it suited Paddy Bawn to the tip-top notch of contentment, for it held the peace that tuned to his quietness and it commanded the widest view in all Kerry – vale and running water, and the tall ramparts of distant mountains, and the lifting green plain of the Atlantic Sea out between the black portals of Shannon Mouth.

And yet, for the best part of five years Paddy Bawn Enright did not enjoy one quiet day in that quiet place.

The horror and the dool of the Black-and-Tan war settled down on Ireland, and Paddy Bawn, driven by an ideal bred closer in the bone of an Irishman than all desire, went out to fight against the terrible thing that England stood for in Ireland – the subjugation of the soul. He joined an IRA Flying Column, a column great amongst all the fighting columns of the South, commanded by Hugh Forbes, with Mickeen Oge Flynn second in command; and with that column he fought and marched until the truce came. And ever thereafter the peace of Knockamore Hill was denied him.

For he was a loyal man, and his leaders, Hugh Forbes and Mickeen Oge Flynn, placed a fresh burden on him. They took him aside and talked to him at Sean Glynn's farmhouse of Leaccabuie above the Ullachowen valley.

'Paddy Bawn, achara,' said Hugh in that booming voice that no man could resist, 'our friend Sean is in a bad way – with a shadow on him.'

'I know it,' said Paddy Bawn.

'And you know that he is a man that we cannot forsake, as he has not forsaken us to the brink of darkness?'

'What do ye want me to do?'

'You will take a job as his land-steward and you will stand by him till the shadow lifts.'

'It will not be long, with God's help,' said Mickeen Oge.

'Long or short,' said Paddy Bawn, 'I will stand by him, for, sure, my own little place will not run away, with Matt Tobin to keep an eye on it – and it will be all the better at the end.'

And, as has been told, he stood by Sean Glynn till the shadow lifted and Sean became a douce married man.

Then at last, and for all time – as he told himself – he turned his steadfast face to Knockanore Hill.

There, in a four-roomed, lime-white thatched cottage, Paddy Bawn settled smoothly into the life that he meant to live till days were done and eternal night quiet about him. Not once did he think of bringing a wife into the place, though, often enough, his friends, half in fun, half in earnest, hinted his needs and obligations. But though the thought had neither web nor woof, Fate had the loom set for the weaving of it.

Paddy Bawn was no drudge toiler. He knew all about drudgery and the way it wears out a man's soul. He hired a man when he wanted one; he ploughed a little and sowed what was needed; and at the end of a furrow he would lean on the handles of the cultivator, wipe his brow, if it needed wiping, and lose himself for whole minutes in the great green curve of the sea out there beyond the high black portals of Shannon Mouth. And sometimes, of an evening, he would see, under the orange glory of the sky, the faint smoke smudge of an American liner. Then he would smile to himself – a pitying smile – thinking of all the poor young lads, with dreams of fortune luring them, going out to sweat in Ironville, or to bootleg bad whiskey down the hidden way, or to stand in a bread line in the gut of skyscrapers. All these things were behind Paddy Bawn forever.

He was fond of horses and he bought an old brood mare of hunter blood, hoping to breed a good-class jumper; he had a black hound dog – out of Master Ross – with a turn of speed, and there were mountain hares to test it; and he had a double-barrel shotgun presented to him by Sean Glynn, and Knockanore heather reared two or three brood of grouse every season; and on summer Sundays he used to go across to Galey River and catch a mess of trout. What more in all the world could a man want?

Market days he would go down and across to Listowel town, seven miles, to do his bartering, and if he met a friend he would have two drinks and no more. And sometimes, in the long evenings slipping slowly into the endless summer gloaming, or on Sundays after Mass, his friends would come across the vale and up the long winding path to see him. Only the real friends came that long road, and they were welcome. Mostly fighting men who had been out in the Tan war: Matt Tobin, the thresher, who had worked a Thompson gun with him in many an ambush; Sean Glynn of Leaccabuie, boasting of his first son; Mickeen Oge Flynn, all the way from Lough Aonach; Hugh Forbes, the Small Dark Man, making the rafters ring: men like that. And once Mickeen Oge Flynn brought Major Archibald MacDonald across from Lough Aonach where he was fishing, and that sound man was satisfied that

Paddy Bawn had found his quiet place at last.

Then a stone jar of malt whiskey would appear on the table for those who wanted a drink, and there would be a haze of smoke and a maze of friendly, warm disagreements.

'Paddy Bawn, old son,' one of them might hint, 'aren't you sometimes terrible lonesome?'

'Like hell I am! Why?'

'Nothing but the daylight and the wind, and the sun setting like the wrath o' God!'

'Just that! Well?'

'But after the stirring times out about – and beyond in the States.'

'The stirring times wore us to the bone, and tell me, fine man, did you ever see a furnace in full blast?'

'Worth seeing, I'm told.'

'Worth seeing, surely. But if I could jump you into an iron foundry this minute you would think that God had judged you faithfully into the hot hob of hell. Have sense, man!'

And then they would laugh and, maybe, have another small one from the stone jar.

On Sundays Paddy Bawn used to go to church, three miles down to the grey chapel above the black cliffs of Doon Bay. There Fate, with a cunning leisureliness, laid her lure and drew her web about him. Listen now!

Sitting quietly on his wooden bench, or kneeling on the dusty footboard, he would fix his steadfast deep-set eyes on the vestmented celebrant and say over his beads slowly, or go into that strange trance, beyond dreams or visions, where the soul is almost at one with the unknowable.

And then, after a time, Paddy Bawn's eyes no longer fixed themselves on the celebrant. They went no farther than two seats ahead. A girl sat there, her back to him. Sunday after Sunday she sat there. Paddy Bawn did not know how her presence grew about him. He just liked to see her sit there. At first his eyes hardly noted her, and then noted her with casual admiration; and slowly that first casual admiration took on body and warmth. She was a bit of the surroundings, she was part of the ceremony, she was secret partner to himself. And she never even looked his way.

On the first Sunday of the month, when she went to early Mass and Communion, Paddy Bawn used to miss her strangely, and his prayers suffered. And gradually he got into the habit of being a monthly communicant himself. Holiness is induced by many road, but seldom by an inclination that way.

She had a white nape to her neck and short red hair above it, and Paddy Bawn liked the colour and wave of that flame; and he liked the set of her shoulders, and the way the white neck had of leaning a little forward, and she at her prayers – or her dreams. And after the Benediction he used to stay in his seat so that he might get one quick but sure glance at her face as she passed out. And he liked her face too – the wide-set eyes like the sky of a quiet night, the cheek-bones firmly curved, the lips austere and sensitive.

And he smiled pityingly at himself and one of her name should make his pulse stir. For she was a Danaher of Moyvalla, and Paddy Bawn was enough Irish to dislike every bone of Red Will O'Danaher of that place who had snitched the Enright acres.

'I'll keep it to myself,' said Paddy Bawn. ''Tis only to pass the time.' And he did nothing.

One person, only, in the crowded little chapel noted Paddy Bawn's look and the thought behind the look. Not the girl – she barely knew who Paddy Bawn was, but her brother, Red Will himself. And that man smiled secretly – the ugly, contemptuous smile that was his by nature – and after another habit of his, tucked away his bit of knowledge in a mind corner against a day when it might come in useful for his own purposes.

The girl's name was Ellen – Ellen Roe O'Danaher. But, in truth, she was no longer a girl. She was past her first youth into that second one that has no definite ending. She might be twenty-eight – she was no less – but there was not a lad in the countryside who would say she was past her prime. The poise of her and the firm set of her bones below clean flesh saved her from the fading of mere prettiness. Though she had been sought in marriage more than once, she had accepted no one, or rather, had not been allowed to encourage anyone. Her brother saw to that.

Red Will O'Danaher was a huge, raw-boned, sandy-haired man with the strength of an ox, and a heart no bigger than a sour apple – an overbearing man given to berserk rages. Though he was a church-goer by habit, the true god of that man was Money – red gold, shining silver, dull copper, these the trinity he worshipped in degree. He and his sister, Ellen Roe, lived in the big ranch farm of Moyvalla, and Ellen was his housekeeper and maid of all work. She was a careful housekeeper, a good cook, a notable baker, and she demanded no wage. Her mean brother saw that she remained without a sweetheart and hinted at his inability to set her out with a dowry. A wasted woman.

Red Will himself was not a marrying man. There were not many spinsters with a dowry big enough to tempt him, and the few there were had acquired expensive tastes − a convent education, the deplorable art of hitting jazz out of a piano, the damnable vice of cigarette-smoking, the purse-emptying craze for motorcars − such things.

But in due time the tocher and the place − with a woman tied to them − came under his nose, and Red Will was no longer tardy.

His neighbour, James Carey, died of pneumonia in November weather and left his fine farm and all on it to his widow, a youngish woman without children, and a woman with a hard name for saving pennies. Red Will looked once at Kathy Carey, and she did not displease him; he looked many times at her sound acres and they pleased him better, for he had in him the terrible Irish land hunger. He took the steps required by tradition. In the very first week of the following Shrove-tide he sent an accredited emissary to open formal negotiations.

The emissary was back within the hour.

'My soul!' said he to Red Will, 'but she is the quick one. I hadn't ten words out of me when she up and jumped down my throat. "I am in no hurry," says she, "to come wife to a house with another woman at the fire corner." "You mean Ellen Roe," says I. "I mean Ellen Roe," says she. "Maybe it could be managed − " "Listen!" says she. "When Ellen Roe is in a place of her own − and not till then − I will be considering what Red Will O'Danaher has to say. Take that back to him." And never asked me had I a mouth on me.'

'She will, by Jacus!' Red Will mused. 'She will so.'

There, now, was the right time to recall Paddy Bawn Enright and the look in his eyes; and Red Will's mind corner promptly delivered up its memory. He smiled that knowing, contemptuous smile. Patcheen Bawn daring to cast a sheep's eye at an O'Danaher! The little Yankee runt hidden away on the shelf of hungry Knockanore! Fighting man, moryah! Looter more like, and him taking the loss of the Enright acres lying down! But what of it? The required dowry would be conveniently small, and Ellen Roe would never go hungry anyway. And that was Red Will far descended from many chieftains.

He acted promptly. The very next market day at Listowel he sought out Paddy Bawn and placed a great sandy-haired hand on the shoulder that hunched to meet it.

'Paddy Bawn, a word with you! Come and have a drink.'

Paddy Bawn hesitated. 'Very well,' he said then. He disliked O'Danaher, but he would hurt no man's feelings.

They went across to Tade Sullivan's bar and had a drink – and Paddy Bawn paid for it. Red Will came directly to his subject, almost patronisingly, as if he were conferring a favour.

'I am wanting to see Ellen Roe settled in a place of her own,' said he.

Paddy Bawn's heart lifted into his throat and beat there. But that steadfast face, strong-browed, gave no sign; and, moreover, even if he wanted to say a word he could not, with his heart where it was.

'You haven't much of a place up there,' went on the big man, 'but it is handy, and no load of debt on it – so I hear?'

Paddy Bawn nodded affirmatively, and Red Will went on, 'I never heard of a big fortune going to hungry Knockanore, and 'tisn't a big fortune I can be giving Ellen Roe. Say a hundred pounds – one hundred pounds at the end of harvest – if prices improve. What would you say to that, Paddy Bawn?'

Paddy Bawn swallowed his heart. Slow he was, and cool he seemed.

'What does Ellen say?'

'I haven't asked her. But what the hell would she say, blast it?'

Paddy Bawn did not say anything for a long time.

'Whatever Ellen Roe says, she will say it herself, not you, Red Will,' he said at last.

But what could Ellen Roe say? She looked within her own heart and found it empty, she looked at the granite crag of her brother's face and contemplated herself a slowly withering spinster at his fire corner; she looked up at the swell of Knockanore Hill and saw the white cottage among the green small fields below the warm brown of the heather – oh! But the sun would shine up there in the lengthening spring day, and pleasant breezes blow in sultry summer. And finally she looked at Paddy Bawn, that firmly built, not-too-big man, with the cleancut face and the deep-lit eyes below steadfast brow. She said a prayer to her God and sank head and shoulders in a resigned acceptance more pitiful than tears, more proud than the pride of chieftains. Romance? Well-a-day!

Paddy Bawn was far from satisfied with that resigned acceptance, but he was well aware that he should have looked for no warmer one. He saw into the brother's mean soul and guessed what was in the sister's mind; and knew, beyond all doubt, that, whatever he decided, she was doomed to a fireside sordidly bought for her. That was the Irish way. Let it be his own fireside then. There were many worse ones – and God was good. So in the end his resignation to Fate was equal to hers, whatever his hopes might be.

Paddy Bawn and Ellen Roe were married. One small statement – and it holds the risk of tragedy, the probability of resigned acceptance, the chance of happiness: choices wide as the world. It was a hole-and-corner marriage at that. Red Will demurred at all foolish expense, and Paddy Bawn agreed, for he knew that his friends were more than a shade doubtful of the astounding and unexpected step he had taken. Except for Matt Tobin, his side-man, there wasn't a friend of his own at the wedding breakfast.

But Red Will O'Danaher, for all his promptness, did not win Kathy Carey to wife. She did not wait for him. Foolishly enough, she took to husband her own cattleman, a gay night-rambler from Clare who proceeded to give her the devil's own time and a share of happiness in the bygoing. For the first time Red Will discovered how mordant the wit of his neighbours could be: and, for some reason, to contempt for Paddy Bawn Enright he now added a live dislike.

Paddy Bawn had got his precious red-haired wife under his own roof now; but he had no illusions about her regard for him. On himself, and on himself only, lay the task of moulding her into wife and lover. Darkly, deeply, subtly, with gentleness, with understanding, with restraint beyond all kenning, that moulding must be done; and she that was being moulded must never know. He must hardly know himself.

First, he turned his attentions to material things. He hired a small servant-maid to help her with the rough work, gave her her own housekeeping money, let her run the indoors as she thought best. She ran it well and liked doing it. Then he bought a rubber-tyred tub-cart and a half-bred gelding with a reaching action. And on market days husband and wife used to bowl down to Listowel, do their selling and their buying, and bowl smoothly home again, their groceries in the well of the cart, and a bundle of second-hand American magazines on the seat at Ellen's side.

And in the nights, before the year turned, with the wind from the plains of the sea keening about the chimney, they would sit at either side of the fine-flaming peat fire, and he would read aloud strange and almost unbelievable things out of the high-coloured magazines. Stories, sometimes, wholly unbelievable.

Ellen Roe would sit and listen and smile and keep on with her knitting or her sewing; and after a time it was sewing she was at mostly – small things. And when the reading was done, and the small servant-maid to bed, they would sit on and talk in their own quiet way. For they were both quiet. Woman though she was, or that she was, she got Paddy Bawn to do most of the talking. It could be that she, too, was probing and seeking, unwrapping the man's soul to feel the texture of it, surveying the marvel of his life as he spread it diffidently before her.

He had a patient, slow, vivid way of picturing for her the things he had seen and felt. He made her see the glare of molten metal, lambent yet searing, made her feel the sucking heat, made her hear the clang; she could picture the roped square under the dazzle of the hooded arcs, with the up-drifting smoke layer above and the gleam of black and with going away up and back into the dimness; she came to understand the explosive restraint of the game, admire the indomitable resolution that in a reeling world held on and waited for the opportunity that was being led up to, and she thrilled when he showed her, the opportunity come, how to stiffen wrist for the final devastating right hook. And often as not, being Irish, the things he told her were humorous or funnily outrageous; and Ellen Rod would chuckle or stare or throw back her lovely red curls in laughter. It was grand to make her laugh.

But they did not speak at all of the Black-and-Tan war. That was too near them. That made men frown and women shiver.

And, in due course, Paddy Bawn's friends, in some trepidation at first, came in ones and two up the slope to see them – Matt Tobin, the thresher, from the beginning, and then Sean Glynn, Mickeen Oge Flynn, Hugh Forbes and others. Their trepidation did not last long. Ellen Roe put them at their ease with her smile that was shy and, at the same time, frank and welcoming; and her table was loaded for them with cream scones and crumpets and cheesecakes and heather honey; and, at the right time, it was she herself brought forth the decanter of whiskey – no longer the half-empty stone jar – and the polished glasses. Paddy Bawn was proud as sin of her.

She would go out and about then at her own work and leave the men to their talk, but not for so long as to make them feel that they were neglecting her. After a while she would sit down amongst them and listen to their discussions, and, sometimes, she would put in a word or two and be listened to; and they would look to see if her smile commended them and be a little chastened by the tolerant wisdom of that smile – the age-old smile of the matriarch from whom they were all descended. And she would be forever surprised at the knowledgeable man her husband was: the turn of speech that summed up a man or a situation, the way he could discuss politics and war, the making of songs, the training of a racing dog, the breaking of colt and filly – anything worth talking about.

Thus it was that, in no time at all Hugh Forbes, who used to think, 'Poor Paddy Bawn! Lucky she was to get him,' would whisper to Sean Glynn, 'Flagstones o' Hell! That fellow's luck would astonish nations.' And the next time the two came up they brought their wives with them, to show them what a wife should be to a man; and Hugh threatened his Frances Mary: 'The next one will be a red-head, if God spares me.'

Wait now!

Woman, in the decadent world around us, captures a man by loving him and, having got him, sometimes comes to admire him, which is all to the good; and, if Fate is not unkind, may descend no lower than liking and enduring. And there is the end of lawful romance. Look then at Ellen Roe! She came up to the shelf of Knockanore, and in her heart was only a nucleus of fear in a great emptiness; and that nucleus might grow and grow. Oh, horror! Oh, disgust!

But Glory of God! She, for reason piled on reason, found herself admiring this man Paddy Bawn; and, with or without reason, presently came a quite liking for this man who was so gentle and considerate – and strong too. And then, one heart-stirring dark o' night she found herself fallen head over heels, holus-bolus, in love with her own husband. There is the sort of love that endures, but the road to it is a mighty chancy one.

Pity things did not stay like that! If they did, Paddy Bawn's story would finish here. It was Ellen Roe's fault that they did not, and the story goes on.

A woman, loving her husband, may or may not be proud of him, but she will play tiger if anyone, barring herself, belittles him. And there was one man who belittled Paddy Bawn. Her own brother, Red Will O'Danaher. At fair or market or chapel that dour giant deigned not to hide his contempt and dislike. Ellen Roe knew why. He had lost a wife and farm; he had lost in herself a frugally cheap housekeeper; he had been made the butt of a biting humour, and that he liked least of all. In some twisted way he blamed Paddy Bawn. But – and here came in the contempt – the little Yankee runt, the IRA ex-looter who dared do nothing about the lost Enright acres, would not now have the gall or the guts to insist on the dowry that was due to him. Lucky the hound to steal a Danaher to hungry Knockanore! Let him be satisfied with that luck, or, by God! He'd have his teeth down his throat. Thus, the big brute.

So, one evening before market day, Ellen Roe spoke to her husband. "Tis the end of harvest, Paddy Bawn. Has Red Will paid you my fortune?'

'Sure, there's no hurry, girl,' deprecated Paddy Bawn.

'Have you asked him?'

'I have not then. I am not looking for your fortune, Ellen.'

'And that is a thing Red Will could never understand.' Her voice firmed. 'You will ask him tomorrow.'

'Very well, so, *agrah*,' he agreed carelessly. He did not foresee any trouble about a few pounds back or fore, for the bad money lust had never touched him.

And next day, in Listowel Square, Paddy Bawn, in that quiet, half-diffident way of his, asked Red Will.

But Red Will was neither quiet nor diffident; he was brusque and blunt. He had no loose money, and Enright would have to wait till he had. 'Ask me again, Patcheen – don't be a bit shy,' he said, his face in a mocking grin, and, turning on his heel, ploughed his great shoulders through the crowded square.

His voice had been carelessly loud and people had heard. They laughed and talked amongst themselves, knowing their Red Will. 'Begobs! did you hear him?' 'The divil's own boy, Red Will!' 'And money tight, moryah! 'Tisn't one but ten hundred he could put finger on – and not miss it.' 'What a pup to sell! Stealing the land and denying the fortune.' 'Ay! and a dangerous man, mind you, that same red Will! He would smash little Bawn at the wind of the word – and divil the care for his Yankee sparrin' tricks!'

Paddy Bawn's friend, Matt Tobin, the thresher, heard that last and lifted his voice, 'I would like to be there the day Paddy Bawn Enright loses his temper.'

'A bad day for him!'

'It might, then,' said Matt agreeably, 'but I would come from the other end of Kerry to see the badness that would be in it for someone.'

Paddy Bawn had moved away with his wife, not hearing or not heeding.

'You see, Ellen?' he said in some discomfort. 'The times are hard on the big ranchers – and we don't need the money anyway.

'Do you think Red Will does?' Her voice had a cut in it. 'He could buy you and all Knockanore and not be on the fringe of his hoard.'

'But, girl dear, I never wanted a fortune with you.'

She liked him to say that, but far better would she like to win for him the respect and admiration that was his due. She must do that now, once the gage was down, or her husband would become the butt of a countryside never lenient to a backward man.

'You foolish lad! Red Will would never understand your feelings with money at stake. You will ask him again?'

She smiled, and a pang went through him. For her smile held a trace of the contempt that was in the Danaher smile, and he did not know whether the contempt was for himself or for her brother.

He asked Red Will again. He was unhappy enough in the

asking, but, also, he had some inner inkling of his wife's object; and it is possible that the fighting devil in him was not altogether subdued to his ideal of quietness – the fighting devil that lifted hackle despite him every time he approached Red Will.

And he asked again a third time. Though Paddy Bawn tried to avoid publicity, Red Will called for it with his loud voice and guffawing attempts at humour. The big man was getting his own back on the little runt, and he seemed quite unaware that decent men thought less of him than ever.

Very soon the issue between the brothers-in-law became a notorious one in all that countryside. Men talked about it, and women too. Bets were made on it. At fair or market, if Paddy Bawn was seen approaching Red Will, men edged closer and women, pulling shawls over head, moved away. Some day, men said, the big fellow would grow tired of being asked, and in one of his terrible rages, half-kill the little lad as he had half-killed stronger men. A great shame to the world! Here and there a man advised Paddy Bawn to give up asking and put the affair in a lawyer's hands. 'I wouldn't care to do that,' said Paddy Bawn. Our Quiet Man was getting dour. None of his prudent advisers were among his close friends. His friends frowned and said little, and were never far away.

Right enough, the day at last came when Red Will O'Danaher grew tired of being asked. That was the big October cattle fair at Listowel. All Kerry was there that day. Sean Glynn of Leaccabuie was there to buy some winter stores, and Mickeen Oge Flynn to sell some, and Matt Tobin to hire out his threshing-machine among the farmers. Red Will had sold twenty head of polled-Angus cross-breds at a good price, and he had a thick wad of banknotes in an inner pocket when he saw Paddy Bawn and Ellen Roe coming across to where he was bargaining with Matt Tobin for a week's threshing. Besides, the day being dank, he had inside him a drink or two more than was good for him, and the whiskey loosened his tongue and whatever he had of discretion.

The first flare in the big man's mind urged him to throw the money in Paddy Bawn's face and then kick him out of the market. No! be the powers! That would be foolish; but, all the same, it was time and past time to deal with the little gadfly and show him up before the crowd. He strode to meet Paddy Bawn,

and people parted out of his savage way and closed in behind
so as not to lose any of this dangerous game.

Red Will caught the small man by a hunched shoulder – a
rending grip – and bent down to grin in his face.

'What is it, Patcheen? Don't be ashamed to ask.'

Mickeen Oge Flynn was, perhaps, the only man there to
notice the ease with which Paddy Bawn shook his shoulder free
– that little explosive jerk with the snap of steel – and Mickeen
Oge smiled grimly. But Paddy Bawn did nothing further and
said no word; and his eyes were steadfast as ever.

Red Will showed his teeth mockingly.

'Go on, you little cleg! What do you want?'

'You know, O'Danaher.'

'I do. Listen, Patcheen!' Again he brought his hand clap on
the hunched shoulder. 'Listen, Patcheen, and let it be heard! If
I had a fortune to give Ellen Roe, 'tisn't a throw-out like Paddy
Bawn Enright of hungry Knockanore would get her. Go to hell
out o' that!'

His great hand gripped, and he flung Paddy Bawn backwards
as if he were no more than the shape of a man filled with chaff.

Paddy Bawn went backwards but he did not fall. He gathered
himself like a spring, feet under him, arms half-raised, head
forward with chin behind hunched shoulder. But, quickly as the
spring coiled, as quickly it slackened, and he turned away to his
wife. She was there facing him, tense and keen, her face gone
pallid, and a gleam of the race in her eye.

'Woman, woman!' he said in his deep voice. 'Why would you
and I shame ourselves like this?'

'Shame!' she cried. 'Will you let him shame you now?'

'But your own brother, Ellen – before them all?'

'And he cheating you.'

'God's glory, woman!' His voice was distressed and angry too.
'What is his dirty money to me? Are you a Danaher after all?'

That stung her, and she stung him back in one final hurting
effort. She placed a hand below her breast, and looked close into
his face. Her voice was low and bitter.

'I am a Danaher. It is a great pity that the father of this, my
son, is an Enright coward.'

The bosses of Paddy Enright's cheekbones were hard as
marble, but his voice was soft as a dove's.

'Is that the way of it? Let us be going home then, in the name of God.'

He placed a hand on her arm, but she shook it off. Nevertheless, she walked at his side, head up, through the jostle of men that broke apart for them. Her brother mocked her with his great bellowing laugh.

'That fixes the pair of ye,' he cried, brushed a man who laughed with him out of his way and strode off through the market place.

There was talk then – plenty of it. 'Murdher! but that was a narrow squeak!' 'DId you see the way he flung him?' 'I'll wager he'll give Red Will a wide road after this day – and he by way of being a boxer!' 'That's a pound you owe me, Matt Tobin.'

'I'll pay it,' said Matt Tobin. He stood wide-legged, looking at the ground, his hand ruefully rubbing the back of his head under his tilted bowler hat, balck dismay on his face. His friend had failed him in the face of the people.

Then Mickeen Oge Flynn spoke.

'I'll take over that bet, friend, and double it.'

The man looked at him doubtfully. He knew Mickeen Oge. Everyone did.

'Is the IRA in it?' he enquired.

'No. Paddy Bawn, himself only.'

'Right, begod! You're on.' THe man was a sportsman. 'An' I won't care if I lose, aither.'

'You'll lose all right, honest man,' said MIckeen Oge, 'and we'll spend the money decently.'

Sean Glynn of Leaccabuie touched him on the shoulder and the two friends went away together.

'Paddy Bawn is in the narrows at last,' said Sean sadly. 'Maybe we were right to be against it in the beginning.'

'We were not,' said Mickeen Oge.

'He will have to do something now?'

'He will.'

'Whatever it is, I'll stand by him as he stood by me. I'm not going home tonight, Mickeen Oge.'

'No?'

'No. I'll go out to see him tomorrow.'

'Very good!' said Mickeen Oge. 'I'll go with you. I have the old car here.'

Paddy Bawn and Ellen Roe went home in their tub-cart and had
not a single word or a glance for each other on the road. And
all that evening, at table or at fireside, a heart-sickening silence
held them in its unloosening grip. And all that night they lay side
by side still and mute. There was but one disastrous thing in both
their minds, and on that neither would speak. He was an Enright
and she was a Danaher, and the feud was on. They slept little.

Ellen Roe, her heart desolate, lay on her side, her dry eyes
closed, repentant for the grievous thing she had said, yet
knowing that she could not unsay it. Disproof had to come first
– but how – how?

Paddy Bawn lay on his back, his open eyes staring into the
dark, and his inner vision seeing things with a cold clarity. He
realised that he was at the fork of life, and that a finger pointed
unmistakably. There was only one thing to do. he must shame
man and woman in the face of the world. He must shatter his
own happiness in this world and the next. He must do a thing
so final and decisive that never again could it be questioned. And
there was just one small hope that a miracle would take place.
He cursed himself. 'Damn you, you fool! You might have known
that you should never have taken a Danaher without first
breaking O'Danaher.'

He rose early in the morning at his usual hour and went out
as usual to his morning chores – rebedding and foddering his
few cattle, rubbing down the half-bred, helping the servant-
maid with the creaming-pans – and at the usual hour he came
in to breakfast and ate it unhungrily and silently, which was not
usual. Thereafter, he again went out to the stable, harnessed the
gelding, and hitched him to the tub-cart. Then he returned to
the kitchen and spoke to his wife for the first time that morning.

'Ellen Roe, will you come down to Moyvalla with me to see
your brother?'

She threw her hands wide in a hopeless, helpless gesture as
much as to say, 'What's the use?'

'I must go,' said he. 'Will you come, please?'

She hesitated. 'Very well,' she said then, tonelessly. 'But, if
I set foot inside Moyvalla, there I may stay, Paddy Bawn.'

'That is on me,' he said bleakly, 'and I will take the blame
now or later. 'Tis Enright or Danaher this day – and Enright
it is before the face of God!'

'I will be ready in a minute,' said Ellen, and her heart stirred in her.

And they went the four miles down into the vale towards the farm of Moyvalla. It was a fine, clear mid-October morning, and a perfect day for harvesting the potato crop or threshing corn. As they turned out of the crossroads at Lisselton they met Sean Glynn and Mickeen Oge Flynn chugging along in an ancient touring-car.

'A slack season of the year,' lied Sean, 'and being as far as Listowel we thought we would come out and see ye.'

'Ye are welcome,' said Ellen Row, and looked at her husband.

Paddy Bawn's heart had lifted in his breast at the sight of his two friends. Whatever befell, these men would stand by him – and God was good after all.

'I am glad to see ye,' he said. 'Will ye come with me now and be my witnesses and –' he fixed them with his eye – 'leave it in my hands?'

'Anywhere – anyhow,' said Mickeen Oge.

The gelding went off at its reaching trot, and the car couldn't do much better than hold its place. So they drove into the big square of cobbled yard of Moyvalla and found it empty.

On one side of the square was the long, low, lime-washed farmhouse; on the opposite side, fifty yards distant, the two-storied line of steadings with a wide arch in the middle; and through the arch came the purr and zoom of a threshing-machine.

As Paddy Bawn tethered the half-bred to the wheel of a farm-cart, a slattern servant-girl leaned over the kitchen half-door and pointed through the arch. The master was beyont in the haggard – an' would she run for him?

'Never mind, colleen,' called Paddy Bawn. 'I'll get him. Ellen, will you go in and wait?'

'I'll come with you,' said Ellen quietly, and, when her husband was not looking, she beckoned with her head to his two friends – and hers, she hoped. She knew the man her brother was.

As they went through the arch the purr and zoom grew louder, and, turning a corner, they walked into the midst of activity. A long double-row of cone-pointed corn-stacks stretched across the haggard, and, between, Matt Tobin's portable threshing-machine was working full steam. The smooth-flying eight-foot driving wheel made a sleepy purr, and the black driving-belt ran with a sag and sway to the red-painted thresher. Up there on the platform, bare-armed men were feeding the drum with unbound corn-sheaves, their hands moving in a rhythmic swing; and as the toothed drum bit at the ears it made a gulping snarl that changed and slowed to a satisfied zoom. The wide conveying-belt was carrying the straw up a steep incline to where many men were building a long rick; other men were perched forking on the truncated cones of the stacks; still more men were attending to the corn-shoots and shoulder-bending under the weight of full sacks as they ambled across to the granary. Matt Tobin himself bent at the face of his engine, his bowler hat on his back hairs, feeding the firebox with divots of black hard peat. In all there were not less than two-score men about the place, for, as was the custom, Red Will's friends and neighbours were choring him at the threshing – the 'day in harvest' that is half work, half play, full of wit, devilment and horseplay, with a dance in the evening and a little courting on the side.

Red Will O'Danaher came round the flank of the engine and swore. He was open-necked, in his shirt-sleeves, and his broad chest and great forearms were covered with sandy hair.

'Hell and blazes! Look who's here!'

He wsa in the worst of tempers this fine morning that was made for pleasant labour and the shuttle-play of Kerry wit. The stale dregs of yesterday's whiskey had put him in a humour that, as they would say, would make a dog bite its father. He took two slow strides and halted, feet apart and head truculently forward.

'What is it this time?' he shouted – an un-Irish welcome, indeed.

Paddy Bawn and Ellen Roe came forward steadily, Sean and Mickeen Oge pacing behind; and, as they came, Matt Tobin slowly throttled down his engine. Red Will heard the change of pitch and looked angrily over his shoulder.

'What the devil do you mean, Tobin? Get on with the work!'

'To the devil with yourself, Red Will! This is my engine.' And Matt drove the throttle shut, and the purr of the flywheel slowly sank.

'We'll see in a minute,' threatened the big man and turned to the two near at hand.

'What is it?' he growled.

'A private word with you,' said Paddy Bawn. 'I won't keep you long.'

'You will not – on a busy morning,' sneered Red Will. 'You ought to know by now that there is no need for private words between me and you.'

'There is need,' urged Paddy Bawn. 'It will be best for you to hear what I have to say in your own house.'

'Or here on my own land. Out with it! I don't care who hears.'

He looked over Paddy Bawn's head at Mickeen Oge and Sean Glynn, his eyes fearless.

'Is the IRA in this too?' he enquired contemptuously.

'We are here as Paddy Bawn's friends,' said Sean mildly.

'The IRA is not in this, O'Danaher,' said Mickeen Oge, and he threw up his lean head and looked slowly round the haggard. There was something in that bleak look that chilled even Red Will. 'If the IRA were in this, not even the desolation of desolation would be as desolate as Moyvalla,' that look seemed to say.

Paddy Bawn looked round him too. Upon the thresher, up on the stacks, over there on the rick, men leaned on fork handles and looked at him; here and there about the stack yard men moved in to see, as it might be, what had caused the stoppage, but only really interested in the two brothers-in-law. He saw that he was in the midst of the Clan Danaher, for they were mostly of the Danaher kin: big, strong, blond men, rough, confident, proud of their breed. Mickeen Oge, Sean Glynn, Matt Tobin were the only men he could call friends. Many of the others were not unfriendly, but all had contempt in their eyes, and, what was worse, pity.

Very well so! The stage was set, and Red Will wanted it so. And it was not unfitting that it be set here amongst the Danaher men. Deep down in Paddy Bawn a hackle lifted.

He brought his eyes back to Red Will – deep-set eyes that did not waver.

'O'Danaher,' said he, and he no longer hid his contempt, 'you set great store by money?'

'No harm in that? You do it yourself, Patcheen.'

'Take it so. It is the game I am forced to play with you till hell freezes.' In stress he used strange little Americanisms. 'You bargained away your sister and played cheat, but I will not be cheated by any Danaher that ever sucked miser's milk. Listen, you big brute! You owe me a hundred pounds. Will you pay it?'

There was some harsh quality in his voice that was actually awesome. Red Will, ready to start forward overbearingly, took a fresh thought, and restrained himself to a brutal playfulness.

'Oho! Yankee fighting cock! I will pay what I like when I like.'

'One hundred pounds – today.'

'No. Nor tomorrow.'

'Right! That breaks all bargains.'

'What's that?'

'If you keep your hundred pounds, you keep your sister.'

'What is it?' shouted Red Will. 'What's that you say?'

'You heard me. Here is your sister Ellen. Keep her!'

'Fires o' hell!' He was astounded out of his truculence. 'You can't do that.'

'It is done,' said Paddy Bawn Enright.

Ellen Roe had been quiet as a mouse at Paddy Bawn's shoulder. But now, slow like doom, she faced him, and he was compelled to look at her. Eye to eye, and behind the iron of his, she saw the pain.

'To the mother of your son, Paddy Bawn Enright?' Only he heard the whisper.

'To my treasure of the world – before the face of God. Let Him judge me.'

'I know – I know. Let Him direct you.'

That is all she said, and walked quietly across to where Matt Tobin stood at the face of the engine. Her two friends went with her, and Sean Glynn placed a firm hand on her arm.

'Give him time, Ellen Roe,' he whispered. 'This had to be, and all he needs is time. He's slow to start, maybe, but he's death's tiger when he moves.'

'Praises be to all the saints and devils that brought me here this day!' said Matt Tobin.

Mickeen Oge Flynn said nothing.

Big Will O'Danaher was no fool. Except when in a berserk rage, he knew as well as any man how far he could go; and somehow, the berserk rage was chilled in him at birth this morning. Some indomitable quality in the small man warned him that brute force would not serve any purpose. He used his head. Whatever disgrace might come to Paddy Bawn, public opinion would flay him alive. He could never lift head again –

and all over one hundred pounds. His inner vision saw mouths twisted in sly laughter, eyes leering in derision. The scandal on his name! Even now, that would come, but there might be time yet to lay the foundation of his future attitude – just a bit of fun at a Yankee upstart. That was it.

Thus the thoughts shuttled in his mind, while he thudded the ground with iron-shod heel. Suddenly, he threw up his head and bellowed his laugh.

'You damn little fool! Don't be taking things so seriously. I was only having my fun with you. What the hell are your dirty few pounds to the likes of me? Stay where you are, blast you!'

He ground round on his heel, strode off with a furious swing of shoulder and disappeared through the arch.

Paddy Bawn stood alone in that wide ring of men. The workers had come down off the rick and stack to see closer; and with the instinct of the breed they knew that no man dared interfere now. They moved back and aside, looked at one another, looked at Paddy Bawn and Ellen Roe, at her friends, frowned and shook their heads. This smallish man from Knockanore was at last displaying the force that was in him. They looked at him again and wondered. Could he fight? Oh, bah! They knew their Red Will, and they knew that, yielding up the money, his savagery might break out into an explosion in which this little man's boxing tricks would be no more use than a rotten kipper. They waited, most of them, to prevent that savagery going too far.

Paddy Bawn Enright did not look at anyone. He stood easily in their midst, his hands deep in his pockets, one shoulder hunched forward, his eyes on the ground, and his face strangely unconcerned. He seemed the least perturbed man there. Perhaps he was remembering the many times he had sat in his corner and waited for the bell. Matt Tobin whispered in Ellen's ear, 'God is good, I tell you.' But Ellen's eyes, looking and looking at her husband, saw their own god.

Red Will was back in two minutes and strode straight down on Paddy Bawn.

'Look, Patcheen!' In his raised hand was a crumpled bundle of greasy banknotes. 'Here is your money! Take it – and what's coming to you! Take it!' He thrust it into Paddy Bawn's hand. 'Count it. Make sure you have it all – and then get kicked out of my haggard. And look!' He thrust forward that great hairy right hand. 'If ever I see your face again I will drive that through it. Count it, you spawn!'

Paddy Bawn did not count it. Instead, he crumpled it into a ball in his strong fingers. Then he turned on his heel and walked with cool slowness to the face of the engine. He gestured with one hand to Matt Tobin, but it was Ellen Roe, quick as a flash, who obeyed the gesture. Though the hot bar scorched her hand, she jerked open the door of the firebox, and the leaping peat flames whispered out at her. And, forthwith, Paddy Bawn, with one easy sweep of the arm, threw the crumpled ball of banknotes into the heart of the flames. The whisper lifted one tone, and a scrap of charred paper floated out of the funnel top. That was all the fuss the fire made of its work.

There was fuss enough outside.

Red Will gave one mighty shout. 'No!' It was more an anguished yell than an honest shout.

'My money – my good money!'

He sprang into the air, came down in his tracks, made two furious bounds forward, and his great arms came flinging to crush and kill. Berserk at last!

But those flinging fists never touched the small man.

'You dumb ox!' said Paddy Bawn between his teeth, and seemed to glide below the flinging arms.

That strong hunched shoulder moved a little, but no one there could follow the terrific drive of that hooked right arm. The smash of bone on bone was sharp as whipcrack, and Red Will, two hundred pounds of him, stopped dead, went back on his heels, swayed a moment and staggered three paces.

'Now and forever, man of the Enrights!' roared Matt Tobin, ramming his bowler hat over his head and levering it loose again.

But Red Will O'Danaher was a mighty man. That blow should have laid him on his back – blows like it had tied men to the floor for the full count. Red Will only shook his head, grunted like a boar and threw all his weight at the smaller man. Now would the Danaher men see an Enright torn apart!

But the little man, instead of circling away, drove in at the big fellow, compact of power, every hackle lifted, explosive as dynamite. Tiger Enright was in action.

The men of the Danahers saw then an exhibition that they had not knowledge enough to appreciate fully, but that they would not forget all their days. Multitudes had paid as much as ten dollars to see Tiger Enright in action: his footwork, his timing, his hitting from all angles, the sheer explosive ferocity of the man. But never was his action more devastating than now. He was a thunderbolt on two feet. All the stored dislike of years was in his two terrible hands.

And the big man was a glutton. He took all that was coming and came for more. He never once touched his opponent with clenched fist. He did not know how. The small man was not there when the great fist came hurtling, yet the small man was the aggressor from first to last. His very speed made him that. Actually forty pounds lighter, he drove Red Will by sheer hitting back and fore across the yard. Men, for the first time, saw a two-hundred-pound man knocked clean off his feet by a body blow.

Five minutes. In five packed minutes, Paddy Bawn Enright demolished his enemy. Four – six – eight times he sent the big man neck-and-crop to the ground, and each time the big man scrambled furiously to his feet, staggering, bleeding, slavering, raving, vainly trying to rend and kill. But at last he stood swaying, mouth open, and hands clawing futilely: and Paddy Bawn finished the fight with his dreaded double hit, left below the breastbone and right under the jaw.

Red Will lifted on his toes, swayed and fell flat on his back. He did not even kick as he lay.

Paddy Bawn did not waste a glance on the fallen giant. He swung full circle on the Danaher men; he touched his breast with his middle finger, his voice of iron challenged them.

'I am Patrick Enright of Knockanore Hill. Is there a Danaher amongst you thinks himself a better man? Come, then.'

His face was like a hard stone, his great chest lifted, the air whistled in his nostrils; his deep-set flashing eyes dared and daunted them.

'Come, Danaher men!'

'*Mo yerm thu, a Phadraig Ban!* My choice thou, white Patrick!' That was Matt Tobin's exultant bugle.

Paddy Bawn walked straight across to his wife and halted before her. His face was still as cold as stone, but his voice, quiet as it was, had in it some dramatic quality full of life and the eagerness of life.

'Mother of my son, will you come home with me?'

She lifted to the appeal voice and eye.

'Is it so you ask me?'

'As my wife only, Ellen Roe Enright?'

'Very well, heart's treasure.' She caught his arm in both her hands. 'Let us be going. Come, friends!'

'God is good, surely,' said Paddy Bawn.

And she went with him, proud as the morning, out of that place. But, a woman, she would have the last word.

'Mother o' God!' she cried. 'The trouble I had to make a man of him!'

'God Almighty did that for him before you were born,' said Mickeen Oge sternly.

An Ciarraíoch Mallaithe

Má leanaim go dian tú siar chun Cairibreach
Caillfead mo chiall mura dtriallfar 'bhaile liom,
Óró, bead a' sileadh na ndeor
Ná tar im dhiaidh gan mórchuid airgid
Stampaí Rí Shacsan go cruinn i dtaisce 'gat
Óró i gcóir costais a' róid
Ní bheidh cloig ar ár ndoirnibh ó rómhar na ngarraithe,
Ná á chruachadh na móna ná 'n fómhar a' leathadh 'rainn,
Beidh rince fada 'gainn más é is fearra leat
Ór a's airgead ól a's beathuisce
Óró fad a mhairfimid beo.

Do shiúlóinn an saol go léir 's an Bhreathnaisc leat,
'S níorbh fhearr liom bheith 'n Éirinn ag éisteacht Aifrinn
Óró ná i Sasana Nua.
Ach ná creidim ó d' bhéal dhá dtrian a n-abrann
Mar is fear magaidh thú a bhíonn a' mealladh ban
Óró le d' racaireacht spóirt.
A chumann mo chléibh a's a réilthion mhaisealach
Ní 'neosainn bréag ó m' bhéal ar chapall duit,
Ar eagla an pheaca 's go mbeimís damanta
Grá tá ceangailte 'm lár ná scarfainn leat
Óró go dtéad síos faoin bhfód.

Ní leogfad faoin bhfód go deo mo scafaire
Ó fuaireas fios aigne mar is é do b'fhearra liom
Óró líon cupán den bheoir.
Glaoigh ar na cairdibh go dtrám an bairille
'S déanfam rírá go mbeidh trácht sa chathair air,
Óró fad a mhairfidh a bhfuil beo.
Seo mo dhá láimh duit go bás ná scarfad leat
Ach ceangailt' go brách leat gan spás fad mhairfimid,
Sin suite ár margadh 's ní dhéanfaidh do mhalairtse
Suí ná seasamh liom ná i bhfaradh dhom,
Óró a's bhfuil agam do gheobhair.

Do shiúileas léi trí shléibhte Callainne
Ag déanamh ranna di a's bréag dá cheapadh dhi
Óró sar a dtitfeadh sí i mbrón
Chun gur bhailíos go géar gach réal 'bhí i dtaisce 'ci,
Gan phlé gan achrann síos am phaba chugham
Óró i gcóir costais an róid.
Do shocraíos féin mo bheabhar hata orm
Mo mhaide 's is calma do léimfinn clathacha
Siar chun Ceanna Toirc d' fhonn bheith scartha lei
Óró a's í ar sodar i m' dheoidh.

Nuair a bhraith an fhaoileann an oíche tagaithe
'S ná fuair sí istigh ná amuigh sa gharraí mé
Óró do chas ologón.
Do phreab sí 'na suí ag caoine' a cod' airgid
Dá rá gur mheallas-sa a croí le m' chleasannaibh
Óró fad a mhairfeadh sí beo.
Éirigí, a chairde ní foláir nó go leanfam é
Cuardóm na bánta a's ard na ngarraithe
Don Chiarraíoch Mhallaithe do mheall mo chuid airgid
Lena bhréithre bladair uaim, ag diúgadh an chnagaire
Óró 's ní fheadar cá ngeobhad.

Ní Fios Cé a Scríobh

TOMMY STACK: RACEHORSE TRAINER

I had my first dreams of the Grand National when I was a boy being brought up on a farm outside Moyvane on the Knockanure road. My parents William and Mary are both dead. My brother Stephen now works the farm and my sister Helen Roche is married in Rathkeale. I was the baby of the family. At national school in Moyvane I was taught by Tom O'Callaghan whose sons Bernard and Colm played for Kerry. Another son, Tom O'Callaghan, was in class with me along with Austin Kearney. I used to play for the under-fourteens in Moyvane. That was the one thing which was marvellous at the time – we had a few county players in the parish. There were good players like Bernard O'Callaghan. Liam Hanrahan was a fine player. The Brosnans were famous.

I remember up in the football field every evening it was an achievement to get a kick of the ball because there were so many players there trying to get it. There would be fifty chasing it. The interest was marvellous and they were tremendously fit and hardy from piking hay all day. If some of them lads hit you a shoulder you would go through the ground. They didn't need any press-ups or weight work. To this day I am still impressed looking back at the fitness and dedication of those lads in Moyvane playing football for hours every evening, They thought of nothing else. That's why they were great footballers because they concentrated on what they were doing. That influenced me. I played but was not a good footballer. But the application these people had rubbed off on me. Every match in the parish league was like an All-Ireland Final. The passion from five teams in a small parish!

I had a piebald pony at home and we used to tackle him to bring the milk to the creamery. I used to look after him and jump him over poles in a field. Every year at the Tarbert Carnival they held a race and I entered my pony and we won. It had a fiver prize-money which was a lot for a young lad. My first win as a jockey. I used to train the pony at night-time. I used to study the photographs in the newspapers of the way Pat Taaffe and Bobby Beasley sat on a horse going over a fence and I modelled myself on them from these newspaper pictures. I followed the racing results from England and Tim Molony was a big figure then.

One of the highlights of the year was the Listowel races eight miles away. The school would close for the three days of the Races and there I saw the real thing. By then the racing bug had gripped me. In 1958 I was sent to Mungret College outside Limerick as a boarder and I was five years there. It was a rugby college and I loved the sport. Exams were tough because I didn't do the work. Fr Cantillon was a very nice man. Fr Jack Brennan was there and in my class the students included Bobby Barry who used to ride while still a student. Barry Brogan came two years after me. When we went to Mungret first you didn't get out until Christmas. The Jesuits were great teachers and marvellous men. I loved rugby and was on the college side playing scrum-half. I played in the junior and senior sides. We had a great junior side. Bobby Barry was wing-forward. We were beaten by Crescent in the Final at Thomond Park and I never cried as much as I did after that game. We were good enough to win.

We beat good teams on the way to the Final despite being a relatively small school with only a hundred and fifty pupils. The school hadn't won a cup for thirty years. I captained the senior side the next year and I also played for the Munster Schoolboys at scrum-half. Johnny Moroney, who played after-wards for Ireland, was out-half on the Munster Schoolboys team. We played in Ravenhill and it was my first time in the North. Frank Hogan, who is now involved with Garryowen, was wing-forward on our side. The Comiskeys from Rockwell were on the team. I used also do the pole-vault and won the North Munster. I won the 110 metres hurdle as well.

I got to know Barry Brogan and his father Jimmy Brogan who trained horses and I used to go up with him and ride at the weekends. Later in Dublin I kept up the contact. Barry Brogan and Bobby Barry had amateur licences while they were in Mungret and Bobby won on Chenille War in Limerick.

Nobody actually gave me lessons on riding style. The pony at home taught me a lot. I had a track going from one field to another and I used to think I was going over Becher's on the pony in a childish way. Pat Taaffe had a great style and Bobby Beasley was great from the last home. So I copied their styles.

During the summer holidays I would milk four or five cows each evening.

When I did my Leaving Cert., I wanted to try and get into the Army Equitation School. I applied for the cadets and I didn't get it and I was so disappointed. It was a kick in the teeth. I got a job with Phoenix Insurance in Dublin. I was in digs in Leeson Street at first and then I went into a flat at 48 Upper Drumcondra Road, Dublin, with three lads from Limerick and one from Cork. There were two Reddan brothers, one was Brian Reddan who was on the Crescent team which beat us in the Munster Colleges Junior Cup Final. He has since died. He was a great out-half and he reminded me of Richard Sharpe, the great England out-half. He was a grand fellow and a fine player. His brother, Pat, was also in the flat and Michael Weekes from Limerick. I was working in the office and I was fine. I used go to Brogan's some weekends. The manager of the Phoenix, Mr Johnson, asked me to join Lansdowne Rugby Club and I did. On Sundays I would go down and play for Abbeyfeale. We were beaten in the Final of the Munster Junior Cup. Dr George O'Mahony had coaxed me to play for Abbeyfeale.

A carload of us would drive down and I drove as I was the only non-drinker. There was a great team in Abbeyfeale. Billy O'Mahony who should have been capped for Ireland was on the side. I was only seventeen or eighteen. Dr George and his wife Betty were two of the most marvellous people you could ever meet. They made Abbeyfeale rugby what it is today. They won the Junior Cup afterwards, but I had gone to Dublin.

While in Dublin I decided to have a crack at the racing and I wrote to every trainer in England. I got one reply back from Neville Crump. I wanted to go over as an amateur. A brother-in-law of mine, the late Paddy Roche in Rathkeale, knew Bobby Renton to whom he sold cattle and got in touch with him. Bobby Renton said he was coming over to Dublin and we met in the Hibernian Hotel. He was an elderly man and was over with Mrs Brotherton, his main owner, looking at horses. He said come over. I handed in my notice to the Phoenix and left for England on 13 July 1965. My mother nearly had a canary over giving up my good job to go to England. My father gave me fifty pounds as my airfare back as he felt I wouldn't last long. He wanted me to get it out of my system.

I didn't know anyone in England and I had only been there once previously for two days on an insurance course. Bobby Renton sent his butler Percy to pick me up at Leeds Airport. I got digs and knew nobody there. That first year I never went out. I said I would have to work hard.

I was given a few horses to look after and ride out every day. Bobby had about eighteen National Hunt horses. After a few days he said he would get me an amateur's licence. He asked me to school a few horses which I did and he said I had done a lot of schooling. I didn't disagree with him, but the truth was I had done little or no schooling of horses up to then. You have to bluff sometimes. He got me my amateur licence and at that time he was paying me four pounds a week pocket money and he bought me a bicycle to get into Ripon for Mass on Sundays. He gave me a ride in September and I was fourth on New Money in a handicap hurdle. I was beaten by a horse ridden by Jack Berry, now the great trainer. I had a few more rides and I had my first winner on 16 October 1965 on New Money at Weatherby. I got a tremendous thrill. That was a big day in my life.

Looking back it was a thousand-to-one chance getting the great start I got. Bobby Renton had never made a jockey before. He always employed outside top jockeys. Here was a young lad from Kerry with a trainer who had no record of cultivating up-and-coming young jockeys.

My first ride over fences was at the October Cheltenham meeting when I won on Well Packed in an amateur's race. Brough Scott and Lord Oaksey rode in the race. My first ride over fences and I won. I won the Grand Annual Handicap Chase on the same horse at the big Cheltenham Festival meeting in 1966. It was unreal. I had broken my wrist a few weeks before and at Cheltenham I rode with a plaster right up my hand to the elbow. I stayed with Bobby Renton after turning professional in 1968.

The first two years were tough and I wasn't going well. Bobby Renton died and I was asked to take out the trainer's licence for a few months. Red Rum was in the yard so I trained him for a period which is not widely known. I didn't win with him. I then went back to riding and rode freelance. Tom Jones retained me for a year, and then I went to Arthur Stephenson where I was stable jockey for the last five years of my career until I retired in 1978.

The moment Red Rum cleared the last fence in the 1977 Grand National was the most memorable moment of my life. For a few moments I had this unbelievable feeling. But after that brief feeling of utter delight, right through to the run to the line I was overcome with concern that something could go wrong. Devon Loch flashed through my mind. And even when I passed the winning post I had a quick look at my saddlecloth to see if it had slipped. I was even worrying that I might had lost some of the lead which is put into a saddlebag to make up the weight the horse had to carry.

Obviously we had been looking forward to the race for some time. I had ridden Red Rum the previous year when he led over the last and we were beaten by Rag Trade by a length and a half. I thought that was my chance of winning a National gone. Brian Fletcher had ridden him in his two previous National wins. I had ridden the horse way back when he was first run in the National as an eight-year-old. I had always ridden Red Rum and I rode him on his first run over fences at Newcastle as a five-year-old when he was with Bobby Renton. Bobby had won a Grand National with Free Booter in 1953. He bought Red Rum off the flat as a three-year-old from Tim Moloney and he won a few hurdle races.

We went to school him once over fences to go chasing with him. He half fell through the first and he refused to jump the second fence. That was the only schooling Red Rum got in his career. Bobby Renton said to forget the schooling and told me I had the ride at Newcastle. He had plenty of experience over hurdles and was cute. He jumped like a cat and had no inclination to stop or refuse. He finished third that day. Then his next race was at Doncaster in a conditions race and he won. He won four or five chases. When Ginger McCain got him I won his first three races and then when he was entered in the National I was asked to ride him, but I couldn't as I was retained by another trainer, and Brian Fletcher got the ride. He won that National and the next one and was then beaten by l'Escargot third time round. Then he hadn't been running well and the owners asked me to ride the horse in the 1976 National in which we finished second.

I was looking forward to riding him in 1977 again after being pipped the previous year. He always improved as the spring went on. That day in 1977 he looked a picture in the paddock and got the best-turned-out award. He really blossomed at that time of year.

I had been racing in Liverpool the day before and went home to Yorkshire that night. We lived in a village called Healaugh. I drove down to Aintree with Liz, my wife, and a friend called Sarah Gardner. We stopped for a cup of coffee at the last service station on the motorway. Before a big event you get tensed up. I was going well and had a good year and was champion jockey. But still, riding a horse like this in a big race, when you know you have a chance, it's a huge responsibility. The horse had plenty of weight so I wasn't wasting to get my weight down. I drove onto Aintree and I took a walk down to Becher's on my own. The best part of Aintree I had always felt was going out through the gates after the race, going home. Over for another year.

There is a big hype leading into the National. I was concerned that I would do my best and that the horse would get back safely and that I wouldn't be at fault if something went wrong. Before the National I rode in two races and finished placed. One of those races was the dead-heat between Monksfield and Night Nurse and I was third. That was a great race. I was third on Peterhoff. There was about an hour between that race and the National. The weighing room has an atmosphere on Grand National day different to any other. There is a cold sense of something about to happen. Nobody is relaxed. People try to make jokes and get little response. People come in looking for jockeys' autographs. The adrenalin is rolling a bit.

I was very tight and I would have been the same before a rugby match. I would be trying to concentrate on what I was going to do. When you have something important to do, you tighten up and get tense. I think this makes you into a better professional, it increases your awareness, and the will to do your best. Before a race I would always be superstitious.

I led the parade because Red Rum was number one on the card. I went down and showed him the first fence. And as it was a cold, dry April day, I got a rug put over his loins down at the start to keep him warm. The ground was drying up fast and that suited. It's like with athletes, the longer you can keep a horse warm the better. He was on his toes and he was wound up. Whatever feeling he got at Liverpool, you knew he sensed the place. He was like a coil under you about to explode. Yet he was not jumping or jigging, but on his toes. With him you kept to the middle of the field for the first circuit. So there were a lot of loose horses to be avoided. Six fell at the first and another six fell at the third which is a ditch.

Going to Becher's for the first time I was to the middle back of the field and another few went there. When I looked up at Becher's there were only seven or eight in front of me and I was very surprised as I felt there should have been a lot more at that stage. After the canal turn John Williams went off a long way in front and we were about sixth, closer than I expected, but I was happy. The race is always dangerous up to Becher's the first time as it is only sorting itself out up to that point with a lot of the less serious contenders falling. The novelty runners are gone by then. Going across the Melling Road there was a horse twenty lengths in front and at the Chair the second horse fell.

Going into the country for the second time I was fourth or fifth. Boom Docker with John Williams, who rides a lot on the flat now, refused after leading. That left Andy Pandy in front. He led into Becher's where he fell, leaving me in front. I had a loose horse in front of me heading for the Canal Turn. I was frightened he could take me out and I raced ahead.

I concentrated on the job. I looked back and saw Martin Blackshaw cantering about three lengths behind me on Church-town Boy. At the second last I jumped it well and I heard a crash and I knew Churchtown Boy had hit it hard. Going to the last I didn't look back and didn't hear him coming. I jumped it well and I looked back and saw we had it.

I can't describe the thrill after the last. I had it then. I pulled the horse off the rail and everything went through my mind. I kept him up the middle. It flashed through my mind that he might duck or somebody might run out. I kept him well off the rail. You could hear the Tannoy, but not clearly as I was concentrating hard. I never touched him with the stick through the race. I think that I have never concentrated so hard as I did in the last two hundred yards of that race.

The lead-in couldn't last long enough, the policemen on horseback, the cheering crowds. It was the result everyone wanted. Things went right on the day and our horse did nothing wrong. Great credit to Ginger, he produced the horse A1 on the day and he delivered. After weigh-in there were television and press interviews. I rode in the last race and finished third.

That night we went back to Southport to a local hotel. I don't drink but everyone was drinking. Then they brought the horse into the hotel at about eleven o'clock. It was unbelievable. I will never forget it. Ginger trained in Southport where he had a garage business. But they brought the horse into the ballroom and everyone was patting him. We travelled home that night. A marvellous day. It was one ambition I had since I started off, to win the Grand National. I thought I wouldn't be good enough to be champion jockey as I hadn't the background or the experience. I was about to become champion that year for the second time. Winning the National was the one I wanted to do, more than becoming champion jockey. It is probably the most famous race in the world.

While I had my greatest high in 1977, winning the Grand National on Red Rum, I also had one of my great lows due to a bad injury at Hexham in September when a horse turned over me in the Paddock. He broke my pelvis in about ten or twelve places and he ruptured my bladder. I had to be put in traction for three months and I had many operations. I was pretty lucky with falls: broken wrists and crushed vertebrae. I never broke my collar bone. I have big, strong bones. I have a seven and a half inch wrist and good boxers wouldn't have wrists much bigger than that. I had an accident after coming back to Tipperary after I went out to see mares in a paddock. I got a kick in the side of the head. Another fraction of an inch and I would have been a vegetable. I was knocked out for forty-five minutes in the field and an artery was severed, but luckily the blood clotted.

I met my wife Liz through racing; she was Liz Townson and was secretary to Ken Oliver. We were married in 1975. She is a farmer's daughter from County Durham. We have two children: James, 'Fozzie' as we call him, is going to Glenstal and our little daughter Serena is fourteen months old. At thirty-two I decided to retire. I had gone beyond my wildest expectation and beyond what I though was possible. I could have ridden for another few years as my nerve was as good as ever. But I got into breeding horses and I was involved in it and that is one of the reasons I gave up. One of my last winners was Rare Gold for Paddy Norris at Killarney. I rode in Listowel also. I enjoyed coming to ride in Kerry and it was nice to have had a winner.

When I took out my trainer's licence in 1986 I found there was no comparison between riding and training. I had a good start winning the Cartier Million at Phoenix Park with Colwyn Bay. As a trainer you have total responsibility.

For seven years or so I had more rides than anyone else in England and I was very fit. It's amazing the fitness levels I got to from riding and that makes you a better jockey. That's why people say amateurs can't ride. After coming out of an office all day what chance have you against a professional?

I liked flat breeding and had been involved before retiring as a jockey. John Magnier asked me if I would manage one of the Coolmore Studs, which I did and I managed Longfield Stud. I stayed there two or three years and we bought this place. We have eighty-five boxes and three hundred acres here at Thomastown Castle in Golden with all-weather and grass gallops. There are about twenty-eight working here.

Training is far more demanding as the buck stops with you and whether you have two or twenty horses you have to deliver and you live by it. A jockey might ride six or seven hundred horses in a year. As a jockey, you get on one, you get off one. For the successes you have, you have so many disappointments. I think the average person does not realise what it takes to produce a horse, fit on the day to win, and the casualties that you have along the way with horses which don't meet that goal. Owners are basically very good, but some don't understand. It is quite an expensive sport. We have some great patrons like Robert Sangster.

I'd like to win a Classic and I get a kick out of watching the home-bred horses progress. In racing I will never stop learning. No matter what level you are at, you never stop learning. I like to win races in Kerry and we have had winners at all three tracks there. I like to go back with horses which have a chance because, being a Kerryman, people in Kerry expect that my horses will have a chance. Kerry people are very proud and have done so well all over the world.

It's great being a Kerryman. Something I always will be. I think that because it has been such a successful sporting county in gaelic football, the major sporting game in the country, a Kerryman or woman has to look at that and say, 'I have to do my piece in what I am doing to maintain that tradition.'

Being from Kerry I have always had an attachment to greyhounds. I had a track dog as a young lad. I am involved in some greyhounds still. I like the coursing and any part of country life.

I was born in the country and I understand it and I know what makes country life tick. I cannot understand how some city people try to run down country life when they don't understand it. They think they understand it, but they don't. I am still a country Kerryman at heart.

When I think of Kerry I think of marvellous characters like Eric Browne, the Listowel bookie. I have known him for a long time, and I think he has great credibility and a marvellous sense of humour and is great company. I have great admiration for Jeremiah Carroll, the man who sent up Master Myles to win the Derby in Clonmel. A more modest man you could not meet and was never given the credit for what he achieved with that great dog. Cormac O'Leary was another teacher in Moyvane. He's a great doggy man and I enjoy meeting these people.

If you had to pick a team to do a job of work tomorrow whatever it might be, as regards loyalty you would put these men on it. The Kerry people would stand by their man, through thick and thin. You certainly wouldn't like them against you, as many a footballer found out.

The Stacks originally came from Springmount, Duagh. They bought the farm in Moyvane. My mother was a Danagher from Athea and she went to America as a child of three. The family returned when she was fifteen. So we used always call her 'the Yank'.

I remember walking cattle into Listowel, seven miles in and seven miles out for the May or October big fair day. I remember marvellous scraps and family feuds which would erupt at the fairs. Dermot Dillon and his brother Kevin are first cousins of mine. Dermot played for Kerry and Kevin played for Cork. Duagh was a great football parish. You had Dan McAuliffe, the Kerry footballer, who was from Duagh. The first North Kerry Final I saw in Listowel was between Duagh and Clounmacon. Dermot, Kevin and Paul, the three Dillons and another player was Tom Costello and Dan McAuliffe. They beat Clounmacon.

Arthur Stephenson, the man I spent the big years of my career with, was a trainer who was a real professional. A hard worker and a great farmer. He told me unless I had the will to win I would be no use to him, He was a hard taskmaster in that

he expected you to deliver when he wanted you to. I admired
him and was very fond of him and the entire family. He worked
hard and his horses were meant to work the same. He would
have one hundred horses in and would go through about one
hundred and fifty in a year. To win a championship you need
a big stable behind you. I rode over six hundred winners and my
biggest tally of winners in a season was ninety-seven in one of
the two years I became champion jockey.

I remember riding in a hurdle for Arthur one time at
Sedgefield. And he said in the paddock just to give the horse
a run and not to get into trouble. When he really expected a
horse to win the only riding orders he would give you were,
'Don't get beat', when legging you up. Coming to the last this
horse was running away and I had to let go his head and he won
by half a length. Coming back in I looked fed-up with myself
and Arthur walked over alongside the horse and said to me:
'Look pleased, you fool.' Concealing our true emotions.

from VOICES OF KERRY (1994)
EDITED BY JIMMY WOULFE

MICHEÁL UA CIARMHAIC
SEANFHOCAIL, NATHANNA AGUS TOMHAISEANNA

Bean rua i dtosach an tslua
Bean ramhar bhodhar bhog bhreimneach
Bean bhuí anteasaí phógach
An bhean gheal dubh an bhean is breátha amuigh.

Bó gan tarbh is fada go mbéarfaidh sí,
Bean gan leanbh is fada di a céalacan.

Cá ngeobhair an tsúil ná feacaigh raidhse?

Chomh líofa le breim bacaigh.

Chomh cam le hadharc reithe.

Chomh hainnis le magairle reithe.

Cos le gach cuileachtain agus lámh le gach locht.

Comharthaí pósta poilleanna dóite.

Chomh balbh le trumpa gan teanga.

Cá raghaidh an fia lena chac?
(Le duine i sáinn a déarfaí é)

Chomh clannmhar le dreoilín.

Chuirfeadh sé clann go colúr.
(.i. le fireannach torthúil.)

Caora mhór an t-uan i bhfad.

Cuireann lodar bruan.

Seacht n-aicidí an tsléibhe: méiscrí, fochmaí, bonnleacaí, lúidíní tinne, oighear, míolcheart agus fríde.

Údarás gan eolas.

Ar thaobh an teampaill agus a dhrandal go fuar.

Ar fhear an tí a théann an chéad scéal d'insint.

Meáigh go maith an chomhairle gan iarraidh.

Gealladh báistí – gealach suaite agus siúl coiligh.

Aghaidh an drochscéil i bhfad uainn!

Bail ó Dhia ar an scéal gan dath!

Tá craiceann air sin mar scéal!

Tá do chomharthaí neamhchruinn agus aghaidh do phoill ó

dheas *(.i. le duine ná beadh an scéal i gceart aige agus ná beadh bailithe aige ach gaoth).*

Ná ligh an mhil den dris le heagla go raghadh dealga id theanga.

Más milis an mhil ná ligh den ndriseoig í.

Ná caith deoch i gcoinne falla ar eagla gur ort féin a thitfeadh sé.

Airgead caillí á mhún cois fallaí!

Bíonn an ghéim is aoirde ag an mboin is caoile sa bhuaile.

Is deacair rogha idir dhá ghabhar chaocha.

Ní chuirfeadh an saol ó thaoscadh an bháid thú!

Nár fheicidh aon drochshúil tú ná aon súil a chiorróidh thú!

Iascaire gan scian nó cú gan eireaball.

Sláinte an bhradáin, croí folláin, bolg lán, agus gob fliuch!

Ar nós coileach ag glaoch ar charn aoiligh.

Átha an bhallaigh ort!

Fuil is liú ort!

Bó-leagadh ort!

Bodhaire Uí Laoire ort!

Casachtach, pocharnach, tochas, is scríobadh! Ach bhuaigh an tochas orthu ar fad!

Tá cluas ar an gclaí.

Tá dhá thaobh ar an gclaí.

Cuirim ort, ligim leat, buail mo sciath!

Buail sa tóin é, seachain sa cheann é.

Srathar na hainnise an cliabh, ach fógraim sa diabhal an beart!

Golb do chníopaire agus blúire don bhfathach.

Bíonn an rath ar an sruimleáil agus clann ag an amadán.

'Ar chaill an láir aon chrú? *(Ceist é seo a chuirtí mar gheall ar an mbean óg nuair a bhíodh cleamhnas á dhéanamh – 'an raibh leanbh aici sarar phós sí?')*

An t-uan ag múineadh méilí dá mháthair.

Is é gol an gháire a bhí aici anuraidh.

Is fearr madraí an bhaile a bheith ag lútáil ort ná ag drantán ort.

Is deacair ceol do bhaint as maidí fuara.

Deireadh seanchapaill bháin deireadh fear léinn.

Buann an t-oideachas ar an gcinniúint.

Neamh-mheabhair an bhairnigh ort ag snámh ar na clocha.

Is moill faobhar agus moill gan é.

Comhairle a thabhairt do mhnaoi bhoirb nó buille ribe ar iarann fuar.

Súgán sneachta nó clathacha baintrí.

Fág fé lic an tinteáin é!

Bíonn cluas eascon ar an bhfeallaire!

Seachain lucht meisce nó leisce nó drúise.

Is fearr tigh beag ar bholg lán ná caisleán mór fé lón beagáin.

Ná bain tuí ded thigh féin chun slinne do chur ar thigh an
leanna.

Aithnítear fear an straoileoige i measc an phobail.

Bean mo thí, máthair mo leanbh, agus céile mo leapa!

Comharthaí aois: fáibrí aois, dronn agus preiceall, casachtach,
clúmh agus breimneach.

Rudaí neamhrathúil: airgead úis, cúr na gcárt agus gaol na
gcnámh.

Oíche na Coda Móire deineadh síoda den triopall agus fíon den
uisce.
Ar eagla na heaspa, is maith bheith coimeádach,
Ach ní abraím leat bheith leamh ná spadánta!

Is ciúin agus sostach sruth na linne láine –
Ní hé sin don sruth éadrom, is ea a bhagras go dána!

Tuiscint is míthuiscint ní oireann siad dá chéile,
Mar is dóigh le fear na buile gurb é féin fear na céille.

Fear an ghabhail stractha agus a bhean gan snáthaid,
ghoidfeadh sé an t-ubh ón gcorr agus an corr féin fé dheireadh.

Dígh gach tine an fhearnóg úr;
Dígh gach díghe meadhg más sean;
Dígh gach ní, sin í an drochbhean.

Adú tine le loch, adú cloch le cuan.

Feadaíl chun gaoithe, feadaíl chun poill,* feadaíl le hathrú
gaoithe, feadaíl fuar na fearthainne!
*(*chun mún a dhéanamh).*

An breim tinn tubaisteach
Do lig an scaidhte ar aghaidh na tine amach –
Níor fhág sé sop tuí ná aoileach comharsan,
Ná an lorg ab aoirde go raibh dá dhroim seolta,
Ná gur raid sé siar do phointe Bhólais,
Le racht gaoithe poill a thóna!
(Nára slán an comórtas!)

Súile gorma lán de ghrá,
Súile dubha lán de dhíomá,
Súile uaithe lán de mhí-ádh,
Súile leisciúla dorcha doimhin.

Ar ghlaoch an choiligh deirtí: 'Tar slán, a mhic na circe!'

Cupán órga is cos as,
Ólann mac rí deoch as!
(.i. an chíoch)

Fear fada donn ina sheasamh sa ghleann
Gan faic ina cheann ach diabhail agus deamhain!
(.i. feochadán)

Fear fada dubh ina sheasamh sa tsruth,
Gan focal ina phluc ach 'dud-dud-dud-dud')
(.i. an maide istigh i gcorcán leitean)

Tugadh bia chun triúir i mbarr Locha Léin,
D'ith an bia an triúr agus tháinig sé féin!
(.i. piscín cait, d'ith sé gearrcaigh an fhiolair)

Fód bog idir dhá bhogfhód agus fód bog,
Bogfód agus fód bog idir fód bog agus dhá bhogfhód!
Cé mhéid fód?

Bhí beirt fhear de mhuintir Chróigh
Ag baint slat lá ceoigh –
Na slata do bhaineadar d'fhágadar ina ndiaidh iad,
Agus na slata nár bhaineadar thugadar leo iad!
(.i. dhá phréachán ag stothadh a chéile)

Cur isteach aige sagart ar cheardaithe go raibh file ina measc:-
Sagart: 'Ceardaithe ag obair go mall, buille acu thall is abhus!'
An Ceardaí: 'Sagairt is Laidean ina gceann, is a mboilg chomh
teann le puins!'

Achaini na seanmhná:
Achnaím ar Dhia mé a bheith óg arís,
Achnaím ar Chríost mé a bheith deas,
M'fhiacla a bheith dlúth daingean geal,
Agus trí thriúr do bheith im shearc!

Abairt é seo, pé brí atá leis:
'Ní raibh ann ach an gréasaí agus an sagart, ach goideadh an
meanaithe!'

EILEEN SHEEHAN
TRESPASS

I would lead you
by the bone
of your finger

to my bed
at the top
of the house

if now
was our time

but another's flesh
holds you

still a warm wind
flows round me

like the dream
of a life
we once shared

and if time is a wheel
then earth
will not hold us

until then
I am the shell that retains
you are the sound of the sea

PADDY FITZGIBBON
from ESTUARY (1993)

[He stands up, takes the shroud and looks at it and throws it back on the coffin]
I am too old for women.

Spring! I wonder is it spring? In rural Ireland spring is that time of year when the thoughts of young men turn to turbary. I remember a teacher who had a cousin who lived in a place called the Whiteloaf Bog. He bought turf from the cousin, and of course he bought it cheap. When he put it in the fireplace it blazed brightly for five minutes and that was that. We called it Morning Glory.

Oh, I remember summer mornings when the sun and I were up at five and I went to fish in the river. People used to say that the sea trout would not run up the river until the wild irises bloomed. I could never figure out how the trout could see the wild irises from the bottom of the river.

One morning very early I hooked a salmon and after ten minutes or so I had him on the bank. For a while I was thrilled by the memory of the silent line stretched taut darting up and down the river as I played the salmon, and then, I was aware only of the salmon himself stretched out on the grass with the morning sun shining on his wet scales out of a cloudless sky. He was motionless and I remembered nothing, not even the excitement of playing him. I was aware only of the salmon and the rest of the day stretching out in front of me forever, laughing and sparkling like the river itself; but of course, night came around eventually and the river reached the curse-of-God, crab-infested, wind-besotted sea.
[He mounts the trestle once more]

As one of the leading intellectuals of his time, Professor James O'Donnell forcefully condemned the sea on several occasions describing it as 'truculent' and 'repetitive'.

He was of course one of Europe's most prominent thinkers and his advice and counsel were sought, not only by the Vatican and Westminster but, according to usually reliable sources, by the innermost counsels of the Irish Rugby Football Union and the Mullingar Tidy Towns Committee as well. In his early years his adherence to the faith was not as tenacious as it might otherwise have been and he was frequently seen lounging outside the back door of the church at Sunday Mass. There is some evidence to suggest that this was for the purpose of obtaining racing tips and also information about the availability and willingness of young women.

His natural intelligence and curiosity soon overcame such distractions and he then carried out a detailed study of the tiny life forms (both current and extinct) to be seen on the external masonry of the parish church. This led to the publications of his first great book, entitled *Fossils and Lichens for Outdoor Catholics*. After that he never looked back. In the scientific area his best known work was his seven volume study *The Quantum Mechanics of Werner Heisenberg* which is remarkable for its many unusual photographs of pre-war Berlin. Moral philosophy was his first love however and in that arena he is best remembered for his early works *Teach Yourself Temperance in Easy Stages* and *Chastity for Beginners*.

[He descends from the trestle]

Did I make my will? I certainly went to a solicitor – old Solon O'Brien who was as dull as the night and as mean as the moon. He never married for he considered matrimony and women to be frivolous compared to the maintenance of a thrift account. He kept a book in which he calculated each evening how much interest his money would earn between bedtime and getting up in the morning. He said that this helped him to sleep and was much cheaper than Ovaltine. 'How many children have you?' he asked. What a stupid bloody question! How do I know how many children I have? Here I am putting my affairs in order, behaving in a responsible manner and the bastard asks me about children! Noisy, smelly creatures, always wetting themselves and then complaining as if it was somebody else's fault! I am certainly not having anything to do with them. Get out of my way you filthy brutes. Look what they do to women – make them all fat and then hang out of them for the rest of their lives.

Still, it could be worse – women should be thankful that they are not marsupial. I did not have any children. I could not have any children. No children! No children! No children! I had no children. Oh crap-filled Christ, tell me I did not have children. Tell me I was too old, tell me I was too mean, too holy, too impotent, too fat, too ugly, tell me anything, please, please, please.

By the Waters of Babylon we sat
And wept when we remembered Sion.
On the willows of that land we hung our harps.
[He has difficulty remembering]
Happy . . . Happy . . . Happy the man who will seize your little ones . . .
and smash their heads against the rocks.

BRIGHID NÍ MHÓRÁIN
OÍCHE NA DTRÍ RÍTHE

Ar lorg na dtrí ríthe
gabhaim tré Dhuibhneach
geal na gcoinnle
Oíche Nollaig na mBan –
Gleann na nGealt taibhseach,
Abhainn an Scáil lonrach,
an Daingean ciúin
ag fanacht le hiontaisí.
Ach ó Mhám an Lochaigh
síneann ríocht an tsolais
fé choróin bhán Bhréanainn
go Barr na hAille siar.
Fé mar stad an réalt
os cionn an stábla
treoraíonn trí choinneall
ar bhonn fuinneoige mé
mar a bhfuil do dhá láimh sínte
ar nós fáilte an rílinbh.

OWEN MCCROHAN
WATERVILLE IS WONDERFUL

Whoever named the village of Waterville must have used Bolus Head as the christening font!

The ideal time to view the scenic panorama that sweeps westward from Bolus Head at the tip of Ballinskelligs Bay, is when the setting sun lifts Waterville out of the Atlantic in a burning embrace, leaving a sunbeam to kiss every window pane. From this vantage point as light begins to fade, one can absorb the stunning beauty of the place as from nowhere else except the sky. In moments such as these, Waterville becomes a veritable fairyland, a bejewelled Aladdin's Cave that beckons the traveller to partake of the treasures that lie stored within.

This is not the jargon of the tourist brochures because it happens to be the truth. A place so beautiful does not need an infusion of blarney to make it acceptable.

Today Waterville is very different from the place where Mick O'Dwyer grew up as a young boy. The years have brought enormous changes, most of them for the better. A thriving holiday resort with many fine amenities has replaced the quaint old village of 40 years ago. In summertime, the place is choc-a-bloc with visitors from many countries who pass their time fishing or golfing by day, and at night, drinking in the pubs and hotels or dining lavishly in the posh restaurants that abound. Fancy prices in the more extravagant eating places do not frighten off the well-heeled Americans, French or Germans who have money to spend. In the main, these are people who are prepared to pay well to indulge their gourmet tastebuds.

The heart of the tourist business is, of course, the bed-and-breakfast trade and this is where Mick O'Dwyer scores with his two hotels, the Strand and the Villa Marie, each of them with good dining and drinking facilities, a night club and a total of 27 bedrooms, all of them en suite. It is a far cry from the bleak days of 40-odd years ago. The small boy who did not recognise an orange when he saw one for the first time, and who sold tomatoes to buy a football, has done very well indeed.

To succeed in big business from modest beginnings is a phenomenon that is well documented in Irish life. It happens all the time.

The success formula is no secret. Hard work, undoubtedly; shrewd judgment, wise investment, a certain capacity for wheeling and dealing, unending determination and, most assuredly, a large slice of good fortune.

O'Dwyer's elevation from garage mechanic to hotel owner provides the archetypal profile of a self-made man. He started from scratch. There was no money in his family. He had a modest education. None of this hindered his development. In business, he showed the same hunger for success that characterised his sporting life. His ambition to succeed was paramount. In fairness, he did it without stamping on too many corns. True, there are some who will say that he used the GAA to make money but even if that were true, it is a mild enough criticism. Being successful in business is hardly a crime although there is a minority everywhere who, according to O'Dwyer, 'will recognise a "nice poor divil" only when he has landed in the gutter'. The one-time garage proprietor and second-hand car salesman is very far from the gutter.

After leaving Waterville Technical School in 1953, he found a job in Lucey's Garage where he trained as a mechanic. It wasn't exactly what he wanted to do but it did get him into the workforce and earning money. Getting some money together was important even if the job satisfaction was less than adequate. However, he was good with his hands and, in time, he became a good mechanic. He knows the intricacies of the internal combustion engine better than most. His approachable demeanour and obliging nature were compensatory factors for the lack of a corporate image. An unknown motorist would be dug out of trouble without any thought of money. After Waterville had lost the All Ireland seven-a-side championship to Bryansford, County Down in 1972 and spirits were low, O'Dwyer found time to go to the assistance of somebody whose car refused to budge. The motorist, with a Northern Ireland registration, did not recognise him. But workwise, he would like to have followed another tack.

'Given a choice, I would like to have been a professional footballer, playing any kind of football – rugby, Australian Rules, American football, soccer, but preferably, of course, Gaelic football.'

That was just a dream. Austin Lucey offered him a job in his garage and he was very glad to accept it. His wages were £2 per week.

The Lucey brothers, Austin, Paddy, Odie and Frank, were prominent businessmen who operated a thriving fish-exporting business that concentrated exclusively on the sale of lobster and crayfish. The fish were bought at various ports around the country and stored in a special pond in Caherdaniel before being shipped overseas on a regular basis. This entailed numerous haulage assignments and the young garage mechanic was given the opportunity of boosting his wages. A trip to Shannon with a cargo of fish paid £2. Longer journeys paid more. Once, he dropped off a load at Shannon before driving to Belmullet, County Mayo where further supplies were available. Next came a long haul across country to Kilmore Quay, County Wexford. After collecting some more fish, he immediately hit out for Waterville, sharing the driving with Frank Lucey. A long journey of more than 500 miles without sleep in a Ford V8 truck was an endurance test that took 31 hours.

In 1956 some things in the life of Mick O'Dwyer were changing for the better. After three years of serving his apprenticeship in Lucey's Garage, he had managed to save £500. Coincidentally, Austin Lucey offered him a readymade investment opportunity. He wanted to get out of the garage business and was intending selling the place as a going concern. O'Dwyer jumped at the chance of becoming his own boss. He bought the garage for the sum of £1,350, much against his father's wishes. John O'Dwyer was one of the old school who abhorred the idea of borrowing money from the bank. His son shrugged off his pessimism and borrowed £850 from the Munster and Leinster Bank in Cahirciveen. In 1956, a sum of that magnitude was a lot of money. At 20 years of age, it took a mixture of gumption, naivety and optimism to shoulder that kind of responsibility. But the gambling streak was in him. He was prepared to take a chance. And as was so often proved in later life, his instincts did not let him down. The garage prospered.

It took long hours in overalls and a lot of hard work to make it tick. But the new owner was not afraid of getting his hands dirty. He never missed a day at work. Even when he was brought to a Tralee hospital with a broken bone in his hand after a

football match, he considered his options before heading for the
fire escape and driving home. A local doctor put the hand in a
cast of plaster of Paris and the filthy bandages were renewed day
after day. The young mechanic kept on working.

Several years later, he was still entrenched in the garage
business. On 3rd October 1970, Jane Reid wrote in *Reveille*:
'Mick O'Dwyer is not one to be found flat on his back on the
football field. But during the week at his garage business in
Waterville, that is often how you will find him – as I did. He
was sprawled beneath a car, his arms covered to the elbows in
oil, his boiler suit spattered with grease.'

Back in the early days, the struggle for survival was often
difficult. Eventually it all came right. As an up-and-coming
footballer, he could claim a certain degree of popularity. Nobody
ever found him in a bad humour. His lifestyle was impeccable.
He did not drink or smoke and like a true GAA stereotype of
the time, he wore a Pioneer pin on his lapel. He had one further
advantage: he was too young to have made any real enemies.

Inside two years, he had cleared off his debt in the bank and
now it was time to negotiate another upward rung of the ladder.
He bought a second-hand Buick from McCairns of Santry and
took over his father's taxi business. It was the best move he ever
made. The GAA connection helped enormously and soon the
taxi business blossomed. For the first time in his life he started
to make real money.

In the early '60s, a growing affluence was mirrored in an
upswing in car sales, both new and second-hand. Gaining a
toehold in this market became a new target for the budding
entrepreneur. He bought cars, mainly in Dublin, and sold them
at the right price. His name as a footballer attracted business.
People trusted him. Well, most of the time, anyway. As a second-
hand car salesman he had the reputation of being fast off the
mark. He would have sold holy water to the Parish Priest.

In 1965 an old Ford Granada was purchased in Dublin for
£150 and converted into a hearse. Overnight he had a new string
to his bow. The gory details of a trade that would not be
everyone's cup of tea did not bother him. There was money to
be made and, like any good undertaker, O'Dwyer had the ability
to put on a solemn face when the occasion demands that it must
be so.

In a few short years a young man who was never squeamish nor compromising in how he earned his living had demonstrated his faith in the Shakespearean philosophy which suggests that 'there is a tide in the affairs of men which, taken at the flood, leads on to a fortune'. Wherever and whenever an opportunity to make money presented itself, he grabbed it with both hands. Every venture of his seemed fated to have a fairytale ending. He was lucky in business.

He was also lucky in love. Mary Horgan remembers how the young football star with the Latin good looks had no interest in girls, much to their disappointment. This was not substantially accurate. True, for a long time, women did not figure strongly in his scale of priorities. Football was his first love. It absorbed every minute of his spare time. A busy work life with the attendant pressures of being self-employed had allowed very little time for gallivanting.

But football and work notwithstanding, it would have been a dull life without a dash of romance. A man who was tall, dark and handsome, who didn't drink or smoke, who was always pleasant and approachable, would have to be made of stone if he didn't fall victim to the tender trap. Eventually he succumbed to the age-old temptation.

When the Kerry left half-back went a-wooing, he didn't travel very far. As an 18-year old he wore out a few sets of bicycle tyres when he cycled to Murreigh to meet Eileen Sheehan. But the course of true love never runs smoothly. She duly left for England. Three years later he became acquainted with Mary Carmel O'Sullivan when they danced in Fogarty's Hall. This liaison was an attraction of opposites, a relationship that was always heading inexorably towards the altar rails. On 20 February 1962 they were married in Waterville parish church. Sean Murphy, one of the great Kerry footballers of his time, was best man. The bridesmaid was Noreen O'Sullivan, sister of the bride. The nuptials were conducted by Rev Fr John Kennelly, a native of Ballylongford and a brother of Colm who played for Kerry and of Brendan who is a well known man of letters and a professor of English at Trinity College.

Several years later, on the eve of the 1976 All-Ireland final between Kerry and Dublin, Mary Carmel O'Dwyer, now the mother of four children and with a husband who was heavily involved in training the Kerry team, was quoted in the *Kerryman*:

'Football, is it?' she asks. 'Sure, I don't know a thing about football. I hardly ever go to a match. I can't stand the excitement; the tension is too much for me. The last time I was in Croke Park was in 1963. When Kerry were being beaten at half-time I tried to get out but found that I couldn't.

I got highly upset, claustrophobia, I suppose, and I said to myself: if I get out of this place I will never be found here again.'

The honeymoon was interrupted by a husband who wanted to play for Kerry against Cork in the National League. Early in the game he sustained a badly broken nose. The *Kerryman* reported:

'Mick O'Dwyer, who had been selected at right half-back on the Rest of Ireland team to play the Combined Universities on Sunday week, may have to miss the game. His nose was broken in the 4th minute of last Sunday's National League game in Cork and it will be in plaster until March 16th. Mick, who is in the Bon Secours hospital, will play if he gets his doctor's permission but this is unlikely.'

Permission or no, O'Dwyer played with his face encased in a mask of plaster. The team sheet read: J. Culloty (Kerry), J. Lynch (Roscommon), L. Murphy (Down), P. McCormack (Offaly), M. O'Dwyer (Kerry), G. Hughes (Offaly), C. Wrenn (Offaly), D. Foley (Dublin) J. Lennon (Down), A. White (Roscommon), J. McCartan (Down), P. Doherty (Down), S. Brereton (Offaly), J. Timmons (Dublin), B. Morgan (Down).

Ten days after their marriage the newly-weds returned to Waterville to start their married life together. The intervening years have been good to both of them despite a serious illness in April 1981 when Mary Carmel O'Dwyer had to undergo open heart surgery at the Mater Private Hospital in Dublin. Happily, the outcome was successful and the patient made a full recovery.

To all outward manifestations, the O'Dwyer marriage is a happy and fruitful union. They are the parents of four boys, John, Robert, Karl and Michael. Both John and Robbie played briefly for Kerry before serious injuries intervened. Karl plays football for UCC. He and Robbie are twins.

Personality-wise and in terms of temperament, Mick O'Dwyer and his wife are two very different people. On the surface, they appear to have little in common. Mary Carmel has no interest in football and rarely travels abroad except on an occasional pilgrimage to Lourdes. It is reasonable to presume that her husband will never see Lourdes unless a football match is staged there. She is a devout Catholic. Mick, on his own admission, is not a spiritual person and rarely thinks about an afterlife. He is not the kind of man who would seek out a quiet corner of a church to pray.

The head of the O'Dwyer household travels a great deal, loves his football and his golf, but admits to being a 'loner'. At times he certainly acts like one. He has, on occasion, travelled to America and to Australia on his own, deliberately avoiding contact with anyone of his acquaintance – and there are plenty of them in every corner of the world. 'There are times,' he says, 'when I want to be alone'. It is a quirk of character that few could reconcile with an outgoing and gregarious disposition. In the ordinary run of life he has a tremendous capacity for people and he does not come across as somebody who would relish his own company for very long. And yet, for whatever reason, he will make an impulsive decision and like John Wayne or Alan Ladd in the best of the old Western movies, ride off into the sunset. All alone.

The O'Dwyers are a formidable husband-and-wife team. In business they have achieved a great deal. Two beautiful hotels, house property and flashy motor cars are the visible trappings of success. Without being ostentatious, they appear to be comfortably well off. Before Easter 1990, the Villa Marie Hotel was gutted from top to bottom and completely refurbished. Nothing was spared.

Nowadays Mick O'Dwyer lives what appears to be an idyllic lifestyle. He is a free and independent spirit, travels a lot, plays a good game of golf, keeps himself extremely fit, stays up late at night and sleeps well into the day. Sometimes, the newspaper is delivered to his bedside. He comes down to breakfast with the easy grace of a man who knows he has it made. The kitchen staff fuss over him. They call him Micko. 'What way would you like your eggs, Micko?'

Some things do not change. He is still an non-drinker and non-smoker. He doesn't worry – ever. He still wears a tracksuit. He has done 200 sit-ups before leaving the bedroom. Today is a new day and life must be lived to the full. Where it will take him depends on whatever whims may assail his subconscious.

The garage is long since closed down and these days O'Dwyer does not work too hard anymore. But as anyone in Waterville will tell you, he works the head. All the time.

from MICK O'DWYER
THE AUTHORISED BIOGRAPHY (1990)

MÁIRE ÁINE NIC GHEARAILT
RÉITEACH

'Táim greamaithe go beo!' ara mise
Ag brú trucaille romham sa phasáiste
'Nil dul uaidh ach dul leis!
Sí mo chinniúint í ar ndóigh!
Sí, agus mo chinneadh fiche blian ó shin'!
Go bás gan scaradh
Go bás . . . go bás!
Fuarallas.

'Níor dibhríodh mo leithéidse as pharthas riamh!
Tuigim rialacha agus téim dá réir
Táim umhal, umhal –
A Dhia cé'n t-úll?'
. . . Agus feicim iad araon ag spréachadh
I solas na reoiteoige!

Mo mhéar ag at i gcoinne an óir
Ar tí pléascadh!
Clástrafóibe!
Ansin chonac é –
An *'Ring Remover'* i *Supervalu.*

KILLARNEY
EDMUND FALCONER

By Killarney's lakes and fells,
Emerald isles and winding bays,
Mountain paths and woodland dells,
Memory ever fondly strays;
Bounteous nature loves all lands,
Beauty wanders ev'rywhere,
Footprints leaves on many strands
But her home is surely there;
Angels fold their wings and rest
In that Eden of the west,
Beauty's home, Killarney,
Heaven's reflex, Killarney.

Inishfallen's ruined shrine
May suggest a passing sigh;
But man's faith can ne'er decline
Such God's wonders floating by;
Castle Lough and Glena Bay:
Mountains Torc and Nagles' Nest,
Still at Muckross you must pray,
Tho' the monks are now at rest;
Angels wonder not that man
There would fain prolong life's span,
Beauty's home, Killarney,
Heaven's reflex, Killarney.

No place else can charm the eye
With such bright and varied tints;
Every rock that you pass by,
Verdure broiders or besprints;
Virgin there the green grass grows,
Ev'ry morn springs natal day,
Bright-hued berries daff the snows,
Smiling winter's frown away.
Angels often pausing there

Doubt if Eden were more fair,
Beauty's home, Killarney,
Heaven's reflex, Killarney.

Music there for Echo dwells,
Makes each sound a harmony;
Many-voiced the chorus swells
Till it faints in ecstasy;
With the charmful tints below,
Seems the heav'n above to vie:
All rich colours that we known,
Tinge the cloud wreath in the sky.
Wings of angels so might shine,
Glancing back soft light divine,
Beauty's home, Killarney,
Heaven's reflex, Killarney.

from INISHFALLEN (1862)

DONAL HICKEY
THE LIFE AND TIMES OF BEATRICE GROSVENOR

A woman of commanding personality and aristocratic bearing, the late and widely respected Beatrice Grosvenor, CBE, was the last of the Kenmare line in Killarney and, following her death in the summer of 1985, the remainder of what was formerly one of the biggest landed estates in Ireland passed into the hands of the Irish Government.

She was president of Killarney Golf and Fishing Club from 1953 until her death and was also chairperson of the club's board of directors for many years, being the holder of the majority of the ordinary shares. Always keenly interested in the club's affairs, the sale of a parcel of land by her to Bord Failte in 1969 enabled the construction of the second 18 holes to proceed.

Beatrice Elizabeth Katherine Grosvenor was born in London on November 6, 1915, the elder daughter of Lord Edward Grosvenor and Lady Dorothy Browne, daughter of Lord Kenmare. Her father was the second son of the first Duke of Westminster by his second marriage. Educated in some of the leading schools in England, she had a conventional upbringing in Britain before World War Two. She met Lady Mountbatten, who was Superintendent of the St John's Ambulance Brigade at the beginning of the war, and became Assistant Superintendent-in-Chief, also being mentioned in dispatches.

Accompanying Lady Mountbatten to the Far East at the end of the war with Japan, she was one of those responsible for organising the care of released prisoners of war.

In recognition of her services, she was awarded the CBE in 1952 and was Deputy Superintendent-in-Chief of St John's Ambulance Brigade, 1954-58, when she resigned on moving to Killarney. Contrary to popular belief in Killarney, where she was popularly known as 'Lady Grosvenor', she had no title. When the last Lord Kenmare, Gerald Browne (7th Earl of Kenmare), her uncle, died without issue in 1952 the entail which directed that the Estate passed on to the next male heir was broken. The Estate was then passed on to her mother, Lady Dorothy, who immediately handed it over to Beatrice. She inherited 25,000 acres in 1953, but death duties were heavy on the demise of Lord Kenmare and she was compelled to sell off a substantial part of the Estate, including the Lower Lake, Ross Castle and the land which the late John McShain handed over to the Government in more recent years. In all, she retained about 6,000 acres.

Since the Deer Park days, the Kenmares had held the presidency of the golf club and she automatically succeeded her late uncle in the position, which she was happy to accept. Along with her sister, Cecily, Beatrice had been an occasional visitor to Killarney before World War Two, mainly during holidays, but she never envisaged in those days that she would inherit the Estate as her life was centred in London. However, when she permanently settled in Killarney she immersed herself in community activities, soon coming to regard herself as a Killarney person and being accepted as such by the people.

As for golf, she played only a little but that did not take one whit from her commitment to the club and she rarely, if ever, missed a directors' meeting. Before the war, she started playing at North Berwick, where her family used to visit every August. Her stepfather, Sir Evan Charteris, KC, had a scratch handicap and she learnt a good deal about the game from him.

But back to more mundane matters. As time passed, it

became increasingly apparent that the debt-ridden Kenmare Estate was not a viable economic unit. In 1958, much of it was purchased by an American consortium, headed by Californian real estate agent, Stuart Robertson, but the property, which included over 8,000 acres, was bought by US millionaire, building contractor and racehorse-owner, John McShain, a short time later. He sold most of the property to Government in 1974.

In the 1960s Mrs Grosvenor acquired a majority interest in the Castlerosse Hotel, which for many years after provided an insufficient return. Consequently, she sold most of the land close to Killarney to the Irish Government and, shortly before her death, also had to sell the great majority of her shares in the hotel. In 1969, she transferred her complete shareholding in Killarney Golf and Fishing Club Limited, with the exception of ten shares, to Bord Failte. This was part of the agreement whereby Bord Failte purchased portion of the Kenmare Estate from her. Some of the land in question was used for the second course. However, the fact that she had no longer a controlling interest in the club did not diminish her interest in the slightest and the annual presentation of her President's Putter continued to be a red letter occasion.

On her death, her interests were inherited by her nephew, Mr Edward Dawnay, of London, and he sold the balance of the Estate, including the Upper Lake, mostly to the Irish Government. The hotel was acquired by Abbey Travel while her private residence, Kenmare House, and its surrounding 50 acres were purchased by Mr Denis Kelleher, of the Wall Street Clearing Company.

An exceptionally tall, articulate woman of striking presence, the late Mrs Grosvenor was a superb ambassador for the club and for Killarney. Always at ease with people, she had the ability to make visitors feel welcome and at home. A big-hearted lady, she was deeply involved in many voluntary organisations; was known for her discreet charity and was also a member of the Southern Health Board.

Dr Billy O'Sullivan, who knew her very well over a long period, said she was more than a figure head. She regarded herself as a Killarney person and always acted in the best interests of Killarney. She was concerned to see that the area progressed and I remember that she took a very special interest in the new course. She had a great brain and was a marvellous extempore speaker. She could talk to everybody and once she met people she knew them for good and glory.

Former club captain and committee member, Gerry O'Sullivan, said she was a rock of commonsense – a person who always knew how to do the right thing at the right time. She was particularly good at meetings and, after a lot of talk by other people, she could always go straight to the point gladly and to her a spade was a spade.

Speaking clearly with a distinct upper-class British accent, Mrs Grosvenor's air of authority – softened when the occasion demanded by her humanity and sense of humour – often came in useful when disputes arose in the community. Also a devout woman, she could sometimes be seen in quiet prayer in St Mary's Cathedral.

The old song 'How Can I Buy Killarney?' would never again have the same magic after her death, for 'Beauty's Home' had, in fact, been sold. It passed on to the Government and would henceforth be administered by the Office of Public Works on behalf of the Irish people, its official owners. Three world-famous lakes and all the land surrounding them – attractions which had drawn millions of tourists for over two centuries – were firmly in the hands of the State, to be preserved as a natural amenity that could not be valued in terms of money.

The then Minister of State with responsibility for the OPW, Mr Joe Bermingham, announced in January, 1986 that the Upper Lake, the Long Range and 4,200 acres of land had been purchased for an undisclosed sum from Mr Dawnay.

It was Mrs Grosvenor's wish that the State should have the first option on the property if her successors did not want it for themselves. The property then became part of Killarney's 25,000-acre National Park, also including the old Bourne Vincent Memorial Park (presented to the State in 1932), the Knockreer Estate, Ross Island, Innisfallen, Glena and the Lakes. Mrs Grosvenor's property, on the southern side of the Park, incorporated much of the area grazed by the only native red deer herd remaining in the country as well as woodlands of high ecological value.

The passing of this remarkable woman in her 70th year was sincerely mourned by the people of her beloved Killarney who recognised her unswerving commitment to the place of her adoption. It was also an historic occasion, for the final trumpet had sounded for the Kenmares. She was laid to rest in the Kenmare family vault in the Cathedral.

Pádraig Mac Fhearghusa
Allagar

'Scaoiltear an saighead!' a d'fhógair an toil,
'Cá treo?' – an breithiúnas a d'fhiarthaigh.
'Fóill, fóill,' a d'éiligh an intleacht,
'Ní féidir go ngluaisfeadh?'
'Éalóm ar a mhuin,' a d'impigh an croí.

Súil agus gualainn a dhein an beart,
Cá luíonn an dairt tar éis an allagair?

Maureen Beasley
Meeting with the Devil

One of the most mysterious, overpowering, frightening experiences I ever had was the night I met the devil, in a place called Killorglin, which holds an annual festival called Puck Fair. After travelling fifty miles through a misty midsummer's evening, I went to see an old friend, who had spent a long term in hospital with me. As I entered her premises I was asked to sit in the room while my friend was busy entertaining her customers. I sat in the chair. The room was big and spacious and beautifully decorated. The drapes were trimmed with Limerick lace and the rest coloured with silvery blue. The floor carpet was a delicate shade of oatmeal.

Suddenly, the door opened and this tall, dark and handsome man entered. He sat down right alongside me in a chair. I just looked at him and no words were spoken. Suddenly there was a knock on the door and Kate, my friend, walked in. *'Céad mile fáilte,' arsa Cáit. 'Go raibh maith agat,' arsa mise.*

I looked at the chair and the man had vanished. I said to Kate, 'Who was that man sitting alongside me?' She said to me,

'I can't see any man.' We sat and talked for a long while and had tea. Then Kate said, 'I will fetch for you the pictures we took when we were in hospital.' Suddenly, the man was sitting alongside me again and he said, 'Come dancing with me to the hotel. All your friends are there.' I hadn't a leg to stand on, never mind dance. And now mind you, I wasn't drunk, at that stage anyhow. I called aloud, 'Come in here quickly, Kate.' She laughed and said, 'Are you all right?' 'Who in the name of God is that man sitting next to me?' I said. She said, 'There is no one there. You're only imagining it.' She then left the room. I turned towards him and said, 'For Jesus' sake, will you go to hell.' His face turned black and his ears, which were as big as saucers, stood up. My friends returned and I told them of my exploits with the devil, but they didn't believe me. 'Yerra, Maureen,' they said, 'you must have been pissed drunk: what in the name of hell would the devil be doing in Killorglin?' 'I'll have a cause to drink after my terrifying night with the devil.' I asked my friends would they help me look for the hotel, the one that the devil told me about, but there was no such hotel. I walked the streets to see if I could see anyone that would fit his description, but he was nowhere to be seen. I can still remember his face, his jet-black suit, shoes with long toes like a leprechaun's and how his good looks changed to those of a horrible animal. His eyebrows stood out like a fox's bushy tail. I wasn't sick, nor pissed drunk, nor hallucinating. I believe myself, to this very hour, that it was the devil himself.

DEIRDRE SHANAHAN
LOGICS

All morning driving around the villages of north Kerry in the rain
fields are being cut up for new houses
and my father talls his interminable tales
of how he went to dances,
cycled this lane or that
and knew a girl at the corner
before she left for Chicago in 1949.

At the pub
where we called several years ago
the owner has passed on
and his niece has taken over.
The whole place has been panelled and smartened
so that I hardly recognise it.

On the way back
I hear about his aunt again
who lived opposite,
how he visited neighbours, criss-crossing roads on his bike
to his grandparents
and theirs before them who eloped
jumping the River Feale on a horse.

Remembering his memories
he replants his youth
with Mickey Bunce, Mickey Joe,
the Bawneens and the girl at the post office
who never married.

Searching out old friends
he visits places which do not exist,
an exiled heart's pilgrimage,
Ossian after the Fianna,
but when I drive these roads in future
there will be his voice
following the logic of hedges and marriages,
their broken stones, their collapsing branches.

MAIDHC DAINÍN Ó SÉ
as A THIG NÁ TIT ORM (1987)

Do shroicheamair Birmingham, Alabama, siar go maith sa tráthnóna dár gcionn. Cuma bhocht go maith ar an ndúthaigh ó d'fhágamair Memphis go sroicheamair Birmingham. 'Deirtear go bhfuil daoine sa stát seo ná feaca raidió ná telefís riamh,' arsa mise. 'Tá mhuis,' arsa Frank, 'agus daoine san áit seo, ná feaca mias uisce riamh.' Bhí an ceart aige mar bhí sé de chuma ar chuid des na daoine nár níodar a n-aghaidheanna ón lá a rugadh iad. Dá bhfeicfeá na sean-ghluaisteáin a bhí ag cuid acu agus d'fhéachaidís go hamhrasach ar aon stróinséir a ghabhadh thar bráid. Ón nóimint a shroicheamair an áit tháinig saghas casadh aigne orm. 'Ní dóigh liom gur mhaith liom an oíche a chaitheamh ar an mbaile seo anocht. Tá seoladh agam anseo a fuaireas ó James Crofton, hillbilly atá ag obair i mo theannta,' arsa mise. Bhí cheithre fichid míle romhainn ach rud amháin ná raibh a fhios againn, gur cúlbhóthar ar fad a bhí san aistear. I bhfad níos measa ná aon bhóthar anseo in Éirinn. Ní raibh aon chomharthaí bóthair le feiscint. Cheapamair fiche babhta go rabhamair imithe amú. Chuireamair ceist ar fho-dhuine a bhuail linn ach ba dheacair freagra a fháil astu. D'fhéachaidís go hamhrasach orainn agus chuiridís cúpla ceist iad féin sula dtabharfaidís aon chúntas. Tar éis bheith ag taisteal tamall fada thánamair ar shráidbhaile beag go raibh cuma na scríbe uirthi. Tig tabhairne amháin ann agus siopa beag grósaera. Bheartaíomair buidéal beorach a bheith againn chun ar scórnaigh a fhliuchadh tar éis an aistir. Chaithfimis eolas na slí a fháil chomh maith dá mba mhaith linn dul go dtí muintir Crafton. Nír raibh aon Chríostaí istigh sa tig tabhairne ach an bheirt againn féinn agus fear an tí. D'fhéach Frank ar chrot na háite agus d'fhéach sé ormsa. Loirg sé dhá bhuidéal beorach. Bhí an bheoir chomh bog leis an aimsir amuigh. Chuireamair comhrá an fhear an tí agus d'inseamair ár scéal. Thug sé eolas na slí dúinn mar bhí aithne mhaith aige ar mhuintir mo pháirtí i Sears Roebuck. Ní fada a thóg sé uainn an áit a shroichint mar ná raibh ann ach an t-aon bhóithrín amháin agus an t-aon tig amháin. Tig adhmaid ná raibh cóir ná slacht air. Seana-*jeep* os comhair an tí amach agus é de chuma uirthi ná déanfadh blúire péinte aon díobháil di. Chnag Frank ar an ndoras ach ní raibh aon fhreagra ag teacht chuige. Cheapas féin go bhfeaca duine éigin laistigh den bhfuinneoig agus sin ag tarraingt isteach. Chnag sé arís níos bríomhaire an turas seo. D'oscail an doras leath-throig. Tháinig barraille gunna amach tríd agus buaileadh suas le srón Frank é. 'Ó Mhuire, maith dhom mo pheacaí,' arsa Frank agus dath an bháis ag teacht air. 'Ní fheadair éinne cá bhfuil fód a bháis agus nára lige Dia gur anseo é, mar ná geobhadh ár muintir tásc ná tuairisc orainn go brách.' Tháinig seanduine amach agus an

gunna dírithe ar Frank fós aige. *'Are you revenuers?'* Thosnaíos
féin ag caint leis ansin. Chuireas in íul do go tapaidh go rabhas
ag obair in éineacht le 'Little Jim' i Chicago. Nuair a chuala sé
é sin chuir sé uaidh an gunna agus d'oscail sé an doras. Mhínigh
sé dúinn cad ina thaobh gur chaitheadar bheith chomh haireach.
B'iad na *'reveneurs'* ná lucht an dlí a bhiodh ina ndiaidh i gcónaí
toisc a bheith ag déanamh *hooch* go meamh-dhleathach. Tine
oscailte a bhí sa tig agus bean an tí ag cócaireacht uirthi. Bhí
cailín óg dathúil ag cabhrú léi. Tar éis fáilte a chur romhainn
cuireadh in ár suí ag an mbord sinn. Chuir fear a' tí dhá mhuga
os ár gcomhair. Thóg sé próca mór cré anuas de bharr an
churpaird agus scaoil sé steall breá galánta isteach sa dá mhuga
as an bpróca. 'Sé seo an braon is fearr a deintear sa cheantar seo,'
arsa an seanduine. 'Ó, dála an scéil, dúirt "Little Jim" galún den
stuif a thabhairt go Chicago chuige,' arsa mise. 'Ar m'anam nár
chaill sé a dhúil ann le cheithre bliana,' arsa an sean-bhuachaill.
Bhaineas slogóg as an muga. Ní túisce a dheineas ná gur
chaitheas amach as mo bhéal arís é, leis an loscadh a fuaireas
uaibh. Ach d'imigh braon beag de síos mo scornach agus chuaigh
le mo anáil. Bhraitheas an stuif ag rith síos trím chorp go barr
lúidíní mo chos ag loscadh a shlí roimhe. Bhain Frank slogóg
as a mhuga féin agus má dhein d'aithníos air go raibh sé ag cur
dhathanna dhó féin. 'Sé an chéad slog is measa,' arsa an seanduine.
'Ní bhraithfir ag dul síos an chuid eile den dtráthnóna é.'

Tháinig fear óg isteach an cúldoras. Strapaire ard lom. 'Sé
seo mo mhac Ralph. Níl aon *revenuer* i Stát Alabama ná
rithfeadh míle uaidh.' Bhainfeadh sé an tsúil as phréachán trí
chéad slat ó bhaile agus an préachán sin ag eitilt tríd an aer.'
Chraitheamair láimh leis. Bheannaigh sé dúinn go tur. Fuaireamair amach gur Joshua ab ainm don athair agus Lena ab ainm
don gcailín óg. Ní fhéadfainn féin ná Frank ár súile ag cur na
súl trínn chomh maith. Ag féachaint timpeall an tí bheadh a
fhios ag duine ná raibh puinn teaspaigh orthu, ach ar a shon sin
bhí sé deas glan. 'Fanfaidh sibh anseo anocht. Tá seomra folamh
againn,' arsa Joshua. Dúrt féin leis go mb'fhearr linn bheith ag
druideam tamall ó thuaidh. Scaoil sé braon eile den stuif
chruaidh chugainn agus an babhta seo scaoil sé braon chuige féin
agus go dtí a mhac. 'Dhera, cá bhfuil ár ndeabhadh ó thuaidh,'
arsa Frank ag baint slog eile as an sáspan agus san am chéanna
ag caitheamh súil ar an gcailín óg. 'Cuir do dhá shúil ar ais i do

cheann a bhuachaill mhaith,' arsa mise i gcogar, 'nó an bhfuil dearmad déanta agat ar an ngunna a bhí faoi do shróin deich nóimintí ó shin. Má thugann tú gean di sin sé'n nós atá sa pháirt seo den ndúthaigh an gunna a dhíriú ar chúl do chinn agus tú féin agus í fén a mháirséail go dtí an altóir.' Dúradh leis na mná greim bídh a ullmhú dúinn. Bean an-chiúin ab ea an mháthair nár bhog a béal ó thánamair isteach sa tig. A chuma uirthi go raibh sí gafa trí chruatan an tsaoil. Bhí an braon ag dul síos níos fearr anois agus faoi mar a dúirt an seanduine ní raibh mórán loscadh orainn tar éis an chéadbhraon a bheith ólta. Chríochnaíos féin an dara braon agus mhothaíos breá súgach ina dhiaidh. Ní fada gur cuireadh an bia os ár gcomhair. Corcán dubh i lár an bhoird agus istigh ann bhí meascán éigin ná feaca-sa riamh roimhe sin. Ar crochadh síos le cliathán an chorcáin bhí spúnóg mhór a húsáidtí chun an pláta a líonadh. Ní fada gur líon an seanduine a phláta féin. 'Seo libh a bhuachaillí, taosc chugaibh,' arsa seisean, ag tabhairt na spúnóige do Frank. Chuir Frank taoscán maith ar a phláta agus dheineasa amhlaidh ansin. Chonac císte mór aráin ar an mbord. Bheir an seanduine ar seo agus bhain sé canta mór anuas de lena dhá láimh. Níor úsáid an mac an spúnóg in aon chor ach bheir sé ar an gcorcán agus d'iompaigh ar a chliathán é agus lig a chuid bídh amach ar an bpláta. D'itheamair lán ár mboilg agus dhiúgamair an braon cruaidh a bhí sa mhuga. 'B'é sin an béile ba bhlasta dar itheas riamh,' arsa Frank agus é ag cuimilt a bhoilg. Ghabhamair buíochas leis na mná a d'ullmhaigh an béile dúinn. Níor stad Frank ach an cur na súl trín gcailín óg. Tógadh anuas an próca cré arís. 'Sea a bhuachaillí, bíodh braon eile againn agus glanfaidh sé síos na scórnaigh,' arsa Joshua ag ligean streancán amach go dtí gach éinne againn ach amháin na mná. Ar m'anam ach nár eitíomair é an turas seo mar d'fhéadfá a rá go raibh dúil ag teacht againn ann. Thugamair tamall ag caint agus ag cadráil agus faoi dheireadh d'éirigh an seanduine. 'Tair linne . . . raghaimíd chun na tabhairne. Tabharfaimíd an sean-leoraí linn mar tá barraille "white mule" á tabhairt agam ann.' Mhol Frank dom an bosca ceoil a thabhairt liom. 'An bhfuil uirlis ceoil libh?' arsa Ralph, nár bhog a bhéal ó dúirt sé "*howdy*" linn nuair a tháinig sé isteach ar dtúis.

Cuireadh mé féin agus Frank in ár suí i dtosach an sean-thrucail agus an seanduine agus an cailín laistiar agus barraille den *hooch* eatarthu istigh i mbosca mór adhmaid.

Sé an mac a bhí ag tiomáint dá bhféadfá tiomáint a thabhairt air. Bhí grean agus smúit á rúideadh uaithi siar ag an sean-leoraí agus an bhróig curtha síos go dtí an urlár ag an bhfear óg. Ar a shon is go raibh droch-staid ar an mbóthar ní thóg sé ró-fhada uainn an baile beag a bhí cheithre mhíle ó bhaile a bhaint amach. 'Ní hé seo an treo a thánamair isteach,' arsa Frank agus é ag caitheamh a shúl timpeall an tseanbhaile go raibh cuma na scríbe air. Foirgnimh adhmaid is mó a bhí ann agus é de chuma ar na tithe gur fada an lá gur cuimlíodh aon scuab péinte dhóibh agus bhí fo-thig anseo agus ansiúd go raibh clár adhmaid nó dhó in easnamh iontu. Tharraing mo dhuine suas an trucail lasmuigh de shean-bhathallach mór tí adhmaid. Is minic a chífeá a leithéid de thabhairne sna sean-scannáin. 'An diabhal,' arsa Frank agus é de chuma air féin go raibh an *hooch* ag oibriú air, 'ba dhóigh leat gur cheart duit Wyatt Earp a fheiscint ag siúl tríd an ndoras, agus Doc Holliday ag siúl ina dhiaidh agus dhá ghunna ag sileadh le gach duine acu.' Scaoileamair na Croftons isteach romhainn agus tar éis iad a leanúint isteach thosnaíos ag tabhairt faoi ndeara i mo thimpeall. In aice na contúrach bhí cúigear nó seisear seandaoine suite, duine nó beirt acu ag cogaint thobac agus an súlach ag imeacht síos cliathán a mbéil. Boladh láidir stálaithe beorach agus deataigh san áit agus é de chuma ar an urlár nár scuabadh ar feadh seachtaine é. D'fhiafraigh Frank dúinn cad a bheadh le n-ól againn agus bhuail sé nóta fiche dollaer anuas ar an gcúntar. Dá bhfeicfeá an fhéachaint a bhí ag na seandaoine ar an nóta. Ní mór ná gur shloig duine acu an blúire tobac a bhí sé ag cogaint leis an anbhá a tháinig air. Chuireas cogar i gcluais Frank ag rá leis gur cheart dó seasamh dos na seandaoine chomh maith. Níor ghá dhom é a rá an dara uair leis. D'ólamair cúpla deoch i bhfochair a chéile agus bhíos féin agus Frank bogaithe go maith tar éis an *hooch* a d'ólamair sa tig agus na deocha a bhí á n-ól anseo againn. Bhíomair ag ól agus ag cadráil linn go dti déanach go maith san oíche. Tharraing seanduine a raibh hata pollta air veidhlín chuige agus is é siúd a bhain rannsach aisti. Ansin a thosnaigh an spórt agus an scléip ar fad. Ba bhreá go deo an ceol é. *'Blue Grass'* a tugtar ar a leithéid de cheol. Fuair an fear a bhí ag freastal trumpa béil agus luig sé isteach ag seinm cheoil le fear an veidhlín. 'Sea anois,' arsa Frank a raibh dhá shúil dhearga go maith aige faoin dtráth seo agus é suite síos le hais leis an gcailín óg de mhuintir Crofton, 'sin ceol de dhealramh agus ní hé an sean-dhiabhal cleatráil a bhíonn tusa ag déanamh le do bhosca, a Mhichíl Uí Shé.' Ba bhreá magúil an gháire a bhí ar a phus. 'Sín chugam an *jug*,' arsa an seanduine a bhí in ár gcomhluadar. B'fhéidir go bhfeacaís na háraistí cré go dtagadh an fuiscí iontu fadó. Bheir sé ar cheann acu sin agus thosnaigh sé ag séideadh isteach sa pholl a bhí ina bharr agus bhain sé glór éigin ceoil as. Is gearr go bhfeaca Frank ag cur a láimh suas go dtí a shúil agus é ag piocadh uirthi amhail is dá mbeadh cuil nó rud éigin mar sin dulta fúithi. 'Cad tá ort?' arsa mise. 'Priosla tobac a tháinig ón bhfear atá ag seinm leis an bpróca a chuaigh isteach i mo shúil agus deirim leat go bhfuil céasadh ag baint leis an bpriosla céanna,' arsa Frank. Tháinig roinnt daoine eile isteach i rith an tráthnóna agus thugamar faoi ndeara orthu ná rabhadar ag meascadh linne in aon chor. D'fhiafraíos do Ralph cad ina thaobh ná rabhadar ag teacht insteach sa chomhluadar. Dúirt sé gur *Hillbillies* ab ea iad féin agus gur River Rats ab ea an dream eile a tháinig isteach. Cheistíos é mar gheall ar na River Rats seo. De réir chosúlachta thánadar ó bhruach abhainn an Mississippi nuair a bhí an cogadh cathartha ar siúl idir Thuaidh agus Theas. Thugadar cabhair agus cunamh don arm thuaidh agus scéidear ar arm Lee. Nuair a bhí an méid sin ráite ag Ralph chaith sé seile amach as a bhéal a chrochfadh páipéar ar fhalla dhuit. Bhraitheas go raibh mearbhall ag teacht i mo cheann faoi dheireadh na hoíche agus maidir le Frank ní raibh sé pioc níos fearr ná balbhán ach bhí an diabhal fós ag iarraidh an cailín óg a ardach leis. Tháinig tinneas uisce orm féin rud nárbh ionadh tar éis an méid dí a bhí caite siar gan trácht ar an *hooch* in aon chor. D'fhiafraíos dhóibh cá raibh tig an asail agus stiúraíodh amach an cúldoras mé laistiar den dtig. Bhí a fhios agam cad a bhíos ag déanamh cé go raibh na cosa guagach go maith faoin dtráth sin. Ní mór an leithreas a bhí amuigh ach falla fada bán agus é tarrálta ina bhun. Fuaireas mo dhóthain cúraim ag iarraidh mo chnaipí a oscailt ach ar deireadh bhíos ábalta an gnó a dhéanamh agus láithreach tháinig sruthán breá sláintiúil is d'imigh leis le fánaigh. Á, do bhraitheas an faoiseamh cheana féin. Dar liom nuair a bhí sé san am agam bheith ag dul i ndísc is ag éirí ar an sruthán a bhí. Má bhíos nóimint ansin agus an sruthán ag imeacht le fánaidh bhíos fiche nóimint ann. 'A Mhuire,' arsa mise liom féin, 'n'fheadar arb é an diabhal *hooch* sin a dhóigh *washer* éigin istigh ionam agus ná fuil ar mo chumas stad.' Chuala glór. 'A Mhichíl Uí Shé, an bhfuil tú titithe i bpoll éigin? Tán tú imithe le leathuair a chloig.' Ba é Frank a bhí ar mo lorg. 'Táim ceart go leor; tá poll dóite díreach síos trím ag an ndiabhal stuif a bhíomair ag ól.' Shíulaigh sé anall chugam. 'Léan ort, a stail amadáin, cas amach an tap uisce atá ag sileadh laistigh duit,' arsa Frank agus é sna trithi. 'Bhuel céad buíochas le Dia . . . cheapas go silfinn a raibh i mo chorp!'

Ní cuimhin liom mórán eile mar gheall ar an oíche. D'fhágamair slán le Muintir Crofton an mhaidin dar gcionn agus mo cheann ag scoltadh le tinneas cinn. Thugamair ár n-aghaidh ar ais ar Chicago.

GEORGE FITZMAURICE
THE MAGIC GLASSES (1913)

The scene takes place in Padden Shanahan's kitchen. Maineen, his wife, comes down from her room. Padden comes in. Maineen places glasses and a bottle on the table.

Maineen   See now, Padden, all is in readiness for Mr Quille, let him come what hour 'twill match him. And, oh hierna! the heart is rising in me at the thought of his putting Jaymony off that habit of going up in the top loft, our fine sons, Roger and Frynk, lighting with shame on account of it, and saying they'll come home to us no more on their holydays if their brother don't get shut of his canter.

Padden   Still, 'tis meself is thinking 'tis a reckless thing to be hysing this Mr Quille on a false pretence that Jaymony has his breast bone down. 'Tis unknown what the stranger will do when he'll know the truth, he an almighty passionate man, they do be saying, that don't like to be deceived.

Maineen   What croaking have you now, and as rejoiced as you were to coax the great man here? 'Tisn't a face we'd have surely to send for a stranger twenty miles away with a high-diddle story of a lad going up in a top loft – 'twould take pains to make Mr Quille believe the like of that.

Padden   Faith, from what I'm after hearing 'twill take pains to please him, whatever way you take him. And 'tisn't alone having the punch steaming on the table for him almost he's over the threshold will do; for Mary Sofine says the half-sovereign must be slipped to him half unbeknownst, the pride is that big in him. To put all words into one, Maineen, the notions and capers of the devil is in this Mr Quille.

Maineen   'Tis the same with all them geniuses, Padden every mother's son of them nothing but notions and capers since the world began itself.

Padden   But, maybe, he isn't the big genius we thought him after all. Sure, some say 'twas the great fame he got the first day from curing the breast bone down made people go running to him with this and that in the line of diseases, and, the pride and gumption rising in him, he couldn't renayge himself attempting all before him – things he was as dull of as the biggest fool walking the road.

Maineen   Glory! Listen to that, and yourself his biggest praiser – drawing down but a few nights ago itself how he cured Mary Canty of the dropsies and the swellings with his dilution of the white heather that does be growing in the bogs; likewise how he set a charm for Looney Carroll put him from going around every tree he'd meet, the fool thinking there was money under it; and making tapes you were itself of the marvel he did entirely with a blue lozenge that made Josie Patt keep his big tongue back in his mouth, and it ever and always going out that length in spite of him with every third syllable he'd speak.

Padden   Maybe I got another account puts a different colour on some of his miracles. Morisheen Quirke wouldn't give in that dilution would cure a boil, and, he told me in private, 'twas no dropsies or swellings Mary Canty had at all, but a bully ball of wind in her stomach, that came up in a hurry, believe you me, at the fright Mr Quille gave her, he to coagle her into a corner, gave her a thump in the middle, and stuck out his tongue at her in the dark.

Maineen   Morisheen is a prime boy.

Padden   If he is itself, 'tisn't Morisheen but another man was eyewitness to the way he managed Looney Carroll, chasing him through a wood in the dead hour of the night till the fool ran up again a tree unbeknownst, was flung back on his back, the blood of a pig spouting out of his nostrils, and, signs by, the fool won't go around a tree since, and it stuck in him that every tree has got a divil. A queerer thing itself he did on Josie Patt. Hit him on the head with a mallet, I hear, when the big tongue was out and the teeth coming together – the Lord save us, half the big tongue fell down on the ground!

Maineen   A likely story! And Josie's people blowing about Mr Quille all over the world, nothing in their mouths but that blue lozenge, talking of it from dusk till dawn at every hour of the day.

Padden   Because they believed Mr Quille, and Josie can't tell whether or which, and nothing but gibberish coming from him since. Sure, they went to Mr Quille about the way he was pronouncing, and what did my boy say but that it was French he was talking – that they all speak French for a while after being cured – and he'd come into the English again in the course of forty weeks. And, when this Mr Quille comes along, I'm thinking it's wise people we'd be if we put the bed and dresser to the door and keep the divil out.

Maineen   Indeed, Padden, we'll do no such thing, and I'm thinking it's something must be rising in your brain to believe the fables going lately about Mr Quille. Isn't it myself heard fables and didn't give ear to them, and isn't it yourself heard fables and didn't give ear to them, and what's come over you all in a hop?

Padden   He's a rogue, Maineen, and a divil of a variegated rogue itself! And with respect to his great speciality entirely of curing the breast bone down – God help

	you! – a man from his own quarter told me, 'You have a better hand at it,' said he, 'up to your own door – a man there's no talk of at all, Michaeleen James O'Toole.'
Maineen	Oh, my shame, Padden, to dare compare Mr Quille with Michaeleen James. Padden, you'll make me say it, but 'tis a bad sign on you entirely to be losing your respect for the great. 'Twould be better you'd lose the brain itself than lose your respect. But it's shivering you are, shaky and shivery all over you are, Padden Shanahan.
Padden	Why wouldn't I be shivering, the ground a cake of frost, and the bitter breeze blowing from the north would perish the Danes or skin a flea itself.
Maineen	Shivering and shaking, and there's a skyon in your eye, Padden Shanahan, glory be to God! 'Tisn't anything, anything airy or fearsome you seen and you are at the fort?
Padden	[hesitatingly] I seen a man, then, a strange man, and he rising like a cloud over the gap in Peg Caxty's bounds ditch.
Maineen	Sure, maybe 'tis Mr Quille himself you seen?
Padden	Well, there's no good in denying it, 'twas the very customer. I couldn't mistake him by the descriptions I got of him – a long black coat on him, and a hat like a parson. Believe you me, 'tisn't long I was putting the legs under me and skelping home by the hedges, for it's a huge man he is, glory be to God! Taking up a big streak of the land itself he was, and he coming and walking through Aeneas Canty's square field. Holy Father, Maineen, he's the biggest and the blackest man I ever seen!
Maineen	[soothingly] What harm, Padden. Like a good man, now, don't let his size be frightening you. Sure, for all we know, though being big he might be as soft in himself as a fool. And, Padden, think of our gintlemen. Be brave in yourself for the sake of having Jaymony cured before our fine respectable sons. Be thinking of Robin, the acting-sergeant, and 'twill put great heart in you to face Mr Quille.

Padden   I'll be thinking of Robin, then, the rosy shine on his face, the clean shoe of his foot, and he sitting down to his bread, butter, tea, and two eggs. A great man for law and order is Robin. Let me be thinking of Robin, Maineen.

Maineen   And Frynk in the London peelers, a bigger man still. Be thinking of Frynk and the night at Mrs Quinlan's wake, and the way he made an ape of Poet O'Rourke in the argument about Dublin and London.

Padden   I will, and how the poet turned as black as the hob, and hadn't a word out of him for the rest of the night when Frynk turned on him in the heel and said, 'You ain't got no 'Yde Park; you ain't got no Rotten Row.'

Maineen   And the chicken, Padden. You mind he didn't know what to make of the chicken and she walking across the floor?

Padden   Frynk lying back in his chair, and he breaking his heart laughing, 'There she goes agin,' said Frynk, said he; 'there she goes agin.'

Maineen   'Tisn't 'agin,' Padden, but 'agyne'. 'There she goes agyne,' said Frynk, and the lovely way he has of talking.

Padden   [rising, pointing out door] Oh, Mineen, look at Mr Quille, look at him now, and he marching down our triangle. Holy Father, you'd think the wide world wasn't in it but himself, he brooding and his head under him!

Maineen   'Tis the proper way for him to come marching, Padden, and all he ever seen retained in his great brain. 'Tis no faith I'd have in him at all if he was going in a little boat peeping about him like a codger. Oh, glory! It must be a wonderful great man he is, surely, and almighty marvels running in his mind.

Padden   [handing her money] Here! Shove the half-sovereign to him yourself whatever, as you can do it nicely, having the slippery fingers of a female. I'll go up in the room for a while, as 'tis an awkward man I am, and shy in myself before strangers. You to be introducing yourself to him, Maineen, and I'll come down after a bit.

Maineen [running after him and catching him] For the love of
God, Padden, stay and welcome Mr Quille! The fine
respectable man, what would he think of the boss of
the house chambering on a fine day? Sit down in the
chair now, for yourself; rise up in your dignity when
he comes in, and bow your respects to him with a fine
smile on your face.

Padden [looking out window] He has lepped off the stile. He
is coming up the bawn. A swarthy devil! Holy Father,
the cut of him and he blowing out of his two yellow
cheeks! Let me go, will you! [they struggle]

Maineen Padden!

Padden Maineen!

[Quille comes in; he stands with his back to dresser
facing Padden and Maineen; he utters a long loud
sound through his nose]

Quille [in a deep mournful voice] Twenty miles of a tramp to
cure a boy with a breast bone down! Twenty miles, and
starting with the streak of dawn! [harshly] Yet there's
devils would say the fame of Morgan Quille would never
pass the bounds of Beenahorna – doctors, priests, and
jealous devils would say Morgan Quille was a quack –
a quack, Padden Shanahan, if it's to you I'm speaking!

Padden It is, sir; welcome here, sir. [aside] Speak, Maineen!

Quille But look at me flourishing like a heap of dock leaves
you'd vainly strive to smother by covering up with
stones, for no man can wither the root or blast the
fame of Morgan Quille of Beenahorna. [blows nose]

Padden [aside] Maineen, the punch!

Quille Twenty miles to cure a boy with the breast bone down!
I would, then, and a hundred miles itself flaking over
a side of a country to come at the stiffest case of that
disease! Where's the patient?

Padden The thing is up in the top loft, sir. Speak, Maineen!
In the name of God explain to his honour about the
top loft!

Quille Is it giggling and sniggering ye are? Giggling and
sniggering at Morgan Quille!

Padden Oh, God forbid, sir! Maineen! – alluding to the top
loft, sir . . .

Quille   [taking a step forward] To the devil with yourself and
         your top loft! Ha! Maybe it's a doubt ye have on the
         powers of Morgan Quille? Some one has belied me
         about the case of Michaeleen O'Rourke.

Padden   That I may be dead and damned if I ever heard a
         syllable!

Quille   You lie, you sheefra! But did Michaeleen obey my
         instruction and come to me the nine mornings fasting
         to be cupped? Didn't the villain do for a twopenny loaf
         on the ninth morning unbeknownst, that made the
         breast bone fail to rise and I having the tumbler full of
         the flesh of his bosom, you brat? The blackguards and
         liars didn't tell you that maybe, the blackguards and liars
         that Christ Almighty will wither off the face of the earth
         as Christ Almighty has withered more than slandered my
         name!

[faces Padden, who hides behind Maineen]

Maineen   Mr Quille – God forgive me! – 'tis no breast bone
         down that's wrong with Jaymony; but 'tis well known
         to us there is no complaint you can't cure through
         means of that inspiration you get when you let yourself
         into the falling sickness. [gives him punch] We know
         'tis only for special people you does it. [giving him
         money] But having the big heart, you might have
         mercy on us and the way we are, Mr Quille.

Quille   Your faith opens my heart, and what can be done will
         be done, Mrs Shanahan.

Padden   [coming forward confidentially] And maybe 'tis more
         merciful you'd be to us still when we tell you it's as
         humble in ourselves we are now in our riches and four
         cows as when we hadn't a cow or a calf; and we does good
         turns for neighbours without looking to be paid back –
         'tisn't like the born farmers that would have to get a
         return if it went to the fourth generation itself.

Quille   [sharply] What are you saying? Isn't all the world born
         farmers in the way you allude, and God help you, if
         you haven't a few tricks of your own!

Padden   [meaning to please] 'Tis you must have some fine
         tricks surely, Mr Quille.

Quille   You snake! [catching him and flinging him across floor] Is it me have tricks? Is it me? Me to stoop to the dirty ways of the things that do be daubing each other in the puddles and the gutters and the sewers of the world? Me that can sweep them clean in the battlefield of the intellect, making them run like rats fleeping into their dirty holes, or cockroaches racing for their dirty lives before the glint of dawn! [music in top loft; he starts] Heavenly Father! What queer music is that upstairs?

Maineen   It's Jaymony, Mr Quille; and that's what we want him cured of, and his fancy for going up in that top loft and making that noise in it.

Quille   [taken aback] Why, that's a fancy complaint entirely. [going and sitting at fire] Hum! But we'll see. [speaking in a professional way] Come here now, and give me the exact rudiments of his case. How long has he recourse to that top loft?

Maineen   God knows, sir, our little boy is going up in that top loft most every day since he was in the fifth book.

Padden   He kept out of it for a while, Maineen, the time he was in his bloom.

Maineen   What signify was that? God knows, sir, counting every absence, he didn't keep clear of it for a twelvemonth.

Quille   His age?

Maineen   What age is on the boy, Padden? He was born whatever the year the bog ran at Cloranmadkeen; the same year that Rourke's son of Meenscubawn knocked the eye out of Timothy Mascal at the election between Hassett and Dayse in the town of Listowel.

Padden   The year the tinkers had the battle with the Moynsha people on the bridge of Lyre.

Quille   [pondering and counting on his fingers] That makes him thirty-eight – a long and a chronic case, faith. Well, what does he be playing in that top loft?

Maineen   I'm dull of it, Mr Quille, for I'm too wide in the girth to get into it, and Padden is too shy in himself to seek out the hidden mystery.

Quille   [meaningly] Maybe 'tis shy for him, Mrs Shanahan. For it's the strange music that is entirely like what they do be playing in Teernanogue, or what they hear them

	that do be drowning to their death. [rises]
Padden	Holy Father! Maineen, is it a fairy, then, that's in the top loft and our Jaymony swept away?
Quille	[walking up and down floor with hands behind his back] We must make out if it is a Christian he is or if it isn't a Christian he is. [looking up at top loft] Is there ere a chance of getting a peep at him now?
Maineen	The dickens a chance, but it's up to the tips for his tea, and, believe you me, he won't forget that whatever else will escape him. There's some stir out of him as it is and you'd hear the boards creaking.
Quille	[walking up and down as before] I'm saying we must first make out if it is a Christian he is or if it isn't a Christian he is. Let me think now – I have it. Put the tongs in the fire and redden it.
Padden	[as Maineen puts tongs in fire] Holy Father, Maineen!
Quille	Put the tongs in the fire and redden it.
Jaymony	[loudly in top loft] Is the tea drawn yet?
Maineen	[putting tea in teapot] 'Tis drawn and shallow drawn.
Jaymony	'Tis not drawn, and 'tisn't wet itself, for it's after washing up the chaney you are with the boiling water, and putting cold water in the kettle. Don't be trying to blink me, for I heard the cover rattling, and 'tis the same with you every day, using the water and leaving me waiting for my tea. The selfishness of this world is a terror, but I'm warning you if the tea isn't drawn the minute I hop down out of this, there isn't a mug in the dresser I won't smash, and I'll break the window, and so every divil around the house will make it the sorry day to you you got into the habit of renayging me in the tea.
Maineen	[to Quille] As peevish as a cat always when coming out of that top loft. [loudly] Here now, you vagabone. [going to table with teapot] Isn't it on the table it is itself, and listen to me putting the sugar into it and stirring the sugar in the cup.
Jaymony	[coming down] And the white bread and the jam?
Maineen	And the white bread and the jam. [he comes down] There now, isn't it quick enough for you, my walking gentleman upstairs?

Jaymony   'Twill do, and 'tis to be hoped you'll be as regular for the future. 'Twould be a great boon to me. [takes off cap and eats and drinks rapidly, Quille from corner watching him intently; when done he blesses himself and puts on cap; meditatively] That jam was damn nice, mother dear.

lights pipe; rises; walks towards dresser; sees Quille. Takes pipe out of mouth and turns his face away from Quille as if ashamed. Quille goes stealthily towards Jaymony; puts hand behind back motioning with finger Padden hands him tongs]

Quille   Down on your knees now, you haunted thing. [Jaymony drops on his knees] Keep looking at me or I'll send this red-hot fizzling down into your baistly guts. *Sacramento, Dominus vobiscum, mea culpa, mea maxime culpa, kyrie eleison, excelsior!* I abjure thee by these words, tell me what you are and what you aren't. Are you Catholic?

Jaymony   [meekly] I am, sir.

Quille   [softly] Are you, faith? Very good. And now, my bucko, if you are, maybe you'll say what I say after me: In the name of the Father.

Jaymony   In the name of the Father.

Quille   In the name of the Son.

Jaymony   In the name of the Son.

Quille   In the name of the Holy Ghost [short pause] Ha!

Jaymony   In the name of the Holy Ghost.

Quille   [pulling Jaymony towards hearth] Come along here, you're some sort of a Christian. Here take this medicine and talk to me.

Jaymony   [drinking] 'Tis you I'd like to be talking to, then, and you a knowledgeable man.

Padden   Holy Father, Maineen! 'Tis working him – the medicine.

Quille   Hush! hush! [to Jaymony] Come, tell me, what's your meaning in going up in that top loft?

Jaymony   [shrugging his shoulders] Wisha, 'tis better than being in the slush – same old thing every day – this an ugly spot, and the people ignorant, grumpy, and savage.

Quille   By the way, they aren't double as bad above in Beenahoran; and I'm telling you it's a happy man you'd be out in the green fields for yourself with the sunny sky over you, if you knew the inside of Tralee Jail where I was landed for six months – [rising in great anger and excitement] – on a false charge brought against me by devils during the time of the Agitation. By devils, I'm saying, by devils! [subsides]

Jaymony   [sadly] Times I know it's a fool I am, surely, but the fancy's got stuck in me for them Magic Glasses, and the sport I had with them up in that top loft.

Quille   From whence, may I inquire, did you procure them Magic Glasses?

Jaymony   From a brown woman, sir.

Quille   [meaningly] From a brown woman, ha!

Jaymony   'Twason a summer's day and we going to the pattern of Lyre – myself and them two brothers of mine that are now ignorant peelers.

Maineen   Oh hierna! Is it reflecting you are on my two fine gentlemen of sons? What learning had you beyond them yourself and you barely out of the sixth book?

Padden   Too much learning he has, Maineen. Too much for sense, sir, and too little for common sense.

Quille   [waving his hand] Be easy now, my good people, and let me examine the patient. [to Jaymony] Proceed!

Jaymony   It's through a wood the brown woman came to me, and it wasn't a crackle or a noise at all she made and she walking on the grass so green. She stood for a while where the bluebells grow.

Quille   Hum! She stood for a while.

Jaymony   Going she was and selling her wares at the pattern of Lyre. And didn't I give her all I had for a set of the Magic Glasses! It put her in great blood, and, said she, "Tis the like of you I always want to meet that has the spunk in you, and I'm thinking you won't get tired of your purchase and fling it away from you in a week like many that haggles over the price of a glass or two, for 'tisn't one in a thousand buys of me the whole set.'

Quille   [wisely] I see!

Jaymony   'For it's the pleasure and diversion of the world,' said she, 'you'll hear and see in them Magic Glasses.'

Quille   Ha! It's more than music is in the glasses maybe?

Jaymony   [laughing] Hold your tongue! – the seven wonders of the world, seas and mountains and cities, grand horses and carriages, and all the wild animals of the earth. Gold and white money you'd see in heaps. Palaces, with the finest furniture inside in them, the best of eating and drinking laid out on tables with the loveliest chaney – all that and more is to be seen in the three brown glasses. Then there's the three red glasses, and the three blue glasses that makes up the set.

Quille   What's in the three red glasses?

Jaymony   Women. Full of the purtiest women was ever seen on the globe. It's myself got very fond of one of them, and maybe of two. And in the glass I could see myself and the one I was doting on, and we together for the six days of the week. Times we'd be talking and times there wouldn't be a word out of us at all, our two mouths in one kiss and we in a sort of a daze. It's after saying I am we'd be together for the six days of the week. But that wouldn't satisfy us, and we'd be together for the three hundred and sixty-five days of the year; and it wouldn't satisfy us, and for ages and ages we'd be in Tirnanogue, and it isn't satisfied we'd be still.

Maineen   [rushing forward] You shameless thing! Don't mind him, Mr Quille, it's ravelling he is in his immoral talk.

Padden   Two months now since he was at church or chapel, and 'tis years since he seen a priest.

Quille   [rising and bending towards Maineen and Padden, who shrink back] Them three blue glasses: in God's name what might be in them?

Jaymony   [excitedly] Ha! It's the rousing wonders is in them entirely. You'd see a dandy army in the grey of the night rising out of the dark glens, and the places where the herons do be screeching.

Quille   [rising suddenly] The inspiration is coming on me, for I knew a sort of a poet – 'Out of the mists they come,' said he, 'one by one – out of the mists and the fantastic quagmires of the South, their sabres gleaming in the light of the moon.' [turning to Jaymony] Isn't it them you see?

Jaymony   The same. [in great excitement] Ah, but I seen more, for 'tis myself I see on a noble horse, spangled and grey; I seen my own bright sabre flashing and I leading the army on, and we driving the Saxon invader before us – through the plains of Desmond, and on and on, even to the Eastern sea.

Quille [flourishing arms] The cloth! The cloth! It's getting convulsed I am! It's getting convulsed I am!

[Padden and Maineen lay sheet on floor; Quille falls on his back on sheet, and works as if in convulsions]

Padden Holy Father! Look at the two terrible eyes rolling in his head, he having no sight in them at all and he convulsed.

Maineen 'Tis like a man of God he is, looking through the rafters, and seeing, maybe, the dome of Paradise itself.

Quille Jaymony, Jaymony Shanahan! Let Jaymony Shanahan drink one wineglassful of the bottle left on the table by one Morgan Quille of Beenahorna – three times a day let him drink one wineglass, in the morning and in the noontime and coming on the fall of night. And the price of that bottle is four-and-six – [Padden fumbles in pocket, hands money to Maineen, who slips it into Quille's hand] – and at the dawn of day let Jaymony Shanahan hop on one leg and make a bow east and west and north and south, and let him pick fourteen red roses and make a garland with ferny leaves and eglantine, and leave it on the thatch. [works again in convulsions] Jaymony, Jaymony Shanahan! Let Jaymony Shanahan go turn the red earth every day will rise over him seven hours between dawn and the time the sun goes down, and in the dusk he'll ramble to the neighbour's houses and discourse on cattle and on crops and all things on the agricultural way. He'll go to market and to fair – take drink – a little – and ketch a woman if he wants to when he is coming home. On the twenty-first day a farmer's daughter is to be made out for Jaymony Shanahan.

[works in convulsions]

Padden We never thought of a wife for him, Maineen.

Maineen Hush, Padden! The great man's jaws are working towards speech.

Quille   Who is the woman to be made out for Jaymony
Shanahan? A lovely woman for a man with four cows,
no blemish on her beauty, but a slight impediment in
her speech. The birthmarks on her are a pimple under
her left ear, three black hairs on her buzzom and one
brown. In Beenahorna this damsel does dwell, and on
the twenty-first day – if Jaymony obey all the
instructions given – one Morgan Quille will bring her
to Jaymony Shanahan, and on the twenty-second day
he'll be cured for ever and live in the grace of God.

Jaymony [clapping his hands] Is it cured I am to be in the heel?
Is it cured I am to be in the heel? [runs and takes up
spade] I will go and turn the red earth! I will go and
turn the red earth! [runs out]

Padden   [running out] And I will rush and tell the neighbours
the marvel of the world done for us this day.

[Maineen goes and makes more punch; she gives it to Quille,
who rises; he drinks and hands her back the tumbler]

Quille   Off with me now and flaking up the long, long
country to Beenahorna; no time have I to waste, and
a witch to prophesy my time was limited. Devils and
curs would say 'tis myself invented the prophecy –
devils and curs! But I am telling you, my good woman,
my time is limited, my time is limited. [makes a spring
out of the door]

Maineen [rushing to door] Oh, Mr Quille, God keep you a
thousand years to work miracles – God keep you a
thousand years! [she goes to fireplace; re-enter Jaymony;
she turns and sees him; wringing her hands] For the
love of God! 'Tisn't renayging you are to turn the red
earth?

Jaymony [shrugging his shoulders] Sick I got of turning it, a
dismal feeling to come over me, after Thade Martin
telling me my two brothers had arrived in the village,
are giving out porter and the people making much of
them.

Maineen Did you hop on the leg itself?

Jaymony I did not.

Maineen Here, take the medicine in the name of God! It might
prevent the charm from being cancelled, and maybe

	after a while you'd go out and hop on that leg. Is it better you feel?
Jaymony	'Tis better I feel.
Maineen	Thank God the charm isn't cancelled. Go out now and hop on that leg in the name of God!
Jaymony	[with sudden elation] Tomorrow I'll do it – tomorrow I'll follow out all the instructions, and it's a great effort I'll make entirely. [sighs] If it isn't too far gone I am to be cured by quackery or the power of man.

[Padden re-enters with Jug and Mary; he goes to table and drinks whisky]

Padden	[giving the women whisky] Drink, Aunt Jug – drink, Aunt Mary – 'tisn't you should be to take a sup the glorious day that's in it. 'Tis in great blood I am, Maineen, I couldn't keep from waving my hat and shouting of the cure to the crowd of labourers on Peg Caxty's turnip garden.
Aunt Jug	[drinking] Isn't it me screeched the good news to Jane Quinlan, the boolumshee that will spread the good news over the known world.
Aunt Mary	[drinking] I found time to screech it to Marse Doolen over her half-door, grigging her I was and a hump on her own son, for 'tis often she was reflecting on Jaymony.

[Jaymony slips up to top loft]

Maineen	And maybe she'll reflect again and the cure not rightly working in him yet. Isn't it up in the top loft he is and playing the music itself?
Padden	The villain of the world, it's now he has us scandalised. [going towards ladder] But maybe he don't know the courage the drop puts in a man. [catching ladder] Come down, will you, from your tingling and your jig-acting, or I'll leather you within an inch of your life!
Aunt Jug and Aunt Mary	That's the style, Padden, up to him and drill the devil out of him itself.
Padden	But I can't go up. I can't even raise a leg. Holy Father, it's paralysed I am, and it must be the devil himself is in the top loft!
Aunt Jug and Aunt Mary	[at ladder] Mother of God, save and shield us! The devil himself above in the top loft!

Maineen [going to ladder] What devil above in the top loft? It's drunk you're all and dazzled drunk itself. The house is creaking – leave go the ladder, I'm saying, or you'll pull the top loft down.

Padden Holy Father! Isn't it the way I can't let go and I glued to it, Maineen?

Aunt Jug and Aunt Mary And likewise glued are we.

Padden 'Tis the devil has us fast. Look through the top loft door. Holy Father! He's up on the table and having every wheel about!

Aunt Jug and Aunt Mary Mother of God! On the table and having every wheel about! [music in loft]

Maineen I'm telling you it's Jaymony is on the table, and better let him be. For it's playing wild he is, and his eyes gone curious mad.

Padden It's a devil that's there, and a terrible devil too.

Aunt Jug and Aunt Mary The devil surely.

Padden Don't I see the horns and the horrid hoofs?

Aunt Jug and Aunt Mary We see the horns and the horrid hoofs.

Padden Brimstone I smell!

Aunt Jug and Aunt Mary Brimstone we smell!

Padden The flags of hell I see and the flames for ever!

Aunt Jug and Aunt Mary The flags of hell we see and the flames for ever!

[They sway about, clinging to ladder, Maineen still exhorting them to leave go and endeavouring to pull them away from it; suddenly ladder gives way, and top loft tumbles down, Padden Maineen, Jug and Mary falling on their backs, in different directions.]

Padden, Aunt Jug, Aunt Mary In the name of God, we're kilt! [they all get up]

Maineen [observing Jaymony's legs, which are seen sticking up above debris of top loft] More likely it's Jaymony is kilt. [goes to ruins of top loft; with considerable surprise, throwing her arms wide] And he is kilt! [bringing her hands together with a slap] Glory be, if it isn't kilt entirely he is, and his jugular cut by the Magic Glasses!

Padden [in terror and excitement] In the name of God don't

lay a hand to him, or it's taken up we'll be for murder,
or manslaughter in the first degree. Leave him in the
position he's in, Maineen, and start rising your
lamentations, and likewise, you Aunt Jug. And let
myself and Aunt Mary go running through the county,
tearing our hair, and calling to the people, wide, the
house fell down on Jaymony. [Padden and Aunt Mary
rush out]

Padden and Aunt Mary   [outside] Our Jaymony is kilt! the
house fell down on Jaymony! Our Jaymony is kilt! the
house fell down on Jaymony!

[Maineen and Aunt Jug commence to ullagone; they keen louder
and louder as tumultous voices are heard approaching.]

ROBERT LESLIE BOLAND
ODE TO A PO

Dedicated to the bedrooms of the world

Loved mother of convention, old as time!
Shrine of our nightly pilgrimage ere sleep!
How often have I pondered, long and deep,
On thee, pale urn; immobile bedroom jeep!
Chamber of music for the feminine,
Who, thy earliest potter, shall I seek?
Thou hast been found in King Tut's ancient tomb
(This mummied monarch, too, should have his leak,
And dared not wet his own sepulchral room).
He was before the Roman or the Greek.
The Chaldees knew thee ere they knew the moon.
Old human vase! For human hemispheres!
Ruth filled thee – with her piss and with her tears!

Brighid Ní Mhóráin
I bhFothair na Manach

Phasálamar na pósaes i dTóin na Fothrach
samhaircíní is púir faille bhí ar tinneall le dúil,
má thug taibhsí na manach fé ndeara sinn
níor ligeadar faic orthu, chaochadar súil.
Ní raibh gíocs as na clocháin;
bhí an dónall dubh ina thost;
dúirís gur mé do leanbh gréine;
nóinín, osclaíonn fén solas buí.
Dá mbagródh an sliabh go dtitfeadh orainn
nó an mhuir go gclúdódh sinn
chuirfimis cluain orthu chun go bhfanfaidís socair,
 – níl ionainn ach leá chúr na habhann,
atáidsean i searc a chéile
ó tháinig ann don domhan.

Fintan O'Toole
Seeing Is Believing

The revelations that week were disturbing. Sergeant Patrick
Reilly told the Kerry Babies Tribunal in Tralee, twenty miles
away, of how he had found the body of an infant on the rocks
at White Strand. Mrs Mary Hayes said that if her daughter
Kathleen had been calling out from the front door to Joanne in
the field, the night Joanne had had the baby, she herself had
heard nothing. A Professor of Oceanography was asked by James
Duggan BL what would happen to an object the size of a
newborn infant wrapped in a plastic bag and thrown into the
sea off Slea Head. Worst was the evidence of Superintendent
John Sullivan, outlining the course of the investigation into the
death of the infant found at Cahirciveen, evidence which
touched on dark things. They had, he said, checked into cases
of incest, of married men known to have been associating with
single girls, of a woman who was pregnant and went to England
but might have returned. The parents of a girl whose diary

contained references to rape were also interviewed. There were even checks on itinerants and hippies. Somebody, he said, had even suggested that it might all be connected with black magic.

When the children of Asdee told their parents of what they had seen in the church, some of them thought of the terrible things that were being dragged to light in Tralee. 'There was all that Kerry babies business,' says one father, 'and there have been other things too. There've been two murders in the Listowel area and over in Tarbert there was a case of a man who was having sex with his two nieces and got one of them pregnant. That's why some of the people here think that what's happened is a sign. There's a message there and it's to do with all the bad things that have been happening.'

At twenty past twelve on the day that Superintendent Sullivan was giving evidence in Tralee, Thursday 14 February, Elizabeth Flynn entered the little church of Saint Mary which is next door to her school in Asdee. Asdee is no more than a dip in the road from Ballybunion to Ballylonford, a tiny line of buildings of which the church, the school, two pubs and the shop-cum-petrol pump are the most notable. From down in the centre of the village's one street there is nothing to be seen but the straggling, sparsely populated dairying land around. From the brow of the hill where the village starts, however, the winking towers of industrial Ireland, the power stations of Moneypoint and Tarbert, loom up from the Shannon estuary. And in the estuary the long dark bulk of a 140,000-tonne coal carrier, the biggest ship ever to dock in an Irish port, lies at Moneypoint, clearly visible.

Elizabeth is seven and she goes to the church every day at lunchtime. She is making her First Communion this month. Mrs Eileen Moriarty, the principal teacher in the school, is a devout elderly woman and she encourages all their pupils to go next door to the church at lunchtime to 'give two or three minutes to Jesus and the church.' Elizabeth prayed to the two statues, painted plaster images of the Blessed Virgin and the Sacred Heart which stand in the alcove at the back of the church on the left-hand side, separated by a brass trolley, surmounted with votive candles and a small round stained-glass porthole which lets in a dim, diffuse light. Then she saw the Sacred Heart crook his finger and beckon her over to him.

When she looked again, Our Lady's mouth was open.

Martin Fitzgerald, who is ten and is one of the altar boys in the church, was playing 'hunting' out at the back of the school when Elizabeth Flynn and the other 'young ones' came up to him. They told him that the statues were moving. He went in with a large group of other children and looked at the statues for a while. He saw the head and eyes of one of the statues move. Some of the other children who were there at the same time saw nothing. Gradually all of the children gathered into the church to look. Altogether thirty-six of them now say that they saw the statue move in various ways. Some, like Blanaid Quane, have had more than one vision, seeing the statues move on different occasions up to the present. A few of their parents say they too have seen movement in the statues.

In the Jesse James Tavern, next door to Saint Mary's Church, the woman of the house keeps a small hardcover notebook behind the bar. The tavern has a low, uneven ceiling, smoke-stained walls and a sign on the wall facing the back door that says 'Please use the toilet'. Apart from the pool table, the jukebox and the framed photographs of Jesse James that hang above the fireplace along with a 'Wanted: Dead or Alive' poster, it is an old-style village pub. The jukebox is on and the air is filled with the nasal tones of Tony Stevens singing a country-and-western song, 'Send Me No Roses', the B-side of the local anthem, 'The Village of Asdee'. The notebook behind the bar is the legacy of the man who put Asdee on the map, the former parish priest Father Liam Ferris. It contains, in bold, clear handwriting, a romantic version of the life and death of Jesse James, along with stories about his Asdee ancestors collected by Father Ferris from old people around the village.

Father Ferris dominated the village from the Second World War until the end of the sixties, and he always believed that Asdee was marked out for a special distinction. A colourful and unorthodox man, he came to believe that the ancestors of Jesse James had come from Asdee and on 4 April every year he would say a solemn requiem Mass, in the same church where the children would see the moving statues, for the repose of the soul of the greatest desperado of them all. He spent many years researching the connection with the James family. He touched the village with a sense of the extraordinary and at the same time tried to encourage a simple piety, organising and encouraging devotion to Saint Eoin's holy well, half a mile from the village towards the estuary.

One of the stories in the notebook in the Jesse James Tavern concerns Saint Eoin's Well. In April 1965 Father Ferris wrote a story he had collected under the heading 'Blindness': 'The James were Protestants. A servant girl of theirs was going blind and she went to the local holy well. She made a "round" there and got her sight. At the same time her master had a horse gone blind. He took it to the holy well and marched it around several times. The horse got its sight, but James, its owner, got blind.'

Many people in Asdee still believe in the magical properties of Saint Eoin's Well, particularly as a healer of the eyes. They say that some years ago a woman called Ellen Welch was praying there when she saw two fish in the water. She was immediately cured of her illness. They say that when the fish appear again in the water whoever sees them will be cured.

The last Saturday in April is one of the traditional days of worship at the well, a worship revived by Father Ferris. This year a few dozen people gathered, walking up the winding tar-macadamed boreen and through the small, rusting gate set among the hedges, where a cardboard sign says 'The Holy Well'. The well is a shallow pool of clear water fed by a sluggish spring. The thick bushes have been cleared from the water but encroach on three sides. On the fourth side some rough-hewn stones serve as a kneeling place for the pilgrims to bend and scoop the blessed water up in a grey smoked-glass coffee cup. In front of them at the far side of the pool is a small plaster virgin and child set on a blue and white square of tablecloth on the top of a rickety chair. The surrounding bushes are tied with clean white rags, pagan symbols of the flowering forth of May. The pilgrims mutter incessant Rosaries. The following morning they will wait back after Mass at ten and mutter the same Rosaries before the statues at the back of Saint Mary's church.

Worship at the well had declined until the arrival of the present curate, Father Michael O'Sullivan, in Asdee a little over a year ago. He not only revived the worship at the well but solemnised it, concelebrating Mass there late last summer with two other priests. There was a large turnout from the village and what one villager describes as a 'tremendous atmosphere'. There was singing in the still air of the holy place and a double rainbow encircled the well while the Mass was in progress. Afterwards, a few of the villagers came to see this as a sign, a portent of what was to come.

The holy well and the notebook in the Jesse James Tavern are not Father Ferris's only legacies. He invested Asdee with a sense of other worlds. Father Ferris's views of the world were so unorthodox that in ecclesiastical circles the term 'feresy' was coined to cover his many sub-heretical opinions.

He believed that all those who attended Mass should share in the sacred mysteries of the priesthood and thus that Communion should be given in the hand. He believed that Moses, Plato and Aristotle should be canonised. He wrote a history of the world, *The Story of Man,* which featured the French Revolution only as a footnote on page 72. He invented a new world, 'pollantory', a place where souls went to have the good knocked out of them before they went to hell, just as they went to purgatory to have the bad knocked out of them before they went to heaven. And once, in one of the sermons in Saint Mary's church, which he would deliver with alternate sentences in English and Irish, he told the people of Asdee, in relation to Jesus walking on the water, that 'anyone could walk on the water if they had enough ESB running through their bodies.'

Father Ferris's many worlds mingled with the worlds of local folklore, which was taught in the school by old Mr Moriarty, who died in 1981, a folklore which still holds a half belief among some of the village people. There are 200 fairy forts in the vicinity of Asdee and some people claim to have seen lights going from one fort to another. There are some stories of a drowned village under the sea between the nearby Beale Strand and Loop Head.

Father Micheal O'Sullivan arrived as curate early in 1984. He had been a curate in Texas and had a strong belief in Padre Pio, the Italian monk who inspired great devotion because he appeared to carry the stigmata of Christ on his body. He himself had come through a serious operation and attributed his deliverance to the intercession of Padre Pio. His arrival sparked off a greater enthusiasm for the church and religion generally. He organised a party of villagers to clean up the small grotto, showing an apparition of the Blessed Virgin, which had fallen into a run-down state. He had Mass said at the Holy Well. And in November he started a Padre Pio prayer group, which would pray fervently every week against the encroaching evils of the world. A few weeks before the miracles of 14 February, Father O'Sullivan had a film about Padre Pio shown in the village and there was a good attendance, including many of the children.

The sacristan is filling the candle stalls at the back of the church with yet another box of votive candles. Forty little flames are flickering around the statues, causing shadowy movements on their painted surfaces. In the three months since the statues moved, the people of the village have come to take the miracles in their stride. 'There have been so many miraculous movements in Asdee,' says the sacristan, 'the people don't remark on them much any more. The only thing we haven't had yet is a cure, and I'm sure that will come. But we've had a lot more movements than Knock has ever had.'

There are now almost as many adults as children who claim to have seen movements in the statues – hands lifting, eyes moving, small spots appearing on the Blessed Virgin's neck. Some say they have smelt heavenly perfumes. 'It's like a reminder that there is another world,' says a woman across the street from the church. 'And these things never happen except in poor little places like Asdee and Knock. Our Lady never appeared in Dublin.'

Shortly after the movements were seen in Asdee, a group of children in Ballydesmond, a village on Kerry's border with Cork, saw the statues move in *their* local church. The people of Asdee are scornfully amused at the Ballydesmond stories. 'Do you know what happened in Ballydesmond a few weeks ago?' asks one local man. 'Two young fellas were in praying in the church one evening and the sacristan locked the door without checking if there was anyone inside. Well, a while later, weren't a few others walking down past the church and they heard these figures banging on the windows from the inside. Well, they ran like the clappers over to the priest's house, shouting. 'Come quick, Father, the statues are trying to get out of the window.'

On the first Sunday after Asdee's apparitions, there were 2,000 people in the village, a bigger crowd even than the one which had gathered the previous September when John Kennedy, who owns the shop and petrol pump in the village, brought home the Sam Maguire cup, which he had helped to win as a member of the Kerry football team. Since then the stream of pilgrims has slowed, but it is still steady. And there have been more miracles. A man from Cavan who came on a Thursday evening to celebrate his wedding anniversary reached up to touch the statue of the Blessed Virgin, placing his fingertips on its hand. His finger and thumb, he claimed, were held firm in the statue's grasp for many seconds while he tried to release its hold. A woman who came in a busload from Newry one Sunday felt the Blessed Virgin take her hand in her own. The statue's hand, she said, turned to warm flesh as it gripped her. She was crying uncontrollably.

The miracles are noted down and placed through Father Sullivan's letterbox. Father O'Sullivan refers all queries to the diocesan office. Matters have been taken out of his hands. For the first few Sundays there were Stations of the Cross in the church and the Rosary was relayed outside to the waiting crowds on a loudspeaker. The speaker still juts from the pebble-dashed church wall but it is now silent. Local people say that the order came from the bishop that the Rosary was no longer to be relayed outside.

Many villagers still expect a message. Some thought there would be a message at Easter. When it didn't come, they simply carried on. 'There will surely be a message,' says a man whose daughter had two visions. 'With all that's happening it wouldn't make sense if there was no message.'

The pilgrims and petitioners who come are drawn not by miracles but by the mundane miseries of the everyday world. From half past two on Sunday they bow their heads and step humbly into the twilight zone around the statues, the light from outside refracted from the rain and strained through coloured glass. The older women cover their heads and mumble Rosaries in unison. The younger women and most of the men stand stock-still, staring at the plaster images, their eyes not revealing whether they are daring or begging the statues to move. Red, plump children play on the floor, their frustration held in check by occasional warnings.

Sometimes the petitioners scribble notes and leave them at the foot of either statue, mostly that of the Blessed Virgin. A woman leaves a leaflet that proclaims the power of holy water – 'the devil cannot long abide in a place or near a person that is often sprinkled with this blessed water.' But mostly the petitions are more personal.

'Our Blessed Lady, please bless all my family and help us sort out all our problems. Make Mam, Dad, better again and let us be one big family together forever.' 'Please, please, help Jim to stop drinking and give us peace in our home.' 'Sacred Heart of Jesus, grant all my intentions and help me pay my bills.' They fondle the hands of the statues continually, rubbing and stroking them. A woman takes a small white child's vest from her bag and rubs it on the statue of the Sacred Heart, then quickly replaces it and moves through the door. Now and then another candle gutters out and sends a last exhalation of smoke towards the roofbeams.

from A MASS FOR JESSE JAMES (1990)

EOGHAN RUA Ó SÚILLEABHÁIN
A CHARA MO CHLÉIBH

Chun Séamais Mhic Ghearailt

A chara mo chléibh 's a Shéamais ghreannmhair ghráigh
d'fhuil Ghearaltaigh Ghréagaigh éachtaigh armnirt áigh,
maide glan réidh i ngléas bíodh agat dom rámhainn
's mar bharra ar an scléip cuir léi go greanta bacán.

M'armsa i ngléas tar t'éis go snasta ó tá
's ó thosach mo shaoil an léann mo thartsa nár bháigh,
ní stadfad dem réim go dtéad don Ghaillimh lem rámhainn,
mar a ngeabhad gach lae mo réal is marthain mar phá.

Ar chaitheamh an lae más tréith nó tuirseach mo chnámha
's go mbraithfidh an maor nach éachtach m'acfainn ar
            rámhainn,
labharfad féin go séimh ar Eachtra an Bháis
nó ar chathaibh na nGréag sa Trae d'fhúig flatha go tláith.

Ar Shampson an laochais déanfad labhairt i dtráth
's ar Alexander tréan ba chraosach seasamh le námhaid,
ar cheannas na Saesars éachtach armnirt áigh
nó ar Heactor an laoch d'fhúig céadta marbh sa pháirc.

Ar Chaitcheann mac Tréan sa bhFéinn chuir easpa 'gus ár
's ar imeachta Dheirdre i scéimh 's i bpearsa rug barr
le bladaireacht chlaon 'na dhéidh sin canfad dó dán –
sin agatsa, a Shéamais, fé mar chaithfeadsa an lá.

Ar chaitheamh an lae dá réir sin gheabhad mo phá
's i mbrollach mo léine déan é a cheangal le cnáib;
don bhaile ar mo théacht beidh mé i meanmain ard
's ní scaipfead ar aon chor réal do dtagad id dháil.

Mar is fear tú mar mé do chéas an seanathart lá,
racham araon faoi scléip go tabhairne an stáid;
is rabhairneach ghlaofam *ale* is dramanna ar clár
is taisce go héag ní dhéan d'aon leathphingin pá.

Thomas Moore
Desmond's Song

By the Feal's wave benighted,
Not a star in the skies.
To the door by Love lighted,
I first saw those eyes.
Some voice whispered o'er me,
As the threshold I crossed,
There was ruin before me:
If I loved, I was lost.

Love came, and brought sorrow
Too soon in his train;
Yet so sweet, that tomorrow
'Twould be welcome again.
Were misery's full measure
Poured out to me now,
I would drain it with pleasure,
So that Hebe wert thou.

You who call it dishonour
To bow to this flame,
If you've eyes, look but on her,
And blush while you blame.
Hath the pearl less whiteness
Because of its birth?
Hath the violet less brightness
For growing near earth?

No – Man, for his glory,
To history flies;
While Woman's bright story
Is told in her eyes.
While the monarch but traces
Through mortals his line,
Beauty, born of the Graces,
Ranks next to divine!

AMERGIN
THE MYSTERY

A Milesian prince, brother of Evir, Ir and Eremon, said to have colonised Ireland hundreds of years before Christ. According to tradition these verses are the first to have been composed in Ireland. They are ascribed to Amergin and are from the Lebor Gebala *or* Book of Invasions.

I am the wind which breathes upon the sea,
I am the wave of the ocean,
I am the murmur of the billows,
I am the ox of the seven combats,
I am the vulture upon the rocks,
I am the beam of the sun,
I am the fairest of plants,
I am the wild boar in valour,
I am the salmon in water,
I am the lake in the plain,
I am the word of science,
I am the point of the lance of the battle,
I am the God who created in the head the fire.
Who is it who throws light into the meeting on the
    mountain?
Who announces the ages of the moon?
Who teaches the place where couches the sun?

                        (If not I)

TRANSLATION BY DOUGLAS HYDE

Biographical Notes

Amergin A Milesian prince, brother of Ir, Evir and Eremon, said to have colonised Ireland hundreds of years before Christ. According to tradition, his verses, beginning with 'I am the wind which breathes upon the sea', were the first to have been composed in Ireland and are said to have been uttered when the Milesians came ashore near Kenmare.

J. J. Barrett (b. 1943) Journalist, poet and prose writer. Son of Joe Barrett of Rock Street and Kerry football fame, J. J. has published a book of poetry, *Not For Dedalus,* and the acclaimed Kerry football saga *In the Name of the Game.* Born in Tralee, J. J. played with Kerry in four All-Ireland Finals, collecting one senior and one under-21 medal.

Maureen Beasley (b. 1918) Poet. Born in Killocrim, near Listowel, where she still lives, she has published collections of poetry and memoirs.

Robert Leslie Boland (1888–1955) Poet and farmer. Born at Farnastack, near Listowel. To the merriment of his friends and neighbours, he assumed the mock-Ascendancy title Sir Robert Leslie Boland Bart. (His real name was Michael Valentine Boland). *Thistles and Docks: The Humorous Poetry of Bob Boland* was published in 1995.

Fiona Brennan Poet. Born in Oxford and reared in Killorglin, County Kerry, she has published poetry in various journals and magazines, including *Poetry Ireland Review, InCognito, Feasta* and the *Cúirt Journal.* A short story of hers was dramatised and televised by RTÉ. She lives in Knocknagree, County Cork.

Paddy Bushe (b. 1948) Poet. Born in Dublin, he now lives in Waterville, County Kerry. He won the 1990 Listowel Writers' Week Award for his poem 'Sceilg' and was runner-up in the 1988 Patrick Kavanagh Award. His 'Poets at Smerwick' was highly commended in the 1987 Arvon International Poetry Competition.

Sigerson Clifford (1913–85) Poet, playwright, short-story writer and balladmaker. Born in Cork, he spent his childhood in Cahirciveen and, having joined the civil service in 1932, served in Dungloe, Tralee and Dublin, which became his home in 1943.

Daniel Corkery (1878–1964) Man of letters. Born in Cork, he was a dedicated enthusiast for the Irish language. He was Professor of English at UCC from 1931 to 1947.

Eoghan Corry (b. 1961) Sports journalist. He dates his infatuation with Kerry football to a long period spent in the Ventry Gaeltacht in 1972. His *Kingdom Come: A Biography of the Kerry Football Team 1975-1988* was published in 1989.

Mary Cummins (d. 1998) Journalist. Spent much of her childhood and youth in Ballybunion, where her father served as a garda sergeant. Was a staff journalist for *The Irish Times* and the paper's Seanad correspondent.

Michael Davitt (rugadh 1950) File. Rugadh i gCorcaigh é. Tá sé ag triall ar Chorca Dhuibhne ó aois na hóige. Bhuaigh sé Duais an Bhuitléaraigh i 1994. Ball de Aosdána isea é. His latest collection *Freacnaircc Mhearcair/The Oomph of Quicksilver* (Cork University Press) is a bilingual selection with translations by Brendan Kennelly, Paul Muldoon, John Montague and others.

Paul Durcan (b. 1944) Poet. Born in Dublin and educated at Gonzaga College and UCC, he is one of Ireland's most individual and widely enjoyed poets.

Desmond Egan (b. 1936) Poet and publisher. Born in Athlone, County Westmeath, he founded the Goldsmith Press in 1972 and edited *Era,* an occasional literary magazine. He gained international acclaim with the publication of his *Collected Poems* in 1983, which won the National Poetry Foundation of America Award that year. Desmond Egan lives in Newbridge, County Kildare.

Edmund Falconer was born Edmund O'Rourke in Dublin in 1814 and went on stage as a boy. He was the original Danny Mann in Boucicault's *The Colleen Bawn* (1960) and was the author of many plays himself. His parlour piece 'Killarney' is still sung. He died in London in 1879.

Micheál Fanning (b. 1954) Poet. A medical doctor, he practises in Dingle, County Kerry. He has published poetry in both Irish and English. Among his collections are *Déithe an tSolais* (1994) and *Verbum et Verbum* (1997).

Piaras Feiritéar (*c.* 1600–53) File, taoiseach de chine Normánach. Mhair na Feiritéaraigh i gCorca Dhuibhne. Nuair a thosaigh an t-éirí amach sa bhliain 1641 thaobhaigh sé leis na Gaeil. Crochadh go poiblí é i gCill Airne sa bhliain 1653.

Paddy Fitzgibbon Playwright. Born in Listowel, where he now lives, his play *Estuary* was premièred by the Lartigue Little Theatre, Listowel, and published by Lartigue Books, Listowel, in 1993.

George Fitzmaurice (1877–1963) Playwright and short-story writer. Born in Bedford House near Listowel, he worked in a bank and in the Land Commission and served in the army during World War I. His later life was spent as a recluse in Dublin. An undeservedly neglected playwright, his collected plays were published posthumously in three volumes by Dolmen Press, Dublin, in 1967 and 1970.

Robin Flower (1881–1946) English-born Celtic scholar, translator and poet. Educated at Leeds Grammar School and Pembroke College, Oxford, from 1929 to 1944 he was deputy keeper of manuscripts at the British Museum. A frequent visitor to the Blaskets, in 1944 *Bláithín*, as he was affectionately named by the Islanders, published *The Western Isle,* an account of his experiences on the Great Blasket.

Patrick Given (b. 1934) Poet. Born in Knock, County Mayo, his family moved to Listowel when he was four years old. He taught English and Greek at Saint Michael's College, Listowel, from 1955 to his retirement. He has published *Poems* (1967) and *Pilgrimage Along the Feale and Other Poems* (1976).

Guistí (Mícheál Ó Conchubhair) (*c.* 1790–1850) File. Mhair sé i bparóiste Chaisleán Ghriaire, Contae Chiarraí. Príomhfhile an Leitriúigh lena linn. Tá Guistí curtha cois farraige i gCill Seanaigh.

Seamus Heaney (b. 1939) Poet. Born in Bellaghy, County Derry, he has earned worldwide fame as a poet, critic, lecturer and teacher. He was awarded the Nobel Prize for Literature in 1995. His *Opened Ground: Poems 1966–96* was published in 1998.

Donal Hickey Journalist. Reared in Gneevguilla, County Kerry, he works as a journalist with the *Irish Examiner.* His book *Stone Mad for Music: The Sliabh Luachra Story* was published by Marino Books in 1999.

Con Houlihan Journalist. Born near Castleisland, County Kerry, he began his journalistic career locally, graduating later to the *Kerryman,* where he was a columnist. He has also written for the *Irish Press* and the *Sunday World,* among other papers, and has published a number of collections of his journalism.

Dan Keane (b. 1919) Poet. Born in Moyvane, County Kerry, he worked for thirty-eight years as. an insurance representative, retiring in 1984. A popular poet, balladmaker, storyteller and broadcaster, he published *The Heather is Purple,* a collection of his poems, in 1986.

John B. Keane (b. 1928) Playwright, short-story writer, novelist, balladmaker, poet and essayist. Born in Listowel, he has lived there most of his life. One of Ireland's most popular writers, he is one of the few who is appreciated by both academe and the academy of the street.

Éamon Kelly (b. 1914) Actor, seanchaí and writer. Born near Rathmore, County Kerry, he has had a varied and successful career as an actor, performing in the plays of, among others, Brian Friel, Tom Murphy and Sebastian Barry. He has published two volumes of memoirs, *The Apprentice* (1995) and *The Journeyman* (1998), both with Marino Books.

Sister Stanislaus Kennedy A native of Lispole, County Kerry, she joined the Sisters of Charity in 1958. A great champion of the needy, particularly homeless people, Sister Stan is president of Focus Ireland, which she founded in 1985. She is also on the board of Combat Poverty and is a member of the Council of State. She lives with other members of her congregation in inner-city Dublin.

Brendan Kennelly (b. 1936) Poet, playwright, novelist and critic. Born in Ballylongford, County Kerry, he is Professor of Modern English at Trinity College, Dublin. He is arguably Ireland's most popular poet - the only one, perhaps, who can fill both the parish hall and the halls of academe when he reads his poems.

Patrick Kennelly (b. 1946) Novelist and playwright. Brother of Brendan Kennelly, he was born in Ballylongford, where he still lives, working as a teacher in one of the parish's national schools. In 1969 he published *Sausages For Tuesday*, a novel.

Collette Nunan Kenny Born in Moyvane, County Kerry, she has published several collections of poetry. She is a regular broadcaster on Radio Kerry.

Thomas Kinsella (b. 1928) Poet. Born in Dublin, he worked for a time as a civil servant. He left the civil service in 1965 to serve as poet-in-residence in Southern Illinois University. In 1970 he became a professor in the English Department at Temple University, Philadelphia, a college of which he opened in Dublin in 1976. Now retired from teaching, he lives in County Wicklow.

Dorothy Macardle (1899–1958) Novelist, historian and playwright. Born in Dundalk, a member of the well-known brewing family, she was educated at Alexandra and UCD and taught at her old school until her arrest for republican activities in 1922. A fervent supporter of Éamon de Valera, she died in Drogheda on 23 December 1958.

John McAuliffe (b. 1973) Poet and critic. Educated at Saint Michael's College, Listowel, UCG and TCD, he has published poetry and criticism in Ireland, England and the US. He won the RTÉ Poet of the Future Award 2000 and lectures in TCD.

Sean McCarthy (1923–1990) Balladmaker and poet. Born near Listowel, Seán McCarthy was a much-loved singer, broadcaster and songwriter.

Mick MacConnell (b. 1947) Songwriter. Born near Enniskillen, he has worked as a journalist with *The Irish Times*, the *Kerryman* and *Ireland on Sunday*. An album of his songs, *Peter Pan and Me*, was released in 1992, and a second is forthcoming.

Owen McCrohan Freelance journalist. A regular columnist on Gaelic football, and particularly Kerry football, in the *Kerryman* newspaper.

Steve MacDonogh (b. 1949) Poet and publisher. Born in Dublin and educated in England, he has lived since 1982 in Dingle, where he founded the publishing companies Brandon and Mount Eagle.

Pádraig Mac Fhearghusa (rugadh 1947) File. Rugadh i mBéal Átha Fhinín i gContae Chorcaí é. Cónaí air i dTrá Lí anois, mar ar bhunaigh sé Scoil Lán-Ghaeilge Mhic Easmainn i 1978.

Thomas MacGreevy (1893–1967) Poet and critic. Born in Tarbert, County Kerry, he served as an officer in World War I and, after being demobilized, was educated at Trinity College, Dublin. In the late 1920s and early 1930s he lived in Paris, where he introduced Samuel Beckett to James Joyce. One of the first, and most important, Irish modernist poets.

Bryan MacMahon (1909–98) Short-story writer, novelist, play-wright, balladmaker and translator. Born in Listowel, where he lived most of his life as a national school teacher. He is generally acknowledged to be one of the few masters of the short story to have emerged in Ireland after Frank O'Connor and Sean O'Faolain.

Máire Mhac an tSaoi (rugadh 1922) file, aistritheoir, criticeoir. Rugadh i mBaile Átha Cliath. D.Litt. Celt. *honoris causa* ó Ollscoil na hÉireann (1992). Áirítear Máire Mhac an tSaoi ar fhilí móra Gaeilge na linne seo.

John Montague (b. 1929) Poet and short-story writer. Born in Brooklyn, New York, and brought up in Garvaghey, County Tyrone. Educated at UCD and Yale, he taught at Berkeley and UCC, retiring in 1988. In 1998 he was appointed Ireland Professor of Poetry. He lives in County Cork.

Thomas Moore (1779–1852) Poet. Born in Dublin, in his lifetime he was the most popular of his generation of Irish writers. His father, a grocer, was born in Moyvane, County Kerry and attended John Lynne's hedge school in neighbouring Knockanure.

Cole Moreton (b. 1967) Writer and journalist. Born in East London, where he still lives. He writes for the *Independent on Sunday*.

William Pembroke Mulchinock (*c.* 1820-64) Poet. Born in Tralee, after an unhappy love affair he became a war correspondent during the British war in Afghanistan. He contributed poems to the *Nation*. Living in America from 1849 to 1855, he became literary editor of the *Irish Advocate*. He died in Tralee in 1864.

Paul Muldoon (b. 1955) Poet. Born near Moy, County Armagh, and educated at Queen's University Belfast, he worked as a producer at Radio Ulster before moving to America in the late 1980s. He is director of the creative-writing programme at Princeton. In the 1980s he lived for a time in Dingle.

Eibhlín Dhubh Ní Chonaill (*floruit* 1770) File. Duine de Chonallaigh Dhoire Fhíonáin in Uíbh Ráthach, agus aintín do Daniel O'Connell, an Fuascailteoir. Sa bhliain 1767, in aghaidh tola a muintire, phós sí Art Ó Laoghaire. Mhair an bheirt acu ar sheantailte Mhuintir Laoghaire in aice le Maigh Chromtha, Contae Chorcaí go dtí gur maraíodh Art i gCarraig an Ime, Contae Chorcaí ar an 4ú Bealtaine, 1773.

Nuala Ní Dhomhnaill (rugadh 1952) File. Rugadh i Lancashire Shasana í. Tógadh í i nGaeltacht Chorca Dhuibhne. Cónaí uirthi anois i mBaile Átha Cliath. Duine de mhór-fhilí Gaeilge na linne seo.

Máire Áine Nic Gearailt (rugadh 1946) File. Rugadh i mBaile an tSléibhe, Fionntrá i gCorca Dhuibhne í. Tá duaiseanna gnóthaithe ag a cuid filíochta i gcomórtas an Oireachtais idir na blianta 1966 agus 1971. Tá cónaí uirthi anois i mBaile Átha Cliath.

Brighid Ní Mhóráin (rugadh 1951) File agus múinteoir. Rugadh in Áth Trasna i gContae Chorcaí í. Tá cónaí uirthi sa Cham tamall amach ó Thrá Lí.

Eibhlís Ní Shúilleabháin Sa bhliain 1978 foilsíodh *Letters from the Great Blasket*, litreacha a scríobh sí chuig George Chambers i Londain. Phós sí Seán Ó Criomhthain, mac le Tomás Ó Criomhthain, agus chónaigh sí in aon tíos leis an Oileánach. Thug sí aire dó i ndeireadh a shaoil. D'fhág sí an Oileán i 1942.

Julie O'Callaghan (b. 1954) Poet. Born in Chicago, she has lived in Dublin since 1974. She works in the library of Trinity College, Dublin.

Pádraig Ó Cíobháin (rugadh 1951) Úrscéalaí, gearrscéalaí, file. Rugadh i mBaile an Fheirtéaraigh é. Ar na scríobhnóirí próis Gaeilge is mó cáil i láthair na h-uaire. Cónaí air anois i gContae na Gaillimhe.

Pádraig Ó Concubhair (b. 1946) Teacher and historian. A national teacher in his native Lenamore, Ballylongford, County Kerry, his publications include *'Thá Sinn Ocrach': Ballylongford and the Great Famine* (1997), *They Kept the Hills of Kerry: 1848 by the Fealeside* (1998), *'Discreet and Steady Men': Kerry in 1798* (1999) and *Leaba i Measc na Naomh: The Story of Aghavallin Churchyard* (2000).

Mick O'Connell The greatest Gaelic footballer of his, and perhaps any other, time. His book, *A Kerry Footballer*, was published by Mercier Press in 1974.

Clairr O'Connor (b. 1951) Novelist, poet and playwright. Born of Listowel stock in Limerick, she was educated at UCC and Saint Patrick's College, Maynooth. Teaches outside Dublin.

Joseph O'Connor (1877–1957). Born in Romford, Essex, of north Kerry parents, his family returned to Ireland when he was nine years old. Having taught in, among other places, Saint Brendan's College, Killarney, for many years, in 1923 he became an inspector of schools, retiring at the end of the academic year 1941-2. In 1952 he published his *Hostage to Fortune*, an autobiography.

Tomás Ó Criomhthain (An tOileánach) (1856–1937) Rugadh ar an mBlascaod Mór é. Iascaire agus feirmeoir abea é. Foilsíodh *An tOileánach* i 1929.

Séafraidh Ó Donnchadha an Ghleanna (*c.* 1620–78) Rugadh é i nGleann Fleisce in oirthear Chiarraí. Ba é taoiseach a chine agus thug sé agus a thriúr mac (in éineacht le Gaeil eile) ionsái ar chaisleán Thrá Li i gcogadh 1641. D'fhan sé ina chónaí i nGleann Fleisce in aimsir Cromwell. Bhí sé oilte i léann na Gaeilge.

Bernard O'Donoghue (b. 1945) Poet and scholar. Born in Cullen, County Cork, he teaches medieval literature at Oxford. He won the Whitbread Poetry Prize in 1995.

Seán O'Faolain (1900–91) Man of letters. Born John Whelan in Cork, he graduated from UCC in 1921, using the Irish form of his name, having been a student by day and a revolutionary by night. He lectured at Harvard and Saint Mary's Education College, Strawberry Hill, Twickenham. He was editor of the *Bell* from 1940 to 1946.

Pádraig Ó Fiannachta (rugadh 1927) File. Rugadh sa Daingean, Contae Chiarraí é. É i mbun an clóphreas An Sagart ar feadh na blianta. D'éirigh sé as Ollúntacht na Nua-Ghaeilge i Magh Nuad cúpla bliain ó shin. Tá sé ina shagart paróiste sa Daingean faoi láthair.

Pádraig Ó hÉigeartaigh (1871–1936) File. D'fhág sé a dhúiche féin, Uíbh Ráthach, in aois a dhá bhliain déag agus mhair sé sna Stáit Aontaithe as sin amach. Tar éis na bliana 1891 is i Springfield, Massachusetts, a chónaigh sé. Foilsíodh an dán 'Ochón, a Dhonncha' ar bhás a mhic sa *Chlaidheamh Soluis* sa bhliain 1906.

Brian Ó hUiginn (1882–1963) Irish-language activist.

Bearnard Ó Lubhaing (rugadh 1928) Údar próis. Tógadh é in Oifig an Phoist i gCeann Trá i gCorca Dhuibhne. Thug sé aghaidh ar Choláiste Íosagáin i mBaile Bhúirne agus ar Choláiste Phádraig i mBaile Átha Cliath mar ar oileadh é ina mhúinteoir bunscoile. Thug sé tamall ag teagasc i gCabrach Thiar sarar fhill sé ar a chontae dúchais. Chaith sé na blianta ag múineadh i Lios Tuathail. Tá cónaí air anois i gCill Airne.

Pádraig Ó Maoileoin (rugadh 1913) Úrscéalaí agus údar próis. Rugadh i nGaeltacht Chorca Dhuibhne é i gCom Dhineoil. Chaith sé thart is tríocha bliain sna Gardaí ach fuair sé post sa Roinn Oideachais tar éis sin ag obair ar chúrsaí foclóireachta.

Aogán Ó Muircheartaigh (rugadh 1948) File. Rugadh i bPort Laoise é. Chaith sé sealanna ina mhúinteoir meánscoile, ag obair i Raidió na Gaeltachta i mBaile na nGall, agus ina eagarthóir ar *Feasta* agus ar leabhair Chlódhanna Teo. Tá sé ina scríobhnóir go lán-aimseartha anois.

Luaí Ó Murchú (1939–1999) Short-story writer and historian. Born in Newtownhamilton, County Armagh, he joined the Irish civil service in 1934. His employment took him to Listowel in 1946. A founder member of Listowel Writers' Week, he was its first chairman. *Journey Home*, a selection of his short stories, was published in 1997.

Aogán Ó Rathaille (*c.* 1675–1729) File. Rugadh é i Screathan an Mhíl i ndúiche Shliabh Luachra, deich míle éigin lastoir de Chill Airne. Tar éis briseadh na Bóinne (1690) ruaigeadh an Rathailleach as a cheantar féin. Do mhair sé ina dhiaidh faoi ainnise.

Seán Ó Ríordáin (1916–77) File. Rugadh i mBaile Bhúirne, Contae Chorcaí é. Níor chainteoir dúchais abea é ach aithnítear é ar phríomhfhilí ár linne. Fuair sé bás den eitinn i 1977.

Mícheál Ó Ruairc (rugadh 1953) File agus múinteoir. Rugadh i dTaobh an Chnoic, Bréanainn, sa Leitriúch. Tá sé ag múineadh i mBaile Átha Cliath.

Maidhc Dainín Ó Sé (rugadh 1942) File, úrscéalaí agus gearr-scéalaí. Rugadh i gCarrachán i gCorca Dhuibhne é. Tá sealanna tugtha aige i Sasana agus i Meiriceá ach tá sé ar ais in Éirinn ó 1969. Bhuaigh sé duais an Oireachtais i 1991.

Pádraig Ó Siochfhradha (An Seabhac) (1883–1964) Úrscéalaí agus údar próis. Rugadh in aice leis an Daingean é. Múinteoir agus timire do Chonradh na Gaeilge abea é. Níos déanaí bhí sé ina eagarthóir do Chomhlucht Oideachais na hÉireann, áit ar chuir sé eagar ar mórán leabhar, *An tOileánach* ina measc.

Eoghan Rua Ó Súilleabháin (1748–84) File. Sa cheantar céanna i gCiarraí inar rugadh Aogán Ó Rathaille is ea a rugadh Eoghan Rua. Bhí sé ó am go chéile ina mháistir scoile, ina spailpín agus ina bhall de chabhlach (no d'arm) Shasana.

Muiris Ó Súilleabháin (1904–50) Rugadh agus tógadh ar an mBlascaod Mór é, ach tar éis bás a mháthar, chaith sé tréimhse i ndíleachtlann sa Daingean. D'fhág sé an t-oileán arís chun dul isteach ins na Gárdaí. D'fhoilsigh sé *Fiche Blian ag Fás* i 1933. Báthadh go tubaisteach é i gContae na Gaillimhe, áit ina raibh cónaí air.

Tomás Rua Ó Súilleabháin (1785–1848) File agus oide. Rugadh i nDoire Fhíonáin in Uíbh Ráthach é. Cara le Daniel O'Connell, an Fuascailteoir abea é. Foilsíodh *Amhráin Thomáis Rua*, bailiúchán dá shaothar, i 1914 agus arís i 1985.

Fintan O'Toole (b. 1958) Critic, essayist and biographer. Born in Dublin, he has been editor of *Magill*, theatre critic for *In Dublin*, the *Sunday Tribune* and *The Irish Times* and literary adviser to the Abbey Theatre. He is at present a columnist with *The Irish Times* and theatre critic with the New York *Daily News*. He lives in Dublin.

Seán Ó Tuama (rugadh 1928) File agus scoláire. Rugadh i gCorcaigh é. Bhí sé ina Ollamh le Gaeilge i gColáiste na hOllscoile i gCorcaigh.

Peig Sayers (1873–1958) Rugadh í i mBaile an Bhiocaire i nDún Chaoin i gCorca Dhuibhne. Phós sí Pádraig Ó Gaoithín ón mBlascaod Mór agus mhair sí leis ar an Oileán. Foilsíodh a scéal féin, *Peig*, i 1936.

Con Shanahan (b. 1911) Prose writer. Born in Moyvane, County Kerry, he has spent most of his life working in England, where he is now retired. He has published articles in the *Irish Post, The 'Boro' and the 'Cross'* and the *Ballyguiltenane Rural Journal*. He lives near London.

Deirdre Shanahan. Poet and fiction writer. Born in London of Irish parents (her father is Con Shanahan), she received an Eric Gregory Award for poetry in 1983. Her first poetry collection, *Legal Tender,* was published in 1988, and a second, *In Parallel,* in 1999. She has published short stories in England and America, and one is to appear in the *Phoenix Anthology of Irish Short Stories* in 2000. She lives in London.

Eileen Sheehan Poet. Born in Scartaglin, County Kerry, she lives in Killarney, where she is a member of the Fia Rua Writers Group. She has published poems in *Poetry Ireland Review, The Shop, Books Ireland* and other magazines.

Pat Spillane (b. 1955) Winner of eight All-Ireland senior football medals and nine All-Stars, he is one of the greatest Gaelic footballers ever. He was still a teenager when he lifted the Sam Maguire (for the injured captain Mickey O'Sullivan) in 1975. With Sean McGoldrick, he wrote *Shooting from the Hip: The Pat Spillane Story,* published in 1998.

Alfred Lord Tennyson (1809-92) Poet. Born in Somersby, Lincolnshire, England, he published his earliest poems at the age of seventeen and in 1829 won the Chancellor's Medal at Cambridge for his poem *Timboctoo.* He left the university without taking a degree. In 1850 he was made Poet Laureate in succession to Wordsworth. He was made a peer in 1883.

George Thomson (1903–87) Scholar. Came to the Great Blasket to learn Irish on the advice of Robin Flower in August 1923 and formed a close and enduring friendship with Muiris Ó Súilleabháin. In 1931 he was appointed lecturer in Greek at UCG, where he taught through Irish. He encouraged Muiris Ó Súilleabháin to write *Fiche Blian ag Fás,* edited the text and co-authored the English translation. In 1937 he took up a position as lecturer in Greek at the University of Birmingham.

Micheál Ua Ciarmhaic (rugadh 1906) File agus údar próis. Rugadh i mBaile na Sceilg é. Seachas ceithre bliana ar imirce i Meiriceá, tá a shaol ar fad caite aige ina áit dúchais mar iascaire. Bronnadh Gradam Bhord Éigse Éireann air i 1993.

Michèle Vassal Poet. In the late 1970s Michèle Vassal left her home town of Barcelonnette in the Alpes de Haute-Provence and moved to Dublin. She now lives and writes in Kenmare. She was the recipient of the 1999 Listowel Writers Week Poetry Prize.

Maurice Walsh (1879–1964) Novelist and short-story writer. Born in Ballydonoghue, near Listowel, he joined the customs service in 1901. He spent twenty years in the Scottish Highlands, which provided him with the settings and themes for much of his fiction. He transferred to the Irish Customs and Excise in 1922, retiring in 1933. He died in Dublin in 1964.

Jimmy Woulfe (b. 1952) Journalist. Born in Listowel, he is a journalist with the *Limerick Leader*.

Index of Authors

ACKNOWLEDGEMENTS

Grateful acknowledgement is made to the following individuals and publishers for permission to reproduce copyright material:

J. J. Barrett for an extract from *In the Name of the Game* (1997); Mercier Press for 'Ode to a Po' from *Thistles and Docks* (1995) by Robert Leslie Boland; Fiona Brennan for 'Feeding the Muse'; Mercier Press for 'I Am Kerry', 'The Boys of Barr na Sráide', 'The Cahirciveen Races' and 'The Ghost Train for Croke Park' from *Ballads of a Bogman* (1955) and 'The Spanish Waistcoat' from *The Red-Haired Woman* (1989), all by Sigerson Clifford; Marino Books for an extract from *The Best of About Women* (1996) by Mary Cummins; the estate of Daniel Corkery and Gill & Macmillan for an extract from *The Hidden Ireland* (1924); Michael Davitt and Cló Iar-Chonnachta for 'Faobhar na Faille siar in Anglia Sheáin Uí Ríordáin'; Michael Davitt for 'Aonach na Súl'; Desmond Egan for extracts from *Peninsula*; Mícheál Fanning and Salmon Publishing for 'Daniel O'Connell at Tara' from *Verbum et Verbum* (1997); Patrick Fitzgibbon for an extract from *Estuary*; Oxford University Press for an extract from *The Western Isle* (1944) by Robin Flower; Pat Given for 'On Visiting the Graves of the Gaelic Poets at Muckross'; Faber and Faber Ltd for 'The Given Note' by Seamus Heaney from *Opened Ground: Poems 1996–1996* (1998); Donal Hickey for 'The Life and Times of Beatrice Grosvenor'; Donal Hickey and Marino Books for extracts from *Stone Mad for Music: The Sliabh Luachra Story* (© Donal Hickey 1999); Con Houlihan for extracts from *Windfalls* (1996); Dan Keane for 'The Kerryman'; Mercier Press for extracts from *The Field* (1965), *Self-Portrait* (1964) and *Big Maggie* (1969) and for 'Death Be Not Proud', all by John B. Keane; Marino Books for extracts from *The Apprentice* (1965) and *Ireland's Master Storyteller* (1998) by Éamon Kelly; Town House Country House Ltd for an extract from *Now Is the Time* (1998) by Sr Stanislaus Kennedy; Bloodaxe Books Ltd for 'Baby' and 'My Dark Fathers' by Brendan Kennelly from *A Time for Voices: Selected Poems 1960-1990* (1990); Patrick Kennelly for an

extract from *Sausages for Tuesday* (1969); Collette Nunan Kenny for
'Weekly Smile'; Thomas Kinsella for 'Ballydavid Pier'; Irish Freedom
Press for an extract from *Tragedies of Kerry* (1924) by Dorothy
Macardle; Owen McCrohan for 'Waterville is Wonderful' from
Mick O'Dwyer: The Authorised Biography (1990); Steve MacDonogh
for 'By Dingle Bay and Blasket Sound'; Padraig Mac Fhearghusa
for 'Allagar'; Elizabeth Ryan and Margaret Farrington for 'Homage
to Marcel Proust' by Thomas MacGreevy; John McAuliffe for
'After Goethe's Fifth Roman Elegy'; the estate of Bryan MacMahon
and Poolbeg Press for extracts from *The Master* (1992) and *The
Storyman* (1994) and for 'A Woman's Hair'; Máire Mac an tSaoi
for 'Jack' and 'Oíche Nollag'; 'Mount Eagle' by John Montague
by kind permission of the author and the Gallery Press,
Loughcrew, Oldcastle, County Meath, Ireland, from *Collected
Poems* (1995); John Moriarty and the Lilliput Press for an extract
from *Turtle Was Gone a Long Time Vol. 1 Crossing the Kedron*
(1996); Cole Morton and Penguin Books for an extract from
*Hungry for Home – Leaving the Blaskets: A Journey from the Edge
of Ireland* (Viking, 2000) copyright © Cole Morton, 2000;
extracts from *Kerry Slides* (1996) by kind permission of Paul
Muldoon and the Gallery Press, Loughcrew, Oldcastle, County
Meath, Ireland; Máire Áine Nic Ghearailt for 'Réiteach'; 'Ceist
naTeangan' le Nuala Ní Dhomhnaill by kind permission of the
author and the Gallery Press, Loughcrew, Oldcastle, County
Meath, Ireland, from *Pharaoh's Daughter* (1990); Mercier Press
for extracts from *Letters from the Great Blasket* (1978) by Eilís
Ní Shúilleabháin; Julie O'Callaghan for 'The Great Blasket
Island'; Pádraig Ó Cíobháin for an extract from *Ar Gach
Maoilinn Tá Síocháin* (1992); Clairr O'Connor for 'Dream of My
Father'; Mick O'Connell for an extract from *A Kerry Footballer*
(1974); 'Munster Final' by Bernard O'Donoghue by kind
permission of the author and the Gallery Press, Loughcrew,
Oldcastle, County Meath, Ireland, from *Poaching Rights* (1987);
Bernard O'Donoghue and Chatto & Windus for 'The Uvular R'
from *Here Nor There*; Poolbeg Press for an extract from *King of
the Beggars: A Life of Daniel O'Connell* (1938) by Sean O'Faolain;
An tAthair P. Ó Fiannachta for 'Reilg Dhún Chaoin' from *Deora
Dé* by Pádraig Ó Fiannachta; Bearnárd Ó Lubhaing for 'Ar Muir
is Ar Tír' from *Ceann Trá a hAon* (1998); Sáirséal Ó Marcaigh
for an extract from *Na hAird Ó Thuaidh* (1960) by Pádraig Ó